To Yanni,

Into the Cosmos

With deep appreciation
for your friendship
& collegiality over the
years since our days
in the Cosmos.

Jim

Pitt Series in Russian and East European Studies

Jonathan Harris, Editor

Into the Cosmos
Space Exploration and Soviet Culture

Edited by **James T. Andrews**
and **Asif A. Siddiqi**

University of Pittsburgh Press

Published by the University of Pittsburgh Press, Pittsburgh, Pa., 15260
Copyright © 2011, University of Pittsburgh Press
Manufactured in the United States of America
Printed on acid-free paper
10 9 8 7 6 5 4 3 2 1

Library of Congress Cataloging-in-Publication Data
Into the cosmos : space exploration and Soviet culture / edited by James T. Andrews and
Asif A. Siddiqi.
　　p. cm.
Includes bibliographical references and index.
ISBN 978-0-8229-6161-1 (pbk. : alk. paper)
1. Astronautics—Soviet Union—History. 2. Astronautics and state—Soviet Union.
3. Astronautics—Social aspects—Soviet Union. 4. Popular culture—Soviet Union. I.
Andrews, James T., 1961– II. Siddiqi, Asif A., 1966–
TL789.8.S65I58 2011
629.40947—dc23   2011020849

The research and writing of chapter 6, Amy Nelson's "Cold War Celebrity and the Courageous Canine Scout: The Life and Times of Soviet Space Dogs," was supported by a Summer Humanities Stipend and a Jerome Niles Faculty Research Award from Virginia Tech
and by the Summer Research Laboratory on Russia and Eastern Europe at the University
of Illinois. Portions of this chapter appeared previously in "The Legacy of Laika: Celebrity, Sacrifice, and the Soviet Space Dogs," in *Beastly Natures: Human-Animal Relations at
the Crossroads of Cultural and Environmental History*, edited by Dorothee Brantz (University of Virginia Press, 2010), 204–24.

"Our space epic has convincingly revealed to the world the upbringing of a new person—spiritually beautiful, courageous, devoted to communist ideals, and having a high sense of internationalism."

—*Pravda*, November 4, 1968, describing
the profession of the cosmonaut

Contents

Acknowledgments

The editors would like to first and foremost thank Peter Kracht, editorial director of the University of Pittsburgh Press. Peter read the entire manuscript and offered insightful organizational and editorial commentary on the work that was invaluable. Dr. Jonathan Harris, professor of Russian politics at the University of Pittsburgh and the series editor of the press's Series in Russian and East European Studies, also read the manuscript carefully, offering critical advice at the early stages of revision. We thank him for his support of the project and for bringing it to the attention of the editorial board.

This project was first conceived as an edited volume at the American Association for the Advancement of Slavic Studies (AAASS) convention in Washington, D.C., in 2006, when both editors began a conversation, as a result of several panels, about the possibility of deepening the literature on the cultural history of the space age. We thank the tremendous diligence of our contributors and commend their patience with our several rounds of editorial commentary and revisions. We wish to thank two anonymous reviewers for the press whose lengthy and supportive critical commentary helped us with the final product. Lastly, we thank our respective families for their patience through the many drafts of this book and accepting the time it took as we moved toward final publication.

Into the Cosmos

Introduction

Space Exploration in the Soviet Context

James T. Andrews and Asif A. Siddiqi

During the Cold War the space program represented an important marker of Soviet claims to global superpower status. The achievements of *Sputnik* and Gagarin were synonymous with a new and dynamic Soviet state no longer hobbled by the devastations of the Great Patriotic War. The Soviet government devoted enormous resources not only to perform its space achievements but also to publicize them in domestic and foreign arenas. Cosmonauts toured the globe, international space-themed exhibitions extolled the technological panacea of modern socialism, and books about the benefits of Soviet space technology surged out of official publishing presses. The rhetoric underlying this extraordinary program of public engagement worked on at least two interconnected levels. On the one hand, the claims made by official mouthpieces were also assertions about the legitimacy, power, and vitality of the Soviet state. These claims depended on an understanding that space technology (and science, in general) represented a powerful and easily understood measure of the future-oriented sensibility of a nation-state. On the other hand, embodied in the artifacts of the Soviet space program—the spacecraft, the rockets, the statues, the posters, the books, the souvenirs, and the text—were particular symbols and stories about the resonance of cosmic travel in Soviet culture; as symbols they spoke in new and powerful languages, and as stories they cradled the anticipations and hopes of Soviet citizens.

The intersections of these two phenomena—one focused on the state and the other centered more on culture—serve as the primary context for the works in this volume. Through interrogations of the connections between the material and the symbolic elements of the Soviet space program—associations operating at the individual, community, and national levels—the contributions in this volume offer fresh insight into an unexplored element of Soviet history, the triangular relationship between science, state, and culture in the postwar era. Many authors have written about the Bolshevik state's love affair with science and technology. A measure of technological utopianism had already emerged in tsarist Russia at the turn of the century, but after the Bolsheviks came to power in 1917, this fascination embodied a millenarian mantra.[1] Some of this obsession with the power of science and technology to remake society was rooted in crude Marxism, but much of it derived from the Bolsheviks' own vision to remake Russia into a modern state, one that would compare and compete with the leading capitalist nations in forging a new path to the future.

Here, the tools of capitalism—Ford's mass production, Taylor's scientific management, the Wright brothers' airplane—were value-neutral systems that could be relocated into a socialist context without the exploitative costs of capitalism; science and technology could, in this way, be delinked from one ideology and connected to another. The Bolsheviks never adhered to a singular and sustained vision of the role of science and technology in building the new Soviet Union; on the contrary, the Communist Party's approach was neither monolithic nor consistent. For example, in the 1920s, during the time of the New Economic Policy (NEP), the Bolsheviks reluctantly embraced the old prerevolutionary scientific elite, conceding that their skills might be of use during a period of reconstruction. But by the 1930s, after the Cultural Revolution, Stalinist imperatives resulted in a backlash against the old intelligentsia who were seen as being divorced from the "real" problems of socialist construction. Instead, party directives embraced a more populist stance on science and technology: "technology for the masses," in the words of a popular adage of the day.[2]

The traumas facing the scientific and engineering communities during late Stalinism have been well documented. During the Cold War pioneering scholars of Soviet science, such as David Joravsky and Loren Graham, underscored the important relationship between ideology and Soviet science.[3] Yet most laypeople typically understood this connection within the Soviet context as discrete and unidirectional. For example, the "failures" of Soviet science, including the disastrous case of Lysenko and the ban on genetics research from 1948 to 1964, represented stark examples of the negative influence of ideology on science. Meanwhile, the successes of Soviet science were seen as exceptions where Soviet scientists succeeded despite the draconic and limiting structures imposed on them.[4] But recent scholarship on Soviet science has completely overturned such views.[5] Besides returning agency to the scientific community and investing our understanding of the role of scientific and engineering practice under Stalin with deeper complexity and nuance, the most important corollary of this new literature has been to dislodge the perception that the Lysenko affair was emblematic of Soviet science as a whole.[6]

If the relationship between science and the Soviet state (and indeed the lack of delineation between the two) has been a subject of much fresh inquiry, mass engagement with science and technology during Soviet times, including popular (and populist) enthusiasm for science, has until very recently been a marginalized field. Mass campaigns involving science and technology were not anomalies during the interwar years but part and parcel of prevailing Soviet culture. James T. Andrews's recent work on public science has underscored the ways in which public enthusiasm was not simply a result of structured state directives but had significant foundation in genuine mass interest in the powers of science and technology.[7] Lewis H. Siegelbaum, Scott W. Palmer, and Asif A. Siddiqi have explored specific dimensions of public engagement with science and technology—with automobiles, airplanes, and spaceships, respectively—deepening our understanding of how Soviet scientific enthusiasm was a peculiar combination of the mundanely practical and the grandiosely symbolic.[8] This new work has not been monolithic. Where Siegelbaum sees automobile users as appropriating automobile technology in ways unanticipated by the state, Palmer views the state as a more powerful force in using fascination with aviation to distract the populace from the earthly realities of the day. Siddiqi's work on cosmic enthusiasm in the 1920s suggests that such popular fascination often stemmed out of deeply mystical notions fundamentally at odds with the Bolshevik project.[9]

Mass enthusiasm for science and technology in Soviet times had its own peculiarities, but this can be best understood as part of broader (usually) state-sponsored campaigns to encourage large segments of the population to invest their work and life with the transformative spirit of the Bolshevik project. The most obvious touchstones here include Stakhanovism, but there were many others, such as the celebration of new secular holidays and festivals, popular campaigns focused on atheism, stratospheric and arctic exploration, literacy initiatives, and industry-related programs such as the shock worker movement.[10] Historians who have investigated these phenomena have contended that mass enthusiasm for these causes were not cynically fostered by a monolithic state exerting power over a passive populace; rather, it was the result of earnest bottom-up zeal that often mutated into forms at odds with the original intention of the campaigns.

Soviet cosmic culture can best be understood as the outcome of similar processes, with two overlapping and often conflicting phenomena, a massive state-directed project, the actual space program, and an equally vast popular response, one whose existence was fundamental to the sustenance of the former. As a number of scholars have shown, popular interest in cosmic themes in Russia long predated any statist intervention. From the late nineteenth century on, Russian readers were first introduced to cosmic themes, particularly through the imported science fiction of such Western icons as Jules Verne and H. G. Wells. This interest exploded after the Bolshevik Revolution (although not necessary because of it) as the gospel of the "patriarch" of "cosmonautics," Konstantin Tsiolkovskii, was taken up by a younger generation of activists. Cosmic fascination in the 1920s took many forms: societies, exhibitions, film, novels, posters, poems, and paintings, for example.[11] Interrupted by the exigencies of industrialization and then the Great Patriotic War, Soviet popular enthusiasm for the cosmos again bloomed in the postwar era, particularly after Stalin's death. The launch of the *Sputnik* satellite on October 4, 1957, signaled not only the birth of the space age, but also evidence of directed state intervention into the idea of spaceflight. *Sputnik*'s trail in the night skies over the Soviet landmass was clear proof that the Soviet state—the party and the government—had made possible the dreams of generations of space dreamers. As the space program became first and foremost identified with state imperatives and ideologies, it became a tool for posturing on the international stage of the Cold War, a point succinctly reinforced by the headline in *Pravda*, five days after the launch of *Sputnik*: "A Great Victory in the Global Competition with Capitalism."[12]

Within the Soviet Union the satellite and its successors invested the rising hopes of a new postwar "Sputnik generation" with a powerful icon.[13] Having passed through the hopes and disappointments of the Khrushchev era, the project of spaceflight was one of the few state policies that united all in its utopianism, heroism, and iconography. By the time cosmonaut Yuri Gagarin returned to Moscow after his historic flight into the cosmos in 1961, more people assembled in Red Square to welcome him than had for the parades celebrating victory in the Great Patriotic War.[14] *Sputnik*, like Gagarin, represented a powerful symbol for restoring Soviet pride in the aftermath of the economic, social, and political shocks of late Stalinism.[15]

Sputnik inaugurated the first triumphant decade of Soviet space exploration, as one after another, Soviet space exploits inscribed a new glorious cosmic future into the fabric of popular imagination. A row of hero cosmonauts circled the Earth in increasingly ambitious adventures in their *Vostok* and *Voskhod* spaceships. After Gagarin there was the first daylong space mission of German Titov, then the first "twins" in space, Andrian Nikolaev and Pavel Popovich, and then the first woman in space, Valentina Tereshkova. There were other nonhuman successes too: the first living being in space (Laika the dog), the first probe to impact on the surface of the moon (*Luna-2*), the first to take pictures of the far side of the moon (*Luna-3*), and the first to land and take pictures of the surface of the moon (*Luna-9*). For a time at least, the Soviet space program seemed youthful, bursting with energy, and limitless in its capacity to dream. The technical achievements were equally matched by a massive industry of popular enthusiasm, as the state-sponsored media produced hundreds of thousands of books, pamphlets, and posters, sponsored museum exhibits, and most important, sent their young hero cosmonauts to proselytize for the space program and its chief sponsor, the Communist Party of the Soviet Union.

Since the collapse of the Soviet Union, historians have produced many works on the Soviet space program, benefiting from a surfeit of information inaccessible during the Soviet period. Few of these works, however, situated Soviet efforts to explore space within Soviet society and culture; most of the literature has focused on geopolitical concerns ("the space race") or narrowly constructed questions of technological development, and have left unquestioned reductive assumptions about the contingent connections between national identity, Soviet culture, and space exploration.[16] In both Russia and the West the topic of Soviet space exploration has generally attracted techno buffs or political historians. The former display a uniformly positivist fetish for technology, terminology, and teleology, while the latter assume that politics alone determined the nature of the program. Both avoid culture as a focus of study unless as an essentializing category to describe ideology (that is, Marxism).[17] Probably the most salient characteristic of this canon has been an overreliance on secondary literature and the inaccessibility of primary archival source material.[18]

The aim of this book is to transcend the shortcomings of the antecedent scholarship on the Soviet space program and to examine the many ways in which space exploration contributed to the construction of a distinct set of markers of Soviet identity at the national, community, and personal levels. The contributions do this by situating the study of the Soviet space program as part of an understanding of broader social and cultural responses to massive statist initiatives in Soviet history. Their goal, however, is not simply to relocate space exploration within the broader currents of Soviet history, but more critically, to use deeply entrenched and iconic aspects of space exploration to shed light on critical questions about the nature of postwar Soviet society—particularly the Khrushchev era—including such aspects as national identity, memory, mythmaking, gender, public culture, consumer culture, and the institutionalization of secrecy.

Scholarly study of the Khrushchev era has typically focused on two broad thematic priorities: the cultural dimensions of the "thaw" (focusing particularly on the activities of newly hopeful intelligentsia who benefited from the looser limits on artistic expression) or politics at the highest level (with Cold War milestones such as the Cuban Missile Crisis and the Berlin Crisis of 1961 as the stock stopping points).[19] The post-Soviet archival revolution has allowed historians to explore this gap between art and politics and to investigate a wider variety of questions on the social, cultural, and economic history of the period. This volume is part of this newer literature on the Khrushchev era whose aims are to bring fresh methodological tools (including archival research) to bear on a period that has typically been overshadowed by the scholarly fetishization of Stalinism. The recent literature on the Khrushchev era has been wide-ranging and ambitious, seeing the Khrushchev era less as a response to Stalinist excesses than a time with its own complex currents that defy easy generalization and periodization. Novel work on such topics as de-Stalinization campaigns, culture and power during the thaw, social, cultural, and educational reforms, the nature of protest and rebellion, atheist campaigns, mass communications, and gender relations have answered old questions and raised many new ones.[20] This volume hopes to add to that scholarship and answer two broadly defined and interconnected questions: Why did space exploration resonate so deeply among the Soviet populace during the Cold War? And what does this deeply embedded current of fascination say about Soviet society and culture in the post-Stalin years?

The contributors, predominantly historians of modern Russia and Europe, have mined a vast trove of untouched archival and published sources from Russia, accessible only since the archival revolution of the 1990s, to bring a unique perspective to Soviet history. At the same time, they benefit from the substantive body of post-Soviet scholarship on the history of the Soviet Union, literature that, based itself on archival research, has raised new and provocative questions on the nature of state, society, and culture of Russia under Communist rule.[21] Similarly, the provocative questions raised by contemporary scholarship on the history of Soviet science and technology, particularly its fresh reformulation of the relationship between science and ideology, also inform the work included in this book.[22]

The volume is divided into three broad thematic components, each represented by a set of chapters. The first introductory part, consisting of pieces by Alexei Kojevnikov and James T. Andrews, provides broad cultural context. At one level both of these contributions work as historical overviews, but they also introduce many of the strands of Soviet space culture taken up in more detail by others in this volume. Kojevnikov combines thoughtful personal reflections with a brief and impressionistic tour through the entire vista of Soviet space aspirations of the twentieth century. The heart of his chapter is a meditation on the generation of the 1960s (the *shestidesiatniki*), their hopes, their disappointments, and their nostalgia. Andrews, meanwhile, grounds the volume in the inchoate cultural beginnings of cosmic enthusiasm, going back to the pre-*Sputnik* underpinnings of popular interest and popularization of space notions, while also looking forward into post-Stalinist times. He argues that, stretching back to the eighteenth-century era of the Romanov tsarist dynasty, Russians had a fascination with the possibility of air and space flight. He believes it was an inherent part of Russians' more general fascination with exploration: on land, air, and in the cosmos. This fascination continued across the 1917 revolutionary divide but began to take on a nationalist component in the Stalin era of the 1930s and 1940s. Yet even during the Khrushchev era of Cold War competition, Andrews believes ordinary Russians exhibited a sincere fascination with space topics in the press, on film, and in popular books—a preoccupation helped in part by the central symbolic role played by Konstantin Tsiolkovskii, considered by many to be the "father" or *Ded* (grandfather) of space exploration.[23] In the end Andrews articulates an overarching theme—namely, that cosmic enthusiasm had been embedded deeply in Russian culture both before and after *Sputnik*'s launching as evidenced by popular journals, magazines, plays, movies, and other diverse venues.

These two chapters set the stage for the heart of this volume, eight additional contributions divided into two parts. In the first part Asif A. Siddiqi, Slava Gerovitch, Andrew Jenks, and Amy Nelson look at the gaps between myth and reality in the Soviet space program and the role of the state apparatus in bridging this gap. Here, the focus spans the gamut from the personal to the institutional. In the second part of the book, Victoria Smolkin-Rothrock, Roshanna P. Sylvester, Cathleen S. Lewis, and Heather L. Gumbert broadly cover the space program's engagement with popular culture, looking at issues as diverse as religion, gender, consumerism, and the appropriation of Soviet space culture for Cold War imperatives.

The first four chapters take up a deeper engagement with the state's role in the Soviet space program, particularly its management of the relationship between myth and reality, between public and private. The Soviet space program differed in one key regard from its American counterpart in its fetishization of secrecy. Almost every aspect of the program was a closely guarded secret during the Cold War. Using secrecy as a lens, Siddiqi deconstructs the process by which state managers tried to create an "official" narrative of the space program. By revisiting the debates over what was considered secret and what was deemed innocuous, he looks at the prevailing tensions and chasms between the secret and public narratives of the Soviet space program. The basic conundrum for managers was how to publicize the program as much as possible while keeping it secret as much as possible, a tension that was sustained throughout the Soviet era. The resourcefulness of Soviet cosmonauts in the light of equipment failures presented a particular challenge to Soviet journalists because the heroism of men (desirable to advertise) had to be contrasted with the failure of machines (unacceptable to advertise). Siddiqi argues that a "public relations commission" of the Soviet space program, organized in 1968 to arbitrate and dictate on the "proper" nature of information disseminated to the public, was only partially successful in managing public opinion despite the draconian limits on open discussion on the space program.

Myth and reality, and the state's arbitration of the boundaries between the two are the subject of Gerovitch's and Jenks's chapters, which explore the problem of identity and the Soviet space program. Recently, a number of scholars have explored the historical connections between identity, self-fashioning, and the Soviet state.[24] In her recent monograph on identity and imposture during the interwar years, *Tear off the Masks*, Sheila Fitzpatrick has explored the tensions between Soviet citizens' self-identifications and the external signifiers bestowed from above during the interwar years.[25] Other scholars, such as Jochen Hellbeck, have investigated the ways in which Soviet citizens (particularly aspiring Communists) wrote their own biographies and thus thought deeply about their own subjectivity.[26] Building on this literature, Gerovitch and Jenks look at similar issues of identity, myth, and social constructs by analyzing the role of the cosmonaut in the era of the Cold War. Gerovitch examines the public image of cosmonauts during the Khrushchev era, focusing specifically on the struggles they faced in finding an empowered voice within the context of highly prescribed technical roles defined for them. Gerovitch argues that the popular picture of the cosmonauts as propaganda icons masked a serious inner tension between the public image and the professional identity of the cosmonauts. Trained as military pilots or engineers, the cosmonauts often were not prepared for the political careers awaiting them.

Jenks's piece on first Soviet cosmonaut Yuri Gagarin touches on the regime's mythmaking and contrasts this process to Gagarin's inner struggles within this constructed image of the heroic icon. Although

Gagarin may have accepted his high-profile public Soviet persona as an honest Soviet hero, his personal life was riddled with ambiguity and struggle. Gagarin's ambivalent persona was a post-Stalinist reflection of earlier life stories from the pre-1941 era. In her recent work on Soviet diaries, narratives, and life-stories, the Russian historian Natalia Kozlova has reminded us that people learned to speak and act "Soviet" on the surface, yet these Soviet heroes and heroines (as well as everyday people) had life histories that have managed to elude fixed meanings.[27] Jenks also deconstructs Gagarin's penchant for telling audiences the "truth-lie," a lie that is justified because it was told in the service of a greater (usually, nationalistic) purpose. Jenks finds that the relationship between political and personal morality was not always a predictable one in a culture whose central pillar was cosmonaut hagiography—that is, overlooking the weakness and shortcomings of the early cosmonauts. Both pieces by Jenks and Gerovitch illustrate the difficulty of these choices (and how the state could constrain their choices, as the literary critic and historian Alexander Etkind has argued) in the context of the struggle between their public and private personas.[28]

Amy Nelson in her chapter on celebrities, canines, and the Cold War argues that because animals could seemingly tolerate the stresses of space, space dogs such as Laika played an important role in the Cold War "space race." Her contribution uses their celebrity and sacrifice to explore the interpretive possibilities and methodological challenges of incorporating animals into the history of the human past. Beyond the scientific significance of the canine cosmonauts, Nelson argues that these dogs captured the public imagination in ways that reinforced Cold War rivalries, and in the process the dogs' achievements and feats celebrated human technological advances. Furthermore, their achievements also raised nagging questions about the ethical treatment of animals and the relationship between dogs and humans.

The chapters in the second part focus on the public culture of the Soviet space program. After the successes of *Sputnik* and Gagarin, the party and government closely identified the successes of the space program with the perceived successes of the Soviet state. Officially sanctioned campaigns tapped into the genuine populist enthusiasm for space achievements in service of particular agendas. One of these agendas was atheistic education, a phenomenon explored by Victoria Smolkin-

Rothrock. By exploring the use of space successes and cosmonauts in the practical application of atheistic education, she recreates the attempts of Soviet ideologists to produce and inculcate a kind of Communist cosmology. As Khrushchev's campaign against religion overlapped with the state's promotion of cosmic themes, Soviet political officials sought to align the two in service of each other. Smolkin-Rothrock finds that the results of such campaigns were entirely unexpected and contrary to the original intentions of the planners.

Roshanna P. Sylvester analyzes the state media's profiling of women cosmonauts—in particular, their public image and their functioning as role models for young Soviet girls. On June 16, 1963, Valentina Tereshkova, a twenty-six-year-old Soviet "everywoman" blasted into orbit aboard *Vostok 6*, thus becoming the first woman in space. Sylvester's chapter studies this crucially important period in Cold War history to understand the impact Tereshkova's flight had on the imaginative landscape of the girls who dreamed of following their heroine into the cosmos. Her research, based on an exhaustive study of popular articles in family- and child-oriented newspapers and periodicals, suggests that Soviet girls in middle childhood harbored a genuine enthusiasm for Tereshkova's achievement and were a "captive and engaged audience" for the insistent claims of Soviet empowerment of female Soviet citizens. At the same time, Sylvester emphasizes that just after Tereshkova's mission press coverage already revealed a marked ambivalence about the role of girls and women in the Soviet Union, particularly in fields of science and technology. That there was no subsequent state commitment to further female cosmonaut missions only confirmed this ambivalence.

In her contribution on the material culture of the Soviet space program, Cathleen S. Lewis situates the production and consumption of collectible ephemera within the broader cultural shifts that took place during the Khrushchev thaw. Such historians as Susan Reid have recently discussed the social transformations in the Khrushchev era with regard to artistic and consumer culture.[29] Lewis sees the infatuation with space-themed memorabilia as part of this broader post-Stalinist phenomenon, where Soviet citizens were beginning to participate in a modern, leisure consumer-oriented process made possible by relative economic prosperity. She finds that although space-themed artifacts embodied a return to a more modernist aesthetic reminiscent of the immediate post-revolutionary era, the message that they conveyed was a "conservative" one, reinforcing rather than challenging the status quo of the socialist regime and thus at odds with the hopeful ethos of the thaw.

In the final chapter on the public culture of Soviet space aspirations, Heather L. Gumbert explores the spatial and cultural dimensions of the visits of Soviet cosmonauts to the Berlin Wall in the German Democratic Republic (GDR) during the Cold War. Beginning with German Titov's historic visit to the Berlin Wall in 1961, and subsequently with Yuri Gagarin's follow-up visit, the GDR could share in the larger metanarrative struggle with the West (the "space race"), a competition at one level about the technical superiority of one global camp over another. Using a rich array of media sources, Gumbert argues that Titov's visit to the Berlin allowed East German leaders to redefine GDR's place in the European context, by reinforcing their allegiance to the larger socialist bloc even as the physical borders with the West were becoming ever more impermeable. Her chapter is a rare and insightful exploration of how the socialist bloc appropriated Soviet space symbols as a tool to legitimize socialist rule.

Part I
The Space Project

Cultural Context and Historical Background

1

The Cultural Spaces of the Soviet Cosmos

Alexei Kojevnikov

In the late 1990s, when I arrived as a postdoctoral fellow at the California Institute of Technology, I found the small Russian-language community of mostly graduate students in Pasadena holding its annual parties on Soviet Cosmonautics Day. Never mind that in the Soviet Union itself, the day of April 12, when Yuri Gagarin first flew into space in 1961—although remembered and commemorated—had not been a major official holiday or a day off for workers. The students who gathered to celebrate did not necessarily see themselves as Soviet or even Russian, coming as they were from different post-Soviet countries. But, in part because some of them worked and studied at the nearby Jet Propulsion Lab, and in part due to its continuing post-Soviet appeal, Soviet Cosmonautics Day served as a cultural marker of their community and of something they shared in background and identities, however else defined.

Upon my coming to Canada ten years later, a university colleague introduced me to the country by presenting a local newspaper clipping. The source's title and the exact date of the publication had been cut off, but the printed story reported the results of alleged research by the

British Association for the Advancement of Science about different nations' propensity for humor. According to a supposedly thorough three-month investigation with thousands of volunteers, of the roughly forty thousand jokes, Canadians liked the following one the best: "When NASA first started sending up astronauts, they quickly discovered that ballpoint pens would not work in zero gravity. To combat the problem, NASA scientists spent a decade and $12 billion to develop a pen that writes in zero gravity, upside-down, underwater, on almost any surface including glass and at temperatures ranging from below freezing to 300 C. The Russians used a pencil."[1]

To my own culturally shaped taste, the joke appeared more realistic rather than outright funny. But this episode also attests to the continuing mythological appeal of the Soviet breakthrough into the cosmos, which does not wane with the decades, even though its meanings have changed with time, place, and community. As the historical dust settles, *Sputnik* and Gagarin increasingly attain the status of the symbol of Soviet civilization in its moment of ultimate glory and historic accomplishment, similar to what for other civilizations, old and new, would be represented by the pyramids, the Great Wall, the *Santa Maria*, evolution, and the atomic bomb. As pertains to such myths, they are constantly rehearsed, retold in dogmatic or deviating ways, and often debunked and denied. This chapter sketches out some of the cultural and anthropological aspects of Soviet efforts related to space exploration as they developed over the decades.

Before *Sputnik*

In addition to his obsessive dream of space travel, Konstantin Tsiolkovskii had another dream that was almost as dear to him: he wished to own a cow.[2] The lifestyle of a schoolteacher on the outskirts of the provincial town of Kaluga was similar to rural life in many respects. Having a cow for Tsiolkovskii would have been, as for many Russian peasants in nearby villages, the sign of his large family's relative well-being, a guarantee his children would have a daily meal, and a security investment in case of emergency or disaster, especially during the turbulent and hungry years of the Civil War. This detail—related by Alexander Chizhevskii, Tsiolkovskii's good acquaintance, younger admirer, and biographer—reminds us that Russian dreams about space developed from the scarcity rather than abundance of resources. Indeed, they almost exactly coincided with the period of most severe deprivations caused by the social, political, and military crises of the first half of the twentieth century. Even the lavish expenditures of the more stable 1960s, when state enthusiasm for space programs reached its peak, exuberant as they seemed to Soviet contemporaries, by others' standards were meager at best.

Tsiolkovkii's commitment to his space dream reflected a kind of escapism that arose from the cultural context of the time. Historians have commented on various aspects on his philosophy—religious, scientistic, progressivist—but have not paid much attention to a recurrent theme of catastrophism in his writings. At least since the time of the revolutionary collapse of the old regime in 1917, Tsiolkovskii increasingly believed that the human race must be prepared technologically to leave the solar system by the time it, too, would be collapsing. Many others who, like him, had survived the combined dangers of World War I, the revolution, and the civil war were prone to obsessive thinking about the cataclysmic historical event they had lived through and often metaphorically exaggerated it into global and cosmic terms. Tsiolkovskii generalized the existential experience of his contemporaries into cosmic dimensions: the universe, for him, was eternal, but stars were not, and any particular solar system, including ours, was destined to die (or rather die and be reborn periodically).[3] The very survival of humanity in the long run thus depended on its mastery of spaceflight. Tsiolkovskii's younger friend Chizhevskii was also thinking in somewhat related ways, as he searched for an explanation and rationalization of contemporary events. In the early 1920s he developed a theory based on massive historical data that such global disasters as famines, epidemics, wars, and major social disturbances occurred periodically on Earth depending on natural causes: they peaked with solar activity, on average every eleven years.[4]

Neither of these views squared very well with the official Soviet ideology. Chizhevskii's theory was explicitly criticized as non-Marxist; many of Tsiolkovskii's millenarian ideas had to be censored when reported in the official press. The meaning of his preaching that could be publicly endorsed in the early Soviet decades was restricted largely to pedagogy, science fiction, and popularization. As an amateur inventor in the fields of aviation and rocketry, he remained throughout his entire life rejected by professional and academic elites. But as the historian James T. Andrews has described in his newest book, *Red Cosmos,* Tsiolkovskii's enthusiasm for space travel inspired many younger students and children, encouraging their general interest in science and technology. In his earlier work Andrews revealed the novelty of approaches and the impressive scope of Soviet efforts in education, propaganda, and popularization of science among the masses during the revolutionary decades.[5] As part of these highly valued and politically supported activities, Tsiolkovskii's devotion and lifelong enthusiasm for flight in the air and in space received official endorsement as exemplary and inspirational, especially for the younger generation, albeit without mentioning that many of his concrete designs and proposals had not been found practical or developed enough to be actually realized.

But inspiring they were, and the culture of the 1920s supported a genuine popular enthusiasm for science fiction and travel to other planets. Similar attitudes developed in several other countries contemporaneously, but in the Soviet Union they enjoyed a particularly strong appeal due to their resonance with other utopian temptations of the time—be they political, social, or technological.[6] Young kids growing up in revolutionary Russia did not have the same existential experience as Tsiolkovskii and were more likely to partake in the dream of space travel as part of the general optimistic vision of humanity's bright future on Earth, rather than as a way of escaping to other worlds from an unavoidable cosmic calamity.[7] A few of them were not only reading and dreaming but also tinkering and materializing some of Tsiolkovskii's ideas in metal, assisted by whatever little infrastructure the Soviet educational establishment could provide for youth activities in the field of amateur technological creativity. Several local groups of engineering students engaged in small-scale rocketry construction as an after-hours hobby, while occupied with more respectable and practical topics in their regular class assignments. Thirty years later, some of these young amateurs would become the leading designers of the Soviet space project, including Valentin Glushko, Sergei Korolev, Mikhail Tikhonravov, among others.[8]

Their utopian fervor receded considerably after the early 1930s, with enthusiastic visions of a bright but distant future overshadowed by the much nearer and frightening prospect of the looming war. With the threat of a military conflict with Nazi Germany becoming ever more real, an increasing part of all thoughts and activities in the Soviet Union turned toward military preparations. Discussions about future travels to other planets, and even science fiction as a literary genre, almost disappeared for about two decades, while practical or more precisely military aspects of rocketry came to the forefront. The German army had developed a serious interest and investment in rocketry research in the 1920s during the Weimar republican period, already before Hitler came to power, because this branch of weaponry was not explicitly prohibited under the terms of the Versailles peace. The Soviet military started showing its interest later, possibly alarmed by the German efforts, but the status of rocketry research remained somewhat controversial. In particular, the notorious tendency of rockets to stray off the course made many military experts skeptical about their potential use as anything more than an auxiliary weapon. To some, especially among artillery professionals, shells looked like much more reliable and useful projectiles.

Nevertheless, the Soviet command gathered existing amateur rocket tinkerers into a special institute/design bureau, thus for the first time granting them professional recognition and institutionalization. The very same military priorities, however, reoriented rocket engineers toward technological tasks and designs quite different from the ones needed for spaceflight. Opinions clashed over which possible weapons were practical and realizable under severe time and resource constraints as the war drew nearer. The routes actually taken reflected important differences in technological culture between Russia and Germany. The German project invested heavily in the technically daunting task of solving the problems of guided and long-distance flight. The resulting famous missile, generally known as the V2, could fly several hundred kilometers and stay more or less on target if the latter was roughly the size of London. This engineering feat constituted a true technological revolution with great potential and promise for the future, yet as far as the ongoing battles of World War II were concerned, was still largely impractical as a weapon and a waste of resources.[9] Prewar disagreements among Soviet rocketry specialists ended up in favor of a different weapon choice, colloquially known as *katyusha*. A battery of trucks, each equipped with a couple dozen small rockets, could fire in salvo thousands of unguided projectiles over a distance of only a few kilometers across the front lines. As much as this design was technologically primitive, cheap, and less prestigious from the engineering point of view than the V2, it proved much more effective as an actual weapon during the war, in particular in situations where large concentrations of troops made precision less important than area coverage, such as the Stalingrad and the Berlin operations.[10]

Yet even before the katyusha system could prove its value in battle, many from the leadership and staff of the military rocketry institute were executed or arrested as part of the broad purges in the Soviet military in 1937 and 1938. Several key engineers survived, but Korolev and Glushko spent the war years as arrestees working on aircraft design—apparently aviation was a better established and recognized (hence also less risky politically) technology on which to work.[11] Soviet science and engineering in the wartime could barely afford the luxury of long-term, grand, and uncertain endeavors and focused primarily on improving mainstream technology that was crucial for the ongoing conflict, rather than future wars. Large-scale and forward-looking projects of the kind exemplified by the atomic bomb received full attention and support in the USSR only after the end of the war. In 1945 the Soviet rocketry team reassembled, too, this time in occupied Germany, to study the enemy's experience and war trophies. The German breakthrough with the V2 then inspired the Soviet Union as well as the United Kingdom and the United States to launch their respective programs that aimed first at replicating and then developing the guided missile technology further.[12]

The best of the war bounty—the chief engineers from the German missile team along with most of the surviving V2s—was acquired by the United States in Operation Paperclip. Having obtained much less, the Soviet military relied mostly on its own engineers, who began by studying the remaining fragments of equipment and documentation in Germany, and in 1946 they moved to a secret research center in Kaliningrad, near Moscow. Despite the initial handicap, in ten years the Soviet team managed to surpass its German-American rivals in developing the world's first intercontinental ballistic missile (ICBM). Part of the explanation comes from the urgent importance of rocketry for the Soviet side due to the asymmetrical strategic balance during the earlier half of the Cold War. American bombers from airbases located in Europe and Asia could deliver their nuclear payloads to cities deep inside Soviet territory, while the USSR lacked any forward bases from which aircraft could reach American shores. In an attempt to accelerate the development of an alternative delivery system, the Soviet officials set the target payload for a future nuclear ICBM as early as 1953, before they actually knew the exact mass of the hydrogen bomb, on the basis of an approximate higher-end estimate of three tons.[13] The assignment pushed Korolev's team to leapfrog several incremental stages and proceed directly to developing the powerful two-stage missile R7 with a seven-thousand-kilometer reach.

This machine was capable of flying to the American continent, thus offering for the first time some possibility of retaliation and deterrence against nuclear bombers targeting Soviet cities.[14]

At least some of the engineers at this juncture had not entirely forgotten their youthful dream of space travel that decades earlier had brought them into the then amateur field of rocketry design. They understood their chief mission to be about strategic defense of the Soviet homeland, not cosmonautics. But a missile with the R7 characteristics was also perfectly capable of delivering its payload into a space orbit. While the missile was still under development, Tikhonravov's small group started working on parallel designs for sputniks and manned-space missions. In 1956, at an opportune moment when Nikita Khrushchev inspected and happened to be particularly pleased with the work on the R7, Korolev requested permission to use one of the future missile tests for a sputnik launch. The Soviet leader needed reassurances that such a distraction would not delay in any way the fulfillment of the main job, but he agreed to reward scientists and engineers in their desire, even if it might appear somewhat childish.[15]

The space race did not exist yet in the minds of most politicians and the public, but Korolev and his top engineers worried about possible American competitors. They decided to forgo the wait for more sophisticated equipment and to go ahead with what their internal documentation referred to as the "simplest sputnik"—a rump satellite able to confirm, besides the fact of the space launch itself, the possibility of radio communication from orbit back to Earth through the ionosphere.[16] The R7 was still at a stage when approximately every second launch encountered some problems, but the one with the first sputnik happened smoothly on October 4, 1957, just six weeks after the first successful military test of the R7 as an ICBM. Even the engineers who knew that they were about to accomplish something important could not anticipate the enormity of the political tsunami that followed. Overnight, *Sputnik* became the chief world media sensation and a public fixation. The dream about the cosmos entered a different cultural realm—no longer a monopoly of science-fiction fans and a few engineers, but a matter of primary attention for the political establishment, mass culture and media, countless children and their teachers, and much of the general population across the globe. Rocketry and space travel became relevant for various areas of cultural life, endowed with many new and changing meanings and uses.

After *Sputnik*

In his contribution to this volume, Asif Siddiqi has reminded us that the umbilical cord linking the ostensibly peaceful exploration of the cosmos with military programs remained its essential contradiction and continued to produce tensions between sometimes conflicting priorities. One can argue that precisely this link, often as unmentionable in public as it was self-obvious, made the space race a useful political trope and a powerful symbol for the rivalry between the Cold War superpowers. By talking about space, one could also symbolically invoke military might and threats without explicitly naming them. Political authorities in the USSR and the United States understood the major importance of *Sputnik* for the strategic balance in the world as well as for the world of public relations immediately, if only post factum. Typically the Soviets looked dismissively on the Western media's propensity for sensationalism, but in this case they found it working in their favor and started supporting it with their own propaganda tools. Soviet spokesmen promoted the achievement nationally and internationally as a demonstration of social-ism's advantage over capitalism.

After the triumph of the first sputnik, Khrushchev was asking Ko-rolev for further spectacular achievements in space scheduled around the days of two major Soviet holidays, November 7 and May 1. The American leadership initially tried to downplay the event but was also worried about the changed dynamics in Cold War technological competition. In 1945 the Soviets were regarded as inherently backward, but they had caught up in the development of the atomic bomb by 1949, pulled even with thermonuclear weapons by 1953, and actually surpassed "the West" in missile design by 1957.[17] The public interest aroused by *Sputnik* and the Cold War mentality thus transformed the idea of space travel from an id-iosyncratic obsession of some into a chief political priority for the existing and eventually other aspiring superpowers. The space race began in ear-nest, primarily aiming at the first human flight, but as Amy Nelson has reminded us in her chapter in this volume, also involving animal heroes.

From a military perspective, as the most visible side effect of the ICBM development, the Soviet space launches signified a gradual shift toward the ever more symmetrical stage in the Cold War's strategic bal-ance, with the USSR achieving a modicum of nuclear counterthreat (although the latter would take several more years to develop from a largely symbolic to a sufficiently serious one). The loss of unchallenged nuclear supremacy was hard for the U.S. leaders to swallow, which produced the dangerous outbreak of the Cuban Missile Crisis.[18] Eventually it had to be accepted as a fait accompli and resulted in a relatively stable state of growing mutual awareness that an all-out thermonuclear war would bring about suicide for all of humanity and could not be won in principle. The Soviet leadership's acceptance of this conclusion earlier, already by 1956, allowed Khrushchev to announce publicly that world wars had become avoidable and to proclaim the policy of "peaceful coexistence" with capitalism as the official Soviet strategy on the world arena.[19]

Another aspect of the war mentality proved unchangeable, however. The generation of Soviet officials who had seen their country half destroyed, hanging by a thread, and just barely surviving in the war against Nazi Germany, could not settle for mere capacity for serious counterstrike as an adequate form of military deterrence. Their experience derived from World War II demanded nothing less than relative parity with the United States—that is, roughly the same actual numbers of warheads and delivery means. At this point the military and space priorities began to part ways, because after the R7 their respective demands required different technological systems and increased competition for resources.[20] The Soviet political and military leaders chose as the country's first priority to catch up with the United States in nuclear capabilities—rather than to compete seriously in the militarily and economically useless moon race. Their culturally defined notion of strategic security required mass production of newly developed missiles that were different from those used in the space launches. A major commitment of efforts and resources toward this task dominated the entire decade of the 1960s. They finally saw such relative strategic parity achieved by the beginning of the 1970s, albeit at a quite burdensome price for the national economy. Such parity in turn created the grounds for détente and for the first serious negotiations with the United States on limiting the arms race.

The space race continued to play a major role in the public perception and the superpowers' propagandistic bickering, where both states celebrated different "firsts" as their respective ultimate victories. The Soviets claimed the main prize on April 12, 1961, when a modified three-stage version of the R7 carried the capsule *Vostok 1* with the first cosmonaut, Yuri Gagarin, who orbited the Earth once and landed safely after the 108-minute flight. In the USSR, as well as in post–Soviet Russia, the success of the first manned flight has been valued as the ultimate victory in the space race, higher than any other possible achievement in space, including *Sputnik*, and commemorated annually as Cosmonautics Day.[21] In the United States the frustration over the defeat made President Kennedy announce the next national priority for country: send a man to the moon. Having committed tremendous resources toward this task, the United States accomplished it with the moonwalk by Neil Armstrong on July 21, 1969. After this triumph or consolation prize, political emotions cooled down somewhat.

Today, fifty years later, the public fixation on manned flights can probably be understood as a misperception, because their actual purpose, economic usefulness, and longtime prospects—apart from the ever declining propagandistic value—have remained as yet rather uncertain. Sputniks, however, proved their practical utility almost immediately with spy, meteorological, and communication satellites. They have become, in the meantime, irreplaceable and invaluable by having changed the essential ways of human life, from allowing for global communications and the Internet to fostering environmental awareness of our common fate on the Earth. In hindsight, it would probably be more appropriate to recognize and celebrate the first little sputnik as humanity's revolutionary breakthrough into space, humble as most true moments of great exploration.

The recent resurgence of popular interest in the Soviet space story in contemporary Russia has brought about new cultural meanings. For example, feature movies by two leading contemporary directors—*Cosmos as Anticipation* by Alexei Uchitel and *A Paper Soldier* by Alexei German Jr.—set their respective plots against the historical/mythological background of the early space launches, which serve as a metaphor for Soviet civilization as a whole.[22] In the latter film the main protagonist, a young physician helping to train the first group of cosmonauts, is torn apart by inner insecurity. He sees in the realization of the space dream the desperate last chance to redeem the Soviet project and return to its original idealistic values after the excesses and distortions of Stalinism, yet unconscious doubts torture him and eventually lead him to death. Artistically interesting, both movies also reveal how hard it has become in the post-Soviet, anticommunist cultural climate, to understand and represent the beliefs and attitudes of the Soviet generation whose formative years of youth coincided with and were greatly influenced by the dawn of the space era and Khrushchev's liberalization. That generational group went by the self-appointed name *shestidesiatniki*, or the 1960s generation (roughly applicable to those who in 1960 were in their twenties), to whom the historian Donald J. Raleigh has also referred as the "Soviet Baby Boomers" and "Russia's Sputnik generation."[23]

Coming of age almost a decade earlier than the American baby boomers, the Soviet shestidesiatniki developed a similarly strong generational mentality to distinguish themselves from older folks. Born mostly before the war, a great many of them were raised by single mothers and without fathers, who were serving or had been killed at the front. Many experienced great deprivation and hunger as young children during the war and the immediate postwar reconstruction, but they also witnessed fifteen years of tremendous improvement in living standards from utter poverty to normalcy and even relative prosperity by the 1960s. This explains the popularity of belief in Soviet values and exuberantly optimistic views of the future. Science-fiction books and futuristic literature were once again the rage, and even Khrushchev may be said to have been carried away by the visionary mood of the time when he foolheartedly promised the Soviet citizen Communism in twenty years.[24]

They saw excesses of Stalinism as violations of the idealistic values of socialism, which Khrushchev had promised to restore. The shestidesiatniki grew up with those values naturally, learning them in school as an already established and settled social norm, without too much of an alternative. Unlike the older generation, the shestidesiatniki were mostly too young during the Stalin years to have been personally forced into difficult moral compromises when those values contradicted with the violent practices of dictatorship. They could thus see themselves as relatively uncorrupted by Stalinism and, living in peaceful time, could optimistically and sincerely believe in a harmonious combination of Communism, morality, and nonviolence.[25]

If this description reminds the readers of Mikhail Gorbachev, it is no accident, for he belongs to the same generation and his views were quite typical of the shestidesiatniki. What is somewhat less usual about him, however, is not the value system itself, but that Gorbachev was able to retain it throughout all the subsequent years deep into the 1980s. Many of the first Soviet cosmonauts came from that very same age group, and as exemplary heroes during the 1960s, they were subject to the cultural expectations of the time. Cosmonauts acted as public promoters of the So-viet values of atheism, feminism, and scientism. Truth and truth-telling received particular praise as the most desirable and required virtues dur-ing de-Stalinization—especially by those who had not had to burden their consciences with unavoidable lies during the earlier era by virtue of their youth.[26] Mass consumerism (in its modest Soviet version) emerged in the 1960s as a relatively new phenomenon. Goods were still scarce, but the absolute amounts mattered less than the rapid upward trend, which the generation of the 1960s had enjoyed for the great part of their still very young lives. As Cathleen S. Lewis aptly tells us in her chapter in this book, the little collection items that became consumer goods, such as stamps and *znachki* (enamel pins) with space symbolism, served as markers for an important social shift.

The cultural nexus of the 1960s would not last very long—it was already disintegrating by the middle of the decade. Economic growth slowed down considerably, while de-Stalinization and other reforms did not go as far as many had hoped and finally stalled, leading to widespread disillusionment and loss of optimism. In subsequent decades some of the typical shestidesiatniki would lose their naïvete and turn cynical or alcoholic; others would become open or closet dissidents; yet oth-ers maintained their beliefs quietly, waiting for more opportune times, like Gorbachev and some of his perestroika team. But by the time they marked their presence in the upper echelons of Soviet power and tried to reform it, popular disillusionment with the regime had already gone too far. Believers in its rehabilitation soon found themselves in an abso-lute minority. With the removal of censorship and deepening economic crisis in the late 1980s, the public mood quickly surpassed the reformist stage and proceeded toward the wholesale rejection of the system. Soviet cultural heritage, however, proved of much more lasting value than the political regime per se. Some of its parts have also been lost or rejected, while others, including space culture and its mythology, have survived and continue to develop in Russia and other post-Soviet countries, even if not necessarily labeled as "Soviet" anymore.

Interestingly, some of the more profound cultural legacies of the So-viet opening into the cosmos can be found internationally. Whereas in the domestic Soviet context the propagandistic potential of Sputnik and oth-er successes in space mostly supported and reaffirmed the already well-established values, on the global arena it served as a vehicle for spreading these ideas into new territories. The highly publicized achievements in space exploration changed the Soviet Union's international image during the 1960s from an "underdog superpower," however promising, to a technologically advanced one, roughly equal in imagination to the United States. The overall attractiveness of the Soviet model increased significantly, influencing many of the cultural reforms and changes in the world of the 1960s.

When Soviet cosmonauts delivered their political message about the advantages of socialism over capitalism to Soviet audiences, they were preaching mostly to the converted. But when they traveled all over the world, then steeped in the process of decolonization and battles over civil rights, they also brought with them a powerful message supporting ongoing struggles for national and racial equality, independence and anti-colonialism, modernization and social justice. For girls in the USSR, as Roshanna P. Sylvester has noted in her chapter in this book, the achievement of the first woman in space offered a powerful inspiration and an affirmation of the socialist commitment to educational and professional equality. For women in Europe and North America the Soviet feminism of the 1950s and 1960s, however incomplete by today's standards, served as an example of accomplishments that were not yet available to them, especially in the public sphere and education, and provided models to follow. Ideological adversaries, too, became affected by parts of the Soviet cultural model, as was evident (even if not explicitly acknowledged) in the post-*Sputnik* changes in educational and science policies in the United States, such as dramatically increased federal support and job opportunities for scientists, government funding for science and engineering education, gradual expansion of racial and gender diversity in science, the establishment of NASA as a centralized (Soviet-type) state agency overseeing research and development, and the decline of the ideology of pure science.[27]

The discussion of space exploration has traditionally focused on the issues of technological competition, Cold War politics, and bickering. Cultural aspects of the story have arguably had a much more important and long-lasting impact on our lives but have as yet remained considerably understudied. This book opens up new questions and helps shift directions of research away from the traditional terrain toward yet unexplored topics, including popular and material culture, social movements, and global cultural change.

2

Getting Ready for Krushchev's *Sputnik*

Russian Popular Culture and National Markers
at the Dawn of the Space Age

James T. Andrews

By the late nineteenth century a myriad of popular science journals started to discuss the possibility of exploring the cosmos. This developing space culture was a natural outgrowth of Russia's interest with exploration on land, and subsequently air, that predated the Soviet era. By the Soviet 1920s a proliferation of popular books, newspaper articles, and pamphlets on air and spaceflight filled the popular press. In the 1930s, however, the state began to sponsor more nationalistic public spectacles canonizing aeronautical heroes and rocket designers alike.[1] Although popular film and theater on Soviet space exploration reflected a dynamic upsurge in envisioning and colonizing space, under Stalin it simultaneously began to reflect more nationalistic, competitive cultural paradigms. In the 1940s the regime's military subsidies to developing rocket programs would certainly peak the government's interest as a corollary in space research later on. However, by the 1950s and the eventual successful launching of *Sputnik*, the Khrushchev regime would direct popular campaigns more aggressively from above in the press. In the Khrushchev era the space program became a national marker for the Soviet Union's technological competition with the Western capitalist world (much like it was similarly for the American polity and public in the West). In essence, this was the only aspect of the grandiose rocket program that could be overtly discussed. However, even with this highly secretive and politicized context in the Cold War era, cosmic visions flourished because they had also been deeply embedded cultural signifiers in late imperial and Soviet culture—enmeshed in popular film, journals, newspaper items, and theater alike.

Rocketry, Cosmic Culture, and the Public

Russian cosmic popularization, which began with Konstantin Tsiolkovksii in the late nineteenth century, borrowed from a tradition of indigenous technical expertise stretching back to the late 1600s. The early popularizers, like Tsiolkovskii, were mostly technical specialists who were deeply influenced by their compatriots who had written on rocketry before the 1880s. The use of rockets in Russia, however, does not date much earlier than the late seventeenth century. Prior to the time of Tsar Peter the Great, Russian rockets were mainly used for fireworks display, particularly for members of the tsar's immediate and extended family.[2] Russian historians of rocketry, such as V. N. Sokolsky, have argued that these firework displays were popular among the aristocracy in provincial areas of the empire as well—noting that well back into the 1670s, even towns such as Ustyuga held these rocket display events generally for the region's nobility.[3] However, in the capital cities on occasion these grandiose tsarist celebrations were interrupted when rockets exploded accidentally, often hurting those lighting the fireworks.[4]

In Moscow in the 1680s the tsarist regime founded the first rocket works factory, where both signal and illuminating rockets were made for the Russian army. After the founding of Saint Petersburg in 1703, Tsar Peter I moved the rocket workshop to his new capital on the Baltic and vastly expanded the production of rockets by the early 1720s. In these newly constructed rocket workshops on the banks of the Neva River in Petersburg, hundreds of rocket specimens were produced in the first quarter of the eighteenth century alone. Although they still served as entertainment at celebratory events for the regime's courtly entourage and the provincial aristocracy, these rockets also were created with the hope of serving future military forces.[5] The first to actually publish detailed designs of rockets was Aleksandr D. Zasiadko (1779–1837), a talented engineer and hero of the Napoleonic War of 1812. He designed, at the turn of the nineteenth century, a high explosive rocket as well as launchers that could fire six rockets simultaneously. He tested these rockets successfully near Mogilev and produced them at the Petersburg Pyrotechnic Laboratory. After 1826 a Saint Petersburg Rocket Institute (the first of its kind in Eurasia) was established on Volkovoye Field near Saint Petersburg.[6]

The military engineer Konstantin I. Konstantinov (1817–1871) really helped expand the design, manufacture, and production of rockets not just in Saint Petersburg, but in other parts of the Russian empire as well. Furthermore, by the 1850s he began to popularize these notions through public lectures he gave in Saint Petersburg, particularly ones at the Mikhailovsky Artillery Academy. Thus in the 1850s an interested educated layperson (mainly officer) could hear about devices that could move into the air at high velocities. In 1864 the first edition in Russian of Konstantinov's collected public lectures on rocketry were published in Saint Petersburg, then translated into French by a Parisian publishing house in the late 1860s.[7] Konstantinov might be considered therefore the first popularizer of rocketry in Russia, as his works appeared in a number of journals in the Russian language. Konstantinov's work, however, was mostly published in an array of artillery and military journals throughout the 1860s and 1870s.[8]

In the mid- to late nineteenth century a host of Russian engineers, technicians, and scientists became interested in the futuristic use of rockets for air flight, and not solely for military purposes. N. V. Gerasimov, a military engineer, was the first in the late nineteenth century to propose using a rocket with a gyroscope inside to assure the stability of the projectile in flight.[9] I. V. Meshchersky (1859–1935), a design engineer, began to investigate the physical dynamics of objects in flight with respect to their weight and the velocity they traveled through air.[10] As these technical specialists began to dream of rockets moving through the air at greater speeds, visionaries started to dream of exploring the cosmos.

It is at this crucial juncture, in the late nineteenth century, when public interest first started to meet indigenous Russian technical vision and invention. Those such as the self-taught math and physics teacher from Kaluga, Konstantin Tsiolkovskii, started to popularize his work in journals and newspaper articles so that interested Russians (beyond the military, the tsar's court, and the aristocracy) could read about these utopian notions. Although Tsiolkovskii's technical ideals built on previous Russian conceptual ingenuity on rocketry, he was obsessed with popularizing these notions. Technically, his innovation was his conception of using liquid fuel as a propellant to catapult rockets through the atmosphere, as well as his equation regarding the velocity it would take to get a projectile to break through Earth's gravitational forces into orbit. Tsiolkovskii, however, also wrote voluminous science-fiction novels about the cosmos beyond and helped expand on the developing Russian literary tradition in this arena. At this time there already was a rich tradition of prerevolutionary utopian science fiction in Russia—this genre intersected with the new and vibrant interest among educated Russians in interplanetary travel and stellar configurations. Beginning with the stories of those such as V. Taneev and V. N. Chikolev, written from the late 1870s to the 1890s, there were many novels written by Russians about themes as diverse as alien life, new forms of energy, and interplanetary travel.[11] The engineer V. N. Chikolev wrote science-fiction tales in Russian in the 1890s, such as his tale about a world and cosmos transformed by technology and electricity.[12]

Editors of such journals as the Moscow magazine *Vokrug sveta* (Around the world) became particularly interested in soliciting articles for their readers on rocketry and the cosmos. *Vokrug sveta* was the most popular late-tsarist-era journal covering global exploration, and its editors thus took an interest in such writers as the young provincial teacher, K. E. Tsiolkovskii, whose visionary fiction on exploring outer space became popular with readers in urban areas. *Around the World* carried articles on world expeditions, geographic and geologic analysis, anthropological logs, space travel, and even travel log narratives of Russians visiting distant lands. Images of traveling into outer space became part of a greater fascination, on the part of the Russian prerevolutionary reading public, with exploratory narratives in general.[13] Later cosmonauts could be envisaged as inheritors of the pantheon of a long line of Russian explorers and heroes, from Tian-Shanskii to Otto Shmidt, from the Caucasus in the nineteenth century to the polar north in Stalin's times.

One of the first space travel stories for popular consumption in tsarist Russia was Tsiolkovksii's *Na lune* (On the moon), which was first serialized in *Vokrug sveta* in 1893. Tsiolkovskii's novel is about our nearest celestial body, Earth's satellite or moon. Its main protagonist is a young astronomy enthusiast (a popular hobby in Russia at that time) who relates a dream he had while in a very deep sleep. The young man dreams that he and his physicist friend had been transported to the moon. There they travel, take observations, perform scientific experiments, and just enjoy their stellar adventure. Toward the end of the story, they are about to freeze during one of the long, cold lunar nights, when suddenly the young man awakes from his dream and writes it down in his journal. This story thus confronts men setting foot on the moon eventually, as they would in the late 1960s. It also provides an imaginative escape for its main character to go beyond what was capable at that moment—much like Tsiolkovskii himself, who constantly envisioned the technical achievements of the future.[14]

An interest in outer space and air flight was only one aspect of a greater interest in astronomy by the Russian reader. Amateur astronomy societies proliferated in Russia in the decades immediately preceding the revolutions of 1917. The Russian Amateur Astronomy Society, founded in Saint Petersburg, published a widely read journal *Mirovedenie* (Study of the natural world) that spread knowledge on astronomy, stellar configurations, and popular information on other planets in the galaxy. This society helped form public viewings through its large telescope on the grounds of the Tenishev School in Saint Petersburg. Furthermore, it solicited articles from astronomy and physics professors that could explain complex stellar configurations in popular, diluted form for its eclectic readership. Saint Petersburg professors, such as K. D. Pokrovskii and A. V. Bochek, wrote enticing articles on the lunar surfaces of the moon as well as topics as diverse as shooting stars and the origins of the planet Mars.[15]

Although World War I (1914–18), two social revolutions in 1917, and a civil war (1918–20) certainly interrupted the cultivation of popular interest in the cosmos, the 1920s would be a time throughout Eurasia when interest in air flight and rocketry expanded dramatically. The air and cosmos fixation became a cultural craze in Soviet Russia during the interwar era.[16] Scientific societies in Leningrad, as well as in Moscow, sponsored numerous events and public disputations on a variety of planets such as Mars. Museums, such as the famed Polytechnic Museum in Moscow, sponsored public lectures by astronomers and physicists on topics of great interest: life on Mars, stellar configurations, rocket flight in interplanetary space, and so on. People waited in long lines at the Polytechnic in Moscow to get tickets to some of these disputations, which generally featured slides and demonstrations. These lectures packed the large auditorium of the Polytechnic, and visitors were eager to see awe-inspiring photographic exhibits on the cosmos.[17]

In the 1920s eclectic groups and individuals made a particularly impassioned effort to popularize notions of cosmic exploration. The biocosmists were interested in both spreading news on interplanetary travel and focusing on cosmic flight as a means to achieve immortality.[18] What is critical about their group of amorphous followers is that it included both the likes of renowned scientists (such as the geochemist Vladimir Vernadskii) as well as influential Bolsheviks (such as Leonid Krasin, the individual who headed the design committee to erect the Lenin mausoleum).[19] Professors like N. A. Rynin in Leningrad became almost full-time popularizers of particularly spaceflight, while the public eagerly consumed journal and newspaper articles devoted to this topic.[20] Rynin, a prolific writer on Russian rocketry and astronautics, was also interested in organizing public astronautical societies in the 1920s. He began to write and publish a multivolume encyclopedia on cosmonautics that placed him at the forefront of the popularization of rocketry in Russia.[21]

During the Soviet 1920s professional science educators also served as popularizers of spaceflight and rocketry. Those Russian intellectuals, such as the Leningrad journalist and public educator Ia. I. Perel'man, had more didactic purposes in mind than Rynin. Perel'man, for instance, published many articles on rocket science and space travel in the widely distributed popular journals he edited, such as *V masterskoi prirody* (In nature's workshop). These articles had an educational focus, attempting to explain the basics of gravitational forces and rudimentary rocketry to a popular audience.[22] Perel'man was ideally suited for this fervent venture because of the popularity of his book series *Zanimatel'naia nauka* (Science for entertainment), which were used as self-education for Russians. Their general circulation in the 1920s and 1930s numbered in the millions of copies.[23]

Perel'man was particularly interested in spreading the ideas of the space visionary Konstantin Tsiolkovskii, and he popularized Tsiolkovskii's theories on spaceflight in his widely read book *Mezhplanetnye puteshestviia* (Interplanetary travel). Perel'man adamantly defended the notion of spaceflight against skeptics, showing readers how rockets could potentially overcome gravitational forces as projectiles traveling at high speeds with the use of liquid fuels.[24] Perel'man was also editor of the popular science journal *Priroda i liudi* (Nature and people), which carried articles on science and the cosmos. During the 1920s Perel'man had served in the Soviet Commissariat of Enlightenment (Narkompros, the Ministry of Education), where he worked on school curricular reform in areas of physics, mathematics, and astronomy.[25]

Leningrad was not the only crucible of space popularization. Many Moscow astronomical, amateur, and space societies actively popularized rocketry and space travel for an eager Russian public. The Moscow Society of Amateur Astronomers had a technical section that was interested in flights to other planets. In 1924 another distinct group of cosmic enthusiasts organized the Moscow Society for the Study of Interplanetary Communication that sponsored public lectures on rocketry and spaceflight by those such as Fridrikh Tsander and M. I. Lapirov-Skoblo. Another Moscow society, called the Society of Inventors, also had an Interplanetary Section under its purview, which was more interested in organizing public exhibitions in the 1920s that had been a Russian tradition well back into the 1880s.[26]

The Interplanetary Section of the Moscow Society of Inventors, however, became famous for its exhibition on models and mechanisms of interplanetary travel that it held between February and June in 1927. The exhibition had "corners" devoted to those great inventors who now are part of the pantheon of the early rocket specialists. The exhibition thus included a corner to the American physics professor Robert Goddard and the Romanian-born mathematician Hermann Oberth. The exhibition had a display entitled the "scientific-fantastic" period with material from Jules Verne's novels. It also included a display on early "inventors," including such Russians as N. Kibalchich, who designed rockets while in a tsarist *okhrana* (literally "The Defense"—the secret police) prison in 1881. Implicated in the assassination of Tsar Alexander II, Kibalchich compiled drawings in his cell of a rocket-powered aircraft while he awaited execution. He also provided mathematical computations for velocity and thrust of a rocket through air.[27]

The exhibit was particularly known for publicizing the work of Russia's own K. E. Tsiolkovskii, with an entire corner of the hall dedicated to the local mathematics and physics teacher from Kaluga. Tsiolkovskii was thrilled to be included and sent the organizers personal letters thanking them and mentioned this was a wonderful way to spread and popularize his ideas among Muscovites.[28] What is fascinating is that a number of famous Moscow poets and literary elites visited the exhibit—and it was particularly mentioned in the curator's notes that futurist poets such as Vladimir Maiakovskii frequented the halls several times taking notes. This alludes to the fact that the modernist literary elite was at least indirectly interested in rocketry and visions of outer space and interplanetary travel.[29] Deeply affected by this exhibit, as indicated by his questions posed to curators, Maiakovskii the very next year in some of his love poetry made allusions to the heavens beyond the Earth in a dreamlike fashion. In his 1928 poem "Letter from Paris to Comrade Kostrov," he wrote, "the sky has a lot of stars. . . . And if I were not a poet, I would surely be a stargazer."[30]

The Tsiolkovskii exhibit had a variety of his rocket diagrams displayed as well as an overview of his writings claiming he had made some of these discoveries as early as 1895. The exhibit also prominently displayed some of his science-fiction novellas that, according to the curator's notes, were of particular interest to futurist poets, playwrights, and novelists, such as Anatolii Glebov, who also visited the exhibition frequently.[31] In the 1920s writers like Aleksei Tolstoi and film directors such as Iakov Protazanov had more complex visions of Soviet theories of outer space. In Protazanov's 1920s film *Aelita*, based on the Tolstoi short story, a Soviet engineer dreams of a space trip to Mars to escape his earthly problems in Russia. Protazanov, one of the most commercially successful Soviet-era filmmakers, was highly criticized by the Soviet press for this "supposed" critique of Soviet society. Protazanov, himself intrigued by Russian notions of spaceflight, had elaborate set constructions for actions on the alien planet that won the film director much technical praise.[32] Maiakovsky, Protazanov, Tolstoi, and Glebov are but a few Soviet-era cultural figures interested in these imaginative dreams. They reflected the countless science-fiction pieces on outer space during this early Soviet era that became popular with the reading public. Even prerevolutionary works were republished for popular consumption, particularly famous ones such as A. Bogdanov's *Red Star*, also about a future utopia on the planet Mars.[33] Spaceflight occupied not only the Soviet public's interest, but it also became embedded in the cultural intelligentsia's utopian dreams and visions as narrative fodder for their poems, films, and theatrical productions.

National Markers, Spaceflight, and the Soviet Public

By the early and mid-1930s a cultural shift had occurred in Russia under Stalin, coined by the historian Nicholas Timasheff as the Great Retreat. Timasheff, and some current cultural historians (such as David Brandenberger), have argued that Russia during high Stalinism embodied a retreat away from socialist cultural norms back toward greater Russian, more nationalistic themes.[34] Yet as the historian David Hoffman so aptly has reminded us, the 1930s and 1940s also witnessed a continued effort on the part of the regime to modernize their society, not necessarily therefore at odds with previous Communist visions.[35] This is particularly true in the way the Stalinist regime embraced technological feats with such fervor. It is within this context that the Soviet aeronautical feats during the 1930s, for example, were glorified and popularized through propagandistic means by the Soviet press.[36] During the earlier 1920s international aeronautical feats (especially those in the West) were covered with the same frequency as equivalent Russian achievements. During the Stalinist 1930s and 1940s, prior to the era of *Sputnik*, however, Russians began to witness a departure toward an increasingly nationalistic, triumphalist tone—albeit the rhetoric maintained a revolutionary ethos—such as "storming the cosmos," "conquering the stratosphere," and "reaching new heights of the cosmos."

Through theater and other media, Stalin-era cultural figures propagated ideas on spaceflight that reflected this triumphant poised paradigm. Most emblematic of this new departure were the Moscow staged plays of those such as Anatolii Glebov, although poets and film directors showed continued interest in the topic as well. The Soviet writer Glebov, who wrote and produced the play *Gold and Brain* at the Zamoskvoretskii Theatre touched on rocketry in many of his works. In a 1932 article in the journal *Tekhnika* (Technology), Glebov noted how "in my latest play *Morning* (shown at the Revolution Theatre in Moscow), I likewise again touch on the issue of rocketry and space exploration. Furthermore, I am always ready to propagandize about Russian achievement in this useful arena."[37] By the 1930s these cultural figures would help the Soviets to figuratively "storm the stratosphere," as Glebov's article was entitled. They reflected a nationalistic tone as well as a radical transformative impulse so indicative of the Stalinist cultural arena of the 1930s. Much like the radical transformation of nature campaigns that invaded the space of ecological nature preserves, so well documented by the historian Douglas Weiner, the Stalinist cultural elite was ready to conquer and transform the cosmos.[38] Furthermore, these cultural signifiers and tropes may have also been part of a general trend, as the scholar Malte Rolf has pointed out, to reduce the number of acceptable cultural features of the Stalin era into a more manageable set of ideological and nationalistic canons.[39]

It is during this era of resurgent Russian nationalism that the visionary rocket and space theorist K. E. Tsiolkovskii was asked by Stalin to give his famous speech on the future of human space travel on May Day in 1935 from Red Square. This was no ordinary speech, nor was its repercussion among the public and physicists alike. Tsiolkovskii's taped speech was also broadcast by primitive wireless (radio waves) throughout the former Soviet Union, across eleven time zones, with an enormous social impact. Both Stalin, and later Khrushchev, would use the figure of Tsiolkovskii to focus on the superiority of Soviet technology over Western capitalism and its scientific system. However, both during this speech and at times before this event, Tsiolkovskii used these Soviet public venues to promote his own ideas about the future possibility of spaceflight. This speech was given while impressive Soviet airplanes flew above Red Square, and Tsiolkovskii described them as "steel dragonflies" that were only a tip of a more profound iceberg.[40] This dualistic tension between the regime's nationalistic and propagandistic canons in the 1930s on the one hand, and the scientist as cultural purveyor of knowledge on the other, created a tension between patron (state) and supplicant (specialist). In subterranean ways figures like Tsiolkovskii thus tried to alter the Stalinist canon, or at least provide it with nuanced sentiments. This process led to a fragmentation of the Stalinist cultural ideal; this is evident even if the canon, as orchestrated from above, reflected a regime-centered technological myopia.

All the same, the common state-constructed trope of the 1930s and 1940s evoked this Promethean metaphor of conquering the cosmos with Soviet technological ingenuity. Unlike earlier Soviet science fiction, artistic productions of the Stalinist era 1930s and 1940s had the requisite myopic ideological components embedded in these narrative plots about outer space.[41] Probably the best example of this genre was the 1935 Soviet film *Kosmicheskii reis* (Cosmic race), which was directed by V. Zhuravlev. Tsiolkovskii actually consulted on the film, which is mythically set in 1946 at the fictitious All-Union Institute for Inter-Planetary Communication. In the movie young pioneers help an inventor overcome his detractors at all odds, even against the wishes of the old conservative intellectual-director of the institute—thus representing the young Communists achieving miraculous feats in space through the use of new Soviet technology. When a successful journey into space concludes back on Earth, there is the requisite Communist festival in their honor, where the elder Tsiolkovskii-like designer of rockets gives a speech saluting Soviet youth.[42] The film thus merged the Stalinist socialist-realist ideological paradigm with the inspirational, less politicized, hopes and dreams of the real-life elder K. E. Tsiolkovskii.

The popular film and state-sponsored propaganda in the 1930s and 1940s operated simultaneously with a major governmental investment in the potential military use of rockets as weapons under Stalin. In the 1930s the popular *katyusha* system, a battery of trucks equipped with dozens of small rockets, was a technically low-grade method of scattering projectiles at enemy forces (and certainly built on Zasiadko's similar, yet even more primitive, invention in the pre-1917 era). Yet the regime in 1931 had already brought together a number of specialists to work collectively in both Leningrad and Moscow on far more sophisticated technology under what became known as GIRD (Group for the Study of Reactive Motion). In 1933 the GIRD groups amalgamated into the Moscow Scientific Research Institute of Reactive Motion (the RNII). Critically, the founders of this organization, including the dean of Soviet rocketry (S. P. Korolev), claimed that Tsiolkovskii was their inspirational leader, and they made him an honorary member of their engineering board in 1934. By the late 1930s the purges would decimate the ranks of this group as rocket specialists, especially the likes of Korolev, would be incarcerated in *sharashki* (the prison design bureau) to work for the regime's militaristic ends in mostly other pursuits, such as aircraft design. All the same, in the 1930s these technical engineers sought more approval for their work, and more funds from the regime itself, by skillfully invoking popular heroes or "father figures" like Tsiolkovskii. In fact, one of the top-ranking Soviet military engineers, I. T. Kleimenov, was the chief of RNII in Moscow; and both he and Korolev actively corresponded with Tsiolkovskii in an attempt to get his pronounced public support for their research initiatives at a time before this research became completely top secret.[43]

During World War II, however, and throughout Soviet reconstruction in the late 1940s and early 1950s, Soviet aeronautical feats were to some extent relegated to the periphery of the public landscape, while the country was rehabilitated physically, politically, and psychologically. This lack of publicity in the public sphere was also primarily a result of the pronounced issue of secrecy employed by all governments on rocket and bomb development internationally, both during and after World War II. Although much of the international press would eventually discover the successful detonation of an atomic bomb by Igor Kurchatov and his team in the Central Asian Steppe in 1949, the rocket specialists were moved to a secret headquarters outside of Moscow near Kaliningrad.[44] The Soviet military would become obsessed with achieving parity with the United States with regard to rockets, although Korolev would use one of his R7 military missiles to catapult *Sputnik 1* into orbit in October 1957.[45] Nikita Khrushchev and the regime monitored closely their clandestine military investments with much anxiety (and expectations) throughout the 1950s. Sergei Khrushchev noted that his father demanded that Leonid Smirnov, the deputy chairman of the Soviet Council of Ministers in charge of missile technology, phone him after every new project development (and later after every successful launch). Khrushchev demanded these updates from Sergei Korolev and Defense Minister Malinovsky as well. According to Sergei Khrushchev, Premier Khrushchev took much personal pride in these developments, even if conducted under such secrecy (and without public disclosure of successes).[46]

Although much of the secretive technology was generated for military purposes in the early Cold War, and could not be publically announced, once *Sputnik 1* was launched in 1957, the country witnessed an array of publicity on Soviet aeronautical (and now cosmonautic) developments. Interestingly, this was the only element—namely, the overt residual success of *Sputnik*—that could be publicized in laudatory terms without revealing top-secret research. However, after *Sputnik*, as part of the myriad of public celebratory events, a host of journals had pages filled with laudatory articles on Soviet rocketry, the history of spaceflight, and the life of the new cosmonaut. They included eclectic journals such as *Ogonek* (Little flame) as well as more politicized official ones, such as *Kommunist* (The communist). All of these journals publicly expounded on Soviet feats in spaceflight, enabling the regime an outlet to boast about its technological achievements in rocketry.

Articles on Soviet feats in outer space appeared regularly from 1957 through 1960 in newspapers and journals from a variety of genres as diverse as the Soviet Red Army's newspaper *Krasnaia zvezda* (Red star) and even literary journals such as *Literaturnaia gazeta* (Literary gazette). As 1957 and 1958 unfolded, the Communist Party newspaper *Pravda* and the governmental newspaper *Izvestiia* were particularly interested in promoting fantastic new feats in outer space. The press was completely engrossed with the canine heroic pursuits of Laika and a literal host of other Soviet dogs that were used experimentally in these test flights before the age of Yuri Gagarin and human cosmonauts began.[47] After Gagarin's 1961 flight Soviet Premier Khrushchev himself would become obsessed with ceremonies in Red Square throughout this period to glorify cosmonauts and their achievements as well as to make these "official" celebratory versions focused on successes (not the equally abundant yet classified failures). So much so, that his son Sergei in his memoirs recalls an incident immediately after Khrushchev's ouster in October 1964 that is revealing of this emotion. Sergei recounts how his father (now officially retired) on October 23, 1964, much to Leonid Brezhnev's consternation, almost had his driver take him to Red Square to partake in the festivities of three new cosmonauts—a staple, celebratory event that he relished in the earlier years and now missed immensely. Luckily for Brezhnev, the new general secretary of the Communist Party, Khrushchev controlled his excitement for the cosmonauts' heroic feats and instead told the driver to go to his placid dacha outside Moscow.[48]

Although most Soviet writers (and journalists) in varied, censored publications glorified Russian achievements in space in the late 1950s and early 1960s before Khrushchev's ouster, there were the occasional letters to editors (published in such newspapers as *Komsomol'skaia pravda*) that questioned the public support of the space effort—yet they were generally anomalies to the norm.[49] Public debate on the efficacy of the space program did exist in the popular press under Khrushchev.[50] Sometimes, ordinary concerned citizens wrote letters to editors of newspapers that questioned why so much funding was shunted to the space program at a time when salaries for workers in factories were woefully low and consumer items so scarce. Slava Gerovitch, a historian of Soviet technology and science, has also argued that a corollary to these debates in the popular press was a developing tension between cosmonauts themselves and Soviet engineers—particularly whether automatons (or computer devices) should be used in space or real-live test pilots, cosmonauts, or animals. Cosmonauts were particularly concerned about their professional role in this development, and wanted to be in control of the flight process itself. But there was also the public concern about the safety for humans (cosmonauts) as well as animals in spaceflight.[51]

With these exceptions aside, public cultural discourse on the space program was mostly constrained and even limited to voices with large public reputations (such as major writers of literary significance). Furthermore, one can argue this discussion in the press was class-specific. Namely, it was the cultural intelligentsia of the 1950s and 1960s who raised these issues and concerns regarding the amount of funds spent on large-scale technologies. Some literary figures, such as Il'ia Ehrenburg, were concerned about how technology and the space race obscured the importance of other aspects of Soviet life on Earth, such as the development of literature and the arts, and questioned the substantial funds and government subsidies put into these technical arenas.[52] These critiques by literary figures and citizens alike may have been a repercussion of the Khrushchev "thaw"—the limited loosening of controls on artistic and public expression in the Soviet Union from 1956 until approximately 1962.[53] The intelligentsia had a strong collective sense of its past and may have felt ostracized by the celebratory focus on Soviet technology. Sometimes these debates raged in popular journals but mainly in those read by a more educated public—this is especially true for a variety of topical issues and debates that appeared in *Literaturnaia gazeta* (Literary newspaper) during this time period. One interesting topical debate became known as the *Liriki-fiziki* or the "lyrical poets vs. physicists," while others dealt with the funding of big science. These debates, also featured in the Communist Youth League press, focused on how the arts could survive in an age where technological feats reigned supreme. Ironically, the cultural intelligentsia was obsessed itself with "cosmic visions" thematically, but at some point rocket specialists (and the regime's prioritized military investments during the Cold War) may have impinged on the cultural intelligentsia's status.

The historian of technology Paul Josephson, in his analysis of the public ramifications of nuclear, atomic, and space science, has argued that celebrations and mass rallies (particularly in Moscow) became an important site for the Soviet "masses" to become involved in the spectacle of display, constructed from above, for Soviet "big science." His work has also touched on themes regarding the efficacy of space research.[54] As Josephson has aptly noted in his diligent research, planetariums hosted lectures on outer space, short stories for adults and children were written with exaggerated platitudes by writers, while Soviet composers created popular songs (especially short *chastushki*) to be sung to children at schools celebrating *Sputnik*.[55]

What is generally left out of the scholarly analysis of the rhetoric of Soviet technological feats in outer space, however, is how official academic institutions, besides the Soviet press and journalistic community, also played a distinct and crucial role in the celebratory theatrics of Soviet space accomplishments. Established scientific institutions, such as the Academy of Sciences, probably became the greatest proponents and conduits for disseminating more detailed public lectures on the significance of these achievements. Furthermore, as proponents of the regime, they carried a level of scientific and technical authority among the general public that may have eclipsed the litany of pronouncements in the press and journals.

In actuality, it was the real father of the Russian space program, S. P. Korolev, the director of the post–World War II Soviet rocket program, who was asked to direct these celebrations at the academy. He gave the 1957 keynote commemorative speech for the capstone series of events planned in the Khrushchev era that honored Soviet space legends such as Konstantin Tsiolkovskii. Fortuitously, some of these highly orchestrated celebratory events were planned by scientists and technicians during the centennial-year celebration of Tsiolkovskii's birth, the year of the launching of Soviet *Sputnik 1* in 1957. Lectures and festivities such as these at the academy mythologized the "founding fathers of Soviet spaceflight and rocketry," thus creating a Soviet pantheon as cultural referent. In the 1940s, primarily after the war and into the 1950s, the Soviets made several public (some unsubstantiated and others not) claims of national priority in scientific discoveries—especially in the era of *Sputnik* regarding rocketry.[56]

Understanding Popular Space Culture in the Era of *Sputnik*

State-sponsored technological propaganda was not unique or exceptional to Soviet Russia. In fact, it was an inherent aspect of Western governmental rhetoric as well as their construction of their own heroes in the press. Scientists in Soviet Russia, however, even the most heralded in the hagiography, such as Tsiolkovsksii, had their own ideas about popularizing notions of spaceflight. Furthermore, they tapped into the popular interest in cosmic flight by an already engaged audience outside of the state's purview or orchestration. This dynamic, however, created a complex and unique duality in Soviet political and cultural life. For instance, while both Stalin and later Khrushchev would use the figure of those such as Tsiolkovskii (or Gagarin) to focus on the superiority of Soviet technology over Western capitalism and its scientific system, figures like these men used these Soviet public venues to promote their own ideas about the future possibility of spaceflight.

Although events like this were certainly propagandistic public spectacle, scientists and future physicists alike were still very impressed with the secondary depoliticized vision that Tsiolkovskii's ideas embodied. In his memoirs the nuclear physicist and science adviser to M. S. Gorbachev, Roald Z. Sagdeev, himself recognized the duality embedded in these Soviet public spectacles. On the one hand, he believes Stalin used Tsiolkovskii's 1935 broadcast from Red Square to further build the notion of the superiority of Soviet technology. On the other hand, predominantly because of Stalin and the Soviet regime's support, Tsiolkovskii's work became better known in the 1930s and 1940s, and many future space scientists read his popular work voraciously. Sagdeev has argued that on May 1, 1935, enthusiastic Soviet citizens, including his own parents (educated scientific academics), were enthralled by the speech. Furthermore, the popularization of spaceflight had a readymade audience that was not inextricably linked to prescribed directions from the regime itself.[57]

Valentin Glushko, the designer of Energiya and many rocket engines that operated on Tsiolkovskii's dream of using liquid propellants, corroborates to some extent Sagdeev's perspective in his own memoirs. Glushko corresponded with Tsiolkovskii as a teenager and was inspired by his popular books in the 1920s and 1930s. Glushko believed that mixed in with the Soviet propaganda and nationalist fervor of space exploration propagated from above was a sheer enthusiasm and pride on the part of future scientists (and young space enthusiasts) from below.[58] Many physicists (and ordinary citizens alike) made pilgrimages to Kaluga (Russia) to see Tsiolkovskii before his death in September 1935, while Tsiolkovskii's funeral in provincial Russia was almost a type of national, cathartic dirge and thus a reflection of the spontaneous interest in local space heroes.

Popular adulation for space heroes continued into the Khrushchev era and beyond in Brezhnev's times. The eminent historian of Russian science Loren R. Graham, in his recent memoirs, had a similar impression on April 12, 1961, when he marched through Red Square at the celebration for the cosmonaut Yuri Gagarin sponsored by the Soviet leadership. Graham found this a mix of propagandistic spectacle from above with a sincere, heartfelt public outpouring of support from below. As Graham looked back at that day and canonization, he also reviewed in his mind the views of Soviet citizens, their pride in Gagarin, and the popular interest in spaceflight: "In later years when the Soviet Union became a decrepit and failing society, I often recall that day as the apogee in Soviet citizens' belief that they held the key to the future of civilization. The celebrations on the street were genuine and heartfelt. Soviet science was, they were sure, the best in the world, and Soviet rockets succeeded where American ones failed."[59]

In the end it is impossible critically to completely separate the regime's nationalist paradigms from the pride generated from below. One cannot also assume that scientists like Tsiolkovskii, who gave heralded speeches on the future of Soviet cosmonautics, only had the regime's agenda in mind when agreeing to propagate messages of national pride. Many of Russia's cultural elites also popularized notions of spaceflight because of the inherent fascination they had with cosmic themes. Besides the politicized message of Soviet competition with the West, the Russian people themselves engaged notions of spaceflight from a sheer human impulse of fascination in exploration going back to the late imperial period forward to Khrushchev's times.

Part II
Myth and Reality in the Soviet Space Program

3

Cosmic Contradictions

Popular Enthusiasm and Secrecy in the Soviet Space Program

Asif A. Siddiqi

Since the collapse of the Soviet Union, *Sputnik* and its successors have been the subject of a vast literature that has generally split into two distinct categories. One body of work, focused on recovering "truth" about the effort, has sought to fill gaps in our knowledge. In the deluge of "new" information available with the coming of glasnost and then continuing into the postsocialist period, historians and journalists have rushed to reveal the "real" story behind the Soviet space program. Another smaller but growing stream of recent literature, favored by social and cultural historians, has explored the meanings behind the undeniably massive cosmic enthusiasm that characterized the height of the Soviet space program in the 1960s. Here, scholars have delved into the social and cultural resonance of space, situating their claims in the broader matrix of postwar Soviet history. In broad terms the first canon has been concerned with production, and the latter with consumption. One obvious bridge between these two literatures has been the figure of the Soviet cosmonaut, who was simultaneously part of the machinery of science, technology, and industry that allowed the Soviet Union to achieve many impressive feats in the early years of the space race *and* a constituent of the machinery of public relations, critical to creating a global wave of popular enthusiasm for Soviet exploits. Despite a widespread fascination with cosmonauts and what they represented, we know very little about the codes that governed their passage from one world to the other, from production to consumption, from the private to the public. Mediating this connection between production and consumption, between "truth" and "image," was the regime of Soviet secrecy, which not only circumscribed the ways in which cosmonauts crossed over these divides, but also (re)constructed text, images, and symbols on cosmic topics in fundamental ways that remain misunderstood.

Secrecy pervaded every single aspect of the Soviet space program.[1] In the early 1960s so much of it was shrouded in secrecy that it seemed that the program could be capable of anything, and its future appeared boundless. The less we knew, the more seemed possible. This heightened level of secrecy, the strictest it was ever to be in the history of Soviet space exploits, was already in place by the launch of *Sputnik*, the world's first artificial satellite. Two years before *Sputnik*'s launch, on August 8, 1955, the Soviet Presidium (as the Politburo was known at the time) approved a project to launch a satellite into Earth's orbit; one of the first problems on the agenda was *what* to say to the world about the event. The final version of the official Telegraph Agency of the Soviet Union (TASS) communiqué, which was approved ten days later with the help of party ideologue and Politburo member Mikhail Suslov, established several precedents for all subsequent official pronouncements on the Soviet space program.[2]

The press release contained no information on who built the satellite, who launched it, what kind of rocket was used, from where it was launched, why it was launched, and who decided to launch it. The final version of the communiqué, issued on the early morning of October 5, 1957, is illuminating in what it *does* say: there is an abundance of arcane scientific and technical data about the satellite and its trajectory, as if to overwhelm the reader with mathematics in the absence of even a picture of the object. What remains of the text is taken up by expressions of pride of the late "father" of Soviet cosmonautics, Konstantin Eduardovich Tsiolkovskii and some final words about possibilities opened up by this accomplishment. These allusions to the past and the future left a discernible hole about information in the present.[3]

Secrecy was not simply a regime for preventing the transmission of information from one community to another; it also encapsulated an ongoing discursive metacommentary about the relationship between the space program and the Soviet populace in the 1960s. In every proclamation about a new achievement in space, in every declaration about the heroic work of a cosmonaut, and in all ephemera of the culture of Soviet cosmic travel was embedded a conversation about the acceptable limits of secrecy. Yet because of secrecy, the Soviet space program was victim to a fundamental contradiction resulting from two countervailing impulses. On the one hand, party and government officials sought to promote the space program as much as possible, aided by rhetoric that repeatedly connected the triumphs of the space program with the power of socialism. On the other hand, those selfsame officials accepted the need to maintain deep secrecy about almost all aspects of the enterprise. These antithetical impulses gave the Soviet space program, both in its internal workings and its public image, a peculiar quality that distinguished it from its American counterpart. The discourse surrounding the space effort was characterized by a "rhetorical tension" that was never fully resolved but embodied and amplified by the frequently ambiguous messages about the program's goals, successes, and values.

This chapter explores this "rhetorical tension" to answer a fundamental question: how was it that the Soviet space program—the central advertising emblem of postwar Soviet Union—was shrouded in the highest secrecy and drowned in draconian censorship at the very time when the controls over cultural production were at their most liberal, during the Khrushchev "thaw"?[4] Any possible answer to this question must lie in a deep exploration of the creation, uses, and repercussions of the secrecy regime in the Soviet space program—in particular, the edicts, prohibitions, and procedures of Glavlit, the main censorship body within the Soviet government, that were embedded throughout the entire Soviet media apparatus, including those publications that consistently extolled the glories of the Soviet space program to the populace in the 1960s and 1970s. The chapter explores the motivations and rationales behind the strict secrecy regime in the space program that were rooted in the larger culture of institutional secrecy in the Soviet Union that originated in the 1920s, soon after the October Revolution. It deconstructs the practice of secrecy as manifested in the space program—its main characteristics, how it operated, explicable patterns, and most important, the effects of the secrecy regime for the public understanding of Soviet cosmic exploits during the 1960s and 1970s. Official pronouncements—whether communicated at a press conference, depicted in a postage stamp, or recounted in a museum placard—were the end results of deeply contested visions of the Soviet space program. These expressions did not reflect a monolithic stand on such issues as modernity, progress, technology, and socialism; rather, they were the outcome of negotiation between various parties invested in maintaining, reinforcing, or undermining secrecy.

Glavlit

Drawing from a long tradition of censorship during the imperial era, the Bolsheviks put their particular imprint on the control of information immediately after coming to power. Only days after the storming of the Winter Palace, on November 10, 1917 ("new style," referring to the Gregorian calendar, which was adopted in Russia in 1918), the Bolshevik Party issued a "Decree on the Press," which, conceding that the "bourgeois press" was "no less dangerous than bombs and machine-guns," prohibited all press that advocated "open resistance or disobedience against the workers' and peasants' government."[5] The culmination of this process was the formation in 1922 of the Main Administration for Literary and Publishers' Issues (Glavnoe upravlenie po delam literatury i izdatel'stva, or Glavlit) as part of Narkompros, the governmental body in charge of cultural activities.[6] Throughout the 1920s Glavlit displayed a noticeable latitude in what was allowed for publication, in line with the economic liberalism of the New Economic Policy (NEP) era, although simultaneously the party *apparat* encoded new rules governing and limiting the circulation of information within the party structure. A whole host of military, economic, political, and "general" information was blanketed under various degrees of classification.[7]

As the historian A. V. Blium has noted, the "era of total secrecy . . . began" by the late 1920s, near the end of the NEP era.[8] Glavlit's work expanded in leaps and bounds, helped by special "lists" (*perechen'*), which themselves were secret, that enumerated the types of information that were considered secret, such as statistical information on the homeless and unemployed, information about sanitary conditions in jails, crime statistics, numbers of suicides, and so on. All "real" economic information, particularly at the national level, was also shrouded in secrecy, while all descriptions of calamities or accidents, especially those dealing with lack of food, were prohibited from publication. Already by the late 1920s any information that privileged the West or showed Western industry in a favorable light, at least as compared with the Soviet Union, was excised from publication. Acting on these lists, Glavlit issued a barrage of directives to control the flow of particular types of information.

The repressive climate in the late Stalin years brought more draconian secrecy measures into law. Concern over revealing scientific secrets may have played a role in this process. After the infamous Kliueva-Roskin affair, when information about a supposed "cure" for cancer was passed on to American scientists during a brief period of openness in 1946, the Supreme Soviet issued a decree the following year intensifying the penalties for revealing "state secrets."[9] In March 1948, Stalin signed a Council of Ministers resolution that enacted a total ban on all information that touched on state interests. The fact that the decree itself was classified top secret was emblematic of the nature of secrecy in the Soviet context. As the scholar Yorlam Gorlizki has noted: "Stalin pressed the [new secrecy] campaign beyond any rational limits so that it assumed a completely inconsistent and illogical form."[10] He notes that the Council of Ministers was flooded with inquiries, "some quite farcical," about the kind of information that needed to be kept secret. Even evidently innocent information about the operation of a ministry had to be kept closely guarded and "de-secretized" if previously out in the open. Given that the Soviet ballistic missile program, which eventually became the Soviet space program, was undergoing its birth pangs at the time, it is not surprising that even "normal" aspects of its functioning, such as recruiting secretarial or custodial staff or housing issues, were shrouded in a blanket of secrecy. The March 1948 decree was strictly enforced at the lowest levels of missile design organizations throughout the 1950s.[11]

The "thaw" under Khrushchev, the zenith of Soviet successes in space, continued the paradoxical and contradictory tendencies of Soviet secrecy. As others have shown, print culture was crucial during this period as a vehicle for assisting in social change, not so much to challenge the norms of prevailing Soviet life but "to reinvest them with the significance they had lost over the previous thirty years."[12] A combination of new publications, a fresh philosophy about the role of the written word for the future of socialism, and fluctuating notions of what was permissible, resulted ironically in a "flood of new instructions from above," meaning that "Party controls over print culture proliferated in the post-Stalin period, even if they did not intensify."[13] A Glavlit report issued in 1965, reviewing its previous two years of operation to "protect military and state secrets in print, radio, television, and cinema, and ... entertainment" and to "prevent the spread of foreign publications in the country containing anti-Soviet anti-socialist materials," underscored just how busy Soviet censors had been. In 1964, Glavlit employees "monitored" nearly 192,000 pages of literature, compared to 186,000 the year before. Their work included preparing a new "List of information forbidden to publish in the open press, transmitted on radio and television" as well as a similar list meant for regional media outlets. Relevant instructions for the space program were enumerated in Glavlit's "Instructions on how to prepare for the publication of information on scientific and technological achievements of the USSR, which can be recognized as patentable inventions and discoveries."[14]

Glavlit had their hands full as the Soviet space program reached its zenith in the early 1960s. The early cosmic successes coincided with a massive growth in Soviet print publications; almost a quarter of the non-specialized popular journals in existence in the late 1980s were established in the late 1950s and early 1960s. Many of these new journals, such as *Iunost'* (Youth, established 1955), *Iunyi tekhnik* (Junior technician, 1956), and *Iskatel'* (Adventurer, 1961) were key avenues for bringing the Soviet space program to the masses. Older journals, such as *Ogonek* (Light), *Tekhnika-molodezhi* (Technology for youth), and *Znanie-sila* (Knowledge is power), continued into the 1960s with the same vein of technologically utopian literature that was characteristic of their articles in the decade before. The popular literature on space that emerged in the wake of *Sputnik* in 1957 did not emerge out of a vacuum but out of a strong and vibrant tradition of space-themed writing that was ubiquitous in the early and mid-1950s.[15]

What changed was the scale and content of it—that is, there was much more of it and there were now "real" events as points of reference, not just idle fantasy. Spaceships replaced airplanes as harbingers of the future, a change reflected in the transformation of the Air Force's banner journal, *Vestnik vozdushnogo flota* (Journal of the air fleet), originally established in 1918, to *Aviatsiia i kosmonavtika* (Aviation and cosmonautics) in 1962. The latter journal served as one of the mouthpieces of the Soviet space establishment. Major General Nikolai Kamanin, the air force official in charge of cosmonaut training who served on the journal's editorial board helped its editor, Colonel Ivan Shipilov, establish "close ties" with highly placed but secret designers and scientists so that Shipilov could "use this connection for the cause [of popularizing space exploration]."[16]

The post-thaw period saw strengthened and more streamlined controls over what was permitted in print. In 1965, although it was technically forbidden to mention the name of the mysterious "chief designer" of the space program, it was still acceptable to note that "owing to abnormalities associated with the situation of the cult of personality, [his] rocket aircraft was flight-tested only in 1940."[17] This oblique allusion to the Stalinist purges was whitewashed out by the time the first biographies of Sergei Korolev appeared in the late 1960s.[18] To eliminate such "deviations" from the correct ideological stance and also to encourage publishing houses and other media organs to take more responsibility for censorship in the post-thaw era, the secretariat of the Central Committee issued a new comprehensive decree on secrecy in January 1969. The new law required Glavlit to "strengthen control over the maintenance of state and military secrets in the press. To establish that all questions arising in the process of preliminary monitoring of works of an ideological and political nature, are to be examined at the level of heads of Glavlit and the heads of publishing agencies and cultural organizations. Comments from [Glavlit] workers are to be brought to the attention of the authors of the works without reference to the censor. Violation of this order shall be considered a violation of state and party discipline."[19]

The decree effectively strengthened Glavlit's control over both information and ideological content. At the same time, the immovable curtain between the author and the censor was rendered further opaque. Eight years later, at the height of Brezhnev's stagnation, the Central Committee department in charge of censorship was able to proudly report that the clauses of the decree had been properly executed and that "Glavlit systematically informs the leaders of the organs of press, information, and culture, and in necessary cases party and Soviet organs on errors of ideological and political nature, contained in materials meant for publication or public use."[20]

The censorship apparatus based around Glavlit remained largely the same throughout the 1960s and 1970s. From 1953 on Glavlit, now with the official expansion Main Directorate for the Protection of Military and State Secrets in Print, was subordinated directly to the Council of Ministers—that is, the highest governmental authority in the Soviet Union.[21] In principle, Glavlit was an execution authority, receiving general ideological guidelines from the Department of Propaganda of the Central Committee of the Communist Party, one of numerous departments responsible for any and every aspect of Soviet society, culture, and the economy.[22] This department was itself overseen by a secretary of the Central Committee, one responsible for "ideological issues" who had the last word on censorship.[23] On paper, these party functionaries were responsible for determining the appropriate ideological content of open expression so that Glavlit could do its mission of censorship, but in practice, Glavlit's functions were a mix of policy and implementation, an overlap that mirrored the connection between two separate but also overlapping functions: ideological policing and protecting secrets.[24]

Why Secrecy?

Iaroslav Golovanov, the famed and now late Russian space journalist, rationalizing why there was so much secrecy surrounding the space program, once astutely noted that: "Secrecy was necessary so that no one would overtake us. But later when they did overtake us, we maintained secrecy so that no one knew that we had been overtaken."[25] Golovanov's half joke was not so far from the truth in that it encapsulated two different rationales: to protect the strengths of the Soviet state, usually of a military nature; and to protect the weaknesses of the Soviet state, sometimes military but more often than not economical or social. Disaggregating these rationales reveals an array of subordinate factors, some of them repeated explicitly in many Glavlit documents in the postwar period and evident in the workings of censorship within the space industry. These rationales include: to protect information necessary for national security; to present the Soviet Union to the outside world in the most favorable light by controlling information seen as damaging to the national reputation; to present a monolithic view of the Soviet Union where there is no dissent over state policies; to convey that the party and government are in control, whether over ideas, technology, or nature, and that there are no accidental outcomes in Soviet society; and to protect Soviet claims to inventions and technologies by not revealing too much information about them—a point mentioned in many Glavlit documents.[26] Ultimately, as the long history of Glavlit shows, secrecy was also endemic because of the enduring tradition of censorship in the Soviet (and before it, the Russian context)—that is, there was a self-sustaining quality to the sheen of secrecy, ensuring that it had an indelible and perpetual presence in the Soviet space program despite the many successes and failures of the effort through several decades.

There were compelling institutional explanations for the regime of secrecy that surrounded the Soviet space program, rationales that transcended any need to maintain the fiction of a Soviet lead in the "space race." The fact that the entire institutional structure supporting the Soviet space program was lodged firmly and deeply in a military setting was undoubtedly the most critical factor. The earliest Soviet successes in space—such as the launch of *Sputnik*, Laika, probes to the moon, Yuri Gagarin, Valentina Tereshkova, and many more—were orchestrated by the Experimental Design Bureau-1 (Opytno-konstruktorskoe biuro-1, or OKB-1) headed by the so-called chief designer Sergei Pavlovich Korolev. OKB-1 was subordinated for many years under the Ministry of the Defense Industry and then eventually, like most other space enterprises during the late Soviet era, under the Ministry of General Machine Building. Both of these ministries were part of the highly secretive military-industrial complex, scrutinized by Western intelligence agencies throughout the Cold War. OKB-1's primary goal, at least until the mid-1960s was not space but rather to develop more efficient intercontinental ballistic missiles for the Soviet Strategic Rocket Forces. Because of its association with such an overtly military project, Soviet space achievements were shrouded in an extra layer of secrecy. In July 1955, when work on the rocket that launched *Sputnik* was reaching peak levels, the Council of Ministers issued a decree "with the goal of ensuring more strict secrecy on work carried out on rocket and reactive armaments" that enumerated a whole host of new regulations at various enterprises, including the appointment of a deputy director at each workplace to oversee secrecy regimes and bringing in KGB personnel to help.[27]

Military secrecy could be justified without much controversy because there was "the legitimate strategic purpose of denying sensitive national security information to potential enemies."[28] Secrecy over military affairs was particularly stringent in the defense industry, which developed weapons. Although the names of certain accomplished designers—particularly aviation designers—were revealed during the interwar years, this practice was abandoned at the height of the Cold War when the identities of such designers as Korolev were unknown to the public. Moreover, all information about the organizations that they headed was kept strictly secret. Real names of weapons were never used in writing. Instead Soviet industrial managers developed an esoteric system of naming weapons that relied on a number-letter-number system that was based on no discernable logic; in all written documents, for example, the *Vostok* spacecraft was referred to as "object 11F63" (*izdelie 11F63*), while its launch rocket was "object 8K72K" (*izdelie 8K72K*). Many workers employed at factories contracted to deliver parts for such spacecraft had little or no idea what the part was for. Draconian rules dictated daily handling of paperwork within defense enterprises, with documents divided into at least five categories of access—none of which were permitted to be seen by workers not employed by the enterprise. Workers in a particular department at an organization usually had no knowledge of what was going on in other departments.[29]

Military secrecy first emerged as a temporary practice as part of the draconian measures adopted during the civil war. These measures were reinforced during the so-called war scare of the late 1920s. In 1927 all defense factories were renamed so that their traditional names were replaced with numbers beginning from one to fifty-six. Eventually, this custom was extended to research and design institutions attached to the factories, which were also given numbers to disguise their work profile. This tradition endured to the mid-1960s so that Korolev's organization was simply named OKB-1, while a competitor organization was named OKB-52. To further obfuscate the mission of these institutions, in the 1960s ministries introduced a wholesale name change to generic "machine building" titles. For example, Korolev's OKB-1 was renamed the Central Design Bureau of Experimental Machine Building, while OKB-52 became Central Design Bureau of Machine Building. Afraid that Western intelligence would pick up even these bland names, workers at such institutions were not allowed to use them in public and instead ordered to use special "post office box numbers" to refer to each institute, design bureau, or factory.

The military secrecy regime far exceeded what was necessary for strategic rationales, indicating that this regime was driven by more than simply a need to protect state secrets about mobilization plans and weapons development. An important driver of military secrecy—and in fact, the entire Soviet secrecy regime—was to maintain privilege of those who had access to decision making. The historian John Barber and his coauthors have noted that "secretiveness was . . . one of the defenses protecting the priority and privilege of the military sector generally, and of the defence industry in particular."[30] Secrecy in the Soviet space program, embedded deep within the structure of the Soviet defense industry, stemmed from a similar rationale, given that the space program received enormous disbursements at times—for example, during the era of "stagnation," when many Soviet citizens might have wished for a better standard of living. In addition, there were many within the space program who insulated themselves from critique not only from the general public but also from their peers within the program who might have threatened their status and privilege. Designers would routinely conceal their own plans or exaggerate their own accomplishments to industrial managers or party leaders; the system rewarded those who clung to secrecy or obfuscation.

One of the most enduring examples of military secrecy—the creation of a fake launch site—suggests another rationale for military secrecy, one that had less to do with protecting military secrets than to project the peaceful intent of the space program to the domestic audience. After the *Sputnik* launch Soviet officials said nary a word about exactly from where all these rockets were being launched, but because they wanted to record Gagarin's flight as a world record to the Fédération Aéronautique Internationale (FAI), they had to submit the name of the launch site, as per the federation's rules. It was out of question for the Soviets to reveal the name and location of the launch range, located in a desolate area of Kazakhstan, whose express purpose was to support the launch of intercontinental ballistic missiles (ICBMs). For years, any speculation in the West on where Soviet rockets were launched from was immediately reported back to Soviet officials, who were extremely sensitive about this information.[31]

Given this conundrum, two junior officers at a military institute were asked to come up with a solution. One of them, Vladimir Iastrebov, later recalled that "we needed to name the launch place for the launch vehicle of the *Vostok* spaceship, but we were not allowed to mention Tiura-Tam, where the cosmodrome (or more precisely, the rocket range) was located. Because of this, [Aleksei] Maksimov and I selected on the map the 'most plausible' [adjacent] point of launch that was not far from Tiura-Tam. It turned out to be the town of Baikonur, and since then, with our casual selection, the cosmodrome got its now well-known name."[32] For more than two decades after the launch of Gagarin, official Soviet media assiduously maintained the fiction that Soviet rockets were launched from a place called "Baikonur" in Kazakhstan, when in fact the town of Baikonur was three hundred kilometers away from the actual launch point. The façade was maintained despite the fact that the actual location was widely known by Western observers already in the 1960s, suggesting that the obfuscation was meant more for a domestic audience rather than a foreign one. Soviet citizens were to believe that their glorious space program had purely civilian purposes while the American one had belligerent intentions.

Space Censors

Glavlit, through its daughter organizations and the publishing-house system, was the ultimate arbiter in directing the censorship apparatus during the Soviet era, but it delegated censorship duties in a number of thematic areas, such as military issues, nuclear weapons, and the space program, to smaller specialized organs.[33] During the early months after *Sputnik*, the process of issuing public communiqués and books on the space program was rather haphazard; senior scientists and engineers within the program typically drew up statements that passed through censors within the Academy of Sciences and the relevant publishing house, with Glavlit checking the results but usually deferring to their authority.[34] The academy posed as a convenient public face of the space program although its institutes and staff had little direct involvement in Soviet space achievements because it was run almost entirely out of the Soviet defense industry.

Because of this public fiction, many of the thousands of young Soviet enthusiasts who wrote to volunteer for the space program addressed their letters to "the Academy of Sciences." These letters were then passed on to an institute within the Ministry of Defense with the descriptive name NII-4 (pronounced *nee-chetyr*), which, not so much from intent but rather confusion, inherited much of the public relations functions of the space program in the early 1960s. NII-4, whose main job was to evaluate and conduct research on the battle-fighting capabilities of nuclear-tipped intercontinental ballistic missiles, was located in the Bol'shevo suburb of Moscow, not far from Korolev's own design bureau. Here, the institute deputy director Iurii Mozzhorin, a colonel in the Soviet artillery forces, was handed the job of drawing up the TASS communiqués that were hungrily pored over both at home and abroad for clues into the Soviet space program. Mozzhorin remembers drawing up the press release for

Gagarin's launch in advance of the event. Three preprepared envelopes were distributed to radio and TV stations and TASS, each containing the text of a particular scenario (complete success, death of cosmonaut at launch or in orbit, or emergency landing of cosmonaut on foreign territory); depending on the outcome, the press was ordered to open one and destroy the others.[35]

Throughout the 1960s each State Commission—the ad hoc group of high-level individuals from different branches of the government that oversaw a particular space mission—had a special "press group" that authored and disseminated information about space events. By mid-decade, however, it had become clear that the Soviet space program needed a formalized system to prepare and control the information that was revealed about the space effort, especially because the amount of information being disseminated increased dramatically every year. The obvious solution was to assign Glavlit this job. In July 1967 the highest industrial officials in the space program drew up a plan to create an "expert commission" attached to Glavlit that would be responsible for coordinating and approving all media on the Soviet space program. Because leading space program officials would head and manage the commission, Glavlit opposed this plan, undoubtedly because it would diminish Glavlit's control over the flow of information. In the end, Glavlit lost this battle, and the job was assigned to the space establishment, with Glavlit maintaining a coordinating capacity instead of a leading one.[36]

Mozzhorin retained the task of managing the public relations capacity of the space program. As he moved from institution to institution, from his original employer (NII-4) to TsNIIMash (the Tsentral'nyi nauchno-issledovatel'skii institut mashinostroeniia, or Central Scientific-Research Institute of Machine Building), the leading research and development institute of the Soviet space program, he took the media job with him. As director of TsNIIMash for nearly thirty years, Mozzhorin played a critical role in arbitrating conflicts within the Soviet space program but also formulating future plans. As such, he was in an ideal position to know the full spectrum of both prevailing and future capabilities of the program. His "propaganda" task was formalized by a Council of Ministers decree on July 1, 1968, when the Soviet government for the first time *officially* assigned his staff at TsNIIMash the mission of "organization and preparation of materials on rocket-space themes for publication in print, transmission on radio and television and for showing in film and in exhibitions."[37] Soon after, a team at TsNIIMash performed a two-year research project (from 1968 to 1970) on the entire spectrum of Soviet space-related propaganda and how to systematize the process. The team prepared a draft decree, later approved by the USSR Council of Ministers, which included a document titled "Regulations on the Preparation for Open Publication of Materials on Rocket-Space Technology."[38]

Secrecy was obviously a central concern here, as Mozzhorin himself recalled. He was responsible "not only for the preparation of drafts of TASS communiqués, [and] headers for scientific and technical articles in the newspapers, but also [for ensuring] . . . that all open publications on rocket-space technology in the Soviet Union and materials exported abroad were technically correct, did not contradict government edicts, and did not violate secrecy."[39] Mozzhorin performed this "thankless" job together with Anatolii Eremenko, "a very smart, principled, technically literate, and literary specialist" who headed TsNIIMash's department of "information, expertise and history." Like Mozzhorin, Eremenko authored many books and articles for the Soviet media on the history of Soviet space exploration.[40] This department coordinated their work with representatives from the Academy of Sciences, the Ministry of Defense, the defense industrial ministries, various ministries responsible for radio, television, print, film, central and local organs of the Soviet press, TASS, the Novosti press agency, and the Znanie (Knowledge) All-Union Society, a major popular science outlet during the Soviet era. Both Mozzhorin and Eremenko remained at their posts until 1990, when the former retired. Eremenko continues to work at TsNIIMash and remains in charge of its museum; in 2004, despite his work in the censorship apparatus or perhaps because of it, he was awarded the Utkin Silver Medal "for many years [of] active journalistic work on rocket and space technology and cosmonautics."[41]

Mozzhorin's group played a key role in articulating the public face of the Soviet space program, but the evidence suggests that high-level party and government officials were frequently drawn into issues that were relatively trivial. The Military-Industrial Commission, the very powerful governmental body that supervised the Soviet military-industrial complex during much of the Cold War, for example, had to approve TASS communiqués on every Soviet space event prepared by Mozzhorin's group. When questions of openness reached the Politburo level, as they did often, they highlighted an acute ambivalence about secrecy that frequently delayed plans. For instance, in February 1964, U.S. and Soviet officials signed an agreement to display space artifacts in each other's countries. The Politburo (then known as the Presidium) met a couple of months later to discuss the issue but deferred to the expertise of rocket designers and administrators who recommended that certain aspects of the *Vostok* spacecraft be declassified for the exhibit.[42]

Despite the recommendations, doubts plagued the main actors for months. The Central Committee and the Council of Ministers adopted a set of guidelines for displaying space program artifacts in museums only on February 26, 1965. Even with these guidelines senior party officials continued to waffle about displaying the *Vostok* and had to be apprised of the most arcane details of exhibitions. When space industry officials organized an exhibit entitled "Man in Space" for foreign audiences, the discussion once again went up to the Politburo level in August 1965. As a result of these discussions, the Central Committee and Council of Ministers issued a further decree three months later approving the *Vostok* exhibit.[43] In all, it took eighteen months to simply find agreement about what to show abroad.

If the Politburo often had to give the final word, Mozzhorin and Eremenko wielded enormous power because they provided the first and most important filter for information that the architects of the space program wanted to publish. As such, every single pronouncement on the Soviet space program—whether in a book, a newspaper, a magazine, a poster, a postage stamp, or a placard at a museum—passed through the hands of these two men, who had a special office in the main TASS building in Moscow. Mozzhorin later recalled that managing this affair was a "nightmare" partly because he was frequently caught between the demands of leading space designers who wanted recognition and glory and party ideologues who decried such attempts because they might violate secrecy edicts. Mozzhorin's group also feared that they would "let" something out and be penalized for it, and thus usually erred on the side of caution, even if the information seemed benign. He was particularly afraid that some or other party member would find something published in a foreign news magazine about the Soviet space program that should not have been there.

In one case Mozzhorin was nearly dismissed from his post. In 1967 he approved an essay for publication in the newspaper *Trud* in which Strategic Rocket Forces Commander-in-Chief Vladimir Tolubko noted that military officers were the ones operating the infrastructure in support of the Soviet space program. Minister of Defense Andrei Grechko insisted that there be an investigation on why this article was published, because he feared it might convey to Americans that the Soviet Union was militarizing space.[44] Several people were reprimanded for the incident but Mozzhorin kept his job, although Grechko proved right to some degree. The article was immediately picked up by the American media, scrutinized widely, and confirmed what Western observers had long suspected: that the Soviet space program was essentially a military enterprise.[45]

Where Mozzhorin and Eremenko were the final arbiters of the public face of the Soviet space program, they rarely ever wrote material personally. For this task the party's Central Committee approved a select few journalists, usually one each from a major newspaper or journal to be privy to secret information. These journalists were granted special permission to travel to secret places, meet people whose identities were still secret, and see classified equipment. Yet such writers as Aleksandr Romanov (TASS), Vladimir Gubarev (*Pravda*), Mikhail Rebrov (*Krasnaia zvezda*), Iurii Letunov (radio), and Iurii Fokin (television) displayed a curious homogeneity in their work, all playing up certain tropes—heroism, the socialist cause, Soviet ingenuity, the inevitability of success—that produced a bland product; volume, vague allusions, and highly technical detail trumped economy, actual facts, and eloquence.[46] Mozzhorin himself conceded as such, remembering that most of the articles "smacked of . . . techno-fetishism. They were too high-level and uninteresting for the broad masses, and [they] poorly advertised domestic space [achievements]." Some of the correspondents, such as those from *Pravda* and *Izvestiia*, were hired on the recommendation of the Central Committee secretary for defense industries and space programs, Dmitrii Ustinov, but secrecy seriously impaired their ability to write meaningful pieces; they were forced, in Mozzhorin's words, to write "sugary streams of enthusiastic text."[47] Ironically, the space program "leadership," who themselves were partly responsible for imposing such draconian secrecy, expressed much dissatisfaction with the "low promotional effectiveness" of the literature, which largely resulted from said secrecy.

Although Mozzhorin's group was to act as censors, they had a symbiotic relationship with journalists. The latter were allowed access in exchange for following the former's mandates as closely as possible. This relationship helped to create a powerful union of censor and journalists, a block of actors who controlled both the content and contours of publicly available information on the Soviet space program. Lev Gilberg, the editor of the Mashinostroenie publishing house, which issued dozens of space-themed books, frequently invited officials from Mozzhorin's censorship group to write for him. Gilberg had a key connection into the inner workings of the space program, being a good friend of Vladimir Shatalov, the general in charge of cosmonaut training in the 1970s and 1980s.[48] This coalignment ensured that those writers who did not participate in self-censorship or "play the game" were excluded from the privileged access given to selected correspondents and writers. It also fed the striking homogeneity in the writing on the Soviet space program in the 1960s and the 1970s, both in terms of content and style.

Secrecy in Practice

As Soviet space exploits began to accumulate, certain guiding principles of the secrecy regime became evident. These obviously reflected the characteristics of the broader Soviet secrecy system, but inflected with the peculiarities inherent in the space program, such as its connection to the military, its association with national prestige, and its high-risk nature.[49] Three broad strategies guided those who produced the public narratives of the Soviet space program: first, they eliminated contingency from narratives of the space age so that all successes were assumed inevitable and the idea of failure rendered invisible; second, they constructed a space (no pun intended) of "limited visibility" for both actors and artifacts (that is, only a few selected persons—usually flown cosmonauts or public spokespersons with little or no direct contact with those directing space projects—and objects were displayed to the public); and third, they constructed a single master narrative or chronicle that included a set of fixed stories in which the central characters were few (such as Tsiolkovskii, Gagarin, and later Korolev) but heroic and infallible.

The first pattern of secrecy, the elimination of contingency, was designed to remove failure from the Soviet space program. With almost no exceptions, coverage of Soviet space exploits, especially in the case of human space missions, omitted reports of failure or trouble. This was the case from the early 1960s to the late 1980s. If a rocket failed to reach orbit, it was never announced; only successes were trumpeted. If a mission was curtailed early, TASS would merely exclaim that the original mission had been scheduled for that length. Because of the fear of conceding any kind of failure, accounts of cosmonauts' missions were so sanitized that reports inevitably veered toward ambience than substance. In this sense books and articles from the 1960s conveyed a kind of "thick description" (to use the words of the anthropologist Clifford Geertz) without the actual object being described. In other words, they contain no details, only settings. Canonical space books from the early years, such as *Nashi kosmicheskie puti* (Our space way, 1962), *Ukhodiat v kosmos korabli* (They leave for space in a ship, 1967), *Na beregu vselennoi* (On the coast of the universe, 1970), and *Letchiki i kosmonavty* (Pilots and cosmonauts, 1971) provide literally hundreds of pages of text of reconstructed conversations among cosmonauts, engineers, and laypeople that touch on a variety of social and cultural phenomena, such as family life, workplace customs, humor, and devotion to the Communist Party. These provide rich context, but they do not convey substance because the central issue at hand— the feats of the cosmonauts—are left to the imagination.

Demands for secrecy may have originated from military imperatives, but they had repercussions on many other dimensions of the Soviet space program. For example, the publicity-versus-secrecy dichotomy was paralleled in another polarity: the need to praise the seamless work of Soviet machines versus the need to extol the heroics of Soviet cosmonauts. The historian Slava Gerovitch has explored these built-in contradictions within the space program, particularly how different constituencies within the upper echelons struggled to find an appropriate balance between man and machine.[50] The public dimensions of this struggle showcase an attendant tension, not so much with man and machine, but between publicity and secrecy. For example, during the *Voskhod-2* mission in 1965, when Aleksei Leonov became the first man to exit his spaceship and "walk" in space, the spacecraft faced a number of serious problems that were not revealed at the time.[51]

One of these problems involved the failure of the automatic orientation system that would position the spacecraft in the proper direction before reentry. Through a very complicated and extremely risky series of actions, the crew was able to manually orient the ship for landing, although they landed nearly four hundred kilometers off course. The cosmonauts were forced to spend two nights in near arctic conditions fending for themselves while rescue services searched for them. After the mission, officials argued over how much to reveal publicly about this and the other lapses of safety during the flight.[52] The two cosmonauts were prepared in advance for a postflight meeting with journalists by rehearsing answers to sixty possible questions. The press conference itself had a vaguely farcical quality about it as the cosmonauts resorted to gross generalities and half-truths. At one point the cosmonaut Pavel Beliaev was forced to say that the crew had been "delighted" that the automatic system of orientation had failed, because this provided them with an opportunity to use the manual system.[53] Here, the fallibility of machinery was removed from the center of the narrative so that failure became peripheral, sidelined, and no longer important. We see how secrecy was not simply a regime designed to safeguard military information but also was invested with a certain flexibility, invoked in different circumstances to arbitrate among a variety of seemingly intractable issues at the forefront of the Soviet space program. In this particular case the invocation of secrecy (not revealing the true extent of the many failures on the flight) allowed man to exercise agency over the machine.

Eliminating contingency also meant not divulging information about future plans because plans inevitably changed, leading to delays. One manifestation of this policy was to say nothing about impending missions. In early 1967, Kamanin noted in his diary that the Novosti press agency received hundreds of queries from foreign news agencies about cosmonauts and future flights into space but that "we give them very little information, and even when we do, it's outrageously late. The CPSU [Communist Party of the Soviet Union] categorically prohibits giving detailed information before a flight, allows very little to report during a flight, and cuts all text on technology."[54] This practice was put to test in the late 1960s, when the Soviets appeared to have fallen behind in the so-called race to the moon. Because Soviet cosmonauts had not displayed anything close to matching their American counterparts at the time, Western analysts assumed that the Soviets had faltered behind the Americans, a suspicion that decades later proved to be true. At the time, however, Soviet cosmonauts were often put in awkward positions of conveying that the Soviet space program was indeed advancing along a deliberate plan despite clear evidence to the contrary.

When cosmonaut Vladimir Shatalov, for example, was visiting Japan in May 1969, he was bombarded by questions about the Soviet Union's recent poor showing in space. Kamanin dourly noted in his diary that "we cannot tell the truth openly about our failures and mistakes—we must beat around the bush, trying to put a good face on a bad situation."[55] Sometimes cosmonauts on foreign goodwill missions, frustrated by such questions, would make brave statements about impending Soviet moon missions, which only raised the ire of party officials back home who demanded more control over cosmonaut statements.[56] Amplifying Golovanov's insightful comment (cited earlier in the chapter), secrecy worked in favor of the Soviet space program when it was ahead because the audience, both home and abroad, could let their imaginations run free as to what was going to be possible in the future. When the Soviet Union fell behind, secrecy became absolutely essential to obscure this situation, which further strained the gap between what was happening in the Soviet space program and what was being told about it.

The second trope of secrecy was to construct a space of limited visibility for actors. In practice, this meant that the real architects behind the Soviet space program were rarely named. Soviet Communist Party First Secretary Nikita Khrushchev famously noted in 1958 that "when the time comes photographs and the names of these glorious people will be published and they will become broadly known among the people. We value and respect these people highly and assure their security from enemy agents who might be sent to destroy these outstanding people, our valuable cadres. But now, in order to guarantee the security of the country and the lives of these scholars, engineers, technicians, and other specialists, we cannot make their names public or print their pictures."[57] An official decree of the Central Committee of the Communist Party and the Council of Ministers expressly prohibited leading space designers, including the many chief designers, from speaking on the radio, on television, and in print under their own names. This is not to say that the space program did not have public spokespersons. Besides cosmonauts, the Central Committee had designated a number of eminent scientists who had little or no connection to the actual operation of the space program, to travel internationally and speak with authority on Soviet space achievements. When they spoke, these academicians—such as Ivan Bardin, Anatolii Blagonravov, Leonid Sedov, Evgenii Fedorov, and Boris Petrov—vacillated between two poles. Either they spoke in the most absurd generalities or they delved into the most egregious detail, usually about scientific experiments. Both were strategies designed to evade questions about the program itself. Some of these men had tenuous connections with the secret world of Soviet space, but as Iaroslav Golovanov astutely noted: "Those who were only slightly in the know . . . were so ensnared by what they had signed about not disclosing government secrets, that they uttered only banalities, and thus differed only *slightly* from the uninitiated."[58]

Naturally, those who were effectively in the driver's seat of the Soviet space program found this arrangement troubling if not insulting. Some of them were, however, allowed to write in public but *only* under pseudonyms. This culture of pseudonyms was a widespread practice that blossomed in the 1970s, when more and more "insiders" sought to bring their literary skills to public attention. Although most of the literature on the Soviet space program in the 1960s was authored by sanctioned newspaper and magazine journalists, by the following decade, a large group of designers began doubling as writers but under assumed names so as not to reveal their true identities. In recent years scholars have mapped the pseudonyms with the real names, but in the glory days of the Soviet space program, Westerners or indeed Soviet citizens had little or no way of judging whether a named author was a fiction or flesh and blood.[59] One outcome of the practice of using pseudonyms, as well as the equally ubiquitous practice of using melodramatic identifiers such as "Chief Designer" or "Chief Theoretician" or of the custom of omitting the biographies of authors, was the emergence of a culture of surrogacy in the literature on the Soviet space program, one that gave Soviet space-themed public culture a kind of disembodied voice. Even during the 1960s, it was apparent to many that the people speaking on behalf of the Soviet space program were not deeply connected to it. The discourse had a given and received quality about it, lacking agency; one could say that there was much said about the Soviet space program but it wasn't clear who was saying it.

The one exception to this rule was, of course, the cosmonauts, since they were the most visible face of the space program. But secrecy presented a set of problems for the public role of cosmonauts. Like their American counterparts, cosmonauts represented the most compelling, appealing, and effective instruments of the space program. Space travelers on both sides of the Iron Curtain had to deal with massive bureaucratic structures that sought to manage their public activity.[60] Because of secrecy, however, the cosmonauts' public stance evolved in markedly different ways from the astronauts. The inhibitions on cosmonauts were numerous and onerous: they could not be photographed with their spaceships, they could not describe them, they could not speak of those cosmonauts who had not flown yet, they could not talk about the military foundations of the space program, they could not refer to the rockets that launched them on their glorious voyages, they could not talk about future plans with any specificity, and so on. Many cosmonauts wrote memoirs, aided by ghost writers and with censors peering over their shoulders, but they mirrored the patterns of the general literature on the space program—context without content. The handicaps they faced were ably underscored by the occasional press conferences. The following exchange between journalists and first cosmonaut Yuri Gagarin at his first post-flight press conference exemplifies the flavor of the public discourse:

—When were you informed that you were to be the first candidate?

—*I was informed in due time. There was plenty of time for training and preparation for the flight.*

—You said yesterday that your friends, pilot-cosmonauts, are ready to complete new cosmic flights. How many pilot-cosmonauts are there? More than a dozen?

—*In accordance with the plan for the conquest of cosmic space, our country is preparing pilot-cosmonauts. I think that there are enough men to accomplish a series of flights into space.*

—When will the next spaceflight take place?

—*I think that our scientists and cosmonauts will undertake the next flight when it is necessary.*[61]

Journalist Iaroslav Golovanov, who was at this press conference, noted in his personal diary that Gagarin seemed "terrified of saying the wrong thing, all the time looking back at [public spokesperson] academician Evgenii Konstantinovich Fedorov, who struggled to pretend that he had some direct relevance to this historic event. The most interesting thing I learned at that press conference was that [Gagarin] weighed 69.5 kilograms."[62]

Cosmonauts in general faced the conundrum of being the most powerful and simultaneously the most powerless representatives of the Soviet space program. They were instruments of political power, coming to symbolize in their bodies new Soviet power and prestige, ambassadors of Soviet socialism to both the Eastern bloc and the Western world. Their utterances, occasionally militaristic and politically minded, were more potent than a dozen *Pravda* editorials. The cosmonauts were, in many senses of the word, the elite of the Soviet space program, in a society that officially disavowed them. The problem of blurred boundaries between being an elite and being a hero was not a new one—famed Soviet aviators in the 1930s negotiated these categories skillfully—but they did not deal with an all-encompassing regime of secrecy. The early aviators carried out their record-breaking exploits in full view of the world, often landing to welcome receptions in foreign lands.[63] Their machines were not only visible manifestations of their achievements but also measures of the power vested in the hands of the aviators. Secrecy divested modern-day cosmonauts of this power—they after all could not pose in front of their spaceships nor be seen at the literal spaces where they performed their heroism, at the launch pad and in their spaceships. They were powerless because of the draconian limitations imposed on their public discourse, for they could never speak freely about anything.

At the same time, although the cosmonauts' public statements, their only tangible instrument of agency, were constricted by secrecy codes, their language was overcompensated, almost overripe, with meaning. I use the word "meaning" here only in the broadest sense, the way that "signified" is more important than the "signifier," to use linguist Ferdinand de Saussure's terms. The variety of the signified was left to the imagination of the consumer, the public, opening up immense possibilities for interpretation. By dint of their vagueness and reach for a grand narrative (of socialism, technology, human evolution, and so on), the words of cosmonauts achieved a level of public, political, social, and cultural resonance that the words of astronauts never did. Secrecy gave cosmonauts' statements a potency of meaning that they might have lacked had they been mired in the details of their missions. Despite the ruthless secrecy and censorship, the many cosmonaut biographies of the 1960s and 1970s communicate an enthusiasm, generalized but irresistible, that undeniably infused the great Soviet cosmic project of the 1960s with a kind of fervor and energy—and mystique—which a completely open program would probably have lacked.

The final dimension of the secrecy regime was the creation of a single master narrative with a set of fixed stories, highly teleological, with all roads inevitably converging to a single transcendental point. The central concern was to ensure that alternative interpretations of received knowledge from official sources were eliminated; the public had to believe in a singular story with no ambiguity about the events, goals, and meaning of the Soviet space program. In describing Soviet censorship in the 1930s, the historian Jan Plamper has described the "abolition of ambiguity" as a "secondary censorship mode," a powerful practice that emerged during the early Stalin era when the party "not only saw to it that heretical cultural products be kept from public view [but] also sought to control the interpretation of those products that actually were allowed to circulate in society."[64] One way of enacting this secondary form of censorship was to use the selective publication of information to construct a master narrative of Soviet space history, one that encompassed priority (before the Americans), progress, and purpose.

The master narrative of Soviet space exploits came under many threats. One of the most rancorous controversies stemmed from an adversarial stance between censors and writers on one side and the space industry designers on the other. In the early 1980s Mozzhorin's press group began to compile essays for a comprehensive encyclopedia on the history of space exploration. More than three hundred eminent authors contributed to the manuscript, planned for publication in 1982, the twenty-fifth anniversary of the space age, but Mozzhorin found fault with many of the works for "popularizing Western achievements" too much. Such a book might put the master narrative of Soviet achievements in space, of unchallenged preeminence, in jeopardy.

Surprisingly, many leading Soviet designers, including the powerful Valentin Glushko, opposed this move, believing that such a stance would actually cheapen Soviet accomplishments. Mozzhorin continued to stand steadfast, at one point even delaying the publication because he objected to publishing the names of important Soviet space designers whose names were ostensibly still secret.[65] Despite the best efforts of Glushko and others, the number and length of essays on the American space program were reduced while the same were increased for Soviet efforts in space. After a long protracted battle between the censors and designers that even drew in the attention of Politburo members, the book, neutered and sliced up, was issued in 1985, the last gasp of the Soviet master narrative of cosmic conquest.[66] It was only after glasnost and particularly after the collapse of the Soviet Union, when the secrecy regime fell apart, that multiple, contradictory, and personalized narratives of the history of the Soviet space program flooded into the public consciousness, "privatizing memory," and creating a market of different accounts that were now valued and traded.[67]

Figure 3.1. This image of first cosmonaut Yuri Gagarin shows another cosmonaut (Grigorii Neliubov) airbrushed out of the background. Because he had not actually flown in space and was still in training, his existence was censored out of the official Soviet narrative of the mastery of space.

These three features of the secrecy regime in the Soviet space program—eliminating contingency, creating a limited space of visibility, and maintaining a master narrative—deeply affected not only the content of Soviet space culture but also its aesthetic qualities, as particularly manifested in the imagery associated with Soviet space exploits. Because the cosmonaut could not be shown next to or in his (or her) spacecraft, Soviet publishers had to be creative in communicating the new and modern symbiosis of man, technology, and adventure that the Soviet space program represented. This creative process was recruited in service of two requirements: to highlight a particular ideological stance; and to not raise any questions in the reader's mind that "something" was missing.

Cosmonaut photographs from the 1960s typically emphasized some familiar tropes of the cosmonaut as a family man—a modest, hard-working and diligent student, one who is agile in training, able to inspire large crowds, and at home with working people. Most of these images are highly stylized and many of them are staged; few had any overt technical associations. Many were embellished with penciled accents as was common for Soviet publications of the period, sometimes to emphasize particular points in a specific picture or to airbrush out aesthetically displeasing features.

Editing or altering images was a common practice, largely to sanitize them of any object or person that violated secrecy codes, a tradition inherited from the Stalinist-era practice of whitewashing important party and government officials from official pictures.[68] Despite the looser cultural restrictions of the Khrushchev's thaw, the space program retained this particular Stalinist trait as unflown (and hence, still secret) cosmonauts were "disappeared" from various pictures whose full vistas were not published until the 1980s or 1990s.[69] In some cases, the adjustments were purely aesthetic: a man might be positioned farther from another to eliminate clutter, or a speech by an air force general might be edited to delete mistakes in his diction (figure 3.1).

Soviet artists and model builders were notorious for producing versions of Soviet spacecraft that often had little or no connection with reality. This practice, ubiquitous in the early 1960s, opened the way for some outlandish depictions of Soviet spacecraft, including a supposed *Vostok* spacecraft shown at air shows or documentary films that bore little resemblance to any real spaceship but that had quite striking and even beautiful fins attached to one end.[70] The tension between aesthetics and secrecy was most starkly evident in the work of Soviet "cosmic" painter Andrei Sokolov, probably the most well-known "space" artist of the period. Sokolov later remembered that because he had no security clearance, he had to paint from his imagination about the Soviet space experience. Once, when he painted a rocket in flight, the painting was censored without explanation. Many years later he discovered that because his image approximated a real space rocket, it was not allowed for public consumption. Sokolov's experience provides a telling counterpoint to that of Aleksei Leonov, the cosmonaut turned painter, who was intimately familiar with secret technology. According to Sokolov, Leonov "deliberately distorted reality [in his paintings] because of the requirements of

Figure 3.2. To celebrate Aviation Day in July 1961, Soviet authorities approved the display of a *Vostok* spaceship at an exhibition in Tushino. The object approved for display had little resemblance to the actual spacecraft and included superfluous additions such as an aerodynamic fin added to the rear. *Source: Soviet Space Programs: Organization, Plans, Goals, and International Implications*, prepared for the Committee on Aeronautical and Space Sciences, U.S. Senate, 87th Congress, 2nd Session (Washington, D.C.: U.S. Government Printing Office, May 1962).

censors, sketching deformed trusses on the launch pad and improbable satellites."[71] The contrast between Sokolov and Leonov encapsulates how secrecy mediated the relationship between artist and the art in the world of secret space: because of secrecy, those who were not privy to secrets had to be careful about unleashing their imaginations, while those in the know had to let their imaginations run free so as not to give away those secrets (figure 3.2).

In addition to editing images, many key events—including, for example, meetings of the State Commission that oversaw the launches of the *Vostok* and *Voskhod* spaceships with cosmonauts on board—were restaged (or in some cases prestaged) for the cameras. After Gagarin's flight, for instance, Korolev was refilmed talking to Gagarin by radio, confidently holding a microphone and reciting the exact words he had said during the actual launch. Gagarin's prelaunch speech, supposedly given at the launch pad right before entering his spacecraft—flowery and hyperbolic—was actually recorded much *earlier* in Moscow.[72] Famous Soviet journalist Anatalii Agranovskii vividly described a scene where a truck driver at a farm stops to hug and congratulate the mother of cosmonaut number two, German Titov, after his launch. Official photographers insisted on retaking the whole scene with both the truck and the driver's clothes washed, and finally denuded the scene of any spontaneity when they objected to the fact that the truck driver's vehicle was an American Studebaker—that is, unacceptable to be seen in print.[73] The final image retained only a ghost of its original intent to capture the joy of a passerby and the gratitude of a cosmonaut's mother.

In all of these and many other cases, the object of re-creation was at one level designed to remove the messiness inherent in everyday life. Images would reflect the fact that the project of Soviet space exploration was literally a cosmic adventure far above and beyond the mundanities of daily existence, one where events unfolded with meaning and deliberation without imperfection and ambiguity, much like the machines and the men who orbited the Earth. Here, the elimination of spontaneity and ambiguity was not simply a structural process but also an aesthetic one. The style of images, film, and text on the Soviet space program created a singular kind of aestheticism that rendered the Soviet space program unusually static and devoid of color. All the vast rhetoric, images, films, posters, and the like on display for the populace at the height of the space race were designed to inspire. But if their dynamism was immediate, it was also only surface deep; beneath the text and the images were lives where life itself seems to have been struck out. Western audiences who saw these pictures saw them as ham-fisted ideologically colored propaganda. But looking deeper, the pictures were much more complex aestheticizations of a fundamental conflict between secrecy and publicity, between fixity and ambivalence. Eliminating uncertainty was central to creating a master narrative of Soviet space history, because that story had to be without defects. These defects were not simply structural, however; they were also aesthetic in nature. Because of this requirement, the architects of the official world of Soviet space created a world of limited visibility, wherein aesthetics and editing were conjoined in unbreakable relationship, one mediated by secrecy.

In the Soviet space program, especially during the 1960s, there was a chasm between what was actually happening and what was being told about it. There were many reasons for this gap between rhetoric and reality—all governments after all seek to control information about activities that are closely identified with the state—but in the Soviet case the central explanatory factor for the chasm was secrecy. The regime of secrecy in the Soviet space program created a fundamental conundrum between the drive to publicize the project as much as possible and the equally firm insistence that everything must be kept secret. This tension was never fully resolved and insinuated itself into all public discussions of the space program for a period of almost thirty years, from the launch of *Sputnik* in 1957 to the beginnings of glasnost in the late 1980s. Secrecy played itself out through the elimination of contingency, through the limiting of individuals who were allowed to speak, and through the creation of master narratives. Each had its own dynamic, a contested space where actors sought to define their places in the public image of the space program.

How was it that secrecy in the Soviet space program was at its peak during the Khrushchev thaw, a period identified with the relative loosening of controls over free artistic expression? One explanation is structural: besides being a period of cultural freedoms, it was a also a time of heightened tensions between the superpowers, manifested in a massive and expensive race to build strategic missiles. In the Soviet Union the same organizations that designed and built these weapons also designed, built, and launched the *Sputnik*s and *Vostok*s that launched the Soviet cosmic project. Given its proximity to weapons making, the space program had to be shrouded in total secrecy.

There is another way to see this apparent contradiction. The heightened secrecy surrounding the Soviet space program peaked along with the most successful period in the Soviet space program. This was also the first burst of public discourse on the Soviet space program, an explosion that was reflected in the euphoric and frequently hyperbolic claims about the program and the equally euphoric and hyperbolic response of the populace, measured in the thousands of supportive letters sent to newspapers, magazines, and the Academy of Sciences by Soviet people from all walks of life. For a brief period, before disillusionment set in during the early 1970s, the official word and the popular response mirrored and fed each other. The official word—what was being told about the space program—was at a fundamental level about "what ought to be happening." Here we are reminded of historian Sheila Fitzpatrick's trenchant observation about socialist realism, that writers and artists were "urged to . . . [see] life as it was becoming rather than life as it was. . . . Ordinary citizens developed the ability to see things as they were becoming and *ought to be*, rather than as they were."[74] Soviet newspapers, magazines, and exhibitions were less a site of "performance," as such scholars as Jeffrey Brooks might say, but rather the principal vehicle to *project* the raised expectations of the thaw generation.

To see the official press narratives on the Soviet space program, filtered through the censorship apparatus, as simply a mode for social control of opinions is to miss the point. As the historian Thomas C. Wolfe has noted, the Soviet press "participated in the cultivation of a complex kind of subjectivity and self-concept that is not seen by the scholarly model of an oppressive state tormenting the lone individual with a press devoid of real content."[75] Here, the condition of what "ought to be" (public) was as important as "what was" (secret); they existed simultaneously and were essential to each other. For Soviet citizens during the thaw, especially young Soviet men and women, the notion that there was an ineffable and secret world behind the rhetoric provided a charge to everything said about the Soviet space program. It is no coincidence that that charge of cosmic enthusiasm was at its height during a period of high success in space, a time of raised expectations of the thaw, *and* a regime of draconian secrecy. Triumphs in space and hope for a better society were given an extra boost by secrecy because it lifted the ceiling on people's aspirations and expectations of the future. Without deep knowledge of the inner workings of the Soviet space program, people believed that anything was possible in the near future. For a brief golden period this cosmic enthusiasm helped merge the visible with the invisible, the private with the public, and secrecy with success.

4

The Human inside a Propaganda Machine

The Public Image and Professional Identity of Soviet Cosmonauts

Slava Gerovitch

On April 11, 1961, as Nikita Khrushchev was resting in his vacation residence at the Black Sea resort of Pitsunda, he received a telephone call. The head of the Military-Industrial Commission, Dmitrii Ustinov, had called to report on the impending launch of the first manned spacecraft with the cosmonaut Yuri Gagarin the very next day. Just a few days earlier, on April 3, Khrushchev had chaired a meeting of the Presidium of the Party Central Committee, which approved the launch but did not set a specific date. Now the date was set, and Khrushchev began to think ahead about the postflight publicity that this event deserved. He flatly turned down Ustinov's suggestion to bring Gagarin after the completion of his mission to Pitsunda. Khrushchev reasoned that this would look like a private event, and he wanted a spectacular public ceremony. He proposed instead that he would fly back to Moscow, greet Gagarin at Vnukovo airport with "as much magnificence as possible: radio, television, and brief speeches," and then bring Gagarin to the Kremlin for a grand reception. Khrushchev also proposed organizing a welcoming mass demonstration on Red Square by assigning a specific quota of participants to various Moscow factories and institutions. Initially Khrushchev thought that the Red Square demonstration might pass without speeches, but an official joint resolution of the party and the government issued the next day specified that speeches must be given.[1]

Organizing "spontaneous" collective expressions of public enthusiasm was a routine Soviet practice. When foreign dignitaries arrived in Moscow, people lined the streets, greeting them with flowers and waving flags. To ensure that an adequate number of enthusiastic citizens would show up, the authorities assigned fixed segments of every street along the route to local industrial enterprises and institutions, which were responsible for hoarding their employees and "covering" a specific section between two designated lampposts. Employees, for their part, often viewed a daytime walk to their familiar lampposts as a welcome diversion from routine work duties.[2] But the reception of the first cosmonauts turned out to be quite different. Instead of trying to induce public sentiment, the authorities faced the problem of containing the mass outpouring of emotions.

On April 14, as the plane carrying Gagarin flew over Moscow, the cosmonaut saw thousands of people flooding the streets and squares of the capital. As soon as the plane touched down, a military brass band began to play the "Aviation March": "Ever higher, and higher, and higher we direct the flight of our birds." The song had been very popular in the 1930s, as part of the Stalin-era "aviation culture."[3] The public ceremony of Gagarin's welcome evoked the mass celebrations of Soviet aviators' feats in the 1930s. The new Soviet hero—the cosmonaut—took the baton from Stalin-era aviation idols and carried it ever higher.

Red Square could not contain all who came to celebrate. The government had planned a two-hundred-thousand-strong demonstration and distributed the requisite number of passes to the square. Yet thousands of people without passes crowded the neighboring streets.[4] After the demonstration Khrushchev hosted a lavish reception at the Kremlin for fifteen hundred people, including the entire foreign press and diplomatic corps. At the reception Gagarin thanked the party, the government, and the people. He toasted to the Soviet people, Lenin's party, and Khrushchev's health. The text of the toast had been approved in advance by the Presidium of the Party Central Committee.[5]

After coming home from the Kremlin ceremony, Gagarin looked in the mirror and saw a different person. A young lieutenant whose name had been known only to a narrow group of cosmonaut trainers and space engineers instantaneously turned into a recipient of the highest Soviet honor—the Gold Star of the Hero of the Soviet Union—and a world celebrity. Barely hiding his embarrassment, Gagarin told his wife: "You know, Valyusha, I did not even imagine such a welcome. I thought I'd fly and then come back. But I did not anticipate this."[6] He did not fully realize the extent of the transformation yet. From that moment on, Gagarin became a symbol, and despite his hopes and efforts to the contrary, his whole life was now subordinated to a single goal: to fulfill this symbolic function well.

As the Soviet government kept the identity of the true leaders of the space program secret, a handful of flown cosmonauts had to stand—literally on top of Lenin's mausoleum next to Nikita Khrushchev—for the entire space program. State-sponsored propaganda of Soviet space achievements turned such staged events as mausoleum appearances into iconic images of the space era, widely disseminated through television, newspapers, posters, and postcards. Throughout Russian history the persona of the explorer had conveyed a variety of ideological messages—from imperial power to reformist drive to socialist transformation to Communist future.[7] The cosmonaut myth played a major role in Khrushchev's attempts to de-Stalinize Soviet society—to break up with the Stalinist past and to reconnect with the original revolutionary aspirations for a Communist utopia.[8] In 1961, soon after Gagarin's flight, Khrushchev ordered to remove Stalin's remains from Lenin's mausoleum on Red Square and to change the name of the city of Stalingrad, the site of a major battle that turned the tide of World War II and a potent symbol of the Soviet victory over Nazism. As statues of Stalin were being dismantled, new monuments of the space age were erected, supplanting the collective memory of Stalinist terror with futurist visions of space conquests.[9]

The Soviet Union's wide use of its technological achievements in space exploration for propaganda purposes is well documented in the political and cultural histories of the period. Groomed by the Soviet political leadership to serve as ideological icons of Communism, the cosmonauts presented a public face of the Soviet regime. The cosmonauts toured the entire world, reinforcing political ties with the socialist bloc, propagating Communism in the Third World, and showcasing Soviet achievements in the West. Inside the country cosmonauts served as a symbol of the New Soviet Man—a true believer in Communist values and a conscientious builder of the bright future. The cosmonauts played an important role in campaigns for atheism and scientific education. They also symbolized the superiority of Soviet rocketry, whose "display value" underscored the might of the Soviet Union as a nuclear superpower.[10]

Like any myth, which is to be believed rather than critically examined, this popular picture of the cosmonauts was full of internal contradictions. The cosmonauts were portrayed as both ordinary people and exceptional heroes. All the first cosmonauts had military ranks, but their missions were presented as entirely peaceful. Their flights were praised as daring feats, while official reports of perfectly functioning onboard automatics did not seem to leave much room for human action. Soviet space technology was hailed as infallible, thus seemingly eliminating any element of danger from spaceflight. The role of a public hero whose mission did not look very risky was uncomfortable for the cosmonauts, who knew full well the real hazards of their flights but could not talk about them.

Most important, the cosmonauts found it increasingly difficult to reconcile their professional self with the ideal public image assigned to them. Trained as military pilots or engineers, the cosmonauts often were not prepared for the public roles assigned to them. They usually preferred training for new spaceflights rather than going on exhausting political speech circuits. Yet their public persona had little to do with their professional skills. The cosmonaut myth was not about their actions in orbit or the technical aspects of spaceflight, but about the Soviet state. As the historian Cathleen Lewis has noted: "Spaceflight was merely an attention grabbing method with which they could gain worldwide notice."[11] This chapter examines the tension between the public image and professional identity of Soviet cosmonauts in the 1960s, drawing on recent literature on identity construction and imposture in Soviet culture.[12] I focus on the interplay between Soviet political culture and the professional culture of Soviet cosmonautics. Instead of being a perfect display model for Soviet society, the cosmonaut myth reflected genuine contradictions and tensions of Soviet politics and culture. The question of how to fit the cosmonaut into an automated spacecraft sparked an internal debate over the cosmonaut's professional role.[13] A similar controversy was generated by the attempts to fit the cosmonaut into the Soviet propaganda machine.[14]

The Making of a Living Symbol

For many people around the world the cosmonauts—young, energetic, good-looking masters of cutting-edge technology—became a living embodiment of the bright, promising future. The party leadership, however, wanted to make the cosmonauts into a very specific symbol—an emblem of the Communist dream come true. Just a few months after Gagarin's historic spaceflight, the Twenty-second Congress adopted a new Communist Party program, which set the goal of building the foundations of Communism in the Soviet Union by 1980. This all-out drive toward Communism had two crucial components: the construction of a material and technical basis of Communism, and the education of a new Soviet man who would "harmoniously combine spiritual wealth, moral purity, and a perfect physique."[15] Who better than the cosmonauts could embody this new ideological construct? The Soviet media quickly generated a propaganda cliché: "The Soviet cosmonaut is not merely a conqueror of outer space, not merely a hero of science and technology, but first and foremost he is a real, living, flesh-and-blood *new man*, who demonstrates in action all the invaluable qualities of the Soviet character, which Lenin's Party has been cultivating for decades."[16] In August 1962, Khrushchev publicly proclaimed that "hero-cosmonauts are people who even now already embody the wonderful traits of the member of the communist society—high intellectual culture, moral purity, and perfect physique. Their deeds are driven by the love for Motherland, sense of public duty, and noble ideals of communism."[17]

The first group of cosmonauts—twenty young fighter pilots—all had similar social and professional backgrounds. Born (with few exceptions) in 1933 through 1935, they witnessed the horrors of World War II but were too young to participate in the war. A few, like Gagarin, lived under Nazi occupation. Many, like Gagarin, came from peasant families and had modest schooling. Most went to a military aviation school right after graduating from high school. By the end of 1959, when they were selected into the cosmonaut corps, most of these young men had served in the Air Force as fighter pilots for only two to three years and had the rank of senior lieutenant. Only two had graduated from Air Force academies; just one had training as a test engineer. Most cosmonaut trainees had little flying experience. Gagarin, for example, accrued only 230 hours of flight time. Sixteen of twenty were ethnic Russians. After the Ukrainian Vladimir Bondarenko died in an accident and the Tatar Mars Rafikov was expelled from the corps for misconduct, only two non-Russians remained in the group.[18] Major General Leonid Goregliad, who participated in the cosmonaut selection, remarked that for all cosmonauts, the life story was the same.[19]

Turning a group of young pilots, inexperienced in public relations, into professional spokespersons for Communism required a serious effort. As the Cosmonaut No. 2, German Titov, confessed, he was "very afraid of journalists. After all, we were trained to fly into space, not to speak at various official or improvised press conferences."[20] Lieutenant General Nikolai Kamanin, an Air Force official in charge of cosmonaut selection and training, carefully scripted cosmonauts' public appearances, wrote their speeches, rehearsed them, and corrected their "errors." In particular, Kamanin staged Gagarin's first public appearance before the Soviet leadership at Vnukovo airport and wrote the sixty-six-word-long report that Gagarin was to give to Khrushchev. Kamanin and Gagarin spent thirty minutes rehearsing it. Kamanin posed as Khrushchev, as Gagarin was getting his intonation just right. Kamanin was satisfied with the training, noting self-contentedly that he had seen an oratory potential in Gagarin even before the flight.[21]

Kamanin used his experience of being a cultural icon of the Stalin era as a model for his efforts to shape the cosmonauts' public persona.[22] Kamanin was a legendary Soviet aviator, a household name in the Soviet Union in the 1930s. In 1934 he was among the first recipients of the newly established title of Hero of the Soviet Union for the daring air rescue of the crew of the *Cheliuskin* exploration ship, crushed by the Arctic ice.[23] Among other famous aviators, Kamanin represented the New Soviet Man of the Stalin era.[24] A decorated air corps commander during World War II, Kamanin served after the war as first deputy to the Air Force chief of staff and air army commander. In 1960 he was appointed deputy head of Air Force combat training for space. Kamanin oversaw the Cosmonaut Training Center and represented the Air Force in all negotiations over crew selection and responsibilities in flight. An unabashed Stalinist, he ruled the cosmonaut corps with an iron fist, demanding strict discipline and implicit obedience and severely punishing any transgressors, up to expulsion from the corps. The cosmonauts, whose chances for future flights depended heavily on Kamanin's favor, were terrified of him.[25]

Kamanin's goals did not always perfectly align with the objectives of Khrushchev's propaganda apparatus. Outraged by Khrushchev's attacks on Stalin and by the vociferous campaigns glorifying Khrushchev's personal accomplishments, Kamanin had little sympathy for official political rhetoric. He knew how to pay lip service to the party line but was adamant in pursuing his own priority—boosting government support for human spaceflight. Rather than following orders from above, Kamanin often put forward new propaganda initiatives. When his military superiors vetoed his proposal to declare April 12 (Gagarin's flight anniversary) an official Cosmonautics Day, he petitioned the Party Central Committee over their heads. Kamanin arranged for Titov to sign the petition, thus adding the cosmonaut's political weight to the proposal, which was accepted.[26] While the Soviet leadership exploited space spectaculars for their political ends, Kamanin and other leaders of the space program skillfully manipulated the symbolic capital at their disposal to elicit much-needed support for the space program from party bosses.

Space propaganda thus had a dual face. It conveyed political and ideological messages to the masses and at the same time boosted the legitimacy of spaceflight as an indispensable component of Communism construction. The new party program proclaimed that "the first triumphal orbitings of the globe, accomplished by Soviet citizens . . . have become symbols of the creative energy of ascendant communism."[27] This not only adorned the image of Communism with space symbolism, but also asserted the highest ideological value of space exploration and thus ensured sustained government support for human spaceflight. The canonization of April 12 as Cosmonautics Day effectively mobilized various government agencies in the service of space propaganda. Party directives instructed that lectures about Soviet space achievements be given at factories, collective farms, and military units; the radio and television broadcast numerous meetings and concerts on space themes; news agencies distribute reports and visual materials; political and literary magazines publish special issues; movie studios create films about cosmonauts; and sculptors erect monuments to Soviet space triumphs.[28]

Kamanin carefully controlled access to cosmonauts and their public image. He signed off on publications about cosmonauts, managed their schedules, and gave permissions for interviews.[29] He even critiqued the work of the sculptor Grigorii Postnikov, who created cosmonauts' busts for public display. Kamanin approved Postnikov's portrayal of the cosmonauts Gagarin, Andrian Nikolaev, Pavel Popovich, and Valentina Tereshkova but found fault with the depictions of Titov and Valerii Bykovskii.[30]

Soviet media gradually shaped a canon of visual representation of cosmonauts. Illustrated magazines, such as *Ogonek*, featured the same types of photographs for every new cosmonaut hero: the hero looking at his or her photograph on the first page of *Pravda*; the hero speaking on the phone to the Soviet leadership, informing them of the successful flight and thanking them for party's loving care; a ritual welcome at the airport; the hero in childhood; the hero in training, preparing for the flight; the hero among the friends, fishing or playing chess; the hero among the family, embracing children. By showing the cosmonauts in everyday situations, the photographs emphasized that heroic deeds were accomplished by ordinary Soviet people. The cosmonauts were not supermen; they symbolized the progress of all Soviet people toward the "new Soviet man," the dedicated builder of Communism.[31]

As living symbols, the cosmonauts had to comply with their prescribed image around the clock. A formal set of rules regulated cosmonauts' daily life. Cosmonauts had to inform their superiors about their whereabouts every time they left the Cosmonaut Training Center.[32] They had to refrain from alcohol and go to bed at 11 p.m., even if they were on vacation.[33] The authorities often forbade cosmonauts to go on private trips (for example, to a friend's wedding).[34] They also tried to dictate whether cosmonauts could take their children with them on vacation.[35] Cosmonauts' appearance also became the subject of strict regulation. The question whether Tereshkova, the first woman in space, would be dressed in uniform or in civilian clothes on her official photo was discussed by the Party Central Committee. It was decided that the official Soviet news report should not mention her military rank, and Tereshkova had to change in a hurry.[36] On another occasion, when Titov appeared unshaven during an interview, Kamanin suggested that the interview be cut from a documentary about the *Voskhod* mission.[37]

Kamanin took upon himself not only the formal supervision of the cosmonauts' selection and training, but also their moral upbringing. He did not spare any effort to make the flown cosmonauts conform to their public image as exemplary Soviet citizens, scolding them for marital troubles and withholding their promotion in rank for drunken-driving incidents. Kamanin treated the cosmonaut trainees even harsher, expelling several of them from the corps for drinking and insubordination. Rules for cosmonauts' behavior during their trips abroad were much stricter than inside the country, because any incident would be immediately publicized and it would be more difficult to do damage control. On all foreign trips the cosmonauts were accompanied by KGB minders.[38] Although KGB personnel were routinely attached to Soviet delegations going abroad, in this case their functions were broader. They not only watched the behavior of the cosmonauts; they were also on the lookout to prevent any "ideological provocations," such as an attempt to photograph a cosmonaut with a bottle of Coca-Cola in the background.[39] Once Tereshkova's minder had left her to the care of a Soviet ambassador's wife for a few hours, and Kamanin was outraged; apparently the KGB watch was to be maintained around the clock.[40]

For every trip the Party Central Committee issued specific behavior guidelines and talking points for the cosmonauts. Kamanin himself drafted those guidelines and, after they were approved by the party authorities, was obligated to enforce his own instructions.[41] For example, when the cosmonauts Pavel Beliaev and Aleksei Leonov were sent to an International Astronautics Congress, Kamanin told them to act toward American astronauts "in a friendly manner, but without praise" and to keep their relationships with the German-American rocket designer Wernher von Braun "polite but strictly official."[42] Kamanin eliminated shopping from cosmonauts' trip schedules, on the ground that this would "belittle" them.[43] When foreign media reported that Gagarin had received a sports car as a gift from the French, the party secretary for ideology, Mikhail Suslov, became concerned and advised cosmonauts to be "careful" about accepting gifts out of capitalists' hands.[44]

Kamanin skillfully crafted cosmonauts' speeches abroad, trying to reconcile contradictory expectations. While Soviet officials insisted on political propaganda, the locals wanted to see a cosmonaut and not an overt political agitator. Kamanin privately remarked, for example, that in his speeches in India, Gagarin "delved into politics more than he should" and put too much stress on Communist ideology. This probably alienated some local politicians, who began limiting Gagarin's public appearances.

Kamanin then advised Gagarin to stick to the basic message of world peace and cooperation in space.[45] Kamanin also pointed out to the cosmonaut Popovich that some statements he had made on Cuba were indiscrete. Popovich had said, "We will help Cuba not only here on Earth, but from outer space as well," which had sounded like a veiled military threat. Popovich had also hinted that the Soviet Union was about to launch a woman cosmonaut, which was still a state secret.[46] On another occasion Kamanin admonished the cosmonaut Leonov for saying that "people in Greece welcomed us even warmer than in socialist countries."[47] The warmth of reception was seen as a political indicator, and it had to correspond to the degree of the country's closeness to the Soviet Union. Cosmonauts clearly had to learn the ropes of public political speech. Kamanin insisted that they had to visit two to three socialist countries before they could be trusted to go on a more challenging mission to the Third World, not to mention the capitalist inferno.[48]

Kamanin made a determined effort to turn former fighter pilots into public figures, skilled at oratory and adept at political language. Political education was made part of the formal curriculum. The first group of six candidate cosmonauts, including Gagarin, received forty-six hours of instruction in Marxism-Leninism, which amounted to 8 percent of their total training time.[49] Under Kamanin's supervision the Cosmonaut Training Center introduced a program of enculturation to broaden the fighter pilots' intellectual horizons. The cosmonauts went on group trips to museums, art galleries, and historical sights, visited the Bolshoi and other theaters, and attended concerts by performers from Czechoslovakia, Cuba, and the United States. They listened to lectures about ancient Greece and Rome, the Renaissance men, Peter the Great, and famous Russian painters and opera singers.[50] The chief of the Air Force, Marshal Konstantin Vershinin, who often felt embarrassed at meetings with foreign dignitaries because of the lack of knowledge of foreign languages, instructed Kamanin to make sure that all cosmonauts become fluent in English.[51]

Cosmonauts' "private" lives were by no means private. Kamanin insisted that Gagarin and Titov treat their wives with greater respect. In a domestic dispute between Popovich and his wife, Marina, Kamanin took the side of the cosmonaut and suggested that Marina, an ace pilot, should quit flying and devote more time to her husband and daughter—a proposal that made Popovich quite uncomfortable.[52] Kamanin took a special interest in the marital plans of Nikolaev, the only bachelor among the first cosmonauts, and even introduced him to the daughter of the Soviet minister of defense, hinting that a marriage to her might prove "useful for cosmonautics."[53] When Nikolaev's affections turned to Tereshkova, however, Kamanin quickly realized that their marriage would also be "useful for politics and for science," even though he had strong doubts about their match.[54] In October 1963 he urged Nikolaev to hurry up with a proposal, since both Nikolaev and Tereshkova were already invited to visit Hungary together in December, on the assumption that they would have got married by then.[55] Kamanin even suggested setting the wedding day in late October or early November to avoid conflict with their foreign trip schedule. Finally the date of November 3 was set by a formal decision of the party leadership. Kamanin suggested that "the wedding cannot be just a family affair, for the entire world is interested."[56] Two hundred people were invited to a government-sponsored banquet; Kamanin handled the invitations. The newlyweds spent their honeymoon on a propaganda trip to India.[57]

Cosmonauts could not speak publicly in their own words: Kamanin wrote their speeches, and journalists drafted their articles and memoirs. Cosmonauts spoke other people's thoughts and copied other people's texts in their own hand before submitting them for publication to preserve the appearance of authorship.[58] Tereshkova pointed out to Kamanin that her ghost-written memoir tells a story of her long-held dreams of space, while in fact the idea of becoming a cosmonaut had never crossed her mind before she was invited to take part in candidate selection tests. Kamanin acknowledged that a journalistic account followed stereotypes and had many discrepancies, but it was too late to make any corrections if the book was to be released by the third anniversary of Gagarin's flight.[59]

Early cosmonaut biographies were all written on the same template, likely borrowed from Kamanin's own 1935 autobiography, written when he was twenty-six or twenty-seven, about the same age as the cosmonauts. The biographies featured an obligatory set of points of passage: humble beginnings, childhood burdened by wartime hardship, encouragement by the family and teachers, good education paid for by the Soviet state, a wise mentor who taught the core Communist values, loyal military service, building up character and physical strength through a "trial of fire," receiving an important mission from the Communist Party, achieving the lifetime dream by carrying out that mission, and finally coming back with an important message reaffirming the Communist values. Both Kamanin's and cosmonauts' biographies contained little detail about the feats themselves but were rich in expressions of gratitude to the party for inspiration and support. The father figure of omniscient Stalin, prominent in Kamanin's account, was gently replaced in cosmonaut biographies by the equally omniscient "chief designer" of the space program.[60]

Kamanin's energetic efforts to publicize the lives of cosmonauts caused discomfort for his military superiors and ideological watchdogs, who were losing control over space propaganda discourse. In 1963 the KGB and the General Staff raised concerns about possible revealing of state secrets—in particular, cosmonaut training methods.[61] Kamanin had to close the Cosmonaut Training Center to journalists, photographers, and movie producers and to start producing publicity materials by the center's staff.[62] Bound by secrecy on one side and by propaganda demands on the other, Soviet media coverage of space was reduced to a set of clichés: flawless cosmonauts flew perfect missions, supported by unfailing technology. As a result, Kamanin privately admitted, "people get the impression of 'extraordinary ease' and almost complete safety of prolonged spaceflights. In fact, such flights are very difficult and dangerous for the cosmonauts, not only physically but also psychologically."[63] Yet Kamanin himself discouraged more controversial public representations of human space exploration. For example, he refused to serve as a consultant for Andrei Tarkovsky's movie *Solaris*, because, as he explained, such fiction "belittles human dignity and denigrates the prospects of civilization."[64]

Idealized media descriptions of cosmonauts' personal qualities closely matched the "Moral Code of the Builder of Communism" from the new Party Program.[65] This code included such ethical imperatives as "love of the socialist motherland," "conscientious labor for the good of society," "a high sense of public duty," "collectivism and comradely mutual assistance," "moral purity, modesty, and unpretentiousness in social and private life," and "mutual respect in the family, and concern for the upbringing of children."[66] Evgenii Karpov, the head of the Cosmonaut Training Center, gave the following list of Gagarin's personal traits: "Selfless patriotism. An unshakable belief in the success of flight. Excellent health. Inexhaustible optimism. The flexibility of mind and inquisitiveness. Courage and determination. Carefulness. Diligence. Endurance. Simplicity. Modesty. Great human warmth and attention to people around him."[67] The Party Program language clearly echoes in this description, suggesting that cosmonaut representations were thoroughly informed by the tenets of political discourse. Gagarin seemed to be specifically selected to match the myth he was to embody.

Gagarin's idealized image reveals a paradox, however. According to the leading space journalist and historian Iaroslav Golovanov, "most studies of Gagarin drive a stubborn idea of Gagarin's exceptionalism and at the same time stress that Gagarin apparently did not distinguish himself among others or 'push' others by the force of his personality; he was 'like everyone else.'"[68] One sympathetic Indian journalist described Gagarin as "normal to the point of abnormality."[69] Gagarin fully shared the experiences and feelings of his cohort. "For all of us, Yuri [Gagarin] personified the whole generation of Soviet people, whose childhood was singed by the war," recalled one cosmonaut.[70] Even Kamanin called him "the most normal of the normal."[71]

Gagarin's natural charisma, geniality, and openness began to shape a new image of the Soviet man abroad. The old imagery—the menacing-looking dictator Stalin, the dogmatic party bureaucrat, and the stern Soviet soldier—was replaced by this cheerful and charming young man. "The first cosmonaut was chosen ideally to represent the Soviet man before the nations of the entire world. His perfect features, pleasant look, his charming smile and even his short height, which stresses his youthful stature—everything makes the most favorable impression on anyone who met with him, saw him in cinema or on television," raved the Indian journalist. "The almost mythical idea of the Soviet man became reality for the people of the world in this unusually humane, modest, and agreeable image of Yuri Gagarin. They can see now that he is an attractive young man, an exemplary son, a devoted husband, a cultured man who loves to read good books and listen to good music. The fact that he is a communist does not mean that he is intolerant toward those who disagree with his ideology, and it does not mean that he lacks a sense of humor."[72] Perhaps it was this "abnormal normalcy," rather than the idealized propaganda image, that endeared Gagarin to millions of people around the world. The story of an ordinary person performing an extraordinary feat felt more humane and inspiring than tales of superman's super deeds. Performing a spaceflight required a lot of courage, but facing worldwide fame presented an even greater challenge.

The Burden of Fame

The Soviet government organized mass manifestations to celebrate space achievements in the same way all mass events were orchestrated. First, the number of attendees was set; usually two thousand to three thousand for the welcome ceremony at Vnukovo airport and sixty thousand to two hundred thousand for the demonstration on Red Square. Helicopters dropped leaflets, organizations received quotas for sending people to greet the cosmonauts along the route to Red Square, columns marched, leaders gave speeches, and music played. The day ended with a gala reception in the Kremlin for the select guests and with lavish fireworks for the masses.[73] "Although the new rituals were artificially designed," the historian Richard Stites wrote, "many of them were sufficiently artful, emotional, and 'authentic' to insure [sic] some success among Soviet citizens."[74] Despite the thorough planning, the public outpouring of emotions seemed genuine. "At the dawn of the Space Age, people were coming out to greet cosmonauts on their own initiative," one memoirist has recalled.[75]

The eminent historian of Russian science Loren R. Graham, then in his thirties, was among the ecstatic crowd on Red Square on April 14, 1961, celebrating Gagarin's triumph. He recalled that day as "the apogee in Soviet citizens' belief that they held the key to the future of civilization. The celebrations on the street were genuine and heartfelt. Soviet science was, they were sure, the best in the world, and Soviet rockets succeeded where American ones failed."[76] For the postwar generation of Soviet people the cosmonauts' triumphs signified an ultimate payoff for years of sacrifice during the war and for Stalin-era privations. "Gagarin's achievement was our greatest pride," recalled a member of the "Sputnik generation."[77] According to the 1963 poll of the readers of a popular youth-oriented Soviet newspaper, Gagarin's flight was named by far the greatest human achievement of the century.[78]

While before the flight the cosmonauts' training was mostly technical, their activity after the flight was to a large extent political. Immediately after landing, the cosmonauts were thrust into a "swirl of receptions, trips around the world, and incessant speeches," as the cosmonaut Konstantin Feoktistov recalled.[79] Thousands of requests for interviews and invitations to visit various factories and institutions poured down on Kamanin, who oversaw the cosmonauts' schedules. The organizers of public events attempted desperately to lure in a cosmonaut or two, using all sorts of leverage on Kamanin, from his military superiors to the connections at the Party Central Committee.[80] The top military brass liked to appear at public events accompanied by a couple of cosmonauts to bask in the cosmonauts' glory, and they often gave Kamanin direct orders to summon cosmonauts to serve as their entourage.[81] In September 1964, Kamanin wrote in his private diary about his meeting with Bykovskii: "We understood each other without words. Bykovskii has been going to receptions and meetings seven days in a row, and he is tired of this. He insisted on letting him do his regular job. I said, 'I know everything. If they send you again tomorrow, you can rebel, but today you must be at the House of Friendship to meet with the Finns.'"[82]

Kamanin tried to keep a lid on what he termed "partying and empty talk" and to allocate adequate time for cosmonauts' flight training and academic studies.[83] The Air Force Engineering Academy, where cosmonauts studied, complained about their absenteeism, and cosmonauts repeatedly asked Kamanin to cut the number of public appearance at least during the final exams.[84] Kamanin attempted to limit their public appearances to one to two per week, rejecting more than 90 percent of all invitations.[85] Turning down high-level requests became so routine that he even refused to allow the cosmonauts Nikolaev and Popovich to meet with the party activists from the staff of the USSR Council of Ministers. The request was granted only after a threatening phone call from the Party Central Committee.[86] From 1961 through 1970 the cosmonauts attended more than six thousand public events in the Soviet Union.[87]

Like any celebrity, cosmonauts soon grew tired of incessant public attention. It became impossible for them to show up in public without causing mayhem. In June 1962, Titov and his wife attended a popular music concert, but as soon as the audience learned that the cosmonaut was present, everybody stopped listening and started searching for Titov. When the concert ended, Titov and his wife had to run for their lives. "The entire crowd rushed to the exit to see Gherman and his wife," recalled an eyewitness. "The railing around a public garden miraculously held under pressure, and a reinforced police unit was able to restrain the excited mass of people for a few moments to give the Titovs an opportunity to jump into their black Volga and to escape the violent expression of universal love."[88] Cosmonauts' private lives became subordinated to the demands of the propaganda machine. They were routinely recalled from their vacations to attend various public ceremonies in Moscow.[89] No wonder cosmonauts soon began to complain to their superiors that they were "dead tired" of "meeting with the people."[90]

When asked in an interview about his most difficult challenge, Gagarin unhesitatingly replied, "it's to carry the burden of fame."[91] He even compared this burden to the heavy g-loads he experienced during his spaceflight.[92] Yet Gagarin took his public mission very seriously. He appreciated people spending hours in line to see him, and he patiently did his duty, giving speeches and signing autographs. He explained to his friends that his activity was necessary to establish a broad public support for the space enterprise: "A person would come home, show my autograph, and tell about meeting a cosmonaut. A conversation about cosmonautics in general would ensue, and such conversations add up to form a public opinion."[93]

Groomed by the Soviet political leadership to serve as ideological icons of Communism, cosmonauts also toured the world, spreading the message of world peace, cooperation in space, and support for the Communist cause. Within four months after completing his space mission, Gagarin visited Brazil, Bulgaria, Canada, Cuba, Czechoslovakia, Finland, Great Britain, Hungary, and Iceland.[94] In every country he visited, Gagarin drew enormous crowds. In Calcutta more than a million people gathered to see him, which prompted Kamanin to compare Gagarin favorably to Jesus. Recalling (in his private diary) that the crowd fed by five loaves of bread counted only five thousand, Kamanin concluded that Gagarin would be a clear winner.[95] On his trip to England in July 1961, Gagarin won universal admiration for his willingness to travel in an open car under the pouring rain. He reportedly said that if the people could get wet waiting to see him, then so should he.[96] As the number of invitations to visit foreign countries became overwhelming, Kamanin had to turn down more than two-thirds of all invitations.[97] Eventually the Soviet authorities introduced a complicated system, by which all cosmonauts' foreign trips had to be authorized by the party leadership. The trips of Tereshkova were authorized by the highest political body, the Presidium of the Party Central Committee.[98] All requests had to receive prior approval from the Ministry of Foreign Affairs, the Ministry of Defense, and the KGB.[99]

Cosmonauts' visits had a particular political importance in the Third World, where their public appearances were carefully planned to support pro-Soviet politicians. During a 1961 trip with his wife to India, Gagarin privately complained to Kamanin about the overloaded schedule: "Too much politics, and nothing for ourselves; we did not even see any elephants."[100] In the course of one day during his visit to Ceylon, for example, Gagarin traveled more than three hundred miles, visited nine towns, and gave more than fifteen speeches.[101] During his numerous foreign trips he endured nearly 150 days of such political marathons.[102] While diligently fulfilling his public responsibilities, Gagarin privately told Kamanin that he was "drained to the bottom."[103] Kamanin had to fight both Soviet ambassadors and local politicians, who pushed Gagarin to perform for fourteen hours a day. In his private diary Kamanin noted: "They do everything possible to squeeze out of Gagarin the maximum support for the government. They don't care how this would affect him."[104] Even in an open publication, Kamanin hinted at the problem: "Meetings and demonstrations follow one another; then come lectures and receptions. The sun is mercilessly burning. Sweat is covering the eyes. The feet are filling with lead. Yet Gagarin, excited and joyous, is standing in the human vortex and responding to greetings. Well, this is his duty."[105] After several years of incessant propaganda trips abroad Gagarin began to have nightmares: "Sometimes I close my eyes and see endless queues of people with burning eyes, shouting greetings in foreign languages."[106]

Soviet officials viewed the reception of cosmonauts in various countries as a litmus test of the political leanings of local politicians. Kamanin observed that Warsaw was the only capital of a socialist country that welcomed Soviet cosmonauts with portraits of both cosmonauts and American astronauts. He concluded that "Poland would easily enter into a closer contact with the West at the expense of the interests of the Soviet Union."[107] Kamanin's deputy, who accompanied the cosmonaut Titov on a trip to Vietnam, noted that some prominent political leaders did not attend any of Titov's appearances, and suggested that this might indicate a split in Vietnam's leadership.[108] While the Soviet government tried to use cosmonauts as "agitators for communism" and to improve the Soviet image all over the world, local politicians often exploited the visits to their own ends, trying to boost their public image. Cosmonauts were greeted with either excessive hospitality or ostentatious coldness, depending on local political rivalries and the relations between provincial elites and the federal government. If Soviet officials perceived that they were being taken advantage of, they tried to regain the initiative. When the local authorities in Bombay deliberately gave Gagarin's visit a low profile, the Soviet delegation immediately stirred public interest by announcing the visit route in local newspapers and thus attracted big crowds.[109]

The propaganda work load on the cosmonauts was enormous. During the years 1961–70, the cosmonauts made two hundred trips abroad; Tereshkova alone made forty-two foreign trips.[110] She received by far the most invitations among the cosmonauts.[111] Kamanin noted that "nobody could match her ability to evoke warm sympathy of the people."[112] As a result of overwork, Tereshkova's postflight propaganda activities tired her out much more than preflight training and the mission itself, and she was growing increasingly irritable and losing her self-control.[113] She was able to escape the political speech circuit only temporarily when she became pregnant. Doctors forbade her to travel after February 15, 1964.[114] Tereshkova was forced to do her propaganda job full-time almost to the last day: she returned from her trip to Africa on February 9.[115] Her daughter was barely two months old, when Kamanin urged Tereshkova to attend a ceremony commemorating Aviation Day, arguing that it was "time for her to show up in public."[116]

Because of the shroud of secrecy that surrounded Soviet rocketry, the leading designers of spacecraft remained anonymous, and the media often presented human spaceflights as cosmonauts' personal achievements. Some cosmonauts felt it was not fair to focus the spotlight on them at the expense of all other participants in the space program. A few weeks after his flight, Gagarin wrote a confidential letter to the chief marshal of aviation, Aleksandr Novikov: "There is a lot being said and written around the world about this event [Gagarin's flight—S.G.]. I do not feel that I can or have the right to accept all this on my own account. If my contribution amounted even to one percent of everything that is being said, this already would have been the greatest reward for my deed. I know what our pilots had to endure during the Great Patriotic War. Their service and their hardships were so much greater than mine. I simply happened to be in the epicenter of events."[117] The more public praise Gagarin received, the more uncomfortable he became with his public image. "It is awkward to be seen as a super-ideal person," he later confessed.

"It's as if I always did everything right. But, like anybody else, I make many mistakes. I have my weaknesses. One shouldn't idealize a person. One should take him just as he is in real life. It's annoying when I'm portrayed as a 'sugar boy,' who is so sweet that it's nauseating."[118]

More than anyone, Gagarin felt the pressure of the propaganda windmill that crushed his dreams for another flight and turned him into a calcified symbol. "Gagarin is still hoping that one day he would fly into space again. It is unlikely that this will ever happen; he is too valuable for humanity to risk his life for an ordinary spaceflight," reasoned Kamanin.[119] "I must try to convince him to give up flying and to prepare himself for the position of one of the leaders of the Soviet space program."[120] A leading space engineer who had many encounters with Gagarin remarked: "Gagarin understood full well that he would no longer be able to serve as an active cosmonaut, that he became a symbol. It was painful, and it made him depressed, and he could not restrain himself from longing for another flight. Just imagine a young, daring, venturesome Gagarin, who says happily 'Off we go!' and flies the first into space, and then, in a little while, he sees himself as a wax figure in Madame Tussauds museum. This is an abomination. A normal man, full of life, cannot live like that; he would look for compensation."[121] And cosmonauts did look for compensation.

The Human Side of a Public Icon

The cosmonauts faced an impossible task—to fit into their assigned image of "an ideal citizen of an ideal state."[122] Even though they were specifically selected to have qualities best matching their future public mission, the challenge of coping with the burden of fame proved too difficult for some. In 1961, Gagarin and Titov were elected delegates to the Twenty-second Congress of the Communist Party. The congress would adopt a new party program, which set a triple goal of creating a material and technical basis of Communism, forming the new communist social relations, and bringing up the New Soviet Man. Gagarin and Titov were supposed to sit in the presidium of the Congress and to showcase the tangible achievements of the regime both in high technology and in the upbringing of the New Man. They were to illustrate the new "Moral Code of the Builder of Communism," with its calls for honesty, sincerity, moral purity, and modesty. A few days before the Congress, however, the plans went awry: Gagarin broke a facial bone when jumping out of the window after what looked like a womanizing incident. Gagarin missed the opening of the Congress, and he and Titov were dropped from the Presidium list. Khrushchev was furious when he learned about the behavior of Gagarin, next to whom he had stood on top of Lenin's mausoleum during the May Day celebrations just a few months earlier.[123]

Once cosmonauts had flown their missions, they became celebrities and their lifestyle completely changed. Kamanin was showered with reports of their excessive drinking, drunken driving, and angry encounters with the police. The KGB submitted reports on cosmonauts' misbehavior directly to the Party Central Committee, which set up a commission to investigate the failure of the Cosmonaut Training Center's leadership to enforce discipline.[124] The irony of the situation was that party and government leaders themselves often invited cosmonauts to their private parties, where cosmonauts "got accustomed to drinking and became corrupted," as Kamanin put it.[125] Kamanin found himself in a double bind: he was reprimanded if cosmonauts misbehaved in public, but when he tried to limit cosmonauts' private contacts with the political elites to contain their "corrupting" influence, he also got into trouble. "The leadership of the country fusses over the cosmonauts like a child over a new toy and showers praise, promotions and invitations on them out of the horn of plenty," he remarked bitterly in his diary, while he was expected "to keep the cosmonauts in check and to be held responsible if they drink too much at an official reception and say or do something inappropriate under the influence."[126]

The cosmonauts received substantial material rewards and privileges, which placed them in the same bracket with the country's elite. Lieutenant General Kamanin's salary was only 15 percent higher than Major Gagarin's.[127] In addition to formal honors, the cosmonauts received handsome remuneration for completed spaceflights: a furnished luxury apartment, a luxury car, a two-year salary bonus, and a long list of gifts for their families—from vacuum cleaners to handkerchiefs.[128] A year of training in the cosmonaut group counted as three years of military service, and cosmonauts received accelerated promotions in rank.[129] They received access to goods that were not available to ordinary Soviet citizens—for example, baby formula imported from Czechoslovakia and paid for in hard currency by special permission from the Ministry of Finance.[130] The top brass of the Air Force and the Ministry of Defense grumbled about the cosmonauts' perks, which were decided at a higher political level.[131] Kamanin privately suggested that the government's provisions gave the members of the cosmonaut group "so much material wealth and so many privileges that there is no motivation for them to fly into space, especially to fly the second time."[132] He believed that an accelerated rise through the ranks could also be detrimental: "The character of most cosmonauts has not quite solidified, and this may damage it by planting the dubious notion that for them everything is permitted."[133]

As the popularity of the cosmonauts grew, it was becoming more and more difficult for Kamanin to control their behavior. He bitterly complained in his private diary that "the cosmonauts overestimate the significance of their personal accomplishments and take at face value everything that is being written, said, and shown about every human spaceflight in the media."[134] "Reinventing" themselves to fit their iconic image, the cosmonauts seemed to gradually internalize their public persona, just as an ordinary Soviet citizen in the 1930s who had to hide undesirable social origins and, in his words, "began to feel that I was the man I had pretended to be."[135] The newly acquired celebrity image did not square well with the daily routine of spaceflight training and strict military discipline. The tension often resolved in violent outbursts.

Excessive drinking and regime violations plagued the cosmonaut corps. When a spree of drinking parties and auto accidents involving Titov culminated in the death of Titov's passenger, Kamanin ran out of patience. He called a meeting of the cosmonaut group and told Titov in front of the whole gathering: "With your own misdeeds, you have put yourself outside the party and outside the cosmonaut group. There is a strong basis for expelling you from the party and depriving you of all your titles: a deputy, a Hero, a cosmonaut pilot, and a lieutenant colonel." But taking into account Titov's world fame, reasoned Kamanin, "Titov's disgrace would be a disgrace for all the cosmonauts, for all Soviet people. We cannot afford that."[136] Titov received a strict reprimand, a demotion, and a temporary ban on public appearances, attending receptions, and driving a car, but his transgressions were kept under wraps, and he continued to represent the New Soviet Man in public. The cosmonaut Leonov's drunken driving led to two serious traffic accidents in four months, and Kamanin personally imposed a six-month ban on his driving.[137] The cosmonaut Popovich also got into trouble for drinking and brawling. He got a black eye and had to miss a session of the Twenty-third Party Congress. Kamanin fired him from the position of deputy head of the cosmonaut team and suspended his training but did not object to electing Popovich a member of the Supreme Soviet.[138]

The attempts to make the cosmonauts into exemplary Communists proceeded with considerable difficulty. Cosmonauts privately exchanged political jokes, such as the double-entendre slogan, "Officers of the Missile Forces, our target is Communism!" Even some of their supervisors laughed at ideological clichés. One cosmonaut recalled that the deputy director of the Cosmonaut Training Center in charge of political education "understood everything, believed that the cosmonauts would not give him away, and did not make pretenses with us. . . . When asked 'How are things?' he invariably replied, 'Our country is on the rise.' If we mockingly asked 'And how is the party?' he replied with an equal measure of irony, 'The party teaches us that heated gases expand.'"[139]

Although cosmonauts were allowed some license in private jokes, any hint at serious political dissent was quickly suppressed. For example, at a political education session in early 1964 the cosmonaut candidate Eduard Kugno raised some controversial questions, such as "Why do we have only one political party?" and "Why do we send assistance to other countries, while there are shortages inside the country?" This was immediately reported to his superiors.[140] Furthermore, when asked why he did not join the Communist Party, Kugno replied, "I will not join a party of swindlers and sycophants!" Kamanin quickly judged that Kugno was "ideologically and morally unsteady" and expelled him from the cosmonaut corps.[141] Kamanin privately used even stronger expressions condemning the incompetence and corruption of the Soviet leadership, but he was outraged by Kugno's unwillingness to play by the rules and to restrict his remarks to the private sphere.

The cosmonaut supervisors' greatest fear was to see a flown cosmonaut use his or her celebrity status for a public expression of political dissent. When the deputy chief of the Air Force heard that two cosmonaut trainees had raised some criticism at a meeting at the Cosmonaut Training Center, he reacted at once: "Expel both. If they give such speeches while still on training, what will they say after returning from space?"[142] These fears were not entirely groundless. After returning from space, cosmonauts did use their newly acquired popularity in the ways that did not always please their superiors.

Cosmonauts Speak Out

The cosmonauts found it difficult to reconcile their professional selves with the ideal public image assigned to them. Many of them felt uncomfortable about the unrestrained public praise and the monuments erected in their honor. The cosmonaut Leonov, for example, defied a government decree and objected to the installation of his bust, which remained in the sculptor's studio for twenty-eight years.[143] The role of a public figure giving incessant speeches did not appeal to the cosmonauts originally trained as fighter pilots. When meeting with American astronauts, the cosmonauts often forgot about their ideological mission and engaged in purely professional talk. Having met the astronaut John Glenn during his visit to the United States in 1962, Titov particularly remarked about Glenn's "tenacious professional gaze of the pilot" and admitted that when the cosmonaut and the astronaut met, they were "connected by everything they had experienced and lived through in space."[144]

Most cosmonauts preferred training for new spaceflights to public appearances. Gagarin, losing patience, once flatly refused to meet with TV correspondents from East Germany, for which he was reprimanded by Kamanin.[145] Tereshkova long resisted Kamanin's attempts to turn her into a professional politician and even enrolled in the Air Force Engineering Academy, hoping to retain her qualifications for another spaceflight. Kamanin was convinced, however, that "Tereshkova as the head of a Soviet women's organization and of international women's organizations would do for our country and for our party a thousand times more than she can do in space."[146] Eventually he prevailed, and Tereshkova left the cosmonaut corps and served as the head of the Soviet Women's Committee for more than twenty years. Tirelessly rehearsing with cosmonauts their speeches, editing their memoirs, monitoring their private lives, and guiding their careers, Kamanin was more than anyone responsible for shaping the cosmonauts' self. He was quite justified in his confession in a private dairy that "it was I who created Tereshkova as the most famous woman in the world."[147]

Cosmonauts gradually developed an independent voice. They started by criticizing the harsh disciplinary regime at the Cosmonaut Training Center. In February 1963 they staged a "battle" (as Kamanin termed it) against the recently appointed head of the Center, Lieutenant General

Mikhail Odintsov. A group of cosmonauts led by Gagarin organized a party meeting, at which they complained about work overload and Odintsov's heavy-handed management style.[148] Kamanin eventually took the cosmonauts' side and, when Odintsov continued to ignore cosmonauts' critique, replaced him.

Soon cosmonauts moved on to more ambitious attempts to influence space policy on the government level. Mingling with the political elite at high-level receptions, cosmonauts enjoyed unique access to the Soviet leaders, which even their military superiors did not possess. In August 1965, after the successful completion of an impressive eight-day mission of *Gemini V*, Kamanin decided to petition the Soviet leadership for a fundamental change in the organization of the space program to catch up with the Americans.[149] He realized that this proposal would be much more effective if it came not from him, but from the well-known flown cosmonauts. He persuaded Gagarin and five other cosmonauts to sign a letter, which Gagarin then passed on to Leonid Brezhnev's aide.[150] The letter warned that the Soviet Union was "losing its leading position" in space and pointed out the "many defects in planning, organization, and management" of the space program, such as the lack of planning of human spaceflight, the absence of a central agency responsible for space efforts, the "scattering of efforts and resources in space exploration," and the prevalence of policy decisions that "often reflect narrow departmental interests." The letter boldly accused the leadership of the Strategic Missile Forces, and even the minister of defense of insufficient support for the space program. The letter concluded with a suggestion to unify all military space affairs under the Air Force command, which would provide the basis for "thoughtful planning of space research."[151]

The cosmonauts' celebrity status gave them many privileges, but it did not translate into tangible political influence. The Soviet leaders passed on the cosmonauts' letter to the top brass of the Ministry of Defense—to the very people about whose indifference to the space affairs the cosmonauts complained. In November 1965 the Military Engineering Panel of the Ministry of Defense discussed the issues raised in the cosmonauts' letter. Of all the cosmonauts only Gagarin was allowed to attend the meeting, and he was not given an opportunity to speak. Kamanin suspected that the top brass were afraid of the cosmonauts' frank and authoritative statements. As a result, Kamanin and the cosmonauts suffered a "crushing defeat."[152] The cosmonauts never received a formal response to their letter from the party authorities.[153]

Outraged by the lack of action on the matters raised in the letter, the cosmonauts decided to pursue a personal meeting with the Soviet political leadership. Kamanin advised them to "cool their heads" and to plan the next step very carefully.[154] Cosmonauts ignored his warning and asked the head of the KGB, Vladimir Semichastnyi, to arrange a meeting with Brezhnev. While the KGB was secretly monitoring cosmonauts' activities and submitting reports to the party authorities, Semichastnyi privately mingled with the cosmonauts, and they felt confident that he would be friendly enough not to report them to their military superiors. Eventually the deal fell through, as Semichastnyi himself soon lost his position and influence.[155]

The Erosion of the Cosmonaut Myth

In the first half of the 1960s the Soviet space program boasted one spectacular success after another—the first man's flight, the first day-long mission, the first group flight, the first woman's flight, the first multicrew mission, and the first space walk. The names and faces of the first eleven cosmonauts were well familiar to any Soviet citizen who read newspapers, listened to the radio, or went to cinema theaters. The myth of the cosmonaut—a perfect hero conquering outer space with flawless technology—fed from and sustained a larger political myth of the Soviet Union as a mighty superpower that produced perfect heroes and created flawless technology.

The cosmonauts—professional fighter pilots—had to reinvent themselves to become public ambassadors, atheism lecturers, and political agitators. They had to assume a new public persona and to learn a new language of public speech, a Khrushchevian variant of Stalinist "Bolshevik."[156] Just like the "confidence men" of the 1930s, they had to pretend to be someone else, for their professional skills as cosmonauts were irrelevant to their public role. The constant tension between their professional identity as pilots and their public persona made the burden of fame suddenly showered on them even heavier. Strict discipline imposed on the cosmonaut corps clashed with the elite lifestyle they came to enjoy as world celebrities. The cosmonauts' role as a symbol of technological progress and bright future brought them popularity, but this popularity created temptations that seriously undermined their ability to represent moral perfection. Moreover, their public duties often interfered with their training for future flights. To function efficiently as symbols, the cosmonauts had to stop being cosmonauts.

Soviet aviation heroes of the Stalin era were not "merely passive symbols in the pantheon of Stalinist propaganda" but took active steps to define their own place in Stalinist culture.[157] Cosmonauts similarly attempted to break out of the assigned role and to use their celebrity status to take an active part in the discussions of space policy. These attempts proved futile—not only because their fame did not translate into power, but also because the Soviet space age was already passing its heyday, and they were losing their emblematic appeal.

In the second half of the 1960s the string of space spectaculars gave way to a chain of unfortunate and tragic events. In early 1966, Sergei Korolev—the legendary anonymous "chief designer," an energetic and charismatic leader of the Soviet space program—suddenly died. His identity was finally disclosed and his contributions widely honored. The focus of space mythmaking began to shift from the cosmonaut heroes to the engineering geniuses behind the miraculous rockets and spacecraft.[158] Yet the myth of flawless technology did not last long. In April 1967 the parachuting system of the new piloted spacecraft, *Soyuz 1*, malfunctioned, and its flight ended in a fiery crash and the death of the cosmonaut Vladimir Komarov. The Soviet authorities had hushed up the first casualty of the space program, the 1961 accidental death of the cosmonaut candidate Vladimir Bondarenko during training, but Komarov's fate could not be concealed from the public. The death of Komarov—one of the heroes of the 1964 *Voskhod* mission—shattered the myth of perfect reliability of Soviet space technology. In March 1968 the nation was shocked by the death of its most beloved hero, Yuri Gagarin, when his aircraft crashed in a training flight. Sad public rituals of state funerals took the place of the former mass celebrations of space triumphs.[159]

In the meantime, the Soviet secret manned lunar program was foundering, as the giant new rocket *N-1* kept exploding at trial launches. These failures went unannounced, but it was difficult to keep from the public the news of the successes of the American lunar program—the circumlunar flight in 1968 and the lunar landing in 1969. The attempts to counter American lunar spectaculars with Soviet orbital missions proved futile. In October 1968 the cosmonaut Georgii Beregovoi misread signal lights and failed to perform a manual docking during his *Soyuz 3* flight. Though Beregovoi's return was greeted with usual fanfare, the public remained puzzled about his seemingly pointless mission. The successful *Soyuz 4-5* mission in January 1969 did not bring the expected propaganda dividends either. The crews showed tremendous courage and skill: Vladimir Shatalov performed the first manual docking of two piloted spacecraft, and Evgenii Khrunov and Aleksei Eliseev carried out a risky spacewalk from one spaceship to the other. Yet the mission almost ended tragically: a technical glitch resulted in a fiery descent and hard landing of *Soyuz 5*, nearly killing the cosmonaut Boris Volynov. Although the flight was touted as a complete success and the accident was hushed up as usual, rumors spread quickly. A popular joke—an elaborate pun on the cosmonauts' names—portrayed the four cosmonauts as "hanging about, slacking, doing zilch, barely landing."[160] The public no longer saw the difference between true accomplishment and a failure dressed up as a success.

Former public enthusiasm was succeeded by cynicism. Gagarin publicly admitted that "overly stormy applause led to the perception of spaceflight as a predictably easy and happy road to fame."[161] As one memoirist recalled, soon after the crash of *Soyuz 1*, in a small group of Komsomol activists, Gagarin raised a toast to his fellow cosmonauts. Someone kept interrupting him, saying that space technology had already been perfected, and that it was not difficult to become a Hero (of the Soviet Union). "Tearing up, Yuri said, 'And what about Komarov who burned up? What do you say about that?' Yuri threw the glass on the table and turned to leave."[162]

As failures of space technology and cosmonauts' errors began to chop away at the mythological perfection of the space program, the propaganda machinery also began to sputter. The finely choreographed public welcome ceremony for the *Soyuz 4-5* crews was ruined by an attempted assassination of the Soviet leader Leonid Brezhnev. At the gates to the Kremlin, a disgruntled military officer mistook the car carrying the cosmonauts Beregovoi, Nikolaev, Tereshkova, and Leonov for Brezhnev's limousine and fired fourteen shots into the car. The driver was killed, but the cosmonauts escaped unscathed.[163] The cosmonaut myth, however, received a decisive blow. Following this incident, top Soviet leaders no longer attended public welcome ceremonies for returning cosmonauts. The political status of public space events was downgraded. The cosmonauts no longer stood on the mausoleum next to the country's leaders. "The cosmonaut became less visible as a symbol of political power, and more visible as a profession," the historian Cathleen Lewis has written.[164]

The public image of Soviet cosmonauts both resembled and deviated from its most salient model—the public image of Stalin-era aviators. According to the scholar Katerina Clark, the hero pilots of the 1930s illustrated a cultural hierarchy of spiritual generations. The "sons"—the Stakhanovites and Arctic pilots—displayed (sometimes reckless) bravery and "spontaneity." The "fathers"—flying instructors, worker mentors, and the ultimate embodiment of fatherly love, Comrade Stalin—represented "'wisdom,' 'care,' and 'sternness' to guide the chosen sons to 'consciousness.'" Clark has stressed the stability of this cultural hierarchy throughout the Stalin era: "Despite the many gradations of maturity, society's sons were not to grow into fathers; rather, they were to be perfected as model sons."[165] At the dawn of the space age, however, Stalin's "falcons" finally acquired their own spiritual sons, the cosmonauts. The young pilots of the Gagarin generation grew up on stories of Stalinist heroes' great feats. Titov, for example, recalled how he was influenced by the Soviet polar exploration tales from his childhood.[166] Kamanin noted with satisfaction someone's comment that Gagarin was setting an example for the Soviet youth, just as Kamanin did for his own generation.[167] After Gagarin's tragic death Kamanin, who had lost his own son, an ace pilot, twenty years earlier, told Gagarin's widow: "Yuri was so dear to me, as if he were my only son."[168]

Called to be harbingers of de-Stalinization, the cosmonauts, ironically, had much in common with icons of Stalinism, their spiritual "fathers." The cosmonaut myth drew on the established canon, imagery, and ritual of Stakhanovism, the aviator myth, and the Arctic myth of the Stalin era. The cosmonauts "received the same honors and celebratory rhetoric that aviation heroes had received a generation before."[169] Like the Stakhanovites, the cosmonauts inspired workers to boost their productivity.[170] Like Stalin's "falcons," who symbolized the union of "fearlessness with training and iron self-control," cosmonauts served as role models for their generation.[171] Like Stalinist propaganda, the cosmonaut myth was sponsored from above, heavily promoted in the media, and reached all strata of the population—from schoolchildren to retirees. It encour-

aged dreams of exploration and skillfully channeled genuine public enthusiasm into actions that affirmed the Soviet technological prowess and
helped legitimize the Soviet regime.

Unlike the Stalin-era icons, however, the cosmonauts faced a fundamental tension between their public persona and their professional identity. The Stakhanovites' mission was tied to their profession: they called
on other workers to imitate their productivity drive. Stalin's hero aviators
attracted masses into aviation clubs to create a large supply of pilots for
the Air Force. Yet the cosmonauts' mission was not to recruit a large number of new cosmonauts. As historian Lewis has remarked, "there was no
state sponsored inducement to adopt spaceflight as a national pastime
in the name of civil defense."[172] The cosmonauts set a moral example
and carried a political message, rather than pointed a career path for the
masses. The cosmonauts' professional accomplishments made them into
celebrities, but in their function as celebrities they no longer needed their
professional identity. To maintain their public credentials, Aleksei Stakh-
anov had to continue setting new records, and Valerii Chkalov had to
keep flying. The cosmonauts publicly acted as propagandists, educators,
and ambassadors—not as cosmonauts. They talked about peace, friendship, and science—not about the details of their flights. Six of eleven first
cosmonauts never flew into space again, despite their best efforts to stay
on the active cosmonaut list.

Paradoxically, Khrushchev's cultural policy of de-Stalinization drew
on quite traditional, Stalinist rituals of hero-worshipping and organized
mass celebrations. Space propaganda was directed by a generation of
ideologues brought up under Stalin, and its leading architect, Nikolai Kamanin, modeled it after his own role in the Stalinist aviation myth. The
cosmonauts took their place in the generational hierarchy of Soviet spiritual heritage as "sons" of the famous aviators of the 1930s, thus becoming Stalin's spiritual "grandsons." The cosmonaut myth was conceived
as novel, futuristic, and high-tech, yet it was constructed out of many of
the same elements as the old propaganda discourse. The medium sub-
tly undermined the message. And the messenger—the cosmonaut—felt
ambivalent about the message. The crucial questions that interested the
cosmonauts—the technological aspects of spaceflight, emergencies in
orbit, and plans for future flights—were left out of their public speeches.
The cosmonauts had to follow the preset agenda of the space propaganda
machine, just as they had to fit into the controlling machinery of their

spacecraft. Neither machine left them much room for initiative. Just as they tried to increase their control over spacecraft, the cosmonauts tried to wrestle greater control over their social role. Just as they were not perfect automatons on board, they were not ideal models in the social arena.

The Sincere Deceiver

Yuri Gagarin and the Search for a Higher Truth

Andrew Jenks

The Soviet cosmonaut Yuri Gagarin once remarked to a curious Canadian journalist: "A lie is never a fair means to achieve a goal. I do not believe that conditions force you to lie. You know, the truth, even the most bitter truth, is always better than a lie." Perhaps in this instance Gagarin spoke from the heart, but on other occasions the world's first man in space played fast and loose with the facts. Although he publicly endorsed a new ethos of openness and sincerity in Soviet culture after Stalin's death, Gagarin also concocted deceptions for purposes of maintaining state secrets. He lied to keep his wife from worrying too much. He created cover stories to protect his comrades and country. And like so many mere mortals, he spun tales to mask personal failings. In the words of one of his admirers, Gagarin was an able practitioner of the "truth-lie" (*pravda-lozh'*): the justified commission of an untruth so long as it was done (supposedly) for noble and patriotic purposes.[1]

Gagarin's penchant for consciously hiding truths was hardly unique—or even venal. Societies have long used national security as a justification for secrecy and obfuscation. Modern politics, regardless of its ideological orientation, "seems to require a recognition that truth-telling at all costs is not possible, indeed not even desirable."[2] A sense of patriotic duty justifies concealment, prevarication, and dissimulation. British political culture, for example, has never endorsed a public right-to-know regarding national security matters. The image of the lying politician, praised for deftly distorting and dissimulating at press conferences, has become a kind of cliché even in supposedly open and democratic societies—famously captured by the American satirist Stephen Colbert in the phrase "truthiness."

This chapter uses the example of Gagarin to examine the relationship between political and personal morality in the post-Stalin era.[3] The goal is not to catch Gagarin in a lie, a futile task since truth is as much a social and political construct as an objective fact. As the philosopher Ludwig Wittgenstein once noted: "Truth is a matter of what the community accepts."[4] Besides, Gagarin may very well have believed many (though not all) of his public utterances. It would therefore be unfair to call Gagarin a liar if he believed what he said—or perhaps even if he thought his lie might serve a noble goal. Nor is the purpose to prove that the Soviet Union was based on falsehoods and lies, as if dissimulation and prevarication were uniquely Soviet. Rather, the aim is twofold. First, the chapter examines the ways in which the perceived demands of national security continually challenged a very different trend in Soviet culture during the Khrushchev "thaw" and early Brezhnev era: the demand that Soviet citizens be more sincere, honest, and open. Gagarin's soul became a kind of battleground between countervailing currents of secretiveness and openness, sincerity, and dissimulation.

Second, following more recent scholarship in anthropology and cultural history, the chapter highlights the absence of a clear dichotomy between public and private Soviet life and between official and unofficial Soviet society. Living in post-Stalinist Soviet society was far more complex than being either a "dissident" (Alexander Solzhenitsyn, for example) or completely selling out and becoming a mouthpiece for the party line (Gagarin). Most Soviets simultaneously absorbed the values and ideals of official culture while also violating and transforming those values in the conduct of their everyday life—sometimes consciously but more often not.[5] Gagarin was no exception; his moral dilemma derived from his attempt to enact broader Soviet cultural and political ideals that demanded, paradoxically and perhaps impossibly, that a Soviet citizen, in public and in private, be both sincere and deceptive.

The Gagarin Cult

Soviets felt genuine affection for Gagarin—a love that was enhanced rather than diminished by his official promotion as Hero of the Soviet Union.[6] Unpublished letters to the editor of the Soviet Union's major newspapers, like those that were published, expressed unbridled joy at Gagarin's feat. Peasants and factory workers, in particular, identified with the provincial lad. Born on a collective farm and trained as a foundryman, Gagarin was the underdog who had conquered Moscow and the world. Even complete strangers forged a bond of familial intimacy with Gagarin, referring to him by his diminutive "Yura" or "Yurochka." Wherever he went, adoring crowds laughed at his jokes, teenage girls swooned, schoolboys pledged to be just like him, and older women shed tears of joy—as if he were the son so many Soviets had lost during the war.[7]

The kinder, gentler, smiling cult of personality embodied by Gagarin—the welcoming cult of the son to replace Stalin's terrifying cult of the father—was well suited to immediate post-Stalin years. Technological accomplishment, a yearning for peace, and the official condemnation of state-sponsored terror had nurtured a climate of hope. As one Soviet journalist remembered: "The thaw and the roar of rocket engines filled this epoch with new content. The cult of personality was condemned, Solzhenitsyn was published, poets and artists created fresh new works."[8] A new emphasis on truth-telling and sincerity, it was hoped, would solidify trust and faith in the party's plans to reach the Communist promised land by 1980. Besides, being sincere seemed to be the right way to live. "The key word of the epoch was sincerity," noted one study of Soviet values during the 1960s.[9] Writers such as Solzhenitsyn and Yevgeny Yevtushenko, among others, began speaking previously unspoken truths about the Soviet gulag and the massacres of Jews during World War II. Even the so-called dissidents of the late 1960s, after Khrushchev had been ousted, initially took their cue from the regime. "The party called upon them to be sincere—and they spoke the truth."[10]

Nonetheless, interpretations of the new emphasis on truthfulness and authenticity in post-Stalinist society varied greatly. In Solzhenitsyn's case, for example, truth-telling was a moral imperative, an end in and of itself. In the case of Khrushchev, however, truth-telling was subservient to political goals, which in turn often masked personal ambitions. He famously condemned Stalin but passed over his own role in Stalin's crimes. For Khrushchev, as for his successor Brezhnev, lies were not really lies so long as they upheld political power. And truths were not really true so long as they jeopardized political power. As the Czech dissident Vaclav Havel once noted, echoing the position of the ancient Greek Sophists: "The principle involved here is that the centre of power is identical with the centre of truth."[11]

To complicate matters, individuals often took poetic license when it came to revealing politically charged truths. The great artist Picasso once proclaimed that "art is a lie that makes us realize the truth. . . . The artist must know the manner whereby to convince others of the truthfulness of his lies."[12] The movie director Grigory Chukrai, in his popular 1959 film *Ballad of a Soldier* (Ballada o soldate) used his simple tale of a soldier who goes on leave during World War II and falls in love as an opportunity to extol the virtues of truth-telling. He tackled problems previously unaddressed in Soviet film: sexual attraction and adultery on the home front. Yet even as Chukrai discussed previously forbidden topics, he closed debate on another matter: not once in the supposedly more realistic representation of World War II does there appear an image of Stalin or a mention of his name. Like so many commissars from the Stalin era, Stalin, the proverbial elephant in the room, was now the commissar whose image and memory had vanished. In the name of one political truth, and perhaps even a sense of justice, another historical truth was suppressed.

Gagarin similarly struggled with fulfilling the new mandate of truth-telling. Publicly he seemed to espouse Solzhenitsyn's notion of truth as absolute: no circumstances could ever justify a lie. Georgii Shonin, a fellow cosmonaut who trained with Gagarin before his flight, said of the original group of cosmonauts that they came from similar backgrounds, experienced the privations of war, were incredibly ambitious and hardworking, and were determined to "live honestly."[13] But then the party and the state asked them to lie, which they felt honor-bound to obey.

The contradiction was embodied in the July 1961 party program, which outlined the moral principles of an ideal Communist. Principle No. 7 proclaimed: "Honesty and truthfulness, moral purity, modesty and guilelessness in social and private life." Yet an ideal Soviet was also expected to have "a high sense of public duty" and unflinching "devotion to the Communist cause," even if that meant being insincere.[14] Handling secrecy with tact and discretion, and using deception to prevent secrets from being revealed, was a positive part of the moral development of "homo sovieticus," of whom Gagarin became the exemplar. Gagarin thus operated in a cultural and political context in which national security required deceptive behavior, while the new emphasis on truth-telling transformed him into an icon of sincerity and guilelessness who always spoke from the heart. Open and closed, honest and insincere, a truth-teller and dissimulator—Gagarin, like so many of his compatriots, was all these things simultaneously.

Duty Made Me Do It

Behind Gagarin's many distortions was the justification that military and political duty compelled it. The idea of duty to others—and above all to the state—runs like a red thread through Gagarin's life. The head of a Gagarin museum in Saratov, who spent much of his life collecting images and reminisces of Gagarin's life, concluded that the core of Gagarin's identity was a sense of obligation and duty, moral Principle No. 1 outlined in Khrushchev's July 1961 party program. "An order is an order," he said. Gagarin once wrote to his mother in 1957: "I have to obey. There is no other choice."[15]

Although the first commands for Gagarin to lie came immediately after the flight, the very nature of the Soviet space enterprise heightened the perceived need for duplicity. The Soviets insisted, of course, that their space program pursued civilian and scientific goals, but its underlying logic and chief rationale was military—to wit: the development of the Soviet ballistic missile program. As a classified military project, there was virtually nothing, according to Soviet censorship rules, that the Soviets could say about the flight—or about Gagarin, for that matter, who was himself a classified object. Reading the sixty-page pamphlet for Soviet newspaper editors that outlined, in small type, all the classified objects that could not be publicly discussed, it seems a small miracle that they said anything at all about Gagarin's flight.[16] Before his postflight press conferences, Gagarin was thus carefully prepped by his commander Nikolai Kamanin and the "competent organs," who found in him an able practitioner of obfuscation. Kamanin, a KGB officer and head of cosmonaut training from 1960 to 1971, was both commander to the cosmonauts and a template for their heroism. Trained as a fighter pilot, he had been awarded the very first Hero of the Soviet Union in 1934 for his rescue of survivors of the Chelyuskin steamship crushed by Arctic ice. As the creator of the public face of Soviet cosmonautics, Kamanin's daunting challenge was threefold: maintaining the integrity of military secrets; spinning Gagarin's biography and feat into a model for all young Soviets to follow; and convincing the world that the Soviet space program pursued exclusively peaceful and scientific purposes.[17]

One solution to the problem of talking about the flight without revealing anything militarily significant was simple and inelegant. The Soviet authorities began a coverup, followed by cover stories. The process began on the very day when the ship, the Vostok, landed on a collective farm outside of Saratov. The authorities covered up the capsule with a black tarp to prevent locals from seeing any of the craft's details. One eyewitness remembered the alarm of KGB officers who arrived at the landing site of Gagarin's charred capsule, which alit about two kilometers away from Gagarin. People were climbing all over it, snapping pictures (photography of military objects was strictly forbidden!), and stripping off pieces as personal souvenirs. Within hours, before a security cordon could be reestablished and a black tarp placed over the capsule, the details of a top-secret enterprise had been dangerously exposed to the public.[18]

The cover-up continued at the first press conference in which Gagarin fielded questions about his flight from those wily capitalist journalists. Like a nimble bantamweight eluding an opponent's jabs, his task was "to find the right answer, that is, to say, not what you are thinking and not what is really the case, but what is necessary and correct in a given situation," said one cosmonaut-candidate from the early 1960s. The process was "no doubt . . . the product of insincerity, but at the time it seemed natural." The cosmonauts especially enjoyed watching their colleagues spar with foreign journalists who tried "to pierce through the wall of secretiveness. . . . We were relieved and ecstatic when one of those answering questions managed to successfully 'wriggle out' of a tough spot."[19] Gagarin's "diversionary" account at his first press conference contained two lies. The first was that he had landed in his space capsule when in fact he had parachuted out before the capsule landed. The fiction was designed to ensure that the Soviets would be officially recognized as launching the first man into space—which required that he land in the capsule (figure 5.1).[20]

Gagarin then uttered another falsehood. He claimed that after landing in precisely "the planned spot" (which was nearly a thousand kilome-

Figure 5.1. The primary portrait in the main exhibit of the Gagarin museum in Saratov maintains the fiction that Gagarin landed in his capsule. When asked about this, the director replied: "It looks better that way." *Source*: Andrew L. Jenks.

ters away from where he landed), he was met "almost simultaneously" by a search party and a film crew. This suggested, contrary to the truth, that Gagarin's ship had landed exactly where its designers had planned. Later cosmonauts joked among themselves, whenever they were lost by foot or car, that they were in the "planned spot again." The games of cat and mouse continued, as Gagarin refused to reveal either the launch site (later erroneously called Baikonur, although it was really in a place called Tiura-Tam) or the landing site. When he was asked when he learned he had been chosen for the flight, Gagarin answered evasively: "In a timely fashion." The Soviets in the audience, incidentally, laughed and applauded. When Gagarin was asked about his salary, he replied: "As with all Soviet people, my salary is enough to satisfy fully my needs." As for when the next flight would occur, Gagarin said: "When it is needed."[21] There was no small irony in the complaint from a *Pravda* journalist at the time that foreigners "know almost nothing about the details of the flights of Soviet space ships," when the Soviets themselves had deliberately prevented those details from being publicized.[22]

In the meantime, Soviet authorities masked the military purpose in the rhetoric of peace. In Bulgaria, Gagarin was photographed releasing a white dove into the air—an iconic image that was reproduced by the thousands. An Egyptian newspaper noted: "A person with a soul like Gagarin's could not drop atom bombs," yet it did not mention that Gagarin had been trained as a fighter pilot. To maintain the pretense of peaceful purpose, the Ministry of Defense's official newspaper, *Krasnaia zvezda*, transferred all the letters to the editors from its readers requesting to go into space to the civilian Academy of Sciences. The academy was similarly chosen as the venue for Gagarin's press conference and as the public face of the Soviet space program, although it had almost nothing to do with its creation or management.[23] Meanwhile, the military logic of the flight often belied the message of peaceful purpose.[24] As the crisis in Cuba mounted after the disastrous Bay of Pigs fiasco, a Soviet general had a moment of candor, now permitted by the shifting demands of national security. He reminded Americans of the flight's underlying military logic: "that the Soviet rocket that had hurled Maj. Yuri Gagarin into space could be used for military purposes 'if necessary.'"[25]

Like a wave originating deep in the ocean and washing ashore thousands of miles away, the obligation to obfuscate moved seamlessly from Gagarin's life in the Soviet military-industrial complex to his personal life. As he prepared for his flight into space, Gagarin's wife did not ask about his job and he rarely talked about it (when old friends from school asked, he said he was a "test pilot"). His wife claimed that as his date for the launch on April 12 approached, he hinted but never stated explicitly that he would be the first to fly into space. Instead, Gagarin gave her the wrong date for this unstated event as he left; he said the "flight" (with a wink and a nod) would take place April 14, so that she would not worry. Gagarin's wife detected in his lie the concern of a loving husband simply doing his duty.[26]

While Gagarin continued to present himself as a paragon of sincerity in Soviet culture, he frequently sacrificed his commitment to the idea that "even the most bitter truth is always better than a lie." To take one example, two days before Gagarin's tragic death in 1968 he arranged to celebrate a colleague's fiftieth birthday. A telegram arrived reporting that his colleague's father had just died. Gagarin's wife brought the telegram to her husband, sitting at the head of the table for the party, and asked: "Should we tell [him] or not?" Gagarin said: "Not under any circumstances."

The news would have to wait until the next morning, "otherwise we'll spoil his party." Gagarin's wife cited the incident in her memoirs as a positive illustration of Gagarin's moral qualities. It was a seemingly trivial lie, a white lie, but it also was emblematic of a distinctive and well-noted aspect of late Soviet culture: good celebrations were not to be interrupted by the truth, whether it was the disastrous state of Soviet agriculture, the May Day celebration just after the Chernobyl disaster, or some piece of unhappy personal news that might spoil a colleague's birthday.[27] A belief that truth could do more damage than "un-truth" thus also defined the moral milieu in which Gagarin was raised.

Of all the people who knew Gagarin, his father seems to have been the most skeptical of Yuri's claims to honesty and openness. The cosmonaut's father, taciturn and gruff by nature, could be crude and cruel. During his son's wedding party, held immediately after Gagarin finished officer training school in Orenburg, he stunned the celebrants by attempting publicly to unmask him and catch him in a lie. According to Gagarin's older brother Valentin, Gagarin was dressed to the nines in his new uniform with lieutenant stripes. He sat at the head of the table with his beautiful new wife—eager to show his relatives that he had made a success of himself. As the guest prepared for the ceremonial first toast, Gagarin's father tapped his glass with a fork, rose, and congratulated his son on the marriage and being commissioned as an officer. "But I simply want to know one thing," he added. "Did you register [the marriage] . . . and do you have a document proving that you graduated from the [military] academy?" A long moment of uncomfortable silence followed. Yuri then reached into his breast pocket and pulled out a document, which his father inspected closely. "Well, everything is clear now! I congratulate you son!" Nonetheless, an air of discomfort lingered, and even Yuri's brother was not sure how to interpret the public interrogation. If it was a joke, Gagarin's brother remembered, it was "crude but from the soul."[28]

When Should I Lie?

Gagarin revealed the complex hermeneutics of Soviet truth-telling in a revealing exchange of letters with a fifteen-year-old Canadian boy from Montreal in 1963. Like so many of Gagarin's fans, the boy sent a letter to Gagarin requesting his guidance. He wanted to know, "is it right to lie for the sake of principle?" Was it right to do whatever was necessary to achieve one's ambitions? The questions, according to Gagarin's wife, agonized Gagarin, who seemed to recognize in them the same issues he had confronted since his flight. Gagarin labored long and hard over his response, composed a letter, and then tossed it, along with many other drafts, into the trash bin. There was really nothing he could say, he admitted to his wife. "He's already discovered the most important thing—he lives in a dog-eat-dog world." But Gagarin, as always, persevered and composed a letter to "my young Canadian friend" in which he emphasized his "comradely" upbringing. He concluded that it was wrong to lie for the sake of "personal interests," but significantly he did not discuss whether it was wrong to lie for other reasons. He ended with two pieces of advice: make sure your goal is reasonable, and surround yourself with comrades to keep you on the right path. The question of whether it was wrong to lie on behalf of others was deftly ignored. "I hope that in the future . . . you will never have to lie and will be lucky."[29] For a time the Soviets put the letter as well as Gagarin's response on display at the museum in Star City—thus transforming Gagarin's private moral dilemma, along with his solution, into a shining example of Soviet virtue in action.[30]

If Gagarin's lies often grew from a concern for the feelings of others as well as from the demands of military secrecy, his own behavior caused him to make lies that entailed more complex personal motives. Gagarin's well-known fondness for drink threatened to tarnish his image and compelled him, for personal and political reasons, to engage in many truthlies. "Everyone wanted to get drunk with Gagarin for his friendship, for his love, and for a thousand other reasons," remembered Kamanin. One army officer recalled how he and his friends tried to finagle visits to Star City to party with the cosmonauts. They stuffed their briefcases full of appetizers and bottles of vodka, just in case a party broke out, which it usually did. Gagarin, in addition, married his love of drink to the cultivation of a new post-Stalinist masculine identity. As head of the Soviet Federation of Water Skiing, he was frequently pictured bare-chested and grinning on water skis. He drove cars fast, taking friends on 160-kilometer-per-hour spins (on Russian roads!) in his fiberglass French Matra (a gift from his French acolytes). And he definitely liked to keep the company of pretty women (figure 5.2).[31]

The cosmonaut Aleksei Leonov remembered one night of hard partying in May 1964. After staying up until four in the morning drinking, Gagarin, "who drank just as much as the rest of us," awoke the entire

Figure 5.2. The "Volga" Gagarin received from the Soviet government is displayed outside his ancestral home in Gagarin (formerly Gzhatsk). His preferred car, however, was a fiberglass red Matra Djet given to him by the French. *Source*: Andrew L. Jenks.

party three hours later to go on a water-skiing trip. Somehow he had managed to assemble liquor, food, and all the necessary equipment for the day's outing. As Gagarin steered the boat, Leonov and the other cosmonauts raised their glasses to toast Gagarin: "Here's to you Captain!" Gagarin, in response, urged them to serenade him with a song. "Boy could he organize a party," Leonov remembered.[32] A love of partying, of course, made him a regular Russian guy—a "man's man," in the words of fellow cosmonaut Vitalii Sevast'ianov.[33] It was also characteristic of the Gagarin clan, who had a reputation back in their native land of Smolensk oblast for hard partying. The trademark smile and the appreciation of a good time was thus a family tradition, an enactment of post-Stalin masculine political identity, and perhaps even a symbolic manifestation of the bright and happy communist future.[34]

But the love of Bacchus might also suggest something darker—less a celebration of success and more an escape from a reality that often did not accord with the official image. Kamanin's diaries, published by his son after the collapse of the Soviet Union, are filled with titillating details about the drunken escapades of Gagarin and his comrades.[35] The most serious incident occurred on October 4, 1961, damaging Gagarin's personal life, his public image, and potentially the image of the entire space program. The day had begun with Gagarin and his comrades getting drunk and taking a speedboat on the water for joyrides—without life vests, far out at sea, doing circles in the water at high speed. After dinner Kamanin went to sleep. At 11:30 he was awakened by his frantic wife who said something had happened to Gagarin. When Kamanin went out into the courtyard, he saw Gagarin lying on a bench, his face covered in blood and a gaping wound over his left eye. Gagarin's wife was screaming, "He is dying!" A naval doctor performed an operation on the spot to stabilize him. He had broken his skull above the left eyebrow and would be hospitalized for at least three weeks.[36]

Kamanin's investigation revealed that Gagarin had arisen after taking a nap and began playing records as the men played chess and the women played cards. Still drunk, he went up to his wife just before midnight and told her to stop playing cards and go to bed. She played on for a few more minutes and then asked where he went. One of the cosmonaut's wives said she saw him walk down the hotel corridor. Gagarin's wife immediately got up and started checking doors, banging insistently on one that was locked. Within moments she was greeted by a twenty-seven-year-old nurse, who said simply: "Your husband jumped from the balcony." The nurse later told Kamanin that she had just returned from her shift and was lying in bed reading with her clothes on. Gagarin barged in, locked the door behind him, and said to her: "Well, are you going to scream?" He then tried to kiss her. It was at that time that Gagarin's wife began pounding on the door and Gagarin made his infamous flying leap from the balcony, stumbling and falling head first onto a cement curb and nearly killing himself.[37]

The Cover Story

Lurid details aside, the incident had political as well as personal consequences. How does one cover up a public idol's broken skull? The most immediate concern was to explain Gagarin's absence from a scheduled appearance at the Twenty-second Party Congress, which for Khrushchev was a key moment in the unveiling of his renewed effort at reform—a program that emphasized technological prowess and a renewed attack on the Stalin cult. Gagarin had been slated for the starring role of trumpeting the Soviet Union's successful mastery of the scientific-technological revolution, so Khrushchev and the Central Committee were understandably irate. Only a lie, they agreed, could solve this problem: they thus concocted the story that Gagarin stumbled and fell while playing with his daughter on vacation. He was fitted with a fake eyebrow and for three weeks after the incident something unprecedented happened: the most photographed person in the world vanished from public view. Finally, a photograph with Gagarin and his fake eyebrow was sent to Khrushchev, who gave permission "to release Yura into 'the world,'" as Kamanin put it. The prosthetic eyebrow, however, only fed the rumor mill, which could not have concocted a rumor more lurid than what had actually happened. The poet Yevgeny Yevtushenko noted in his 1981 work *Wild Berries* that the whole world could now "see the scar which gave rise to so many rumors."[38] One delegate at the Twenty-second Party Congress who escorted a wobbly and woozy Gagarin to his seat remembered that "the efforts of doctors and make-up artists did not produce 100 percent results. The deep gash, filled with a dark brown substance, really stood out."[39] Gagarin's scar was a constant visual reminder that the real Gagarin was quite different from the iconic image, that the truth-lie of this image, like so many of the late-Soviet era's claims, was "truthy" at best but certainly not "truthful." "Everyone paid attention to the scar," wrote one Russian many years later. Yet he also remembered that the scar, like rumors of Gagarin's partying, may have enhanced rather than diminished Gagarin's popular appeal—that he was considered by many a real man precisely because there was much more to him than met the eye.[40]

Perhaps rumors of Gagarin's drunken escapades unintentionally reinforced the image of Gagarin as a "man's man," but they also threatened the official narrative of Gagarin's triumph. Being known for daring and risk taking was one thing; engaging in drunken orgies quite another. When the Twenty-second Party Congress was completed, the party and Gagarin's commander once again addressed the issue of Gagarin's conduct—and that of his partying fellow cosmonaut Titov. In accordance with the demands of *samo-kritika*, a Soviet ritual in which an individual admits to personal faults and failings before comrades, Gagarin and Titov admitted their drunken excesses in a closed meeting of the party cell. Gagarin claimed he went into the nurse's room as an innocent practical joke on his wife. Kamanin was only partially convinced, but he kept his doubts to himself—or rather, he recorded them in his diary.

Gagarin's explanation, Kamanin reasoned, "may lessen the impact of the incident and will not be a reason for family discord." Besides, fulfilling the role of a paragon of socialist virtue had greatly complicated the moral complexity of Gagarin's situation. The first cosmonaut was not merely lying for personal reasons but to protect the honor of family and country. And so, for the sake of communal harmony, the truth had to be suppressed. That same day Gagarin gave a speech at Moscow State University and received a medal. The next day the papers carried a text of Gagarin's speech and also his response to a question concerning that funny-looking eyebrow. "At a resort in Crimea I was playing with [my daughter] Galka and tripped," said Gagarin, who then added another touching detail that converted the incident into an act of heroic self-sacrifice. "Trying to save my daughter, I raised her high and fell face first on a rock. It will heal before Galka's wedding and even before the next flight into space."[41]

Interestingly, Kamanin's acceptance of Gagarin's lie mirrored the logic behind his own critique of Khrushchev's second wave of de-Stalinization, which coincided with the aftermath of the Gagarin incident. Making Stalin a scapegoat for the "tragic events of 1937 to 1939" not only tarnished Stalin's glorious accomplishments, it also represented a "short-sighted and stupid politics" that would cause problems abroad and erode the faith of youth in Soviet power. "It won't do anyone any good, and even more it could spoil our relations with China and cause new complications." If Khrushchev really wanted to tell the truth, he should admit his own guilt in the purges and "do the only correct thing—give up leadership of the party and the country." Given the potentially disastrous consequences of telling the truth, the only sensible solution was to continue telling lies—truth-lies, white lies, for the good of the country.[42]

If Gagarin's incident was a personal embarrassment, it was also emblematic of broader problems for the Soviet regime when it came to revealing uncomfortable truths about its icons. Because a Soviet icon symbolized the perfectibility of human nature, the myth-making apparatus of the Soviet regime could not account for evidence of Gagarin's fallibility.[43] In Gagarin's case, however, no amount of spin control, or cosmetic surgery, could completely submerge the uncomfortable truth that Soviets—and in particular the most ideal of them all—were no closer to achieving human perfection than their nonsocialist counterparts. As one Central Committee member noted when first learning of the incident: "We can manage in space, it's on Earth that we act like fools."[44] It was telling, of course, that party figures kept such thoughts to themselves and worked vigorously, as they would until the era of glasnost, to maintain the truth-lie of developed socialism.

The Public and Private Gagarin

In his last years Gagarin's signature trademark smile often disappeared in the morning of a hangover. Being a "man's man"—enacting the role of a Soviet playboy—was clearly taking a toll on his iconic image as a Soviet superman. He gained weight after his flight (from 64 to 73 kilograms, or about 141 to 161 pounds) and his face became visibly bloated. Adding to the other mark of imperfection over his left eyebrow, he acquired a paunch and his hair grew wispy thin—physical facts that eroded the believability of his public biography. In the meantime he fell on and off the wagon. In his personal journal from 1967, Gagarin ranked as one of his more significant accomplishments that he went to a party "and drank juice." His personal struggles with alcohol, however, could not be incorporated into his official persona. While Hollywood stars could humanize themselves before an adoring public by declaring their weaknesses and going into rehab, Gagarin remained a privately drunken model of public sobriety. His only possible redemption came through another questionable public utterance. As he said to a group of foreign reporters: "I do not have time for wine or cognac."[45]

Drunkenness, tight living quarters, constant surveillance, marital spats, public speeches—it was all so exhausting. Gagarin's wife remembered that he was sometimes "devilishly tired, upset and even angry." When Gagarin's mother noticed his unhappiness and asked him what was wrong, he jokingly asked her if she had been sent by foreign spies. Or *was* it a joke? The only way he could make time for all the demands placed on him—including living up to his image as a partier with all the right stuff—was by cutting back his sleep to just a few hours. He once complained bitterly about being diverted from his studies because of a summons to Moscow to autograph pictures. "I wasted four hours. I'll have to make it up at night." He lamented that he did not have time to fully develop his thoughts or write his memoirs.[46]

Although Gagarin's public persona symbolized spontaneity and the promise of freedom under Soviet rule, his private life was completely controlled, which was perhaps appropriate for a system that consciously eroded the boundaries between public and private life.[47] In her memoir Gagarin's wife hoped that "it would not appear strange that in these purely personal remembrances about Yuri two things, so to speak, are intertwined: the public and the private." But that was characteristic of Gagarin, she said. "As concerns public life, with him it was never separated from private life." Vacations were invariably interrupted by calls to return to Moscow for this or that duty. He wrote in his diary from 1963 that he was beginning to lose his bearings. "Everything is mixed up together in one big pile: studies in the academy, flying, training."

Gagarin said to one friend in January 1965 that his greatest desire was to just go somewhere and relax "incognito." He tired of the constant visits to the doctors that now marked his life after the flight—his transformation into a human guinea pig, the constant prodding and poking and measurement of his vital signs. Like Lenin's body, even Gagarin's own body was no longer his own property. "The doctors make you do all sorts of useless things. In a word, idiocy. I really can't stand people who say one thing to your face and do another behind your back."[48] But of course he had on many occasions said many things that did not accord with what he actually did. And he continued to report for his daily regimen of prodding and poking by the doctors. One of those doctors remembered how difficult Gagarin's situation must have been: constantly asked to conceal the truth of his flight and life from the public even while his doctors "demanded from him the truth, and only the truth."[49]

If the public face of Gagarin was one of youthful, albeit rapidly dissipating, energy, his journal entries from the mid-1960s lamented his passing youth. "Life is going by so fast," he wrote in 1963. In 1965, at the "advanced" age of thirty-one, Gagarin remarked: "Oh youth, how quickly you are disappearing." The death of Korolev in 1966, the chief engineer for the Soviet space program and a man Gagarin greatly admired, was especially traumatic—not only because of what it meant for the space program but also because of what it revealed about the real state of Soviet technology. Korolev died under an incompetent surgeon's knife (the minister of health!) during a routine operation for hemorrhoids. The truth, of course, could not be told, just as Korolev's identity or critical role in the Soviet space program was concealed as a military secret. Public meetings, Gagarin remarked in private, were a farce, an exercise in feigned sincerity. "The hen praises the rooster for the fact that the rooster praises the hen." Shortly before his death in 1968, he complained that his "popularity and fame" had made it difficult for him to do anything other than be a living monument.[50]

But even earlier Gagarin had grown weary of the accolades and attention, of the competing demands of being sincere and deceptive. The glowing accounts, he remarked shortly after his flight, made him "feel embarrassed. You can't idealize a person. You have to accept him for what he is." The idealized portrait of himself, he wrote in 1962, "makes me sick." Not long before his death, a jaded Gagarin returned from another trip abroad where he was awarded yet another "Gold Medal of Heroism." His voice dripping with sarcasm, Gagarin flipped it over and read aloud the etching on the back: "No. 11,175." He remembered stopping in a village during a road trip and knocking on a door for a bite to eat. The elderly woman greeting him at the door refused to believe he was Gagarin—although she did admit there was a vague resemblance. He often seemed to wonder the same thing about himself: Was he that same Gagarin they write about in the papers?[51]

The truth-lie was also apparent to Gagarin as he traveled abroad immediately after his flight. He encountered a "carefully guarded border" that seemed to function as much to keep people in—to prevent them from seeing "forbidden zones"—as to keep foreign invaders out. His spaceflight, he once joked, was the only time he was allowed to go abroad "without any permissions or visas."[52] His press conferences during his world tour were exercises in planned spontaneity where, as if on cue, he "started acting as he was taught." While he was constantly watched and coached, he appeared to his hosts in Canada, England, France, Italy, and Japan as a refreshing and spontaneous breath of fresh air, a proletarian chap who could cut through the stifling protocol and formality of an official bourgeois reception (although not a Soviet one). There is a revealing photo of Gagarin and his commander/handler Kamanin on the streets of Havana, both dressed to the nines in their lily-white, newly knit, short-sleeved uniforms. Gagarin is smiling and waving. Kamanin—his commander, watcher, and speech writer in the background—wears a stern, suspicious, and weary look. People saw Gagarin, but with few exceptions they did not see his alter ego Kamanin.[53]

Irreconcilable Contradictions

If Gagarin dutifully played his appointed role, the spaceflight none-theless gave him a cosmic perspective that allowed him to distinguish representation from reality, to catch a glimpse, as one acquaintance put it, of "the disharmony of society, the absurdity of its arrangements."[54] Yet Gagarin was also a willing participant in the absurdities and "truth-lies" he sometimes condemned. He had internalized the values of a system where lies were not just lies but essential tools for achieving higher po-litical ends. Vladimir Vysotsky—like Gagarin, a postwar icon who par-tied hard and died young—may have best captured Gagarin's dilemma in a 1970 song entitled, "I First Measured Life Counting Backwards." Vysotsky's lyrics created an image of Gagarin as a confused and tragic figure. In it Gagarin was complicit in his fate but he was also innocent; like everyone else, he had no choice but to do and say as he was told. In such a situation "not guilty" could not mean the same thing as "not complicit," wrote Vysotsky. One could therefore lie and still be a decent, upright person.[55]

It was difficult, however, for Gagarin to distance himself entirely from responsibility for his own actions. If the growth of the Gagarin cult in the 1960s reflected the logic of the truth-lie, it also paralleled a new dialogue about the nature and function of the truth. Not just writers such as Solzhenitsyn but even the party had suggested that lies were morally indefensible under any circumstances. Gagarin was not immune to such notions—ironic, because it was the party's own morality campaigns, for which he was the front man, that had made the truth-lie potentially prob-lematic. Gagarin's scar, in this new cultural context, could easily become a metonym for falsehood, a window into the mendacious nature of of-ficial image and public celebrity. Khrushchev's policy of de-Stalinization, meanwhile, raised the problem of whether a partial truth—Stalin's part in the crimes of the Great Terror but not Khrushchev's own—was just a lie. Was a smaller lie better than a bigger one? Was a partial truth some-times better than a whole truth? How could one determine if a liar was lying for public benefit or personal gain—or both simultaneously? Finally, what happens when people begin to suspect that everything is a truth-lie? In the words of one philosopher: "Once it is accepted that there are 'different kinds' of truth, some superior to others, then truth acquires the advantages of falsehood in being multiple, not single. It is hard to distinguish one from another."[56]

French journalists, according to Gagarin's wife, once asked him why he was so active in so many spheres of public life. "That's a complex question," he said. "If I say that I am a communist and I act out of a sense of duty, they will say: 'Communist propaganda.' If I say I do it because it is interesting to me, they won't believe me. All those additional obligations and social work, which I perform, are not unpleasant to me. On the contrary, I love to work with young people, with Komsomol members, I love sport and I find it interesting to take trips and meet with people of labor . . . all of this is tremendously satisfying." But the condition of the truth-lie made it impossible to know if he was telling the truth—and, indeed, if public service itself was not a kind of lie. Following the exchange, Gagarin was frustrated that no matter what he said, people would not believe him.[57] His frustration reflected another problem with the truth-lie: once everyone believed public statements had to be deceptive, even for legitimate national security reasons, the foundation for faith in the system and its claims no longer existed. Purity of motive, and perhaps even a community of interests, was no longer deemed possible.

Even long before the notorious cynicism of the late Brezhnev period some Soviets expressed disappointment in unpublished letters to the editor of *Komsomol'skaia pravda* that they were not getting the full truth about their idol. One letter writer, a pensioner named Aleksei, addressed his letter of April 16, 1961, to "Dear Newspaper People." Calling himself a confederate (*edinomyshlennik*), to stress his loyalty, the writer challenged the versions he had recently read in the newspaper point by point. He wanted to go beyond the "ceremonial stories and parade speeches" that had filled the pages of the press and get to the truth, which Khrushchev's policies had led this man to expect from his government. Based on what he had read about Gagarin's biography, he wondered how someone could finish military school so quickly, in just two years, and then get a promotion from lieutenant to major just three years later (Gagarin was promoted to major in space, thus skipping a full rank). "Did he study, using the language of our time, at a cosmic speed?" A proper education for a major would have to be at least five years, making Gagarin's precipitous promotion another example of "hastiness." "After this I truly see that miracles occur on Earth!" He could understand such a promotion in wartime, but in peacetime it made no sense. "Something is not right here." Even more, the hasty promotion to major seemed to demean the much more deserving service of those who had fought in the war, a point echoed by another letter from a group of war veterans, who wondered why "his title does not correspond with the rules of protocol in the Soviet army."[58]

He also smelled a new personality cult in the making—something he thought was not supposed to happen with living people following Khrushchev's denunciation of Stalin's cult of personality. "And so this Gagarin, like Stalin, will get to the rank of Generalissimus. And it's the same thing. Both were never soldiers. They didn't smell gun powder. But still they went right up to the rank of Generalissimus." He wasn't sure how Gagarin's promotion to major happened, but he suspected someone pulled him aside and said, "If you fly, we'll make you a major, if you don't, you'll rot forever in the rank of a lieutenant. Of course, all the newspapers say he flew, risking his own life, and not for the sake of glory and fame, but for the sake of the motherland, the people, the party, the government, and so on and so forth." The letter writer also did not buy official newspaper accounts about Gagarin's landing—a point repeated, it should be noted, by a number of other readers who admired Gagarin but wondered why something in the official reports of the landing did not add up.

"Where is the so-called 'planned spot'" where Gagarin was said to have landed, he asked. Did he really land in the capsule? The newspapers provided not a word about this, or about the point of launch. "Why can't they talk about this honestly and openly?" The answer, he said, had nothing to do with protecting state secrets, as he was sure he would be told, because the "American spies surely know the launch site." The real reason was that the government did not trust its own people—and that is why they hid the truth. Finally, even if everything the newspapers wrote was true, it still avoided the main issue. "How many of the peoples' kopeks have been wasted on the launch of these satellites into space, how many billions of rubles have been and will be spent on these sensations?" If Lenin were alive, the letter continued, "he'd probably hop right back into the grave. . . . And so we have atomic bombs, rockets, and spaceships. But how often do you see automobiles for sale? Every year they make the promise. And refrigerators? The same thing. And sewing machines? Even worse! Not in one store will you see even a meat grinder or an electric iron." There was plenty to do on Earth, he concluded. "We need to take care of that and not stick our nose into the heavens, the cosmos. Let's fix things first on Earth, where the cows on collective farms are starving, where there is a housing crisis, where there is a shortage of school buildings, and then we can crawl into space, to Mars and Venus."

The writer declined to offer his name and address, "for reasons that are completely clear to you, even more so since you would never print my letter, because, as they say, 'truth stings the eyes.'" It should be noted that the letter writer in early 1961 was in a very distinct minority; most Soviets in the early 1960s seemed content with the official coverage of Gagarin's flight.[59] Only during the long collapse of the Soviet Union in the 1980s did those early feelings of betrayal—expecting to hear the truth and being told a lie—become more and more common. That was especially the case when Gorbachev's policy of glasnost inadvertently confirmed what many now suspected: much of what they were told, it seemed, was just not true.

The popular mythology of Gagarin, which by the late 1970s and into the era of perestroika spun a portrait of Gagarin as a womanizer and monumental drunk, seemed closer than the official mythology to a fundamental truth: that Gagarin was a human being, capable of great feats and colossal blunders.[60] Even so, it was not the truth, at least as professional historians understand it. It was based on rumor and hearsay; and just as fables and hideous sea creatures grew on the edges of medieval maps, so too had rumors multiplied in the mysterious realms of official silence surrounding the Soviet space program. Indeed, rumors had emerged since the day of the flight on April 12, 1961 (encouraged, it should be noted, by Voice of America broadcasts): stories that an earlier unsuccessful flight had preceded Gagarin's, that Gagarin was a stand-in for a critically injured cosmonaut from an earlier flight. "The world is filled with rumors," as one eyewitness noted, regarding Gagarin.[61] If those rumors had sowed doubts about official campaigns for truth-telling in the early 1960s, by the 1980s they had blossomed into the cynical view that fact could never be distinguished from fiction, truth from lies. As the old saw went, there was no news (*izvestiia*) in the newspaper *Pravda* and no truth (*pravda*) in the newspaper *Izvestiia* (News). In such a context, anything could be true—and anything could be a lie. And no one could be trusted.[62]

The circumstances surrounding Gagarin's tragic death in March

1968 illustrate the point. Gagarin died on March 27, 1968, while on a routine training flight. His death was officially reported in *Pravda* on March 29, which also announced the formation of a commission to investigate the accident. Although *Pravda* devoted most of its coverage through March 30 to the funeral and condolences from around the world, it did not make any further mention of the reasons for Gagarin's death. Nothing. For those accustomed to the detailed speculations and analysis of the reasons for tragic deaths (from President John F. Kennedy to Lady Diana) the absence of any public discussion or explanation of the accident for nearly two decades is astounding. No wonder there were rumors! The official investigation, whose results were only partially published in the Gorbachev period by one participating investigator, clearly pointed to a combination of technical errors on the part of air-traffic controllers, maintenance crews, and aircraft design.[63]

The truth was suppressed for so long, according to one commission member, because it cast an unflattering light on Soviet technological systems. To reveal that truth, it was believed, would only play into the hands of the Soviet Union's enemies. In addition, the investigating commission was paralyzed by a fear among many of its members and their organizations that they might be held responsible. "In the work of the commission ... there was felt a terrifying fear of looking anew at what had happened, at an independent opinion. .... As a result there was no official publication of the results of the commission." Fear of retribution induced silence and passivity among those investigating the tragedy, just as it had put a stop to the investigation of Stalin's crimes after Khrushchev's ouster. Many commission members "literally thirsted for a showcase punishment (and a public one!)." The atmosphere of grief and anger ultimately prevented anything remotely resembling an objective analysis. "As a result, a 'diplomatic balance' was established, and there was formed a passive exit from a difficult situation—the position of silence." The silence itself only created a vacuum of information that was filled, yet again, by the rumor mill.[64]

Almost immediately there emerged a legend that Gagarin had been seized by angels—or that he was the victim of an alien abduction. Many in the military continued to blame Gagarin's lack of preparation and carelessness, thus deflecting blame away from themselves and onto Gagarin. Another popular version claimed that Gagarin took a drunken flight to watch a soccer match in Alma-Alta and crashed on the return. Some people swear they saw him at the match. Another version echoed the legends of tsars who supposedly faked their deaths to escape the burdens of their official position and take up a humble position among the masses. According to one variant, he had plastic surgery after successfully ejecting from the plane and took on a new identity. A Soviet émigré playwright staged a play in New York City in 1981 about Gagarin in which the cosmonaut "invited death by hunting animals from a low-flying jet." In Saratov during the 1980s residents remember a touched elderly man who everyday paced the city streets and announced in a stentorian voice: "Gagarin Lives!" During perestroika a person in Moscow claimed to be Gagarin. His voice was similar to Gagarin's and he often made calls to cosmonauts. Another version suggested that Brezhnev locked Gagarin up in a psychiatric hospital as punishment for an incident in which Gagarin supposedly threw a glass of champagne in Brezhnev's face during an official reception. The story itself is indicative of the kinds of hopes and ideals that ordinary people, and not just those in the regime, invested in the myth of Gagarin. He dared to challenge and humiliate the domineering bosses.[65] But that was also not true. The truth-lie of Gagarin's public life was thus countered by the rumor and innuendo of popular urban myth.

As the Soviet Union collapsed, the stories became more and more fantastic, spilling onto the pages of the late-Soviet and post-Soviet press. The head of the Gagarin museum in Saratov offered a sociological explanation: "The chaos in our life, the dissatisfaction with the social order, the profound feeling of many injustices, the lack of full and accurate information have made people vulnerable to sensations, and therefore they readily believe absurd rumors about the reasons for Gagarin's death." One editor at the end of the Soviet period remarked to a level-headed investigator of the crash, who had participated in the official investigation, that his version of the events was too complex and technical. "The reader won't accept it in this form." It needed to be more sensational, less reasonable. In 1994 the journal *Svet* published an article claiming that Gagarin's brain had been downloaded into another person—and that Gagarin, languishing in an insane asylum, was struggling to escape from the alien host. Another article in 1998 claimed Gagarin was a drug addict. It was accompanied by an illustration of his rocket as a hypodermic needle. Rocks scattered on the ground are in the form of tablets, which presumably explained why Gagarin always had a smile on his face. The shift from enforced silence to anything goes told volumes about the transformation of Russia in the three decades after Gagarin's death. In 1968 nothing could be publicly asserted about his death; in 1998 people could publish anything about him. And in both instances there was no verifiable truth.[66]

If there is a common element to many of these explanations, it is the presumption of a vast conspiracy to hide a damning truth. The conspiratorial mind-set was a by-product of a tendency, going back to the show trials, to explain all misfortunes as a result of evil, enemy intent. It was also a logical outgrowth of a system obsessed with secrecy, where vast areas of public life belonging to the Soviet military-industrial complex—of which Gagarin was a part—were declared off limits to the public. It therefore seemed perfectly logical to many that a conspiracy of power could have killed Gagarin for some good reason. "The success of the conspiracy [theory]," remarked one anthropologist, "is rooted in the leaps of imagination that establish similarity between apparently unconnected events, objects, and people." Even the more level-headed observers, who had studied the technical details of the crash and dismissed the notion of a conscious conspiracy, nonetheless felt that Gagarin's death was akin to a kind of premeditated murder. As one Soviet aeronautical engineer who knew Gagarin noted, the system of technical incompetence, which was the result of political imperatives winning out over technocratic expertise, made Gagarin's death "objectively similar to murder." In his view a system that could not tolerate an alternative technocratic authority therefore had to eliminate those who objected to political decisions on technical grounds. "In the framework of these rules of the game there was no place for Korolev or Gagarin," the supposed "sources of scientific-technological progress" that "semi-literate" party hacks could not tolerate.[67] Gagarin thus died because he supposedly resisted an irrational and unjust system in the name of technocratic competence.

It is perhaps an appropriate tribute to Gagarin's life that his death has become inscrutable: Gagarin had been hoisted upon the petard of his own truth-lie. During his seven years as a Soviet celebrity, patriotic pretext had given Gagarin a license to prevaricate. To the extent that he protested against the mendacious aspects of the Soviet order, he (like millions of other Soviets) was always compromised by his own participation in their construction. In the end his belief that truth is whatever enhances Soviet power made him unable to tell the truth about himself. Perhaps like the Manhattan Project's J. Robert Oppenheimer in 1945, Gagarin believed that from the moment of his initiation into the supersecret world of the Soviet military-industrial complex, he could be permitted to experience "only classified thoughts."[68]

The legacy of the truth-lie lives on in post-Soviet society—minus the Communist Party commandment to be sincere and honest. Those close to Gagarin, including the Russian Federation government, cling ferociously to the ideal image of Gagarin. Gagarin's daughter Elena, the director of the Kremlin museum today, said that Gagarin was a completely blameless figure—and she has successfully sued those who claim otherwise. He was the same person in private, she claimed, that he was in public. "And this is not because propaganda made him this way, but because he was such a person." For many former and present cosmonauts, protecting the "sacred" achievement of Gagarin is a matter of professional honor, of defending "the honor of the uniform" (chest' mundira). The truth is beside point.[69]

The revival of the Gagarin cult has required both a suppression of negative moments in Gagarin's life and attacks on those "who have besmirched the name of our first cosmonaut." The Russian Federation has revived the cult of the ideal Gagarin and planned a high-profile fiftieth anniversary of Gagarin's flight on April 12, 2011. Through a combination of public and private resources, former cosmonauts, Komsomol, party and KGB officials, as well as Gagarin's relatives are using Gagarin's exploits as the foundation for a new Russian patriotism. As one former secretary of the Komsomol Central Committee remarked, the American media company CBS pulled its unflattering biopic of Ronald Reagan after complaints from advertisers, so why shouldn't Russians prevent similar public attacks on Gagarin?[70]

The managers of Soviet archives have also joined the revival of the Gagarin cult, among other things, by preventing access to archival sources that might taint the image. The Russian State Archive of Scientific and Technical Documentation on its Web site celebrates the heroic image of Gagarin, using a selective culling of images and documents to maintain the truth-lie of Gagarin's feat and life.[71] It addresses neither the reasons for his death nor the personal challenges of his life (and an exhibit it sponsored in 2007 repeated the claim that Gagarin landed in his capsule!). Among other things, the selective culling of documentary evidence perpetuates the practice of using historical documentation to manipulate and erase inconvenient memories.[72] Presumably, a sense of duty justified the omission.

6

Cold War Celebrity and the Courageous Canine Scout

The Life and Times of Soviet Space Dogs

Amy Nelson

In the gripping Cold War contest that was the space race, the feats of astronauts and cosmonauts marked some of the most iconic moments of the twentieth century. The race to send humans beyond the Earth's atmosphere shifted the battlefield of the Cold War, focusing the energies of the two superpowers on a struggle for scientific and technological supremacy at once more compelling, and thanks to the mass media, more accessible than conventional warfare. Contoured by personal and geopolitical rivalries and fueled by the superpowers' shared aspirations and values—including a faith in progress, the veneration of science and technology, and a commitment to harnessing nature to human ends—the space race might be considered a quintessentially human drama.[1] Yet in the years before Yuri Gagarin's 108-minute flight ushered in the era of human space travel, many of the milestones in the quest to make that era a reality were claimed by dogs. Indeed, from the initial clandestine launches of "rocket dogs" in 1951, to the highly publicized, doomed voyage of Laika in 1957 and the celebrated journey of Belka and Strelka in 1960, the prospects for human spaceflight were measured against the fates of the stray dogs Soviet researchers used to test life-support systems and investigate the effects of spaceflight on living organisms.

This chapter considers the life and times of ordinary dogs enlisted in the extraordinary quest to send humans into space. Building on an emerging literature in animal studies, it addresses the possibilities of integrating animals into the history of the human past by reconstructing the history of the space dog program.[2] It examines the global fame of the canine cosmonauts, especially Laika, to show how competing images and public discourses situated the canine cosmonauts at the nexus of several related but sometimes dichotomous categories. Many of these representational categories circled around the concept of the "canine hero" or celebrity. For example, Western criticism over the use of dogs as experimental subjects in space research played against the Soviets' promotion of the brave canine "scout" and their adept manipulation of the dogs in the Cold War propaganda war. At the same time, the dogs served as a catalyst and provided a template for the paradigm of the heroic space traveler commonly associated with Yuri Gagarin and the cosmonauts.

The dogs were also scientific research subjects. The decision to use them to learn about the possibilities of human survival in space rested on pragmatic grounds (stray dogs were hardy and in abundant supply) as well as on the traditions of Russian-Soviet physiological research, particularly the work of Ivan Pavlov. Like Pavlov's dogs, the space dogs became subjects of "chronic experiments" designed to yield reliable information about the effects of particular stimuli and conditions on specific physiological processes. The dogs were surgically modified to provide researchers access to information that would help them evaluate the potential for humans to survive in space. As living organisms modified by humans to serve human ends, they might even be regarded as creations of the laboratory—a kind of "biotechnology" in an updated Pavlovian physiology factory.[3]

Like other objects of scientific inquiry, the space dogs functioned as "boundary objects" a concept that has been used to show how the same specimen, exhibit, or research subject means different things to different people.[4] Various human constituencies on both sides of the superpower divide saw the dogs in often contradictory ways—as experimental animals, brave scouts, hapless victims, faithful servants, or stellar exemplars of the family pet. This chapter suggests that these sometimes divergent meanings converged in ways that made the space dogs effective boundary objects in the complex and politically charged enterprise of Cold War public science. Although they meant different things to different audiences, the concept of "dog" underpinned all of these meanings, allowing the space dogs to serve as an interface or "translation" between otherwise divergent social worlds.[5] The canine cosmonauts' status as dogs established a measure of mutual intelligibility across the diverse but intersecting perspectives of engineers, politicians, medical personnel, scientists, and the general public.

The multivalent and historically conditioned relationships between humans and the dog (*Canis lupus familiaris*) informed the space dogs' media-mediated celebrity and fueled their ongoing fame. As the oldest domesticated species, dogs' ecologies have been intertwined with human societies since the Upper Paleolithic.[6] Its long cohistory with humanity has made the dog a profoundly social creature. Most dogs spend most of their lives in mixed-species groups, whether as scavengers, herders, haulers, guardians, pets, or laboratory research animals.[7] They are implicated in a myriad of human activities and undertakings where the dynamics of dependency and exploitation can tilt toward either party.

As social domesticates, dogs offer the historian an important, possibly unique wedge into the nexus of nature and culture. Unpacking the complexities and significance of the space dogs' role requires us to think about the concept of "companion species"—not just as "companion animals" (like the ones with whom many of us share our domestic space), but rather as historically situated animals in companionate relations with humans whose actions are also conditioned by a particular set of historical circumstances.[8] In the case of the space program, those relations brought humans and dogs together in decidedly unequal ways in an effort to overcome not just the "great divides" of human/nonhuman and nature/culture, but also the forces of gravity that tether all beings to their terrestrial home. It is precisely this intertwining that explains the global resonance of the space dogs and the enduring fame of Laika.

Dogs in Space

Long before the launch of *Sputnik 2* catapulted Laika to global celebrity, the possibility of extending and transcending the bounds of Earth's environment by travel into space had captured the Soviet imagination.[9] In the 1920s "biocosmists" promoted the idea of space exploration in popular science journals, drawing on the utopian visions of Nikolai Fedorov (1829–1903), who foresaw space travel as a way to achieve immortality and proposed that space colonization might relieve Malthusian pressures on an overpopulated Earth. The mass media also publicized the more practical theories of Konstantin Tsiolkovskii (1857–1935), who suggested that rocket fuel propulsion could make spaceflight a reality and developed a plan for an artificial satellite as early as 1879.[10] Efforts to realize these ambitions after World War II approached space both as an extension of the "nature" humans had subdued on Earth, and as a decidedly "unnatural" (or certainly inhospitable) realm that might be exploited if not conquered.[11] The guiding force behind these efforts was the "chief designer" Sergei Korolev (1907–1966), a gifted rocket engineer and visionary, who was incarcerated in one of Stalin's special prisons for scientists during much of World War II.[12] Released from prison in 1944, Korolev was asked by Stalin to develop the Soviet missile program. Besides putting his considerable talent to use in the development of rockets for military and weaponry purposes, Korolev also pursued plans for space travel and exploration by humans.

In 1948, Korolev enlisted the veteran surgeon and army doctor Vladimir Yazdovsky (1913–1999) to head up the biological program for space research at the Institute for Aviation Medicine in Moscow. From the beginning, dogs figured prominently in the quest to determine the potential for humans to survive in space and in the development of the "closed ecological systems" (space capsules) that would make that possible. While researchers in the United States preferred small monkeys and later chimpanzees for space research, the Soviets found that dogs' physiology and ethology made them ideally suited for investigating the effects of spaceflight on humans.[13] As Yazdovsky later recalled: "We selected dogs as biological objects because their physiology is very well-studied, they adapt well to training, and are very communicative and social [kontaktny] with people."[14] They were also cheap and readily available. Yazdovsky's team acquired a raft of strays from the streets of Moscow, selecting dozens of healthy young adults by weight (six to seven kilograms, or thirteen to fifteen pounds, maximum), and for light coat color (which would facilitate filming during flight). Researchers preferred mixed-breed dogs for their hardy constitutions, and females, because their anatomy made fitting the antigravity suit and sanitation equipment easier. In the decade leading up to Gagarin's flight, they sponsored missions with passenger slots for more than seventy dogs, including twenty who were put on flights between Laika's launch in 1957 and Gagarin's successful flight nearly four years later.[15]

While the dogs were being trained and tested, engineers worked with biologists and medical doctors to design a life-support system and a container that could be safely recovered. This involved refining the nose cone separation mechanism of R-IB and R-IV rockets, installing air brakes, and developing a reliable parachute system. Among the issues that most concerned the designers were the potentially deadly effects of radiation, extreme temperatures, and the environment of vacuum, as well as the stresses of vibration, noise, and weightlessness on the dogs, who would be confined in a very small space. Work on the rocket dog program proceeded in conditions of utmost secrecy, with the overall goal concealed not just from the public but from many of the researchers as well. The physician Alexander Seriapin, for example, recalled that Yazdovsky asked him to design flight "clothing" for the dogs but did not tell him when or how the suit would be used.[16]

The public would not find out for several years, but for Seriapin, who helped design the life-support system for the space capsules, the answer became clear in the summer of 1951, when the first set of "biological launches" took place on the desolate steppe southeast of Stalingrad (now Volgograd). Nine dogs flew in six vertical flights between July and September 1951, with somewhat mixed results. The first launch, on July 22, had the dogs Dezik and Tsygan ("Gypsy") aboard. They reached an altitude of 101 kilometers (62 miles) and experienced four minutes of weightlessness before their parachute deployed and observers rushed to their cars and sped out across the desert to find them. When the hatch was opened, the dogs barked, wagged their tails, and became the first living beings successfully recovered from spaceflight. Although dogs returned safely from three of the remaining five launches, four died when the parachute mechanism on their capsule failed to open properly. Among the victims was Dezik, who was redeployed for the second launch on July 29.[17]

Although the vertical dog flights of 1951 provided valuable data, for the next few years Korolev's team focused its energies on improving missiles and weapons technology, concentrating in particular on the development of the intercontinental ballistic missile (ICBM). Only after Stalin's death did Korolev renew his ambitions for space travel and exploration. Since the first set of dog flights indicated that successfully recovering biological payloads would be a daunting task, the next series tested new air brakes and recovery mechanisms as well as a novel method of providing life support during the flight. In these nine flights, conducted between 1954 and 1956, the dogs were again sent up to an altitude of 62 miles (100 kilometers) but were harnessed to separate "sleds" and ejected separately. Their parachutes also deployed at different altitudes during the capsule's descent. Whereas dogs in the first set of flights were harnessed into a hermetically sealed cabin with an air regeneration system, for the second series the canine subjects received life support via space suits with removable helmets. Of the twelve dogs used, five perished.[18]

In this same period Korolev worked with Mikhail Tikhonravov (1901–1974) to develop plans for an artificial satellite. Their proposal attracted little attention from Soviet authorities, who remained focused on purely military objectives until the United States announced plans to launch its own artificial satellite in conjunction with International Geophysical Year in 1957. This gave the Soviets the motivation to move forward with Korolev's own dreams, and the space race entered a new phase.[19]

As engineers tested and refined the R-7 rocket, which would soon power orbital flights with canine passengers, a third set of vertical dog flights commenced. For this series of five flights, which ran from May through September 1957, the ejectable capsule was abandoned in favor of a larger, hermetically sealed cabin inside the rocket's nose cone that separated for landing. The altitude almost doubled, with each flight reaching a height of nearly 132 miles (212 kilometers). The dogs again flew in pairs, all of them at least twice. In an effort to isolate the physical effects of weightlessness from the general trauma of flight, one of the two dogs was anaesthetized before launch.[20] Oleg Gazenko (1918–2007), a physician with a background in aviation medicine who joined the institute's staff in the fall of 1956, assumed a prominent role in selecting and testing the dogs, who were now separated into two training cohorts—one for vertical launches and one for long-term flights on satellites.

In the months leading up to the launch of *Sputnik 1*, the secrecy around the rocket dog program gave way to a carefully calibrated publicity campaign. Geared for a global audience, media coverage of the program celebrated Soviet technological achievements, portrayed the dogs as unique individuals, and linked their journeys in rockets to the advent of human spaceflight. A few weeks after Alexei Pokrovsky, the director of the Institute of Aviation Medicine, reported on the first two flight series at a scientific conference in Paris, an interview with him appeared in the Soviet newspaper *Trud*.[21] Photographs of dogs called Albina and Malyshka, both veterans of the second test series, depicted healthy, alert animals that could have been mistaken for "lap dogs," confirming the claim that they were well-treated "conquerors of the cosmos." Echoing the popular song "Vse vyshe" (Ever higher), which described the destiny of a generation born "to make fairy tales come true," Pokrovsky clarified that "we do our work in order to bring the time nearer when human flight in space will move from fairy tales to real life."[22]

In the West news that dogs had been sent as high as sixty miles above the Earth and parachuted back safely accompanied announcements that Malyshka "enjoyed" high altitude flights.[23] A front-page photo in the *New York Times* showed a petite canine clad in a modified diving suit, licking her nose, and sitting next to the plastic helmet that protected her during the flight.[24] In June three of the rocket dogs, including Malyshka, were introduced to the foreign press in Moscow.[25] The launch of *Sputnik 1* on October 4 was initially downplayed in the Soviet Union, becoming headline news there only after the American press heralded the satellite's success as a major technological and political triumph.

Following the *Sputnik 1* sensation, Khrushchev asked Korolev if another satellite could be launched in time for the celebrations of the fortieth anniversary of the revolution in early November. Korolev quickly agreed, suggesting that this apparatus, too, could carry a dog. The symbolic and scientific significance of sending a living being into orbit was enormous and would solidify Soviet preeminence in space research. On October 27, Moscow Radio announced that a second satellite would be launched soon, and introduced Kudriavka (Curly), a small shaggy dog who barked into the microphone, as its likely passenger. When the successful launch of *Sputnik 2* was announced a week later, the Soviet news agency, TASS, confirmed that an experimental animal was on board the five-hundred-kilogram spacecraft orbiting Earth every two hours.[26] The dog's capsule had a life-support system, including an oxygen generator and carbon dioxide absorbing device, as well as an automated feeding apparatus. Radio transmitters enabled scientists on the ground to monitor the dog's vital signs and movement.

In the West interest in the dog was intense. The *New York Times* headline on November 4—"Dog in Second Satellite Alive: May Be Recovered, Soviet Hints"—suggested widespread preoccupation with the dog's condition and future. Although official Soviet sources insisted that the animal was in good condition, speculation and skepticism about the possibility of its survival abounded. Western scientists doubted that the return of the space capsule was technically feasible, although a lecturer at the Moscow planetarium suggested that a safe return might be planned.[27] On both sides of the Atlantic animal welfare groups protested the use of the dogs in space experiments, denouncing them as cruel, unnecessary, and of little benefit to human health and well-being. In London the National Canine Defense League demonstrated in front of the Soviet embassy. In New York a canine picket line circled United Nations Plaza, bearing placards reading "Be Fair to Our Fellow Dogs" and "We're Man's Best Friends—Treat Us Accordingly."[28] Soviet children, who worried the dog might starve, suggested that a camel should have been sent instead. Some volunteered themselves as test pilots on future flights.[29]

By November 5 details about the dog and its fate began to emerge. A photo of "Laika" was published in the Soviet army's newspaper, *Krasnaia zvezda* (Red star), and a leading Soviet scientist discussed the mission's progress "while the dog is still alive."[30] Knowing the name of the satellite's celebrated passenger dispelled rumors that the space dog might answer to "Limonchik" ("Little Lemon"), "Linda," or "Kozyavka" ("Gnat"), and prompted Western media to cease referring to it as "Muttnik." But there was still debate over whether "Laika" was the same dog who had barked over the airwaves as "Kudriavka." The fact that "Laika" is both the term for "barker" and the general designator for a number of Husky/Spitz-type dogs used for hunting and transport in the Russian north remained confusing for Westerners, even after the Soviets clarified that the dog's name reflected both breed characteristics and individual traits.[31] The mass circulation magazine *Ogonek* described Laika as a small mixed-breed dog, with a calm, phlegmatic character, who never fought with her kennel mates.[32]

The time and circumstances of the dog's demise also remained uncertain. For the first four days after the launch, TASS communiqués described Laika's condition as "satisfactory."[33] On November 8 the official update indicated that physiological data were still being collected but did not comment on the dog's condition.[34] Three days later TASS announced that all of the experiments had been completed successfully and transmissions from *Sputnik 2* had ceased.[35] It was assumed that Laika was already dead or would die soon. The audience at the Moscow planetarium gave a collective sigh when the news was announced. In a press conference for foreign journalists a few days later, Soviet scientists reported that Laika had died when her oxygen ran out and insisted that her demise had been painless. They announced that developing a way to return space capsules to Earth safely was now a top priority and indicated that many more dogs would fly in space before the first human was sent.[36] Laika's satellite, which American reporters had dubbed a "rocket-shaped dog house," remained aloft until April 15, 1958, when its decaying orbit caused it to reenter Earth's atmosphere and incinerate. Although other dogs would perish in the quest to make space travel a reality for humans, Laika was the only one deliberately sent to her death.

Over the next two years dogs remained central to Soviet efforts to master space, with work proceeding along two fronts. Scientists resumed vertical launches into the upper atmosphere using dogs to gather data about the effects of weightlessness, radiation, g-forces, and extreme temperatures on living organisms. Engineers continued to design larger vehicles for orbital deployment and develop insulation and braking mechanisms that would make the safe return of these crafts possible. In August 1958, Belianka (Whitey) and Pestraia (Spotty) survived a suborbital flight that carried them nearly three hundred miles above the Earth. Like Laika, the dogs underwent extensive training to accustom them to the cramped conditions of the space capsule, the noise of its instruments, and the vibration and pressure they would experience in the initial phases of the flight. Although their flight was widely acclaimed, their fame paled in comparison to that of Otvazhnaia (Courageous), who weathered five suborbital flights to "great heights" between June 1959 and July 1960, earning her the moniker "world's most travelled space dog."[37] In the London *Times* a picture of Otvazhnaia and the rabbit (Marfusha) that had been her crewmate ran directly adjacent to a photograph of (Malcolm) Scott Carpenter, one of the seven men in training for flight on an American satellite.[38] The Soviets pointed to Otvazhnaia's continued good health and Marfusha's litter of healthy kits as evidence that humans could also be protected from the potential environmental dangers of space.[39] "Space Is Getting Closer," proclaimed a Soviet headline after the dog's third flight.[40]

Meanwhile, a spacecraft had been developed with a system of retrorockets that would serve as a braking mechanism and allow it to reenter Earth's atmosphere. The first "spaceship" (*korabl-sputnik*) that was launched in May 1960 carried a "dummy astronaut" but no dogs. It failed to respond to ground control and was never recovered. In July a test of the second *Vostok* spacecraft ended in disaster when a booster rocket exploded during the launch, killing the two dogs on board.[41]

Success came on August 19, when a ten-thousand-pound spacecraft carried Belka (Squirrel) and Strelka (Little Arrow) on seventeen orbits and returned them safely to Earth after twenty-four hours in space. Although an assortment of rats, mice, fruit flies, and plants accompanied the two dogs, acclaim for becoming the first living beings to return safely from orbital flight focused almost exclusively on Belka and Strelka. The dogs made front-page headlines in the United States and the Soviet Union for days and were the subjects of a press conference at the TASS building in central Moscow on August 22. Dressed in civilian clothes, Gazenko and Liudmila Radkevich presented the dogs, still clad in their flight costumes, to an adoring public and the Soviet media. TASS broadcast the affair on the radio, and that evening Soviet citizens watched the celestial travelers on television.[42] American and French correspondents delivered photographs of the dogs to media outlets in the West, where information about the dogs and the details of their training, behavior, and response to the flight were eagerly sought after. The dogs' "normal" behavior in public, television images showing their calm reaction to weightlessness, and the Soviets' assurances that postflight physiological tests (including electrocardiograms) revealed no abnormalities suggested that spaceflight was safe for canines and might soon be a reality for humans as well.[43] The articulation of this expectation in Soviet headlines, such as "A new step on the path toward human space flight" and "Astronaut, get ready to travel!" was underscored when a photograph of the dogs appeared on the cover of *Ogonek* over the caption "Space, expect a visit from Soviet man!" (figure 6.1).[44]

Following the triumph of Belka and Strelka's safe return, several additional missions were scheduled to perfect the ground control and braking mechanisms and to reconfirm that humans could expect to survive the conditions of rocket launch and weightlessness without any ill effects. The first of these launches suggested that the new systems were far from foolproof. On December 1, 1960, a five-ton spacecraft carrying two dogs went out off course during reentry, activating a self-destruct mechanism that kept the capsule from landing in foreign territory.[45] A second launch later that month began auspiciously, but the third-stage rockets misfired,

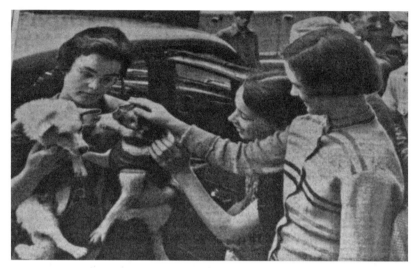

Figure 6.1. Fans greet Belka and Strelka before their press conference, August 1960. *Source: Pravda*, August 23, 1960.

triggering an emergency-landing mechanism. After a four-day search the craft's canine passengers were recovered cold, but alive, in a remote region of Siberia near the Tungus meteorite crater.[46]

Space dogs next appeared in the news in January 1961, when the birth of Strelka's six healthy puppies provided further proof that space travel posed no reproductive health risks. Two successful orbital flights with dogs and dummy astronauts in March raised expectations that a flight with a human passenger was imminent. When Chernushka (Blackie) was successfully recovered from her spaceship on March 9, a cartoon in *Krasnaia zvezda* depicted a space dog walking out of its ship and handing off a suitcase of "data on the results of spaceflight" to a space suit–clad human.[47] Zvezdochka's (Little star) safe return on March 25 after eighty-eight minutes in orbit was hailed as the "latest great victory of Soviet science." A few days later, the Academy of Sciences hosted another press conference to show off the two newest space travelers as well as Strelka's furry, barking brood (figure 6.2).[48]

As the focus of the Soviet space program shifted to manned flight, some hallmarks of the space dog program remained, even as the dogs receded from the limelight. Like the space dogs, Yuri Gagarin's name was announced only when his historic voyage on April 12 was under way. Also like the space dogs, and despite his extensive training as a pilot and

Figure 6.2. Strelka's puppies check out "space mice" at a press conference, March 28, 1961. *Source*: RGANTD, 1-19651.

astronaut, Gagarin was a passenger rather than the pilot of his spacecraft, which was controlled from the ground. Flying in the same craft used by Chernushka and Zvezdochka, Gagarin acknowledged the role the dogs had played in bringing about his triumph. Others concurred that "man's path to space had been laid by his faithful friend, the dog."[49]

But inevitably, once human spaceflight had been accomplished, the centrality of nonhumans to that endeavor began to be minimized in the master narratives of the space race. A significant step in this process was taken as early as June 1961, when officials from the Soviet embassy presented Pushinka, one of Strelka's puppies, to the Kennedy family along with a model of a nineteenth-century whaling ship carved from walrus tusks.[50] Her mother might have been a "fearless space scout," but Pushinka—"a fluffy white puppy of distinguished parentage but undistinguished breed"—was merely a memento of the Soviets' temporary superiority in the race for the stars. Pushinka later had puppies sired by Caroline Kennedy's Welsh Terrier, Charlie.

Although the Soviets continued to send animals into space through the 1980s, Gagarin's flight marked the end of an era, as the fame and bravery of human cosmonauts quickly overshadowed the celebrity of the space dogs. In 1966 canine cosmonauts claimed a final milestone when Veterok (Little wind) and Ugolek (Little coal) spent twenty-two days aboard *Kosmos 110*, setting a record for canine spaceflight—one that was broken by humans in *Skylab* only in 1974.[51] Unlike their predecessors, however, these dogs were identified more as experimental animals than as canine celebrities. Indeed, the research on Veterok's and Ugolok's response to long-term spaceflight supplemented a much larger study of the effects of prolonged radiation conducted on 330 anonymous dogs at the Institute of Bio-Medical Problems beginning in 1965.[52] The renown enjoyed by Pushinka and her puppies as presidential pets exploited the space dog legacy, even as it tokenized the contribution of the individual dogs who helped make space travel a reality for humans.

Constructing the Canine Hero

In a pithy assessment of the synergy between technological advances and the global distribution of the sounds and images that made them "real" to ordinary citizens in the postwar period, Svetlana Boym has asserted that for Soviet citizens "the 'Space Age' began not with Gagarin's flight but with the moment the flight was reported. From then on, the age was associated with the triumph of communism on Earth."[53] No less than Gagarin, the space dogs' fame was inextricably linked to the nearly immediate mass distribution and endless recirculation of their images on film and in photographs as well as their satellites' distinctive "bleeps," which were monitored by amateur radio operators around the globe.[54]

That fame drew on a number of interlinked discourses, including changing human attitudes toward dogs, the traditions of Russian-Soviet science, and superpower rivalries. Most obviously, the canine cosmonauts served as ideal foils for a regime intent on protecting scientific secrets and trumpeting its accomplishments.[55] The dogs' names, photographs, and some details about their training and temperament could be broadcast safely, without compromising the security of the human forces behind the missions' success. Focusing attention on the dogs also made it less obvious that little other meaningful information about the space program was available. Immediately after the launch of *Sputnik 1*, the

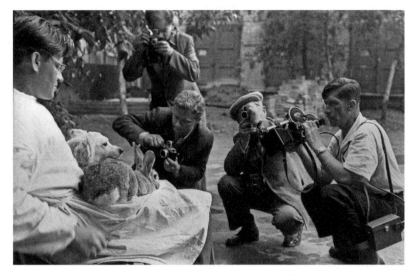

Figure 6.3. "Orchestrating Celebrity": Otvazhnaia and a rabbit pose for cameramen. *Source*: RGANTD, I-19550.

identities of the people most responsible for its success were classified as top secret. For many years Korolev, Tikhonravov, Valentin Glushko, and Mstislav Keldysh were never identified by name and were referred to in the press only by such anonymous titles as "chief designer of rocket-space systems" or "chief theoretician of cosmonautics." Public speaking about the program was delegated to politically reliable spokespeople with little direct involvement in its operations. The veil of secrecy extended to specific information about the design, function, and physical location of spacecraft as well as the broader objectives of the space program.

Of course, information about the dogs also was carefully controlled. Their anthropomorphic celebrity was crafted to facilitate a connection between the dogs and ordinary people who were interested in space exploration or might have a pet dog at home. In most cases the first photographs of the dogs were published when their mission was announced, usually on launch day. Invariably, these were close-up "headshots," clearly modeled on the formal portraits of humans that often accompanied news stories. Sometimes these images were fairly nondescript and served primarily to link "a name with a face" and provide "proof" that the individual existed. In the case of Laika the angle of the image and the pose of the dog in the photo published on November 5, 1957, were carefully calculated to convey a sense of the dog's confidence and alertness. In contrast, postflight photographs showed relaxed, happy, and often panting pooches. Photos of Otvazhnaia lounging underneath Marfusha, the rabbit, and next to her canine comrade, Malek, betrayed no sign of the animals' involvement in rocket launches. They could have been members of a circus act or an unusual trio of pets. When the dogs were displayed for journalists, their handlers described their behavior and relationships in anthropomorphic terms, insisting that Otvazhnaia's name (Courageous) reflected her bravery and enthusiasm for flying in rockets. They also poked fun at Malek's "cowardice," noting that he had whimpered as the crane lifted his capsule onto the top of the ballistic missile that would send him to the outer reaches of the atmosphere (figures 6.3 and 6.4).[56]

Anthropomorphism was just one strand of a media campaign that tapped the multivalence of dogs in Soviet society, framing the canine cosmonauts simultaneously as brave scouts and ordinary heroes while deploying visual associations with technology and spaceflight to maximum effect. On the one hand, the space dogs' handlers portrayed their charges as "normal dogs," emphasizing their interest in treats, petting, and other "normal dog" behavior. They were described as "quick-witted, obedient, and healthy," suggesting the desired traits any dog lover would seek in a pet. After Strelka's puppies were born, photos of the canine "family" emphasized Strelka's attentive maternal instincts, the puppies' physical vitality, playfulness, and that inescapable "cute factor."[57] On the other hand, "the most famous dogs on earth," wore flight suits to their press conferences and were photographed standing atop scientific equipment. Cartoons of the dogs suggested that spaceflight was challenging but fun. When journalists viewed television images of the dogs lying inert and helpless in the first moments of weightlessness during the flight, they were told that the dogs were "resting" before settling down to their "breakfast."[58]

In addition, the dogs' triumphs competed and were intertwined with other Cold War milestones. In the Soviet Union news of Laika's voyage in *Sputnik 2* vied for top billing with photos of Mao Zedong greeting Khrushchev and other dignitaries assembling to commemorate the fortieth anniversary of the Bolshevik Revolution. In both the Soviet Union and the United States, news of Belka and Strelka's successful return ran on equal footing with coverage of the sentencing of the American U2 pilot Francis Gary Powers to ten years in Soviet prison. President Kennedy's

Figure 6.4. Zvezdochka, the last space dog before Gagarin, March 1961. *Source*: RGANTD, 1-19639.

inauguration received scant notice in Soviet newspapers, which elected to run photos and news of the birth of Strelka's puppies instead. Clearly, political agendas in Moscow and Washington drove a considerable part of the dogs' fame.

Besides being the focus of a carefully crafted media campaign, the space dogs tapped into a broader tradition of canine renown in the Soviet Union. The mass circulation press and popular science publications invariably portrayed them as courageous "scouts of the cosmos," validating a model of canine heroism that mirrored popular constructions of canine virtue and informed a resurgence of pet keeping in the Soviet Union after World War II.[59] Although the Bolsheviks had stigmatized keeping pets for pleasure and companionship as decadent and bourgeois, the family dog made a cautious comeback in the postwar period.[60] Among the many factors influencing this newer trend was an ethos of utility, which stressed the practical value of dogs as "workers" who helped humans hunt wild animals, herd livestock, and protect socialist property. Socialist ideology also valued dogs' contributions to the military during the war and their long-standing importance to scientific research.

To offset the narrowly individualistic motivations of "bourgeois" pet keeping, postwar dog care manuals cited dogs' long-standing collaboration with humans and their "service" to the Soviet state as evidence of canine loyalty and devotion.[61] The celebrity of individual dogs and the contributions of dogs to military endeavors and Soviet science validated the status and reinforced perceptions of the ideal pet. Dogs' service during the war as messengers and bomb detectors, as well as in first aid and search-and-rescue was particularly important, serving as a starting point for many postwar commentaries on the place of dogs in contemporary urban life.[62]

Ironically, the heroism of the canine veterans was grounded both in their contribution to the decidedly human enterprise of the Soviet war effort and the fact that the dogs' nonhuman status and distinctively canine qualities made these contributions possible. They were used as mine detectors and messengers because they had physical attributes humans lacked (such as a keen sense of smell). They were deployed in missions deemed too dangerous for people (such as taking medical supplies to besieged troops). With the space dogs this appreciation of canine achievement precisely for its incalculable service to human causes was even more pronounced. When the National Canine Defence League protested on Laika's behalf in front of the Soviet embassy in London, the Soviet spokesman passionately insisted that "Russians love dogs too," but asserted that sacrifices had to be made. He claimed that his own family had donated its German shepherd to the army during the war.[63] After

1957, Soviet dog-care books invariably paid homage to the space dogs, especially Laika. Using the quintessentially Russian concept of the *podvig* (feat) to characterize the space dogs' exploits, these books extended the recognition of the extraordinary courage and self-sacrifice displayed by saints and military heroes to dogs. [64] Official canine heroism and sacrifice for the greater Soviet cause reinforced and mirrored the personal loyalty and devotion of the family dog.

Companion Species in Cold War Science

Cold War enmity provided ample fuel for Western outrage over the use of dogs in space research, and the Soviets were quick to confront the hypocrisy of Western concerns about Laika.[65] After all, the United States was using animals to develop its own manned space program, and biomedical research was undergoing massive expansion in the industrialized West. Yet the outcry over Laika arose precisely at the moment when an ongoing struggle between researchers and animal welfare groups over the use of dogs, especially stolen pets in medical and pharmaceutical research, was entering an acute phase.[66] In an effort to counter activists' criticisms of the cruelties sustained by "man's best friend" in the laboratory, the National Society for Medical Research had recently inaugurated the Research Hero Dog program to recognize dogs who had made important contributions to scientific research. At the same time journals such as the *Journal of Experimental Medicine* were adopting editorial guidelines intended to make published material about laboratory procedures and experimental animals more innocuous and generic.[67]

Domestically, the Soviets did not face the same constraints that researchers in the West were working so diligently to neutralize. Opposition to vivisection had been effectively eliminated by the Bolsheviks, and in the 1950s such movements were scorned as sentimental bourgeois impediments to the advance of scientific knowledge. Nonetheless, publicity about the dogs was sometimes ambivalent, reflecting the unique contours of a rich scientific tradition founded by Ivan Pavlov, whose research on conditional reflexes, digestion, and the nervous system was largely based on experiments on dogs. Indeed, dogs were chosen for space research in part because, thanks to Pavlov, so much was known about their physiology and their suitability to "chronic" experiments.[68]

Researchers' treatment of the space dogs and discussions of the dogs in the Soviet press perpetuated one of the most distinctive qualities of Pavlov's own practices—namely, the tension between his stance as a neutral scientist investigating indifferent, natural material and his involved even sentimental attachment to experimental subjects.[69] Rather than deny that the lives or treatment of the dogs mattered (because they were not human), publicity about the space dogs reflected a recognition of canine-human interdependence, and the unique capacities of dogs as "friends" of humanity and "servants" of science.

In response to Western criticism, Soviet journalists claimed that scientists had taken great care to ensure that Laika would not suffer, citing one of Pavlov's well-known sayings inscribed on the memorial to his laboratory dogs at the Institute of Experimental Medicine in Leningrad: "Let the dog, man's helper and friend since prehistoric times, be sacrificed for science. But our dignity obligates us to do this only when necessary and always without unnecessary torment."[70] Others lauded the "trust" humans had invested in the dogs chosen to perform this "service to humanity" by citing Pavlov's claim that "the dog, thanks to its long attraction to humans, and its quick-witted patience and obedience, serves the experimenter with a certain joy . . . sometimes for its whole life."[71] This tension between regarding dogs as helpmates, servants, and friends and the compulsion to "sacrifice" them for science had complex and often contradictory implications. On the one hand, the dogs were treated and represented as unique individuals. Detailed records were kept of their individual preferences and responses to experimental conditions. They were given names and interacted with in ways that enabled the people who worked with them to describe their "personality." Yazdovsky remembered Laika as a "delightful, calm, sweet dog."[72] Scientists described Belka as "happy" and "gentle," while Strelka was "sharp-witted."[73]

On the other hand, in keeping with Pavlovian tradition, contemporary practice turned an assortment of unrelated stray dogs into an array of collaboratively manufactured biotechnologies designed to generate correct (*pravil'nye*) scientific data. Dogs selected for orbital flights underwent surgery to have the carotid artery rerouted to the outside of the neck inside a fold of skin. Once the wound had healed, the dogs were trained to tolerate the attachment of a blood pressure cuff to the fold. They also had monitors implanted to enable researchers to assess pulse, respiration, and heart function before, during, and after flights. The "space suits" they wore for press conferences concealed the monitoring wires and scars associated with these implants. Underpinning discourses about the individuality of these exceptional but "ordinary" dogs, then, was a powerful impetus to use them as a "technology."[74]

Published information about the dogs' "training program" often made them sound like athletes or circus animals, and Gazenko did enlist the aid of an experienced trainer from the legendary Durov circus to work with the dogs.[75] But the experimental regimen of the institute's laboratory could be brutal and often had devastating consequences. To accustom the dogs to the cramped quarters of the space capsule, they were confined in increasingly smaller cages, for up to twenty days at a time, usually in complete isolation and silence. They were "conditioned" to withstand the stresses of rocket launches in centrifuges, catapults, and on vibrostands.[76] Television monitors of Belka and Strelka in flight revealed terrified, helpless animals, who tried to bite through their shackles, twitched convulsively, and vomited, prompting Yazdovsky to limit the first human flight to a single orbit. Very few of the many deaths and injuries sustained by the dogs were acknowledged in the press.

Privately, recognition of the "sacrifices" made by the dogs and the emotional bonds that developed between test animals and researchers became evident at multiple levels, beginning with the first vertical flights in 1951, when Anatoly Blagonravov, who chaired the state commission overseeing the biological launches, decided to adopt Tsygan as a pet rather than subject the dog to more rocket launches.[77] The rocket designer Boris Chertok recalled the tenderness with which the normally gruff Korolev caressed his "favorite" dog, Lisichka, just before her disastrous launch in July 1960.[78] Before Laika's journey Yazdovsky took her home to play with his children because he "wanted to do something nice for the dog. She had only a very short time to live, you see."[79] On the morning of the launch, after Laika already had been confined to the space capsule for three full days, technicians scrambled to pet the dog and ordered her a "last supper" from the cosmodrome's cafeteria, consisting of soup, a main course, and dessert.[80]

Although everyone knew that Laika was doomed, the details of her fate remained a secret until 2002. For decades published sources in the Soviet Union maintained that Laika died painlessly after her oxygen supply ran out on the seventh day of her flight. But speculation about what had "really happened" abounded. Some maintained that Laika's final portion of food was poisoned or that a deadly gas was injected into her capsule.[81] In the 1990s Russian sources revealed that problems with the thermal-control system had caused overheating in the dog's capsule, causing her to succumb to heat exhaustion after four days in orbit.[82] Finally, in 2002 a researcher at the Institute for Biological Problems in Moscow revealed new information about the design of Laika's spacecraft, including details of the life-support system and the monitoring of the dog's movements, respiration rate, maximum arterial pressure, and electrocardiogram values via telemetry to the ground. She had indeed survived the launch into orbit, although increased pulse and respiration rates indicated that she was stressed during the peak acceleration phase of the flight. At the start of weightlessness, these values returned to near normal. But telemetry also showed that the temperature and humidity inside the dog's cabin increased steadily. When the satellite was on its third orbit of Earth, the transmissions from the dog ceased. She had survived for about six hours after the launch.[83] Although the value of Laika's "sacrifice" was immediately acknowledged, that recognition was qualified with a regret best articulated in 1998 by Oleg Gazenko, one of the physicians who oversaw the space dog program: "The more time passes the more I am sorry about it. We did not learn enough from the mission to justify the death of a dog."[84]

A Legacy of Celebrity and Sacrifice

For nearly all of the space dogs, fame would be fleeting, as the world's attention quickly shifted from their exploits to the even more compelling drama of human space travel and exploration. Laika, however, proved to be the exception. The significance of her voyage and the fact of her death informed an enduring celebrity and complex memory. Soviet tributes to the canine pioneer began within a year of her journey. Soon after her flight a brass tag was attached to her kennel with the inscription: "Here lived the dog Laika, the first to orbit our planet on an Earth satellite, November 3, 1957."[85] In keeping with a well-established tradition of commemorating historic events and individuals, the Soviet mint issued an enamel pin of "The First Passenger in Space," showing the dog's head and a rocket hovering over Earth on a field of stars. Official commemorations in other countries soon followed, as stamps bearing the dog's likeness were issued in Romania (1957), Albania (1962), Sharjah/Mongolia (1963), Poland (1964), and North Korea (1987).[86] In the fall of 1958, the Soviet Union began to market its first filtered cigarette, using Laika's name and image on the wrapper and initiating a now fifty-year-old process of commodification and "branding" of the space dog.[87]

While pins and stamps provided fairly straightforward mementos of a famous individual and a significant milestone, other tributes to the first space dog support this chapter's claim about the dog's unique place in human history. Laika is the only nonhuman depicted on the high-relief at the base of the monument "To the Conquerors of Space," which was dedicated at the Exhibition of Achievements of the National Economy in Moscow (VDNKh) in 1964. Since the late 1980s, echoes of Laika's immediate celebrity have inspired an array of creative endeavors, including a number of literary works, Web sites, and a diverse and expanding corpus of music emanating from various points around the northern hemisphere and the transnational arena of cyberspace.[88]

The original scholarly conception of "boundary objects" and practices of translation examined the process by which such objects funneled conciliation from different social worlds inward to the nexus of scientific work in a natural history museum.[89] Turning this process on its head, this chapter has shown how the space dogs' liminal status resonated outward from scientists and engineers in the laboratory and the dogs' space capsules in the heavens to the public sphere of politicians, concerned citizens, and other human constituencies around the globe. As boundary objects, the canine cosmonauts played an important role in the production of knowledge about outer space and the quest to send humans there. They also provided a flashpoint for debates about the use of animals, especially dogs, in biomedical research and the mobilization of public interest in the space race. Their exploits helped shape the geopolitics of the Cold War. Foreshadowing staple features of the popular imaginary about cosmonauts and astronauts, the media cast the space dogs as "heroes" and "brave scouts." Photographs, cartoons, and other representations of the dogs consistently situated them at the nexus of the fundamental yet contested domains of humans versus animal, natural versus technological, and terrestrial versus outer space. Once the era of human space travel was at hand, however, the dogs' role as scouts and heroes quickly faded and was replaced with images of them as experimental animals.[90] The master narrative of the space race needed to be a human drama after all.

Like other boundary objects, the space dogs were effective because they were simultaneously concrete and abstract—specific individuals representing both the general category of research subject and the even broader category of "dog" with all of its attendant resonances.[91] As dogs, they originated in and inhabited multiple social arenas, providing an intelligible interface between the conceptual worlds of scientists, adventurers, politicians, and pet lovers. Of the many artistic tributes to Laika that have appeared since the launch of *Sputnik 2*, perhaps Leonid Vyshslavsky's poem "In Memory of Laika" best evokes the ways in which her contemporaries saw their dreams and destinies linked to and carried out by a diminutive dog: "In your eyes I did not see fear / as they heeded the human call / licked sugar from a palm one last time / and—set off for the constellation of the Hunting Dogs!" Sketching in the evolutionary ties binding humans to domestic canines, the poem celebrates a long history of collaborative life and labor: "In the darkness of the ages, I—the woodcutter and the plowman— / shared my roof and food with you / with you I fell and rose from the ashes / for new trials and labors." The space dogs functioned variously and sometimes simultaneously as human stand-ins, technologies, servants, and victims, but Vyshslavsky locates Laika the dog as an essential companion to human history: "And so today, having become a giant / I go with you, my friend into space!"[92]

If, as Walter A. McDougall has famously suggested, the advent of the space age caused a cleavage in natural history comparable to the Devonian leap that created the first land-dwelling animals 360 million years ago, Vysheslavsky's poem helps us understand why the unenviable but perhaps inevitable task of opening that breach for humanity fell to the courageous canine scout.[93]

Part III
The Soviet Space Program and the Cultural Front

7

Cosmic Enlightenment
Scientific Atheism and the Soviet Conquest of Space

Victoria Smolkin-Rothrock

Listen!
If, stars are lit—
Then—someone needs it?
Then—someone wants them to exist?
Then—someone calls these bits of spit
pearls?
"Listen!" by Vladimir Maiakovskii

If, as Oscar Wilde said, a man is half of what he is and half of what he wants to be, wrote the Russian writer Viktor Pelevin, "then the So-viet children of the Sixties and Seventies were all half-cosmonauts."[1] Im-ages of cosmonauts—on newly erected monuments, the walls of schools, pins, postage stamps, or the mosaics that decorated metro stations—en-sured that most Soviet citizens living through the space age had "one foot in the cosmos," their everyday realities "a tent camp, in which people lived temporarily, until the sun city was built."[2] Most Soviet people lived somewhere along the spectrum between their everyday existence and the socialist realist "dreamworld" promised by Marxism-Leninism.[3] Some-times, as Pelevin notes, cosmonauts came alive on television, waving to the crowd before launching into the sky. As they stood in their space suits at the rocket entrance, one accessory, a piece of cosmonaut equip-ment, seemed especially interesting to the young Pelevin—the small, pot-bellied titanium suitcases that the cosmonauts carried with them. The question of their contents—star charts, codes, secret weapons?— only added to the general mystery and symbolic power that captured the imagination of Pelevin and millions of people both within and outside the Soviet Union. For Soviet citizens in particular, the achievements of the Soviet space program were proof of what had just recently existed in the realm of hope and possibility. Cosmonauts were the incarnation of utopian promises, surrounded by an aura of potentiality. Set in various ideological contexts, they were used to confirm Soviet political, economic, and technological supremacy in the Cold War.[4]

But the ideological capital of cosmic exploration reached beyond the material—a fact that quickly became apparent to Soviet ideologists. The potential of man's "conquest of the cosmos" to enthrall the imagination, to fill a spiritual longing, became a subject of investigation and discussion. In an extensive web of "Communist education" conducted in schools, libraries, Communist youth organizations, and young cosmonaut clubs, Soviet youth were presented with hagiographies of cosmonauts, whose modeled lives were meant to have a transformative effect on the next generation of Soviet citizens. What made cosmonauts such an effective model for the average Soviet citizen was that they were socialist realist heroes come to life.[5] Much like their forefathers in the 1930s, the Soviet aviators, cosmonauts made the fantastical world of socialist realism more real and seemed to herald the arrival of Communism.[6] Indeed, socialist realism and socialist reality were never closer than in the age of cosmic enthusiasm, and the relationship between Soviet cosmonauts and Communist ideology was reciprocal. In April 1961, Yuri Gagarin blessed Communism by dedicating his historic spaceflight to the Twenty-second Party Congress. Three months later, during the congress, Khrushchev shocked and enthralled Soviet society when he introduced the Third Party Program and announced that "the present generation of Soviet people would live under Communism," which he predicted would be built within two decades.[7]

Khrushchev's confident assertions were accompanied with alarm within the party ranks. Despite more than forty years of Soviet power— during which the party-state secularized bureaucracy and education, conducted several antireligious campaigns, and promoted atheism as part of the broader enlightenment mission—many Soviet citizens continued to turn to religion.[8] As Khrushchev stressed in his congress speech, "survivals" of the former worldview, "like a nightmare, hold sway over the minds of living creatures, long after the economic conditions which gave them birth have vanished."[9] The Marxist schema whereby religion would die out when its social and economic roots had been eliminated needed revision. It was not enough to develop socialism's material-technical base—the Third Party Program underscored—to build Communism, the *spiritual world* of Soviet society had to be transformed. Among the other ideological functions of cosmic exploration, then, atheists mobilized Soviet space achievements to affirm the correctness of the "scientific materialist worldview." The philosophical significance of man's new ability to leave the Earth—the cosmonauts' literal "storming of the heavens"—was intended to deal the final blow to religion, which, against Marxist predictions, continued to frame the everyday cosmologies of many Soviet citizens.

Numerous studies have applied the conceptual frameworks of religious studies to the analysis of ideological regimes, yet scholars of religion, ideologies, and secularization have generally ignored the role of atheism in Marxism-Leninism. While on the surface Marxism-Leninism outlined a clearly materialist conception of the world, the relationship in Communist ideology between the material and the spiritual, the profane and the sacred, was far from unambiguous. In rejecting the religious cosmos, Soviet ideologists were left to see if it were possible for scientific materialism—which laid bare the constitution of the natural world—to mobilize the enthusiasm and belief that had for ages been cultivated and harnessed by religions. Indeed, while Communists generally saw Marxism-Leninism as a science that repudiated metaphysics, the questions Soviet theorists inherited from religion were as much philosophical as they were scientific. Could scientific materialism be infused with a spiritual component and remain scientific and materialist? Did belief in the Communist project unequivocally demand religious unbelief (and vice versa)?

By investigating the use of space conquest and cosmonauts in the practical application of atheist education, this chapter examines Soviet attempts to create and inculcate an atheistic Communist cosmology. It also analyzes the obstacles they encountered along the way. While the overlap of the Soviet space age with the revival of the campaign against religion during the Khrushchev-era "thaw" were no coincidence, the precise nature of the relationship between these discrete phenomena—how they influenced, reinforced, and undermined each other—has not yet been examined. When taken in concert, the proclamation of the open path that human space travel opened to the future, and the inherent admission that tradition—in the form of "survivals"—still exercised a hold over the minds of Soviet people, produced a contradictory picture.

On the one hand, according to the widely accepted narrative of modernity, the march of progress—industrialization, bureaucratization, the development of the welfare state, and the achievements of science and technology—should have rendered religious beliefs, indeed all beliefs that addressed themselves to supernatural forces and relied on faith, both intellectually obsolete and practically unnecessary. In the Marxist vision of modernity in particular, the transformation of the economic and material base of society, which, in the Soviet case, meant the construction of socialism, should have transformed the consciousness of individual citizens, leaving no room—and perhaps just as importantly, no need—for religious faith. Surely, this logic went, the triumphs of science and technology, exemplified by Soviet space conquests, proved the boundless potential of humankind. Soviet cosmonauts triumphed over nature not by God's will but by the power of reason and enlightenment.

On the other hand, the persistent fact of Soviet religiosity—a fact that became an ever more apparent part of Soviet reality as the regime began to investigate this question on the ground—was an unsightly stain on the light of a secular modernity guided by human reason and developing according to patterns revealed by Marxist scientific study of society. Faced with this contradiction within the Marxist-Leninist ideological blueprint, the Soviet elite had to make a choice. Either the narrative had to be made to fit social reality, or social reality had to be made to fit the narrative. This was a familiar crossroads, one that had shadowed the regime from its inception, and would continue to create a tension within Soviet ideology until the regime's revolutionary demise. Much like their counterparts elsewhere, then, Soviet political officials, sociologists, and cultural workers struggled to understand and manage changing landscapes of religious and political beliefs, and to reconcile these with prevailing ideological narratives. An examination of their approaches provides a revealing comparative perspective on the universal questions addressed by all modern societies.

"The Sky Is Empty!"

In October 1962—five years after the Soviet Union launched *Sputnik*, the Earth's first artificial satellite, on October 4, 1957; a year and a half after Soviet cosmonaut No. 1, Yuri Gagarin, completed the first manned spaceflight on April 12, 1961, to be followed shortly after, in August, by German Titov, Cosmonaut No. 2; and two months after cosmonauts No. 3 and 4, Adrian Nikolaev and Pavel Popovich, completed the first group orbit of the Earth—the Soviet popular journal *Science and Religion* published a lengthy editorial taking stock of the "first Cosmic Five-Year Plan."[10] "Five Years of Storming the Heavens," as the editorial was called, marveled at Soviet accomplishments in an area that had until recently only existed in the realm of fantasy: human space travel.[11] More specifically, the editorial readdressed the question that had been haunting the imagination of both East and West in the course of these five space years: How did it come to be that the Soviet Union managed to do what "tsarist Russia could not even dream about"—namely, "the accomplishment of such heroic feats in the fight for progress, the competition with more technologically and economically developed countries"?[12] Why was it that it was *Soviet* cosmonauts who managed to fulfill the long-cherished dream of humankind, when they "ceased to envy the bird" and flew, "relying not on the power of [their] muscles, but on the power of [their] reason"?[13] And finally, what did it mean that the first man who "stormed the heavens" was "Gagarin—steelworker, son of a steelworker, from a peasant family, Russian, Soviet, Communist, [and] 'godless'"?[14]

In the ideological opposition of two world systems that defined the Cold War, Gagarin's alleged "godlessness," and the godlessness of cosmonauts in general, was not insignificant. The editorial claimed that Soviet supremacy in space had a direct connection to the system's "scientific, materialist, and therefore . . . atheist worldview"—indeed, that this was "the logic of modern history." Humankind's path to the cosmos was lined with the "fierce resistance of religion," yet "he chased out the mythical god from the boundaries of the earth," made nature submit to his will, and "became a giant, victorious over the elements, directing the laws of nature and society." Finally, when he mastered the Earth, humans began their conquest of the heavens, the "holy of holies." Material objects "created by the sinful hands of the godless" broke through to the celestial spheres, and humankind, "whose insignificance the clergy has reiterated for centuries, is accomplishing spaceflights, creating and controlling artificial planets, and conquering the cosmos."[15] This teleological narrative left little room for interpretation or doubt—it called for believers to abandon their "dark superstitions" and it urged atheists to combat religion, which remained an obstacle in the path to the enlightened society of the Communist future. With the dawn of the space age, atheists were mobilized to intensify atheist education, so that "the sun of Reason" would shine upon those who lagged behind the march of human progress.[16]

The narrative of secularization presented secularism as a force that both made *possible* the scientific and technological feats of the space program and made *impossible* the continuation of religious beliefs. This was a prominent and, importantly, not exclusively Soviet, response to space exploration. It cast the cosmic implications of human space travel as an advancement of science and technology that marginalized divine activity from everyday life, leaving a cosmos that, in the words of the sociologist Peter Berger, "became amenable to the systematic, rational penetration, both in thought and activity."[17] Yet as science progressively conquered the heavens and collapsed the "sacred canopy," it also undermined the existential foundations of individual life, leaving a "sky empty of angels" that became "open to the intervention of the astronomer, and, eventually, of the astronaut."[18] Examined within the framework of religious belief, space journeys raised questions about man's place in the cosmos and the function of religiosity in modern life. In the Soviet Union these new issues gave birth to a new genre within popular scientific literature that explored the philosophical implications of human penetration into the cosmos in publications with provocative titles like *The Conquest of Space and Religion, Science and Religion on the Meaning of Life: Answers to Questions*, or *Space, God, and the Infinity of the Universe.*[19] Within the context of the space age, interactions between science and religion also shed light on the rise and wane of cosmic enthusiasm and perhaps even on the life cycle of Soviet utopianism in general.[20]

Stories that conformed to the master narrative of cosmic enlightenment—that Soviet space travels destroyed the boundary between the terrestrial and celestial and transformed the primitive cosmologies of believers—were gathered and widely publicized in press, radio, and television. The formula was reproduced in popular periodicals that attacked religious worldviews by giving voice to scientific experts, cosmonauts, ordinary citizens, and even former clergy. Indeed, the argument was believed to be all the more convincing if it came from the mouth of a Soviet everyman, or, even better, an apostate convinced by scientific achievements to abandon religious beliefs.

Even before Gagarin became the first person in space, *Science and Religion* published a letter to the editor from one Ivan Andreevich Dovgal, a worker from Cherkassy region, who argued that the penetration of artificial satellites into outer space was a powerful argument against religious belief. Dovgal wrote that "the persistent religious beliefs of his coworkers truly made him incredulous; he could not understand how they could continue to believe in a heaven after death in light of the fact that Soviet satellites circling the Earth at great heights have not discovered any heaven, that the Soviet rocket, flying around the sun, likewise did not discover heaven."[21] Such rhetoric became much more common after Gagarin's flight, when humans who had traveled to space could report on what they saw (or, more accurately, did not see) in the skies. An editorial in the central state newspaper, *Izvestiia*, exclaimed: "Yuri Gagarin really has given a terrible headache to believers! He flew right through the heavenly mansions and did not run into anyone: neither the Almighty, nor Archangel Gabriel, nor the angels of heaven. It seems, then, that the sky is empty!"[22]

Testimonies by space travelers about the contents of the cosmos on both sides of the political divide inevitably carried ideological weight, and were a crucial, if peculiar, component of Cold War politics. Soviet Communists capitalized on Soviet space firsts to promote the truth of scientific materialism, arguing that Soviet atheism removed the hurdles to space technology that still constrained the capitalist world with its religious reverence. Such statements were intended to provoke and indeed did get responses from both the religious and the secular communities in the West. American astronauts, politicians, and even NASA officials countered Soviet attempts to marry space exploration with religious unbelief by describing American space missions using religious rhetoric. Furthermore, they famously emphasized the religious worldviews of American astronauts in public press conferences and publications, and explicitly cast their belief in a higher power as compatible with scientific and technological progress. As the spiritual debate between the two world systems escalated, leaders on both sides weighed in on the issue of space exploration and human cosmology. The Soviet Union had asked Gagarin and Titov to keep an eye out for heaven, Khrushchev told the American press, and the cosmonauts reported that "there was nothing there."[23] President Kennedy, meanwhile, chose the Presidential Prayer Breakfast to tell those gathered that religion was "the basis of the issue that separates us from those that make themselves our adversary."[24] Their differences on the matter were cast as central indicators of their opposition in worldview and way of life.[25]

Pronouncements attributed to Gagarin about the cosmos being devoid of God and angels took on a life of their own, and the claim that Gagarin made these statements came to be accepted as fact.[26] Meanwhile, German Titov's actual statement, at the Seattle World's Fair on May 6, 1962, that during his spaceflight he "look[ed] around very attentively" but did not detect any deities caused a minor sensation in the American and foreign press. Accompanied by his announcement that he did not believe in God, but "in man, his strength, his possibilities, and his reason," Titov's words made him into the most public atheist cosmonaut.[27]

Titov seemed to accept, perhaps even to cultivate, this role. Shortly after he accomplished the second Soviet space journey, a short article was published in *Science and Religion*, titled simply, "Did I Meet God?"[28] Authored by the cosmonaut himself, the article provided a direct answer to a question that he was asked often, wrote Titov. The universe opened up to man, Titov pointed out, not to "a ghostly inhabitant of the heavens," and he himself hoped at least to make it to the moon. During his flight, he told readers, he heard a radio program in Japan that was discussing "god, saints, and other sly things." He wanted to send them a greeting, but then thought, "What's the point? What if they think that it's true, that God does exist?" Regardless, Titov continued, "the prayers of believers will never reach God, if only because there is no air in that place where he is supposed to exist. So whether you pray or you don't, God will not hear you. I never met anyone in space, and of course, it is impossible that I could have."[29]

After successful Soviet spaceflights, letters about the effect of space achievements on religious worldviews poured into newspapers, journals, and the mailboxes of cosmonauts themselves.[30] The *Science and Religion* editorial cited letters from former believers—often elderly women but sometimes "sectarians" and even priests—who described how their beliefs were called into doubt by scientific evidence received in enlightenment lectures and, in particular, by what they learned about Soviet space travel. One letter, from E. Danilova, a seventy-three year-old woman from Kuibyshev province, fit the conversion narrative so perfectly that it was not only printed in *Izvestiia*, but then cited and reproduced in numerous later publications, lectures, and even party meetings.[31] Written in a colloquial even folksy tone, Danilova's letter described her thoughts on the day of Gagarin's flight:

> On the 12th of April, in the morning, I was sitting on a little stool and heating the oven. Suddenly I hear the call sign on the radio. My heart stopped: could something have happened? . . .
>
> And suddenly I hear: Man is in space! My God! I stopped heating up the oven, sat next to the radio receiver, afraid to step away even for a minute. And how much I reconsidered over the course of these minutes . . .
>
> How can this be?—Man wants to be higher than God! But we were always told that God is in the heavens, so how can a man fly there and not bump into Elijah the Prophet or one of God's angels? How can it be that God, if he is all-powerful, allow such a breach of his authority? . . . What if God punishes him for his insolence? But on the radio they say he has landed! Thank God—he's alive and well! I couldn't hold myself back and crossed myself.
>
> Now I am convinced that God is Science, is Man.
>
> Yuri Gagarin overcame all belief in heavenly powers that I had in my soul. He himself inhabits the skies, and there is no one in the sky more powerful than him. Glory to you, Soviet man, conqueror of the skies![32]

Nikolai Fedorovich Rusanov, a former priest who after Gagarin's flight renounced religion and became an active atheist agitator, described his own path toward faith in science as a journey of liberation. In a 1962 letter to the editor of the party journal *Kommunist*, Rusanov cast himself as a "'prodigal son' who has returned, after his delusions, to the unified Soviet family."[33] Traveling around Russia as a lecturer, Rusanov was one of many former priests and seminarians who contributed to atheist education by publicly proclaiming their break with religion. Rusanov described himself in the twenty years of his previous (religious) life as having been "removed from the world, bringing no benefit to myself, to society, or the government." It is only after he opened his eyes to the disgraceful, scandalous lives of the clergy and the "glaring" contradictions between the

Bible and science that he gradually lost his belief. "Is it even possible," Rusanov asks, "in this century of the atom, of artificial satellites, the century of the conquest of the cosmos, of flights to the stars, to believe in [the idea] that somewhere there is a God, angels, devils, an 'afterlife'?"[34] In light of these scientific discoveries, Rusanov writes, religious belief is impossible, and the clergy, which knows this, continues to serve the church because of financial incentives. Rusanov's narrative, typical of the times, depicted the church as fundamentally tainted by corruption and hypocrisy, and religious belief as inherently deluded and antisocial.[35] As a result, atheist education gained a missionary urgency.

> The people want to know the truth about religion, especially now, when it is becoming clear to many that religion is a lie and many cease to believe in God. It is in this period that it is necessary to make antireligious propaganda more aggressive, to have more individual conversations with believers, more accessible lectures that would force the believer to think about his situation, so that he understands the harm of religion, so that he knows how he is deceived by the clergy, so that he is convinced that man's life is guided not by God but by man himself. It is man who, without the help of God, builds a new and joyous life. The believer should not wait for a heavenly paradise, because it does not and will not exist, but an earthly paradise, which will be built within the next fifteen to twenty years here, in our godless Soviet country. The name of this paradise is Communism.[36]

Conversion narratives such as Danilova's and Rusanov's are both striking and peculiar for their conflation of what are typically considered two distinct, even contradictory, modes of thought—the scientific and the magical. Danilova's rhetoric, despite her newly found faith in science, can hardly be described as secular. It is imbued with an exalted language that replaces religious faith with a millennial belief in the redemptive potential of scientific progress and substitutes one charismatic figure in the heavens (God) with another (Gagarin). Likewise, Rusanov, with his conviction that a Communist paradise is immanent, uses an exalted, almost evangelical, language. In such conversions, one could argue, the object of devotion had been transformed but not the pattern of thinking.

On the one hand, conversion testimonies of this nature—whether they came from ordinary people, scientists, cosmonauts, or priests—were often pronounced crude and simplistic even at the time by religious, secular, and even some Soviet atheist commentators.[37] On the other hand, ruminations about the metaphysical implications of human space travel fell within a long tradition that saw technological developments as a means to achieving utopian ends—extraterrestrial colonization, overcoming death, the evolution of a qualitatively new kind of human being, or any combination of the above. The relationship of the magical and the scientific is not only central to human thought about space travel; it is also inseparable from the technological utopianism of the founding fathers of rocket science. This paradoxical coexistence of the religio-magical and the scientific-technological propelled space enthusiasm in the public imagination. Such metaphysical claims not only provoked strong, polarized responses, but also caused both believers and atheists to reexamine their assumptions about the relationship between science and religion and the nature of an individual's faith in either or both. And nothing had the potential to enact the drama of the individual's place in the cosmos than the stories of actual individuals who physically traveled to the frontiers of the technologically possible and the philosophically imaginable.

Pioneers of the Universe, Cosmic Horror, and the Soviet Moral Universe

In November 1960, on the cusp of history's first manned spaceflight, the journal *Vorposy filosofii* (Problems of philosophy) published an article that explored the "social and humanistic" significance of man's conquest of the cosmos, titled "Man in the epoch of cosmic flights."[38] The author, Ernst Kolman—a Czech-born professor of mathematics and an old Bolshevik who had once been a confidant of Lenin and a student of Einstein—put forth a set of prognoses about the future of space exploration.[39] He saw human space travel as the "first steps" toward man's final triumph over nature and the exploration and gradual colonization of outer space.[40] In a mystical tone reminiscent of Russian Cosmism, the scientific-utopian philosophy that had been popular in the early twentieth century, Kolman proposed that humankind, standing at the top of the evolutionary ladder, mastered technology to conquer nature, thereby making it possible to overturn the trajectory of biological development. "Why then," Kolman asks, "would he be unable to turn the course of events, to overcome death, which like a mystical fate threatens him?"[41]

Kolman explored the necessary moral, physical, and temperamental

makeup of the potential cosmonaut, and suggested the possible physiological and psychological effects of space journeys.[42] He took it as self-
evident that space travel would produce different effects based on
whether the space traveler came from a capitalist or a socialist society,
and suggested that produced persons better equipped for the hardships
of space exploration.[43] Naturally, Soviet "pioneers of the universe" would
have a highly collective mentality and superb control over machinery, but
they would also be immune to certain emotions—fear, cowardice, lone-
liness, or the sense of abandonment. "In their consciousness," Kolman
wrote, "there will be no room for any kind of religious survivals, and everything 'supernatural' will be alien to them."[44] Most important, the ideal
socialist cosmonaut would not be susceptible to the "atavistic, mystical
feeling of 'cosmic horror,'" but would manifest an entirely new perception of the world.

Kolman's description of the "horror" that threatened those who confronted the cosmos brought attention to the philosophical and psychological dimensions of cosmic conquests and, after Gagarin's flight, discussions about "cosmic horror" echoed in the semipublic world of the
official Soviet intelligentsia. A "Knowledge" Society Plenum that took
place on April 20–21, 1961, underscored the significance of Soviet space
victories for the inculcation of the "Communist worldview." Mark Borisovich Mitin, a prominent Marxist philosopher in the Soviet academic
establishment, described "cosmic horror" as an affliction that was profoundly foreign to the worldview of Soviet cosmonauts.[45] The essence of
"cosmic horror"—the panic that threatens to overtake the space traveler
when he observes his own planet from beyond—was "characteristic of
that mood which currently exists in the capitalist world." This unearthly
emotion, moreover, was itself "a bright expression of the collapse of heroism in which bourgeois philosophy finds itself," and of the "horror [and]
despair that grips those who think about the course of events . . . that
the world of capitalism is rolling toward absolute annihilation."[46] Soviet
scientific materialism, however, "inspires man with boundless perspectives, gives him faith in knowledge, gives him that conviction with which
man accomplishes his heroic deeds." This is why, Mitin puts forth, when
Gagarin was asked what he saw during his trip in space, he said he saw
"great beauty."

While "cosmic horror" was presented as the dominant mood of the
capitalist world, Gagarin's wonder at the beauty of the universe was pre-

sented as the "mood of the Soviet person, who constantly opens new horizons." The mission of ideologists, Mitin emphasized, was to harness the charisma of Soviet space achievements and of heroic cosmonauts, and to "present [the audience] with the proper appraisal of events, to show them the meaning of what has occurred, [and] to tie these events with our socialist system, for only socialism can give birth to such people, such technology, and such heroic deeds."[47] The cosmonaut A. A. Leonov described the emotional, psychological, and physiological effect produced by his own space travel. He emphasized that during his famous space walk, he did not succumb to the primitive, reflexive fear of infinite space that humankind inherited from its animal ancestors; and was able to "remove the psychological barrier upon existing the spaceship" as a result of his training. Instead of "cosmic horror," Leonov likened his space walk to "swimming above an enormous colorful map."[48] Soviet cosmonauts, as ideal products of socialism and model Soviet citizens, coauthored scientific publications, published statements about their own paths to atheist conviction, and even weighed in on immortality and the meaning of life.[49]

The War of Science and Religion in Soviet Atheism

The Bolshevik assumption of power revolutionized the relationship between religious and secular institutions and beliefs. Administratively, Bolsheviks secularized the country's bureaucracy and educational institutions shortly after October 1917. Culturally, atheism was recast from a radical intellectual platform, as it had been under the imperial order, into its opposite—a state-supported ideology promoted through the entire bureaucratic apparatus of the new regime.[50] During the first two decades of Soviet power, atheist propaganda approaches—most prominently coordinated by the Communist Youth Organization (Komsomol) and the League of Militant Atheists—generally fell into two categories: politically motivated antireligious agitation and scientific enlightenment. The first approach cast atheists as merciless crusaders whose primary objective was to unmask church dogma and the clergy to destroy religion's influence among the population. Religious institutions were depicted as a politically subversive even antirevolutionary force, and the battle against them focused on the repression and persecution of the clergy, the requisition and destruction of church property, and the undermining of belief in material manifestations of the supernatural (such as the relics of saints, holy wells, or miraculous icons).[51]

Although the iconoclastic antireligious campaigns of early militant atheists are generally well known, the second approach—scientific enlightenment—has received less attention.[52] The historian James T. Andrews has argued that Bolsheviks "saw science enlightenment as an inherently transformative venue for shaping Russian culture."[53] Unlike politically motivated antireligious rhetoric, scientific enlightenment cast religious believers as victims rather than perpetrators, and atheism as the war of light against darkness. Such popular science education had its roots in the prerevolutionary decades and mobilized both those who propagated a utopian view of the potential of science to triumph over nature, as well as those who saw their work as a civic mission and were more committed to the practical, rather than the ideological, function of scientific. The objectives of the scientific intelligentsia—who did not necessarily see the eradication of religion as an end in itself, but rather as a means for overcoming nonscientific thinking, dovetailed with the explicitly antireligious mission of Bolshevik atheists.[54] For Bolshevik atheists the story had clear heroes and villains: unlike science popularizers, they presented science as the untiring enemy of religion, a constant thorn in the sides of religious authorities who persistently sought to circumscribe and silence scientific advancement. Religion was embedded into a narrative of humankind's historical attempts to manage its powerlessness in the face of the sublime forces that governed the universe, and depicted atheism as the gradual evolution of humankind's understanding of the cosmos. Naturally, this tale of progress concluded with the human triumph over nature.[55]

What makes the early Soviet enlightenment project peculiar, though, is that the dream of scientific enlightenment was never dependent on the cult of pure reason. Alongside the efforts to disenchant the universe by laying bare its foundations ran a related, but not overlapping, current of scientific thought—a mystical, utopian understanding of science and technology and its potential to overcome space, time, and death itself.[56] Popular scientific enlightenment, the historian Jeffrey Brooks has noted, put forth science as a modern ideal but it also represented its virtues as more akin to magic than logic.[57] The boundaries between scientific enlightenment and technological or mystical utopianism were especially permeable in the case of speculation about cosmic journeys. Russian and later Soviet scientific thought was propelled by fantastical leaps of imagination—most famously, the cosmist philosophy of Nikolai Feodorov—that was central to Russian visions of human space travel.[58] Indeed, as the historian Asif Siddiqi has shown, it was an enchanted cosmos that propelled the imagination of Konstantin Tsiolkovskii, the "grandfather" of Soviet space technology, and made the space program possible.[59]

Perhaps because the border between these two traditions was so porous, the battle over the cosmos was often depicted quite literally. The stakes of the conflict hinged on the question of who ultimately had authority over the cosmos and its contents, and Soviet atheist rhetoric mobilized art, science, and even military technology in the service of antireligious agitation.[60] The atheist journal *Bezbozhnik*, for example, illustrated deities and angels fleeing the heavens as they are being chased and assaulted by proletarians, "godless" airplanes, and even artists. One cartoon depicted an artist who had climbed an enormous ladder beyond the clouds in order to beat emaciated angels out of the heavens with an oversized pencil.[61]

Early atheist propaganda is also striking for the way it mobilized professional scientists in the mass campaign against religion. Nikolai Petrovich Kamenshchikov, a professor of astronomy at Leningrad University and a public atheist, published works that exploited astronomy in the service of atheism, as did a number of other prominent scientists of the time. Such publications, usually intended for uneducated and often illiterate audiences and written in an accessible vernacular, outlined the blows astronomy dealt to religion, beginning with Copernicus's heretical heliocentric cosmos.[62] They sought to undermine religious cosmologies by attacking popular understandings of time and space.[63] Exemplary of this genre was Kamenshchikov's book *Chto videli na nebe popy, a chto videm my* (What the priests saw in the skies, and what we see), whose purpose was to unmask such concepts as heaven, hell, purgatory, and apocalypse.[64] The cover illustration showed the night sky split in half: on one side, a distraught priest raised his hands to a heaven occupied by angels, saints, and even a Buddha; on the other, the skies, empty of deities and seemingly infinite, await discoveries by the enormous telescope in the foreground. For these early atheists the battle with religion was not just historical. Indeed, in perhaps one of the most peculiar episodes of engagement of scientists in antireligious work, Soviet astronomers (Kamenshchikov among them) critiqued the Vatican's historical relationship with scientific progress in an open, published letter addressed to Pope Pius XI.[65] By asserting the authority of astronomy over the past, future, and nature of the universe, atheists sought to win a battle for the hearts and minds of the population, which they seemed to believe hinged on their ability to claim the heavens.

At the end of the 1920s, during the height of atheist enthusiasm, the Commissariat of Enlightenment proposed the construction of "a new type of enlightenment institution," a monument to technology and scientific materialism: the Moscow Planetarium.[66] Designed according to the most progressive principles in Soviet construction and city planning, and armed with the latest German equipment, the planetarium concentrated the hopes of the Soviet enlightenment project and the individuals whose task it was to make it reality.[67] The planetarium's location, next to the Moscow Zoo, was emblematic of the didactic vision planned for the space: a visitor, with the guidance of educational lectures, could physically and intellectually follow the path of evolution and uncover the material nature of the universe. Underscoring the ideological significance and transformative potential of the planetarium, the constructivist Aleksey Gan described it as "an optical scientific theater" whose primary function was to "foster a love for science in the viewer."[68] In this new "mechanized" theater the workings of the universe would be revealed to the masses; the experience enlightens the viewer and "helps him forge within himself a scientific understanding of the world and rid himself of the fetishism of a savage, of priestly prejudices, and of the civilized Europeans' pseudo-scientific worldview."[69]

When the first Soviet planetarium opened its doors in Moscow in November 1929, the confidence that the light of science would defeat the darkness of religion was paramount. In the years before World War II the planetarium hosted more than eighteen thousand lectures and eight million visitors. It organized a young astronomer's club; a "star theater," comprised of Moscow actors, that put on plays about Galileo, Giordano Bruno, and Copernicus; and a "stratospheric committee" that investigated the atmosphere and issues of reactive motion. Among its members the committee could count the mechanical engineer and "tireless space crusader" Fridrikh Tsander as well as the "father" of the Soviet space program, Sergei Korolev.[70] The main question that worried atheists was not *if* their conquest of the heavens, the assault of scientific materialism on religious mentalities, would ultimately be victorious. Rather, the question was *when* and through what means victory would finally be achieved. By the time Ostap Bender, the paradigmatic Soviet conman of Il'ia Il'f and Evgenii Petrov's novels of the period, waged war with Catholic priests for the soul of his accomplice Kozlevich, he simply declared the nonexistence of God a "medical fact."[71] After winning the stunned Kozlevich away from the priests, he tried to comfort Kozlevich's fears that "he would not make it to the heavens" by confidently stating "the heavens are becoming desolate. It's no longer that epoch . . . Angels now want to come to earth . . . , [where] there are municipal services, a planetarium, where it is possible to look at the stars while listening to an antireligious lecture."[72] Whether Kozlevich would have found these assurances comforting is another question.

The Death and Rebirth of Soviet Atheist Education

Despite auspicious beginnings, Stalin's reign did not turn out to be a fortuitous time for the new theater of scientific enlightenment, and Moscow's planetarium remained the only planetarium in the Soviet Union for nearly twenty years. The consolidation of the Stalinist regime in the mid-1930s was accompanied by the rejection of early ideological utopianism in favor of a more conservative, traditionalist position and more immediate priorities: industrialization and the inculcation of Soviet patriotism.[73] Stalin's need to mobilize the population for war, and later to reestablish control in formerly occupied areas, precipitated a reevaluation of the Soviet state's relationship with the Russian Orthodox Church, with the expected ramifications for atheist propaganda.[74] As a result, Soviet atheism, despite protestations of service to the Communist project, was marginalized throughout the 1930s and 1940s. After the destructive antireligious campaigns of Stalin's "cultural revolution" during the First Five-Year Plan, atheist agitation largely ceased, as did ethnographic studies of religion and sociological investigation in general.[75]

While Stalinist propaganda maintained the commitment to enlightenment by advocating literacy, hygiene, and education in the natural sciences, the specifically atheist conclusions to be drawn from scientific propaganda were for the most part cast aside. The successor of the league, the Society for the Dissemination of Scientific and Political Knowledge, was formed in 1947 as a voluntary association of Soviet intelligentsia committed to mass enlightenment through lectures on foreign and domestic politics and the natural sciences.[76] Prominent scientists, like the astronomer B. A. Vorontsov-Veliaminov, continued to give periodic lectures and publish rare pamphlets on science and religion, but explicitly debunking religious conceptions of the natural world was no longer their primary task.[77] Throughout the 1940s and early 1950s the low priority of scientific atheism was tacitly understood by the people whose mission it was to enlighten the population.[78]

Two new developments converged to bring atheism back into the spotlight of Soviet public culture: the ideological destabilization initiated by Stalin's death in 1953, and Khrushchev's initiation of de-Stalinization shortly thereafter; and the growing awareness that while religion showed no sign of dying out, the state's methods of atheist education and enlightenment were outdated and ineffective. In the new historical context of postwar reconstruction and ideological transformation, Soviet ideology in general, and atheist theory and practice in particular, were in desperate need of revision and reform. The revival of the campaign against religion under Khrushchev, after a nearly thirty-year hiatus during the Stalin era, might appear peculiar in the context of the political and cultural "thaw," but it was intimately connected with the moral mission to cleanse Marxist-Leninist ideology of corruption and fulfill the authentic vision of Leninism. As the private, spiritual world of Soviet persons—their values, emotions, and worldviews—became a central policy concern in the party's top echelons, the campaign against religion became one of the primary instruments to revitalize Soviet ideology.

The problem was that, according to reports provided by the Council on the Affairs of the Russian Orthodox Church (CAROC) and the Council on the Affairs of Religious Cults (CARC)—which included statistics on the incomes of religious institutions and clergy, pilgrimages to "holy sites," and the observance of rituals—religiosity persisted among a significant percentage of the Soviet population. Indeed, by many measures religion showed signs of revitalization during the postwar period, for which the party blamed "insufficiencies" in atheist education and called for a serious improvement in the intellectual, theoretical, and practical quality of "scientific atheism." The party's famous 1954 decrees on religion and atheism—the first on July 7, 1954, and the second on November 10, 1954—certainly announced a reversal of fortune for religious institutions and believers within Soviet borders.[79] Yet they hardly pointed to a new direction in policy. The party again brought attention to the problem of religion and atheism in the July decree "On Great Insufficiencies in the Propagating of Scientific Atheism and on Measures for its Improvement," and then scrambled to correct the fallout of its own directives in November with "On Errors in Scientific-Atheist Propaganda among the People." By the mid-1950s Soviet ideologists began to suspect that if the final revolution was to take place within the realm of worldviews, which were to become scientific materialist through a targeted and comprehensive antireligious campaign, then they had to work to uncover and understand the reasons behind the widespread existence of "survivals." And yet, among the "survivals" held responsible for the population's passivity toward building Communism, religion was perhaps the most scrutinized and the least understood.

The revival of the campaign against religion under Khrushchev, after a nearly thirty-year hiatus during the Stalin era, might appear peculiar in the context of the political and cultural "thaw," but it was intimately connected with the moral mission to cleanse Marxist-Leninist ideology of corruption and fulfill the authentic vision of Leninism. The Third Party Program, announced at the Twenty-second Party Congress (1961), was the official articulation of new ideals that had been promoted throughout the 1950s: the abandonment of coercion as a primary tool of government, increased welfare provisions, and material abundance. Tying together utopian and pragmatic promises, the program heralded vast increases in consumer goods, housing, government benefits, and the cultivation of leisure. Yet what made the program so peculiar was the central importance of morality in Khrushchev's promoted vision of modernity.[80]

To resolve the moral paradox of consumerism, the Soviet abundance promoted in the Khrushchev era hinged on personal moderation.[81] Thus the satisfaction of Soviet wants depended on transformed personal perceptions of Soviet needs. In a kind of inversion of the Protestant ethic, which made a private vice (greed) into a public virtue (work ethic), Communist morality made a public vice (scarcity) into a private virtue (asceticism). These ideals were cemented in the new era's official manifesto, the "Moral Code of the Builder of Communism," which prioritized the state's dependence on loyal, efficient, and morally superior citizens. The private, spiritual world of Soviet persons—their values, emotions, and worldviews—became a central policy concern in the party's top echelons. The final revolution was to take place within the realm of worldviews, which were to become scientific materialist through a targeted and comprehensive educational campaign that was to reach into almost every realm of Soviet life. The revolution of the cosmos hinged on the reformation of cosmologies.

When atheist education was revived in the mid-1950s, Soviet atheists were working with two conceptions about the nature of religion, both of which they had inherited from the early Soviet period. The first held that religion was a product of poverty, misery, and the fear engendered by life's unpredictability. In this context the solace provided by religion served as an "opiate" for people afflicted by war, acts of nature, or personal trauma, and the proposed antidote was the continued economic growth and construction of the material-technical base promised by Communism. As people's lives improved, this theory held, they would experience less need for the solace provided by religion. The second theory presented religion as a product of darkness and superstition. According to this model, religiosity was the result of ignorance about the mysterious forces that govern nature and the universe and was to be fought with scientific enlightenment. These understandings of religion and atheism in general, and the role of science in the greater enlightenment project in particular, were so deeply rooted in Soviet atheist thought that they never stopped guiding the approach to atheist education.

This is not to say that atheist education did not evolve. On the contrary, the Khrushchev era is marked by a growing awareness of the ways in which atheist education fell short, as well as concerted efforts to address these shortcomings. Increased scrutiny of enlightenment work in light of the new political responsibilities of ideological organizations resulted in an increased level of attention to the theory and practice of atheist education. Broadly, the party relied on two kinds of measures to combat religion and religiosity throughout the 1950s. These measures might be classified as "negative" and "positive," respectively, but were by no means allotted equal importance in the first stages of the second atheist campaign. In practice, considerably more emphasis was placed on negative measures: administrative and legal regulation of religious organizations and individual believers. The Council on the Orthodox Church and the Council on Religious Cults (later united into the Council on Religious Affairs) and their local representatives directed the closing down of churches and the registration of religious communities, kept statistics on church attendance and ritual observance, and generally controlled the increasingly strict legal and semilegal measures propagated

Figure 7.1. Village planetarium lecture, Kharkiv region, Ukraine, in the early 1960s. *Source*: Image courtesy of Kharkov Planetarium imeni Iu. A. Gagarina.

against the church.[82] Positive measures, which grew in importance by the late 1950s, entailed a campaign of mass enlightenment. In practice, this meant a calling to arms of the "Knowledge" Society (Obshchestvo "Znanie"), the primary Soviet institution charged with the development of the new Communist citizen on the ground and, until 1964, the largest institution involved in the theoretical development and practical application of atheist education.[83]

Party cadres and intelligentsia enthusiasts were urged to form local-level organizations (atheist clubs, Houses of Atheism, atheist departments in educational institutions, and atheist sections in local party organs, among others). These new institutions held atheist film screenings, hosted debates, and question-and-answer sessions that brought together believers and atheists, and staged atheist holidays to compete with their religious equivalents, and—in what was the most frequently employed form of atheist education—organized lectures by members of the "Knowledge" Society.[84] With the intensification of atheist propaganda over the course of the 1950s, the "Knowledge" Society received a new journal, titled *Nauka i religiia* (Science and religion), which after several years of discussion and preparation began publication in 1959. The journal was aimed at both the mass reader and the propaganda worker and covered the history of religion, the party's evolving position on religion and atheism, and of course the popularization of scientific achievements and the scientific-materialist worldview. It also explicitly addressed the philosophical and religious issues raised by space exploration in periodic articles on the subject that fell under the rubric "Man: Master of Nature."[85] The inside cover of the first issue proudly displayed the blueprint for the monument to Soviet space exploration planned for construction at Moscow's Exhibition of National Economic Achievements (VDNKh).[86] At the turn of the decade, the society was given the brand-new Moscow House of Scientific Atheism as well as the administration of the Moscow Planetarium, which became a critical site of atheistic activity—a catalyst for linking cosmic enlightenment with antireligious thought (figure 7.1).[87]

A Planetarium for Believers and Bibles for Cosmonauts

In the post-Stalinist Soviet Union, the planetarium was widely considered to be one of the most effective spaces in which to conduct atheist work, admired for its aesthetically pleasing and intellectually engaging methodology that emphasized the experiential component of education. The leadership's faith in the atheist potential of the planetarium was made evident by the state's significant investment of resources into the construction of planetariums, despite the fact that as late as 1959, even the most central Soviet planetarium—the Moscow Planetarium—continued to operate at a loss.[88] With the revival of the antireligious campaign in the mid-1950s, the number of planetariums was expanded, as was the scope of their atheist work. The thirteen planetariums that existed in the USSR in the early 1950s were considered insufficient, and atheists called for a planetarium in every major Soviet city.[89] By 1973 the Soviet Union had more than seventy planetariums, the majority of which were constructed over the course of the Khrushchev era.[90]

The state's investment in the planetarium's atheist function was likewise evident in the fact that in the spring of 1959 the Soviet Council of Ministers transferred the Moscow Planetarium from the cultural organs of the Moscow city administration (Mosgorispolkom) to the All-Union "Knowledge" Society with the purpose of making it a more effective tool in the "propaganda of natural scientific knowledge on the structure of the universe (*stroenie vselennoi*)."[91] Indeed, the state hoped that the transfer would help bring order to the society's atheist work, and to atheist education in general, and that the Moscow Planetarium would become the coordinating center for Soviet atheism. As the All-Union "Knowledge" Society leadership stated: "This government decision gives the Society the ability to use the planetarium as a base for a considerable expansion and improvement of natural-scientific and scientific-atheist propaganda."[92] While the Moscow Planetarium was constructed from the ground up according to avant-garde principles of constructivist architectural design, it was, in this respect, almost unique. A significant number of the planetariums constructed after the war—in Gorky (Nizhnyi Novgorod), Kiev, Riga, Barnaul, and others—occupied former church spaces, a fact that had both practical and ideological significance.[93]

Conceived as explicitly atheist spaces, planetariums hosted enlightenment lectures, film screenings, question-and-answer sessions and debates, youth astronomy clubs, and, most prominently, enlightenment lectures geared toward the mass visitor. Planetariums were also attractive because they not only invited believers to attend lectures, but also brought the planetarium to believers. The so-called mobile planetarium could organize lectures and exhibits beyond the confines of its central location, on "agitation-bus" trips to Houses of Culture, pioneer camps, pensioners' homes, military complexes, student dorms, schools, libraries, red corners, parks of leisure and culture, factories, and even local housing administration offices. Using mobile planetariums, planetarium lecturers made expeditions to collective farms in a mass populist drive to educate the rural population that began in the late 1950s. There they would attract an audience by combining the chance to use a telescope and learn about the most recent achievements of Soviet cosmonauts, as well as by giving workers the opportunity to take a break from farmwork. After listening to a lecture, audiences could relax in the field, listen to festive music coming from the loudspeakers provided by the visiting planetarium, and even conclude the night with a dance party.[94] Most of all, the planetarium was also the perfect place to mobilize the enthusiasm generated by the Soviet space program and the most popular lecturers were, of course, Soviet cosmonauts. Audiences were drawn in with technologically advanced equipment and, most of all, with the opportunity to hear about what cosmonauts encountered in their celestial journeys.[95]

Yet the work of the planetarium in general, and its atheist focus in particular, was not without problems. Atheist education in the planetarium was criticized for relying almost exclusively on the natural sciences, lacking "militancy" and avoiding "worldview" issues.[96] It was not enough to read lectures on chemistry and physics, the argument went, without explicitly addressing their atheist significance by tying them to religion and idealism. In 1955 the mathematician and member of the "Knowledge" Society, B. L. Laptev brought attention to the importance of making clear the *atheist* significance of lectures on the natural sciences, pointing out that without this, scientific enlightenment could not be used effectively in the battle against religion. "We conducted [scientific enlightenment] lectures for years," Laptev said, "and it still took a Central Committee decree to reveal to us that we do not conduct scientific-atheist propaganda."[97] Such criticism was especially directed at cadres, as not all planetarium lecturers seemed to understand the importance of explicitly connecting atheism to, for example, lectures on astronomy or physics. This was a common complaint about scientists, who, in offering their knowledge in the service of enlightening the masses were, more often than not, unwilling to exploit the opportunity to agitate explicitly against religion.[98] To illustrate the repercussions of avoiding direct battle against religion, Laptev described a planetarium lecture on the creation of the galaxy that he read on a collective farm. When he was done, he asked his audience whether they liked the lecture, which was accompanied by audio and visual materials. The audience answered that they did, but when asked what exactly they liked about it, his listeners informed him: "We liked how gloriously God constructed the universe."[99]

This was not the first time that Soviet atheists encountered the idea that scientific enlightenment did not necessarily constitute atheist propaganda, but, given the long hiatus in atheist work in the Stalin period as well as the acknowledged shortcomings of atheist education during the Khrushchev-era antireligious campaign, it was a point that seemed to need reiterating. To show cadres the proper way to exploit the planetarium, the Moscow House of Scientific Atheism (Dom nauchnogo ateizma) hosted a discussion of veteran planetarium worker I. F. Shevliakov's lectures: "Science and Religion on the Universe" and "The Atheist Significance of Discoveries in Astronomy and Cosmonautics."[100] After working at the Moscow Planetarium for more than forty years, Shevliakov observed that in the "battle between idealism and religion," both the target of enlightenment measures, as well as the adversary, had evolved. On the one hand, audiences had become both much more educated in the sciences and much less knowledgeable about religion. "If in the first years after the revolution we had to prove that the Earth is round and other elementary things; if we had an auditorium that was informed about the Bible, the Gospels, the Old and New Testaments, the commandments, the Apostles' Creed [*simvol very*], and so forth, then at the present time even the clergy say that the audience knows almost nothing [about religion], and we propagandists are reaping the fruits [*pozhinaem plody*] of this revolution in the consciousness of the growing generation, which began life after the October revolution, after the separation of church and state, and [of] church and education."[101]

On the other hand, the church had become a different kind of opponent since it no longer had a hostile attitude toward science—something that atheists could see for themselves, Shevliakov pointed out, if they leafed through the pages of the journal of the Moscow Patriarchate. In fact, Shevliakov observed, religion had long sought to accommodate science. Even in his gymnasium days in prerevolutionary Russia, "no one defended Bible stories in the literal sense that they are put forward." He recalled how, having learned that Earth was six billion years old in science class, Shevliakov wondered how this could be reconciled with the Bible's teaching that the world was created in six days. In religion class Shevliakov asked the priest whether this was "a contradiction between science and religion," to which the priest answered: "There is no contradiction—what for God is one day, is a million years for man."[102] Then the priest told him to sit back down. "And this is not today, but in 1916," Shevliakov reminded the audience. The need to explicitly draw atheist conclusions during planetarium lectures was also pointed out by Nadezhda Konstantinovna Krupskaia—Lenin's widow and a central figure in the Soviet education and enlightenment campaign—during an early visit to the Moscow Planetarium. After attending an astronomy lecture read by an "inexperienced" lecturer, Krupskaia observed that after a lecture that did not draw out atheist conclusions, "every believer will leave, cross himself, and in his soul say that God's world is great and beautiful."[103] Astronomy alone, Shevliakov concluded, was not enough to "demolish the religious worldview."[104]

Over the course of the antireligious campaign, atheist lecturers across the Soviet Union encountered obstacles in their crusade to obliterate religious belief. A lecturer from the Tambov region reported that although their mobile planetarium attracted visitors of all ages during trips to the countryside, he still had reservations about proclaiming success, since the atheist message of planetarium visits often did not come across. He described a ninety-five-year-old man in one village who "could not be removed from the apparatus for thirty minutes" because, as the old man explained, "I'm going to die soon, and I refuse to go to the other world until I see what's there."[105] Another lecturer reported that their mobile planetarium was very popular with collective farmworkers, especially with those of them who belonged to "sects." Yet during planetarium visits sectarians would ask many questions and try to "corner the lecturer," in which case, "If they [got] the last word, they consider[ed] it a victory."[106] The reactions of planetarium visitors brought to light a phenomenon that Soviet atheists should perhaps not have found so surprising—namely, that the cosmological connection between space exploration and atheism was neither necessary nor entirely obvious. The history of science provided numerous examples where the elegant construction of the universe was indeed taken to prove the existence of an all-powerful creator rather than his absence.

The unexpected results of atheist education brought to light the degree to which agitators were missing a clear sense of their audience. Indeed, one of the most frequent criticisms of atheist propaganda was that too much energy and too many resources were spent preaching to the choir of unbelievers who constituted the vast majority of lecture audiences.[107] As Soviet atheists began to work out new programs, they recognized that they needed to acquire knowledge about the religiosity of Soviet citizens. At a Central Committee conference, Aleksandr Osipov—a former professor of theology at Leningrad Theological Academy who had publicly broken with religion and become one of the most famous atheists of the Khrushchev era—highlighted that the difficulty of atheist work was finding the appropriate tone for an audience spread across a broad spectrum of education: "Every propagandist encounters both [types of] persons. . . . Three days ago in Kiev, [I] simultaneously [received] two notes [from the audience]: 'What do you think about Feuerbach's theory of atheism?' And next to it [another note], 'So tell me, former little father, do witches exist in the world?' Laughter could be heard in the hall. 'So that,' Osipov pointed out, 'is our range.'"[108]

Speaking at the same party conference, the cosmonaut German Titov concurred that on the whole atheist agitators were unprepared to conduct effective propaganda. Even cosmonauts, Titov admitted, had not done everything to ensure that the results of their flights were productive for ideological purposes. When, after returning from a flight, cosmonauts were asked whether they had encountered god, he realized that their assertion that they had not remained unconvincing, especially to believers. Yet, Titov pointed out, cosmonauts did not have the tools to give their assertion more force, because of their fundamental ignorance about religion.

> I do not know even one prayer and have never even heard one, because I, like all of my cosmonaut friends, grew up in our socialist reality and studied in our Soviet schools. Later, when I was getting higher education, and now at the Academy, no one ever spoke to me about this religion—and it seems to me that the situation is similar in all educational institutions.

> And if by chance I came across some books, then, with rare exception . . . these books were so boring that, unless there was a real necessity, one doesn't really want to read them. (Laughter in the hall, applause).

> We consulted with our boys, the cosmonauts, . . . and we realized we had to petition the Ideological department to help us acquire bibles. (Laughter). Now we have received them, and I have a bible in my library, because when I speak in public, especially abroad, we find ourselves in difficult situations. This is why we discussed whether cosmonauts, in the course of their studies and training, should somehow be informed a little about all this God and religion business.[109]

In a brilliant inversion Titov's request for Bibles for cosmonauts underscored the basic fact that atheist education could not be conducted without a fundamental familiarity with religious history and dogma, as well as with the transformations taking place in religion under modern conditions.

Because an accurate understanding of their audience was vital to the success of their work, atheists believed it imperative to learn about the quantity and quality of the population's religiosity. For these purposes, statistics and episodic reports provided by local Komsomol and party organs as well as "Knowledge" Society lecturers and CAROC and CARC representatives only told part of the story. Beginning in the late 1950s, a massive effort was coordinated to educate atheist educators. Publications on religion and atheism increased exponentially. The journal *Science and*

Religion concentrated its efforts on providing the material on the history of religion and atheism as well as methodological recommendations for effective propaganda. Regular workshops, conferences, and seminars for training atheist cadres began to be held in both central and local-level enlightenment organizations and party organs. Finally, cultural enlightenment workers, folklorists, ethnographers, and sociologists "went to the people" on expeditions whose primary purpose was to study the role of religion in everyday life.[110]

The party's ideological interest in the religiosity of Soviet citizens precipitated a "reanimation" of the sociology of religion—a field that had been practically dormant since the mid-1930s.[111] The need to gather accurate information in the practical absence of a generation of sociologists specializing in religion required both a new cohort of trained cadres and a revived discussion of sociological methodology. Councils, sectors, and groups for the study of religion and atheism were formed in the Institute of History, the Institute of Philosophy, and the Institute of Ethnography of the Academy of Sciences and their republic-level equivalents. Sociological research of religion and atheism was given priority on the agenda of the Academy of Social Sciences of the Central Committee of the Communist Party (AON), the party's top institution for training ideological cadres, which eventually formed a separate Institute of Scientific Atheism in 1964. Ethnographic and sociological expeditions lasted anywhere from several days to several weeks, and usually consisted of researchers being placed with families that had been identified as believers to observe their everyday lives and interview individual members. Researchers were occupied with several fundamental questions: What was the worldview of believers, their understandings of the origins of nature, the social world, and humankind's role in it? What were the worldviews of former believers and what brought about their break with religion? And finally, what kept believers tied to religion despite the mounting scientific evidence against religious conceptions of the world, of which space exploration constituted such an essential part (figure 7.2)?

Cosmic Contradictions

Beyond widely disseminated atheist conversion narratives of believers who broke with religion as a result of space conquests, researchers discovered that the effect of Soviet space achievements on the everyday

Figure 7.2. Mobile planetarium lecture at a dairy farm, Kharkiv region, Ukraine, in the early 1960s. *Source*: Image courtesy of Kharkov Planetarium imeni Iu. A. Gagarina.

cosmologies of ordinary people was considerably less linear and logical than they had imagined and expected. Indeed, many reports described their frustration at the stubborn superstition they encountered on the ground. One local party worker relayed a conversation he had with a sectarian woman in Irkutsk who, when told that a rocket was being launched to the moon, replied: "This never happened and will never happen. God will not allow a foreign body to come to the moon." When asked whether she would abandon her belief if a rocket actually went to the moon, she only replied: "This never happened and will never happen, because it is impossible."[112]

Sociological research on the cosmologies of believers, conducted in the village Tretie Levye Lamki in the Tambov region, revealed that in those rather rare instances where believers considered the opposition of science and religion at all, most of them saw no contradiction between their belief in Soviet space achievements and religion. A typical example was fifty-two-year-old Anna Ivanovna Dobrysheva, whose answer to most of the researcher's questions was "Who knows?" She did not understand, even after repeated explanations by the researcher, the contradiction between the religious and the scientific worldview. As the researcher described in his report, Dobrysheva "believes in spaceflights, but cannot seem to understand why [atheists] don't believe in God and why they oppose science and religion."[113] In her view "if we [believers] believe you [atheists], then you need to believe us as well."[114]

One of the more "unbelieving" interview subjects, Petr Alekseevich Meshukov, was described as "not belonging to a religion although he keeps icons [in his home]," and in his understanding of the natural sciences is said to "fully support Darwin's theories about the origins of man, which, when he is in an unsober state, provokes him to call people who offend him 'a degenerate product of simian genealogy.'"[115] Regarding various processes in the natural world, he "has some vague notion, although is certain that 'god has as much connection to them as the tale of a crocodile does to a person.'"[116] Overall, the position of the villagers interviewed was best summed up in the words of one Matrena Petrovna Arkhipova, who stated that "Communists are good in every way, except that they don't believe in God, [and] that is bad."[117] In what became a perennial thorn in the side of Soviet atheists, believers—even when they believed in the achievements of the Soviet space program—still managed to reconcile it with their religious worldviews.

Cosmonaut German Titov encountered a similar situation during the numerous occasions when he was expected to clarify the contents of the cosmos to waiting audiences.

> The fact that ordinary inhabitants of Earth have been to the skies, the holy of holies of all religions, the space of God, has an enormous effect on believers, does not leave any one of them indifferent, and forces them to deeply think about their views and convictions. And many believers are struck by the fact that god did not manifest in response to the fact that ordinary mortals intruded into his estate.

> I would also like to cite one letter which a sixty-seven-year-old inhabitant of Kazan wrote to us. He sent it simply to the address "Cosmonaut." He writes this: "I am already sixty-seven years old, I am illiterate, and yet I would nonetheless would like to be taken on a cosmic flight. I understand that I can contribute nothing from the point of view of science, so to speak. But yet, it is said, that there is no God. I believe that there is no God, but all the same, as the years wear on, I would like to make certain that God doesn't exist."

(Animation and laughter in the hall.)

Ilyichev: Trust, but verify.[118]

No one could argue, Titov concluded, that the scientific achievements of Soviet spaceflights had been amply and correctly highlighted in Soviet enlightenment work, but the atheist significance of space exploration had yet to be fully explained. It seemed, then, that even when believers were enthralled with the technological achievements of Soviet space exploration, they continued to miss the correct philosophical conclusions.

Problematically, from the point of view of atheist agitators, neither did the church. Congresses gathered to discuss the evolving relationship between science and religion that emphasized the danger of the church's "accommodation" of scientific and technological advances and the attempts of religious organizations in general to "adapt" to the modern world. At a conference convened in Moscow in May 1957, shortly before the USSR launched *Sputnik*, M. B. Mitin, the chairman of the "Knowledge" Society, stressed that the battle with religion had transformed and was no longer (primarily) political, but ideological. In light of these developments, Mitin warned agitators to be vigilant to the evolving tactics of religious organizations that "prefer not to openly speak out against science, [and] to present themselves as 'friends' of science, striving to 'prove' the connections between science and religion, the possibility of unifying the two, based on mutual respect and 'noninterference', . . . and seek to prove that science and religion are not opposed to each other, but on the contrary, need one another."[119] In response, atheist agitators were urged to clarify for audiences the irreconcilability of science and religion, to stress that while the religious worldview proclaimed the finite nature of the universe, scientific materialism revealed its infinity in both space and time. In lectures that critiqued religious conceptions of the beginning and end of the world, popular among propaganda workers at the time, agitators were encouraged to critique the religious notion of the primacy of the spiritual over the material.[120] Once it was taken as fact that the cosmos followed the same laws as the Earth and were composed of the same materials, the Estonian astronomer G. Naan put forth, "nothing heavenly really remained in the 'heavens.'"[121]

Yet sociological studies suggested that the transformations that took place within the mind of a believer did not necessarily follow this same logic. Indeed, research on sermons in the Vladimir province described religious functionaries who either dismissed the relevance of space achievements for religion, or, worse yet, presented Soviet space achievements in a religious context. A report of the Council for the Affairs of Religious Cults, for example, described a Belorussian Catholic priest who refuted the notion that space achievements provided proof of God's nonexistence: "Nature has not yet been fully studied by man, [and man] is not yet able to control it. Then there exists some sort of power that controls nature. Sending satellites and people to space does not mean that there is no God. God exists, but he is invisible and not in man's likeness."[122] Archbishop Onisim of Vladimir-Suzdal diocese, however, underscored the need of propagandizing the great achievements of Soviet spaceflights, especially to the rural population. Archpriest L. A. Taranovskii was purported to proclaim: "Flights to space are new proof of God's great power, and the idea that cosmonauts did not notice God, well, it is not as if he sits in one place. One cannot see God, he is a spirit. And if life on other planets is discovered, then their existence also involved the participation of God, he is all-powerful. Even if God walked on the shores of the river Kliazma, people still would not believe that this is God."[123]

Many agitators complained that the church was more difficult to combat when it attempted to coexist peacefully with science, because then religion managed to co-opt technological progress and paint it as a manifestation of God's will. According to this position, God performed his work through unbelievers, and "the unbelieving Gagarin flew to space because it was advantageous to our God."[124] Yet what worried Soviet atheists even more was when religious organizations responded to scientific progress by making the boundary between the material and the spiritual more defined, and in effect, claiming for religion a "monopoly" over the spiritual world.[125] These unexpected and contradictory reactions of both ordinary believers and the church to scientific achievements forced atheists to question their understandings of religion and their predictions about its future in modern society. It also forced them to reconsider their belief that science was the most powerful weapon in atheist work, and turn their hopes to the transformative potential of philosophy to cultivate the Communist worldview of the future.

The Dystopian Cosmos

The Soviet leadership presented space achievements as material proof of the great strides the country was making toward Communist modernity, but their new attention to the persistence of "survivals" in the consciousness of Soviet citizens, as well as the efforts to exorcize these with more and better atheist education, cast a (not entirely intentional) light on the distance that separated the new Soviet person paraded on the world stage from the ordinary Soviet people in the audience. Indeed, reconciling the ambitions of Khrushchev-era utopianism with the unsettling fact that the "human material" that was supposed to actualize these ambitions was still profoundly riddled with "survivals" required an audacious leap of faith. For this reason the optimism of the party's ideological pronouncements tended to be tempered by attention to the obstacles to be overcome along the way. The Communist project, as outlined in Soviet ideology of the early 1960s, required nothing less than a spiritual transformation within each individual separately, and all individuals collectively—a reformation of social behavior and relations, morals, and values, without which the collective utopia remained unattainable. The Soviet space program manifested almost miraculously to provide a platform from which such a leap could be made. Immediately, popular ideological discourse represented Soviet supremacy in the exploration of the cosmos as an almost millenarian inevitability. The series of Soviet space "firsts"—the first artificial satellite, the first human in space, the first woman in space—were credited not just to the superiority of Soviet science and technology, but to the very spiritual fabric of Soviet socialist society.[126]

Soviet atheism sought to offer its own epistemological and moral positions and, over the course of the Khrushchev decade, saw the real and symbolic force of Soviet space achievements as the most powerful weapon in antircligious propaganda and atheist education. In the utopian universe of Marxism-Leninism, cosmonauts—perhaps uniquely—bridged the distance between the scientific and the philosophical, the real and the ideal. Their fearlessness and positive, life-affirming attitude made them icons of the limitless human potential that Marxism-Leninism promised to all Soviet citizens. Their voyages, both in life and to space, were put forth as a counterexample and an antidote to the fear and weakness that atheists claimed were cultivated by religion. This fact not only makes Soviet cosmic enthusiasm an important prism through which to study the process of ideological socialization; it reveals important insights into how atheists understood the nature of religion and the social function of religiosity.

The story of space enthusiasm in Soviet atheism highlights transformations in how religion was understood and approached over the course of the Khrushchev era and suggests the implications these transformations had on the future of Soviet atheist education and the fate of Marxism-Leninism. The Khrushchev-era atheist campaign produced two distinct yet related results. The trials and errors of atheist agitators initiated a reconsideration of Marxist-Leninist positions on the nature and future of religion. The failure of religion to "wither away"—even under the seemingly conclusive blow dealt to religious cosmologies by scientific progress in general and Soviet space exploration in particular—needed, on the one hand, a better explanation and, on the other hand, more effective methodological approaches. While the beginning of the Khrushchev-era atheist campaign was driven by a view of religion as a set of unenlightened beliefs and primitive practices that continued as a result of a kind of historical inertia, Soviet atheists soon realized that the very essence and dynamics of religious belief had transformed. Indeed, they came to suspect that it was their own theories and methods that were primitive and that needed to be modernized to keep pace.

When Soviet atheists attempted to fight faith with fact, they encountered a population that often seemed untroubled by the contradictions they so ardently tried to unmask and instead reconciled scientific and religious cosmologies in unexpected ways. The worldviews Soviet atheists found on the ground ranged from unsystematic, to eclectic, to what today would probably be called secular—that is, worldviews that relied on science for explanations of the material world and religion for explanations of the spiritual realm. Indicative in this respect are the responses of Ul'iana Andreevna Lukina of Ivanovo region to a sociological survey on the "Contemporary believer's perception of God" (Predstavleniia sovremennogo veruiushchego o boge) conducted by the Institute of Scientific Atheism in 1964 and 1965. When asked how she combines, in her mind, the idea of God with the laws of the universe, Lukina replied that "she never occupies herself with speculations about the universe." When asked what she thought about the fact that spaceships had flown to space, Lukina's answer was: "So they flew, so what? There was a time when I barely made it from here to Ufa, and now it is possible to go twice a week. God has nothing to do with it. God, after all, is within us." When asked for her thoughts on the subject in general, Lukina concluded: "What is the point of thinking about this? It's just somehow more peaceful with God."[127]

New attempts to address and reconcile the paradox of modern belief continued to occupy Soviet ideologists until the end of the Soviet period as various hypotheses for the persistence of religion in the modern world were tried and disproved, and atheist methods tested without producing desired results. Moreover, throughout the 1960s novel theories about the nature of religion led to new methods in atheist propaganda, so that the main weapon in the arsenal of atheist education was increasingly seen to be philosophy rather than science. This shift in atheist theories and practices significantly transformed the landscape of Soviet belief, both religious and atheist. Finally, it also made Soviet atheists aware of the philosophical, or perhaps more accurately spiritual, vacuum that opened up when religious cosmologies were contested by atheist propaganda, although few at this point articulated the implications that this vacuum, if taken to its logical conclusion, might have for Marxism-Leninism. Nevertheless, having reached a zenith in the early 1960s, cosmic enthusiasm began to wane. One important reason for the decline in enthusiasm is that the narratives of Soviet space achievements and of Soviet atheism, until this point fellow travelers, experienced a parting of ways.

The story of the conquest of the cosmos in Soviet atheism also lays bare the paradox of the attempt to invest scientific materialism with a spiritual center. Not only did Soviet space achievements fail to produce mass religious disbelief, they also revealed the ideological pitfalls of the utopia promised by Marxism-Leninism. Cosmonauts occupied the space between utopia and reality, and became a vehicle for the management of the desire, longing, and faith generated by religious, ideological, and cosmological utopias. In the broader project of scientific enlightenment, cosmonauts became the consecrated objects of popular devotion. Through their charisma, the average Soviet person could access the ideological enthusiasm that was habitually required in Soviet citizens, and in effect be transformed, even converted, by the experience. Yet, as ideological models, cosmonauts remained removed from the Soviet masses by an impenetrable curtain. The path to the heavens was available to the few, not to the many, and ultimately the vast majority of Soviet citizens remained at best only "half-cosmonauts."

As time passed, the distance between Soviet reality and Marxist-Leninist ideals grew so great that the iconography of cosmonauts and space exploration began to get primarily *ironic* treatments, indicating that Soviet space enthusiasm was coming to an end. Vladimir Voinovich's dystopian novella *Moscow 2042* (1982) depicts Communism as having finally been realized in the future, except that it is concentrated in one postapocalyptic city-state: Moscow. The city's Communist leader, while revered on Earth, is essentially exiled to a spaceship to keep his sacred aura intact and is, in effect, a permanent if unwilling cosmonaut.[128] The Moscow conceptualist Il'ia Kabakov, meanwhile, constructed an individual dystopia in his 1981–88 installation, "The Man Who Flew to Space from His Apartment." His installation depicts a homespun contraption for space travel created by an impatient Soviet citizen, a person the critic Boris Groys describes as an "illegitimate cosmonaut."[129] Finally, returning to Pelevin's childhood utopia, the contents of the mysterious suitcase that the cosmonauts carried with them on their journeys are finally revealed to the curious Pelevin to be . . . excrement—a revelation that transforms cosmic enthusiasm into a parable of dystopia. "The fact that some system for waste disposal was necessary was impossible to deny. But a cosmonaut with a little suitcase full of shit seemed to me so unthinkable, that in that moment, my clean star world got a clear crack," writes Pelevin. "From that moment on, whenever a new cosmonaut walked toward his new rocket, I could not take my eyes off that suitcase. Perhaps this was a result of the fact that I grew up and had long ago noticed that it was not just cosmonauts who carried such suitcases with them, but every Soviet person."[130]

8

She Orbits over the Sex Barrier

Soviet Girls and the Tereshkova Moment

Roshanna P. Sylvester

On June 16, 1963, Valentina Vladimirovna Tereshkova, a twenty-six-year-old Soviet "everywoman" blasted off aboard *Vostok 6* to become the first woman in space (figure 8.1).[1] Her mission was to join fellow cosmonaut Valerii Fedorovich Bykovskii, who was already in orbit at the helm of *Vostok 5*. Despite the notable fact that Bykovskii was in the process of setting a new record for the longest space voyage in human history, it was Tereshkova, not her male comrade, who captured the attention and imagination of the terrestrial public. A Cold War variant of the new Soviet woman, Tereshkova became an instant celebrity, portrayed to the world as both a master of technology and a feminine flower in the garden of cosmonauts. A flurry of articles, speeches, and decrees hailed her as a "hero of the cosmos, a hero of the people" and "a model for Soviet youth."[2] Congratulatory telegrams and letters flooded in from around the world commending the USSR on its scientific prowess and Communist commitment to gender equality.[3] Meanwhile, at home Soviet children, especially girls, were swept up in the general euphoria, enthusiastically cheering the successes of "our Valia," the USSR's newest space star.[4]

Figure 8.1. Valentina Tereshkova during training for her mission to space in 1963. *Source*: NASA.

What did Tereshkova's celestial journey mean to the generation of Soviet schoolgirls who saw her venture into the cosmos?[5] This chapter analyzes the burst of Soviet press coverage about Tereshkova that appeared in child- and family-oriented newspapers and periodicals in 1963. Its findings suggest that Soviet girls in middle childhood were genuinely thrilled by the female cosmonaut's triumph and were a captive and engaged audience for the messages of empowerment that engulfed them in the heyday of the Tereshkova moment.[6] News items and feature stories openly encouraged girls to strive for the highest levels of achievement in science and technology, loudly affirming that in the USSR there were no limits on female aspiration. Girls of the Tereshkova generation responded to the euphoric rhetoric, embracing their interests and the new horizon of possibilities opened up for them by the advent of female space travel.

They availed themselves of the considerable opportunities afforded to them in the USSR's educational system, achieved near parity with their male counterparts in a mastery of scientific and technologically oriented fields, and in greater numbers than ever before moved into careers that put their knowledge into action.

Despite these real achievements, however, the question of whether Soviet girls could in fact grow up to be cosmonauts was of course out of their hands. Scholars have consistently noted the distance between official propaganda that celebrated Tereshkova's accomplishment and the tense behind-the-scenes controversies among those in the upper echelons of the Soviet space program and the Communist Party concerning the development of the female cosmonaut corps.[7] Even in the first blush of the Tereshkova moment, press coverage revealed a marked ambivalence about the role girls and women should play in Cold War society, especially in the much-vaunted worlds of science and technology. Unfortunately for girls, it soon became abundantly clear that among decision makers at the highest levels there was no real commitment to robust female participation in the Soviet space program. As others have shown, Tereshkova herself quickly faded from the headlines, definitively so after her much-publicized November 1963 wedding to her cosmonaut "brother" Andrian Nikolaev and the birth the following year of the couple's daughter, Lena. Although she remained on the rolls as an inactive cosmonaut, the first woman in space was thus quickly recast as a wife, mother, and cultural ambassador—roles more in keeping with the resurgent gender traditionalism that would mark the Brezhnev years.[8] It would be two decades more before a second female cosmonaut made it into orbit.

Although one could focus on what went wrong in the late Soviet period, especially with respect to the distance between ideological promises and women's real experiences, my purpose is to consider instead what went right for Soviet girls of the Tereshkova generation. Despite subsequent developments, evidence suggests that girls themselves held on to a more expansive view of their life possibilities at least in part because of Tereshkova's accomplishments in space. Although the world's first female cosmonaut never again mounted a rocket, the sheer fact that she had done so once inspired girls to dream big. For an instant, the girls who saw Tereshkova fly were part of a universe in which reality and promise converged, with vistas of opportunity available to them that were unique in the world.

"The Girl from Iaroslavl"

The Soviet public knew essentially nothing about Valentina Tereshkova when she rocketed to celebrity in June 1963. But thanks to the efficient work of journalists, readers were soon acquainted with the new
cosmonaut's exceedingly correct and very Soviet biography. Early press
coverage stressed the virtues of Tereshkova's family origins, childhood,
and youth, portraying her as the politically impeccable heroine in a Communist fairy tale. *Pionerskaia pravda*, a twice-weekly newspaper aimed at
school-aged children, introduced its young readers to Valentina, or Valia
for short, by explaining that she was born in 1937 in the village of Maslen-
nikov of good proletarian stock: "Her father was a tractor driver and her
mother a worker in a textile enterprise." The family had three children:
Valia; her sister, Liuda; and a brother, Volodia. Tragedy of the heroic variety struck the family during the Great Patriotic War when Tereshkova's
father was killed "at the front." But her brave mother soldiered on, moving the family to nearby Iaroslavl', where she could get better work. Valia
herself was portrayed as a diligent student who after leaving school at seventeen became a model worker, first in a tire factory and then in a textile
complex. She also joined the Komsomol in Iaroslavl', serving as secretary
of her factory committee in 1960 and 1961. Bent on self-improvement,
Tereshkova returned to her studies in that same period, graduating from
a technical school in 1960. Two years later she solidified her spotless
credentials by becoming a member of the Communist Party. In her spare
time Valentina enjoyed outdoor activities and displayed an adventurous
side by taking up sky diving. Unbeknownst to her, these hobbies made
her an outstanding candidate for the female cosmonaut corps.[9]

As this brief sketch makes clear, press biographies meant for children played up Tereshkova's image as the consummate Soviet youth:
hardworking, studious, politically loyal, and healthy. By stressing these
values, writers fit Tereshkova neatly into the well-established repertoire
of ideal childhood types long emphasized in Soviet publications aimed
at the young.[10] But unlike its typical coverage, *Pionerskaia pravda's* celebration of Tereshkova was aimed squarely at girls, standing in striking
contrast to the paper's normal pattern of primarily addressing an implied
male reader.[11] Girls and women did appear with some regularity in the
newspaper's pages, both in illustrations and photos and as the subjects

of stories. But such representations tended to shoehorn girls into a limited number of roles and were significantly fewer in number than those focusing on male subjects. Girls were most commonly shown dressed in school or pioneer uniforms, sitting at desks, greeting distinguished (usually male) visitors with bouquets of flowers, or on parade for public holidays.[12] Another frequent motif involved girls in the outdoors, picking flowers, displaying the fruits of the harvest, or doing agricultural work.[13] Other activities perpetually associated with girls included sewing, knitting, fashion, and hair styling as well as arts and crafts, music, drama, and dancing.[14] The newspaper also encouraged girls to keep themselves in shape, showing them engaged in a variety of sports and recreational activities deemed appropriate for their gender: swimming, boating, volleyball, skiing, ice skating, and gymnastics.[15]

By emphasizing Tereshkova's accomplishments as a worker, sportswoman, and political activist, *Pionerskaia pravda* successfully packaged the cosmonaut as a tried-and-true role model for girls. Although not as pervasive as positive images of teachers and mothers (by far the most consistent presence), female sports champions were regularly profiled in *Pionerskaia pravda*, as were World War II–era heroines, political figures such as Nadezhda Krupskaia, and female Komsomol leaders or Communist Party members.[16] Women workers also appeared with some regularity, especially those in occupations that in the USSR were traditionally female: textile workers, tractor drivers, secretaries, medical personnel, and the like.[17]

Although the latter set of representations demonstrated that women could and did acquire technical knowledge and operate machines effectively, articles about females working in higher-level scientific specialties or studying physics, chemistry, mathematics, or the other hard sciences were relatively rare.[18] *Pionerskaia pravda*'s editors and writers evidently considered scientific and technical fare to be more appealing (and appropriate) to their male readers. For instance, it was common to find an article such as the one that appeared in a February 1963 issue instructing boys on how to build their own machines juxtaposed against images of girls working in the fields or gardening at home.[19] As for stories of any genre in the pre-Tereshkova era concerning space exploration and rocketry, girls were practically invisible except as starry-eyed observers of male daring and accomplishment.[20]

As *Pionerskaia pravda*'s coverage reveals, it was something of a paradox that Tereshkova was portrayed as operating within the convention-al Soviet mold of female aspiration and heroism while simultaneously shattering old paradigms of female possibility. The first woman in space was quickly established as the newest link in an infamous chain of dar-ing Soviet heroines that included aviation pioneers as well as the much-celebrated female pilots and partisans of the World War II years. And yet in the Cold War context of the early 1960s, evidence suggests that it was the marriage of Tereshkova's "everywoman" persona with more un-conventional aspects of her profile—especially her affinity and apparent aptitude for science and technology—that made "our Valia" an appealing and especially significant role model for girls.[21]

Sveta's Dream

Even before the USSR had sent a woman to space, Soviet girls had shown themselves to be as susceptible as boys to the wave of cosmic en-thusiasm that swept the Soviet Union after *Sputnik*.[22] Tereshkova herself cited "the heroic exploit of Yuri Gagarin" as a personal inspiration.[23] But girls much younger than she also felt the pull and promise of Soviet space achievement at a personal level. For instance, when *Pionerskaia pravda* queried children about which events they thought they would remember their whole lives, Tania Arakelian from Krasnodar replied: "When Gaga-rin flew into space and when revolution came to Cuba."[24] Writing much later, the cultural critic, theorist, and media artist Svetlana Boym remem-bered that she and other "Soviet children of the 1960s did not dream of becoming doctors and lawyers, but cosmonauts (or, if worse came to worst, geologists)."[25] Girls' cosmic imaginings were likewise revealed in an April 1963 issue of *Ogonek*, which featured a selection of children's letters to cosmonauts, including one from Valia Larshina in Orsk: "I am ready to fly to the very largest planet and study it. . . . I wouldn't be ter-rified to fly to space. When the rocket is ready, I will be trained." Mean-while, Liusia Zorina from Yalta imagined weaving together two seem-ingly irreconcilable career aspirations: "I want to be a ballerina and fly to space. I don't even know which I want more."[26]

With Tereshkova's emergence as a "sister" cosmonaut, these occa-sional references to girls' desires for cosmic adventures became a fre-quent feature in children's and family newspapers and magazines. In the heat of the Tereshkova moment, *Pionerskaia pravda* openly encouraged such dreams. Its front page on June 18, 1963, was dominated by a large photo of Tereshkova accompanied by a drawing of two Soviet rockets flying through the cosmos. Next to these dramatic images was a small item penned by R. Kovalenko, who reported that the children in Krasnodar School No. 2 had recently completed a questionnaire that asked what they wanted to be when they grew up: "219 of 300 boys answered, 'We dream of flying a space ship.' But among the girls only Sveta Beliaeva from seventh class wrote, 'Cosmonaut.' And in parentheses explained, 'If that is impossible, then an astronomer.' It is possible, Sveta, it is possible! Your dream will come true," Kovalenko enthused.[27]

One of the most immediate signs that Tereshkova's journey to space had broadened the landscape of girls' imaginative possibilities was the profusion of cartoons portraying girls in space. *Pionerskaia pravda* featured two such offerings on June 21, 1963. The first showed a drawing of three girls and two boys standing in a circle playing a counting game. The caption relayed the words of the eldest girl: "One, two, three, four, five. I will fly you into space." The second cartoon that day was titled "Magic Words." In the first frame an older sister was portrayed tugging at the arm of her screaming younger brother: "If you don't obey, I won't take you to space with me when I grow up." The second frame showed the boy standing up and walking hand in hand with his sister, still looking grumpy but at least cooperating.[28]

Print cartoons of girls taking the lead in space exploration frequently linked standard symbols of girlhood with those associated with the cosmos. Festooning the front cover of the June 30, 1963, issue of the weekly humor magazine *Krokodil* was a full-color cartoon showing a school-aged girl in a polka-dotted dress clutching a stuffed bear while thumbing her nose at two boys who stood alongside holding their toys—a model rocket, plane, and helicopter. The caption reads, "Where's your advantage in the cosmos now?" The second and third pages of the issue were completely taken up with other Tereshkova-themed cartoons, one of which depicted a young girl holding a cosmonaut doll outside the door of her school saying, "There is nothing interesting here. Let's find out where the cosmonaut school is!"[29] The back pages of *Ogonek*'s June issue included a dozen Tereshkova-inspired cartoons, one of which portrayed a girl cozily asleep in bed. Above her head was a dream bubble showing her smiling in a spacesuit, striding purposefully away from her rocket on the surface of the moon.[30]

Readers of these cartoons could hardly miss the point that girls were being encouraged to compete with boys at the very highest levels of scientific and technological achievement. But even more telling than comical representations were items that suggested just how powerfully real girls responded to Tereshkova's accomplishment. For example, an *Ogonek* photo spread featured interviews with five Moscow girls, all of whom were planning to follow Tereshkova's lead. Galia Pankova was photographed standing in front of a *Pravda* front-page picture of her heroine: "I really like Valentina Tereshkova. I will try to imitate her in everything and also fly. . . . In my opinion, I even look a little like her!" Other girls explained that they wanted to be space scientists or rocket engineers. Tania Klokova, pictured with her hands on a model rocket lying before her on a desk, said, "I want to become Chief Designer [of a rocket ship] . . . and invent a ship that I'm satisfied with." Sveta Solov'eva and Nina Savchuk, photographed pointing at a spot on a huge lunar globe, reported that they wanted to study the surface of the moon to select the best landing sites. Meanwhile, Tania Safronova announced her intention to invent space binoculars "so that I can see it all when I myself fly to the stars!"[31]

"A Soviet Woman Has Stormed Outer Space"

Even a brief survey of popular press coverage of Tereshkova's flight suggests that Soviet girls enthusiastically embraced the new world of possibilities opened up for them in science and technology by the female cosmonaut's accomplishment. Meanwhile, Tereshkova herself reveled in the spotlight, enhancing the stature of women throughout the USSR. "A Soviet woman has stormed outer space," Tereshkova exclaimed to a euphoric audience in her Red Square speech on June 22, 1963. Heaping praise on her Communist sisters, Tereshkova celebrated female successes in all realms of Soviet society: "[Women] are participating actively in state management, in the social and political affairs of the country, they are working enthusiastically in the economy, science, culture, education, and upbringing of the younger generation." She was equally full of praise for the scientists, engineers, and technicians who made Soviet spaceflight possible, expressing heartfelt thanks to "all who took part in the development of our wonderful rockets and spaceships, all who equipped and prepared us for our complex journey into space, who ensured our successful fulfillment of this responsible assignment."[32]

Given the context of the Cold War space race, it is unsurprising that Tereshkova and those who commented on her successes were quick to valorize the accomplishments of Soviet science for audiences at home and abroad. In his Red Square speech Communist Party leader Nikita Sergeevich Khrushchev was effusive in his tribute, singling out for special praise the contributions of the rising generation: "the spaceships, the engines for them, and the fuel were developed mainly by young people" who worked "side by side with the experienced workers, scientists, engineers and technicians" to make the future happen now.[33] Valentina Vavilina, the editor in chief of *Rabotnitsa*, reminded readers that women were among the active participants in these scientific accomplishments: "There are some spheres in which women are the main force [in Soviet society]: the textile and the food industries, schools, and medical institutions. But women have also helped create space rockets and the atomic icebreaker. All professions are open to them."[34] "Women are a mighty detachment of our Soviet science," confirmed Vasili V. Parin, a member of the USSR Academy of Medical Sciences and chief physician in charge of monitoring the cosmonauts' medical condition during their training and mission periods. "They are wonderful pilots of the latest high-speed aircraft. And here, following right after the men into the stellar heights, soars Valentina Tereshkova, a glorious Soviet woman" (figure 8.2).[35]

Press biographies of Tereshkova underscored the point that the Soviet system successfully nurtured female accomplishment in the realms of science and technology and that the cosmonaut herself was a master of both. Newspaper readers were told that from an early age little Valia "fell in love with the machines" at the textile mill where her mother worked. She became infatuated "with their noise like falling rain with the twinkling streams of thread, the sweet smell of fresh flax, and the deft skill of the women's hands" as they worked the looms. It was precisely Tereshkova's love of machines that took her ever higher, first as a parachutist then as a cosmonaut.[36] "My most interesting orbits were when I was controlling the ship manually," Tereshkova reported in her first postflight press conference. "It is very exciting to feel such an intricate, complex machine respond to your will." "I have got two wishes," she commented later in the interview, "to study and to fly. In the future space flights will become even more interesting. There will be flights to the Moon, Mars and Venus, and of course I am eager to go on all of them."[37]

The question of the female cosmonaut's own prowess in the realm

Figure 8.2. Valentina Tereshkova, adorned with a panoply of medals and awards, was a visible ambassador for Soviet women on the international stage. *Source*: NASA.

of science and technology was affirmed as well in *Izvestiia*'s coverage. The joint mission of *Vostok-5* and *-6* was a scientific one, the paper reported; its main objective was to enhance medical-biological knowledge of how spaceflight influenced "the organisms of man and woman." The bodily functions of the two cosmonauts were continuously monitored, the ensuing data allowing scientists and physicians to conduct comparative studies that would enable spacecraft designers and engineers to perfect piloting systems and pave the way for further space exploration and colonization.[38] But press reports stressed the cosmonauts were not just passive objects of scientific research. Bykovskii and Tereshkova were actively involved in expanding the frontiers of knowledge. An open letter signed by the Central Committee of the Communist Party of the Soviet Union, the Presidium of the Supreme Soviet of the USSR, and the Council of Ministers of the USSR declared as much: "The feat of the cosmonauts is of unmatched significance. In the multiday joint flight cosmonaut comrades Bykovskii and Tereshkova fulfilled an extensive program of scientific research, making a new outstanding contribution to the treasure-house of world science and culture." Their "unparalleled feat . . . has displayed with renewed force the genius of the Soviet people, a fighting people, a working people. Once again the infinite superiority of the socialist system over the capitalist and the might and grandeur of our country, the Union of Soviet Socialist Republics, have been convincingly and clearly revealed to the world."[39]

Tereshkova's participation in the space program markedly elevated the currency of Soviet women in science and technology. But the fact of her accomplishment was exploited most thoroughly in the Cold War competition with America to win the propaganda wars in the developing world. The female cosmonaut's value as a cultural ambassador was immediately apparent. After lavishly toasting his female space star, Khrushchev quickly dispatched her to the World Congress of Women, which not by coincidence convened in Moscow on June 24, 1963. Tereshkova's appearance there was greeted with euphoria by delegates, many from the developing world, who saw her success as a breakthrough for all women everywhere. Beyond this, they applauded the Soviet Union and Communist ideology for making female equality a reality.[40] As the journalist Stanislav Shcherbatov pointed out to English-language readers in the *Moscow News*: "A flight by a woman into outer space is no mere gesture. It is a logical development of our society. In our country equality of women, like atomic fission, has set free tremendous energy. Consequently in the Soviet Union progress is inconceivable without the participation of the women."[41]

For children experiencing the Tereshkova moment, there was little cause to doubt that Soviet girls would have an opportunity to follow the first female cosmonaut into space. *Pionerskaia pravda*'s June 25, 1963, issue greeted the young eyes and imaginations of its readers with two photographs of Tereshkova. Stretching across the top of page one was an image of the six cosmonauts and Khrushchev on the Kremlin wall—hands linked and upraised in a triumphal gesture. The second photo showed

Khrushchev folding Tereshkova into a fatherly embrace. "We celebrated this time like never before," began the accompanying story, which described the Red Square festivities and parading motorcade. "Here she is, our Valia, the first woman to have visited the stars!" "She is so beautiful, so simple [*prostaia*]! And her smile is bright and dear, and her voice clear, tender, and familiar [*rodnoi*]."[42]

A particularly vivid anecdote included in the piece captured the hopes and enthusiasm of the children who saw Tereshkova in her moment of glory. The reporter described seeing four children "clambering up to the roof of a newspaper kiosk. One of them was a slip of a girl [*devonchka*]. In her hands was a small basket. At the moment when the ceremonial motorcade drove past, the girl threw into the sky white-winged pigeons and cried with all her might: Long live the cosmonauts!" Tereshkova noticed the girl and waved. "Who knows, maybe this slip of a girl with the ardent face and short hair cut will someday fly to space," the columnist concluded.[43]

An Earthly Flower in the Garden of Cosmonauts

Despite the rhetoric of inclusion and unabashed trumpeting of female possibility that flooded the Tereshkova moment, the question of whether girls and women should actually be encouraged to aspire to leadership in the predominantly male preserve of science and technology remained unresolved at best in the upper echelons of party and state power. Soviet girls' ambitions to follow their hero into the cosmos thus stood in marked contrast to the notably ambivalent attitudes expressed in private by some of the USSR's most important political leaders and top scientists toward female participation in the space program. On the one hand, there were certain highly placed hopes that the Soviet Union would outpace the Americans when it came to building colonies in space, an endeavor that if successful would necessarily involve couples and families living beyond Earth. Indeed, the desire to accumulate data about the effects of space travel on the "female organism" was part of what motivated Soviet decision makers to send a woman to space in the first place.[44] But with Nikita Sergeevich Khrushchev at the helm of the Communist Party in the early 1960s, there was on the other hand a concerted effort to recast the young Soviet woman as not only hardworking and politically reliable but also as chic and feminine. In popular representations drab was out while Dior was definitely in.[45]

The project of redefining Soviet womanhood in a space age Cold War fell in part to those writing in the Soviet press about Tereshkova. The biographical profile that ran in the popular illustrated weekly magazine *Ogonek* in the immediate aftermath of her flight sought to integrate the young cosmonaut's unfeminine love of technology with emerging motifs of Soviet femininity. The result was a revised portrait of the ideal new Soviet woman that emphasized "our Valia's" softer side while still celebrating her tenacity, strong will, intellect, and scientific aptitude. The two-page spread titled "I Am the Seagull" (a reference to the cosmonaut's radio call sign "chaika") ran below a large soft-focus photograph of a beautiful, white-clad Tereshkova in a flower garden. The caption read: "Earthly flowers in 'the garden of cosmonauts.'" In striking contrast to that image, the essay's author, Aleksei Golikov, chose to open the piece with a dramatic description of Tereshkova boldly facing her first parachute jump in May 1959. Up until that time, Tereshkova's friends, family members, and coworkers thought of Valentina as an "artistic, fragile looking girl [*devushka*] [who] played volleyball, sometimes engaged in light athletics, but most of all loved music and to stroll around town," Golikov informed his readers. But Valia had her own ideas about whom she was and what she would become, challenging herself to be daring, to overcome her fears, and to strive for perfection. Thanks to her strong character, the profile continued, Tereshkova became a Communist Party member, an excellent parachutist, and finally a cosmonaut. Yet even as she declared herself "ready for a spaceflight," Golikov summoned up for his readers an image of Tereshkova "in a cozy, girlish room" in Star City, sitting at a desk that held "a vase with a lilac branch [and] a pile of abstracts on air navigation, astronomy, medicine, higher mathematics, and astrophysics." Tereshkova passed her exams and kept up with her physical training, Golikov continued. "And so came the day when for the first time in the history of the planet a radio communication emerged from space in a female voice: "I am Chaika. I see the horizon. It is Earth! It is so beautiful!"[46]

The attempt to harmonize Tereshkova's femininity with her scientific and technical prowess became an essential component of official narratives of her accomplishments, part and parcel of the Cold War iteration of the new Soviet woman. But not all writers shared Golikov's felicity of expression, especially those who penned the texts of the spate of official speeches and proclamations that filled Soviet newspapers and airwaves during and immediately following the flight of "the seagull." Predictably, some chose to plot a safe course by placing Tereshkova firmly into the well-established line of inspirational female role models so well known to girls in the early 1960s.[47] It came as no surprise, then, that in their carefully scripted triumphal speeches in Red Square on June 22, 1963, both Tereshkova and Khrushchev referenced the martyred partisan Zoya Kosmodemyanskaya, the storied tractor driver Pasha Angelina, the hero textile workers Valentina Gaganova and Dusia Vinogradova, and other famous Soviet heroines of the World War II and Stalin eras.[48]

Other speakers and writers, including those who addressed children, chose to emphasize a different set of antecedents, inscribing Tereshkova into a line of female accomplishment explicitly connected with science and technology.[49] For instance, a July 1963 issue of *Znanie-Sila*, a popular science magazine aimed at young people, included an article titled "Her Predecessors" that joined a drawing of Tereshkova in her space helmet with a profile of nineteenth- and early-twentieth-century Russian female aviation pioneers.[50] Likewise, *Pravda* special correspondent Nikolai Den- isov reported in an *Ogonek* column "from a journalist's diary" about a press conference with the Soviet cosmonaut corps attended by "academ- ics, leading Soviet scholars, specialists in various branches of learning . . . and, of course, we journalists." One of the highlights of the event was an address given by "a venerable scholar" who after congratulating Bykovskii and Tereshkova spoke "with enormous feeling about the great role of women in Soviet society, recalling too the work of the famous Russian mathematician Sofiia Kovalevskaia, who in the years of tsarism was forced to leave her mother country in order to continue her scientific studies."[51]

For his part, Soviet Premier Nikita Khrushchev seemed particularly ambivalent about the extent to which Tereshkova should be cast as a mas- ter of science and technology. "I am very happy and as proud as a father that one of our girls [*devushki*], a girl from the Soviet Union, is the first, the first in the world, to travel in space, to be in command of the most highly perfected machinery," Khrushchev enthused in a widely publi- cized in-flight telephone conversation with his newest space star on June 16.[52] At first glance the statement suggests that the Communist Party leader was happy to publicly acknowledge and celebrate female aptitude in the realm of science and technology. And yet Khrushchev's use of the term *devushka* bears scrutiny. Literally translated, the word means "an unmarried girl." But in common usage, *devushka* is highly flexible, with tone and context making all the difference in whether it is understood as a straightforward label of age and sex, a term of endearment, or a patronizing, even offensive slur. While in this case Khrushchev used *devushka* in an explicitly paternal voice, perhaps as a way to express his fondness for Tereshkova, it is worth noting that Nikita Sergeevich also regularly referred to her with the familiar diminutive "Valia." But when he addressed the *Vostok-5* cosmonaut Bykovskii, it was with the more formal and respectful first name and patronymic: Valerii Fedorovich.[53] Whether intentional or not, this bit of sexism served to emphasize the more conventionally feminine aspects of Tereshkova's persona, perhaps moderating to some extent whatever threat she might have posed to the masculinized world of science and technology.[54]

Ambivalent as they may have been about how girls would fit in to the USSR's Cold War future, Soviet officialdom clearly hoped that Tereshkova's accomplishments and the associated triumphalism would prove to be inspirational to everyone in Soviet society, including its youngest female members. In actuality, the decade after Tereshkova's entry into space appears to have been the high watermark for Soviet girls and women in terms of female aspiration and accomplishment in science and technology. A long-term study conducted by a team of sociologists in Novosibirsk found in 1963 that both girls and boys desired careers in science and technology.[55] When asked to rank their preferences, girls' top choices were mathematics, medicine, chemistry, and physics.[56]

These positive attitudes were transformed into real career paths as young women began to pursue higher degrees and professional employment in the sciences. Of all the advanced university degrees awarded to women in 1962 through 1964, more than half were in applied sciences and more than a quarter in the natural sciences. At the doctoral level, although only one in twelve physics and math degrees went to women, female chemists constituted 40 percent of recipients in that field.[57] These numbers were particularly impressive given that in the United States, only about 5 percent of PhDs in chemistry and math, and fewer than 3 percent in physics, went to women.[58] By 1970 the census shows that more

Soviet women than ever before were engineering-technical workers, their numbers more than doubling in ten years from 1.63 million to 3.75 million. The 1960s had also seen continued increases in the number of higher degrees earned by females in science, engineering, and technology fields. From 1971 through 1973 three of every four women awarded candidate and doctoral degrees were in the natural and applied sciences.[59]

These statistics alone offer compelling evidence about girls' desire and capacity to move ahead in the realms of science and technology. And yet ambition in and of itself cannot fully explain girls' successes. Something clearly went right in the Soviet 1960s when it came to enabling girls to fulfill their dreams. Although a full investigation of the constellation of factors that led to female achievement is beyond the scope of this chapter, the evidence collected here suggests several preliminary conclusions. Before pursuing them, it is helpful to take note of recent research by a variety of scholars in the United States and internationally who have been studying the question of why females do or do not choose educational and career paths in science and technology fields. The factors cited most commonly in that literature are the influence of parents, teachers, and peers on occupational choice; the shaping power of stereotypes promulgated at home, school, and in the broader sociocultural environment, especially through mass culture; the quality of science teaching in schools; the overall image of science and scientists in society; and the presence of positive role models who demonstrate that science- and technology-focused careers can lead to success and happiness.[60]

Bearing this in mind, one can postulate that Soviet girls' shared quest for advancement in the 1960s was aided by the USSR's standard school curriculum, which demanded that both girls and boys from first grade on spend more than half their time studying math and science.[61] But for the Tereshkova generation, other powerful factors were also in play. First, girls were immersed in propaganda that told them Soviet women could do it all. Second, the Communist system did in fact provide real-life role models—most important, Tereshkova—for girls' emulation. Third, the imperatives of the Cold War, with its valorization of science and technology, afforded girls a range of opportunities to put their knowledge to higher use.

Unfortunately, this empowering combination of factors was relatively short-lived. The gains of those years in which girls achieved near parity with their male counterparts in the realms of science and technology education simply did not hold up. By 1973—the tenth anniversary of Tereshkova's flight—the Novosibirsk study showed that girls were less positive than they had been the decade before toward hard science and math occupations. Moreover, by the late 1970s sociological studies found that despite the fact that Soviet women tended to be better educated and trained than men, when it came to employment prospects in the "thinking professions," women were increasingly confined to lower- and mid-level positions.[62] The attitudes of young people in Russia today underscore the depth of the loss. A recent study sponsored by the European Union found that although both girls and boys in Russia believe that science and technology are important for society, few girls (ages fourteen through sixteen) want to be scientists. Moreover, the study reveals that more than twice as many Russian boys as girls want to work in technology jobs, demonstrating that the gender gap in Russia is the most severe of any of the twenty-five countries surveyed.[63]

The findings presented in this chapter hint at some of the reasons for this dramatic reversal, which cannot in any event be understood in isolation from the larger dynamics that ultimately led to the collapse of the Soviet system. Yet it is clear that part of the explanation lies in the sexism of Soviet political leaders and high-level decision makers among the USSR's scientific and technical intelligentsia. As the historian Sue Bridger has reminded us, in the aftermath of Tereshkova's flight, controversy raged in the inner circles of the Soviet space program about the fitness and capabilities of female cosmonauts.[64] Although none of this was public, no one could miss the fact that Tereshkova never returned to space and that the four other women who were part of the cosmonaut corps in the early 1960s were retired without ever getting the chance to follow her. The next three female trainees were not recruited until the early 1980s, and it wasn't until 1982 that the extremely well-connected Svetlana Savitskaya became the second Soviet woman to make it into orbit. Meanwhile in America, the June 1983 flight of thirty-two-year-old Sally Ride, a Stanford PhD in physics, reinvigorated interest in NASA and opened up new possibilities for girls. "I never even imagined I could be an astronaut," Ride confided in a preflight interview widely quoted in the American press. "I guess because I just assumed there would never be a place for women."[65] But unlike in the Soviet Union, dozens of American female astronauts emulated Ride's accomplishments. By July 1999, when U.S. Air Force Lieutenant Eileen Collins first took command of a space shuttle mission, more than a third of NASA's astronauts were female. Although still certainly an elite profession, "astronaut" had become a viable career path for girls in the United States, something that never happened in the USSR.[66]

One could dwell (as many have) on what went wrong in the late Soviet era. And yet the crucial point remains: the USSR was the first country in the world to send a woman into space. For the girls who saw it happen, that mattered a lot. In those days when possibility was so alive in young female minds, girls plotted their own course to success in the "scientific-technological revolution," their personal missions sustained at least in part by a vision of their hero's cosmic triumph and high-profile reassurances that true equality was the law of the land. And so they played with their cosmonaut dolls, climbed atop rockets at their local playgrounds, competed against boys in math, physics, and astronomy, and with pride and ambition worked toward their dreams of reaching the stars.

From the Kitchen into Orbit

The Convergence of Human Spaceflight and Krushchev's Nascent Consumerism

Cathleen S. Lewis

The Cold War over consumer goods between the United States and the Soviet Union literally began in the kitchen. It was in the American kitchen that U.S. Vice President Richard M. Nixon and Soviet Premier Nikita Khrushchev had a public and impromptu discussion through their interpreters at the opening of the American National Exhibition at Sokolniki Park in Moscow on July 24, 1959. Their discussion over the relative industrial accomplishments of their respective countries took place at an American exhibition of a modern, affordable, and well-equipped kitchen that had been on display at the 1958 World's Fair at Brussels. In Belgium the United States had displayed the latest in American consumer goods. The Soviet Union had displayed cars and airplanes that were not yet available to the public and models of the first three spacecraft that the USSR had launched into space, which had ushered in the space race.[1] At the end of the Brussels exhibition, both sides agreed to open a portion of their own exhibition in each other's country.[2] By the time that the exhibitions had opened in New York and Moscow, the United States had finally successfully launched a satellite into space.[3] In Moscow, however, displays of consumer goods remained the subject for exhibitions and not the contents of stores.[4] The absence of consumer goods in the USSR was as much of a sore point for their population as had been the U.S. failure to be the first in space for Americans.

Collectibles and spaceflight share historical associations in the Soviet Union. Both emerged during the post-Stalin era of Khrushchev. Each came to symbolize the optimism of the era, and each served as a distraction from the realities of Soviet life. The growth of space-themed collectible consumer goods in the Soviet Union coincided with the post-Stalinist effort to create a sense of contentment and modernity for the war-weary population. By participating in a culture of leisure activities that had not existed before the war, the Soviet population could consider itself modern. Leisure and spaceflight represented modern living to Soviet citizens similar to that of Americans. This illusion of affluence and progress could distract the Soviet population from the lingering sacrifices of the war. These efforts to convince the population of their good fortune extended beyond the small items that the average Soviet citizen could purchase. During the Khrushchev era, propagandists made every effort to identify leisure and recreation activities with cosmonauts. Furthermore, unlike much of Soviet culture these objects have endured the collapse of the Soviet Union, retaining significance from a brief optimistic period in Soviet history.

Scholars have recently reexamined the social and cultural shifts that took place during the Khrushchev era during the late 1950s and early 1960s, often known as "the thaw." The current scholarship places greater emphasis on Khrushchev's attempts to change public expectations of the state as part of his movement away from Stalinism.[5] Some historians, most notably Susan Reid and David Crowley, have turned attention to the material culture of the former Soviet Union, emphasizing discussions of consumerism and aesthetics and how they were used to satisfy the national hunger for a private life.[6] Others had pointed out the extent to which these changes touched the day-to-day lives of Soviet citizens.[7] Post-Soviet attention to the preservation and conservation of the material culture of the previous era offers the opportunity for a closer examination of shifts in aesthetics and consumerism in the Soviet Union during the 1960s. One aspect of Khrushchev's thaw was a limited return to the modernist aesthetic that had accompanied the Bolshevik Revolution. Khrushchev's relaxation of Stalin's cultural restrictions did not mean a wholesale

return to the prerevolutionary and early Soviet modernist thought. However, it was an opportunity to shed both the aesthetic and sumptuary
practices that had symbolized Stalinism.

The material culture of this period of spaceflight came from less
tightly restricted circumstances than had previous Soviet material culture. The resulting artifacts displayed less of the Stalinist socialist realist
norms than other forms of culture did and thus took on the appearance
of the neoconstructivist style that was gaining acceptance in the Soviet
Union in the late 1950s and early 1960s. In addition, the designers of
these new modernist styles did not have the intellectual baggage that had
burdened the previous generation. They could create designs that were
constructivist in form but were devoid of ideological content. In contrast
to their modernist appearance, the message that these objects conveyed
was the same conservative one that the cosmonauts spoke, acted, and
lived. These conservative messages did nothing to challenge the current
state of the Soviet Union but sought to reinforce the regime. The material
culture of the space program, however, was unique in that it was ubiquitous and unavoidable for the Soviet population. The museums, exhibits,
and collectibles were widespread, sprouting up in towns and cities all
over the USSR that claimed an affiliation with spaceflight. They combined the constructionist images and conservative message to create a
long-enduring symbolism that would not disappear as other symbols of
the USSR did.

This chapter applies the lens of recent research on the changes in
material and public culture in the USSR during the 1960s to analyze a
unique collection of spaceflight-related collectibles. Each item represents
the efforts to promote spaceflight in the USSR. The biographies and idealized lives of the cosmonauts had mimicked those of the previous generation on Stalin's aviation heroes. In contrast, these new products did
not resemble similar items from the previous generation. They were produced for individual consumption and not for collective use. The public
impact on material culture was very limited under Stalin. After his death
the Soviet party and government were willing to make concessions to
consumer demand, but only in small ways. One of their major concessions was the release of collecting societies from close police scrutiny
that the party had established in the 1930s as a guard against unregulated
consumerism.[8] Another was the abandonment of Stalinist neoclassical

style and allowing architects and designers to return to constructivism. Although these changes did much to change the presentation of cosmonaut culture, they did not change the content meaningfully.

Khrushchev had learned from Stalin that the most effective domestic propaganda involved the promotion of mass celebrations.[9] By enlisting public participation, government programs gained credibility while undercutting the potential for alternative public cultures to emerge. For the human spaceflight program to have effective propaganda, it was necessary to encourage as wide participation as possible among the Soviet population. However, the space program operated in semisecrecy and did not allow popular participation in planning and staging activities. Mass participation in the space program had to take place after the fact. One way in which the Soviet population could share in the growing momentum of the space program was to read cosmonaut biographies, but reading was a solitary act that did not generate the synergy of a group activity even when done so among school groups and youth organizations. And books, even when they did impart lasting memories, did not have the staying power of material goods. Group demonstrations were ideal, but the number of successful missions limited their occurrence. At its peak in the 1960s the Soviet human spaceflight program had two missions per year. Yet the USSR did have a well-established collection of social organizations through which to stage mass activities. Beginning at school age with the Young Pioneers, and through young adulthood in the Komsomol and the Communist Party, information and activities could be channeled to all ages of the Soviet population.[10] The Pioneer and the Komsomol organizations had been previously instrumental in the organization of mass activities of the Soviet Union.[11] They had contributed to the reduction of illiteracy in the 1920s, facilitated political indoctrination in the 1930s, and organized the war effort among youth during World War II. Youth organizations sought to unify Soviet young people in the aftermath of the devastation of the war.

Books, magazine articles, and speeches had been the traditional modes of dissemination of Soviet culture. However, in order for books, articles, and speeches about spaceflight to be effective, people had to invest a significant amount of time to read or listen to them. More visceral, enduring, and unavoidable contact comes with the very visible material culture that rose out of this period. The small collectible items that pervaded Soviet society at the time contributed to this culture. Their origins were the loosening of political mores on personal collecting within the USSR. One of the ways the late 1950s differed from the Stalinist era was that the postwar generation was not as malleable as previous generations. The revolution was ancient history, as was industrialization and collectivization. The Soviet Union had been the victor in World War II. This generation had no reason to sacrifice as their parents and grandparents had. And Khrushchev had publicly abandoned the overt use of terror to enforce party rule. The Soviet leadership recognized that young people would require some liberalization of government policy to maintain support. The most readily accomplished and least socially disruptive areas of liberalization were the relaxation of laws and rules governing hobbies and contacts with the outside world. By relaxing rules concerning hobbies, the Soviet government sought to encourage the limited acquisition of personal property, including collections. The controlled international contacts with the world would take place under the auspices of well-orchestrated international youth events, such as biennial socialist World Festivals of Youth and Students, in which the USSR was an active participant since its inception in 1947. These two shifts in policy set the stage for a groundswell of collecting activity that became the centerpiece of Soviet spaceflight popular culture.

The most personal way to promote participation in space activities would be the encouragement of collecting memorabilia about programs. However, the Soviet Union was distinctive among Western cultures at the time for its tradition of prohibiting or discouraging individuals from collecting trinkets. From the late 1920s individual collecting of such common items as stamps was discouraged, but in the early 1960s the Soviet government sought to reverse this policy and encourage personal collecting.[12] Personal collecting was a small concession to consumerism that could act as a pressure valve for frustration with conditions in the country.[13] Conditions in the Soviet Union had not improved significantly since the death of Stalin, as the Soviet regime had promised. This relaxation of restrictions against private ownership also coincided with the space program, providing an additional justification for allowing individual celebration. Two fields that received the most official encouragement were postage stamps and *znachki* (small lapel pins).[14] Stamp collecting had remained a controlled activity in the Soviet Union since the 1920s. The government introduced the collection of lapel pins as souvenirs as a new activity in 1957, just before the launch of *Sputnik*.

The Changing Aesthetics of the Thaw

By the 1930s the modernism that had once led the way in revolutionary aesthetics had all but ceased activities in the Soviet Union in the fields of art, architecture, and design. Increasing Bolshevik dominance of civil society, culminating in Stalinism, discouraged the freethinking ideology of modernism. Some proponents of the movements left the country; others gradually burrowed into their respective professional infrastructures, adapting to the changing political aesthetics of the time.[15] Experimentation with the modern idiom continued for some time into the 1930s, but it did not meet with any degree of success. Architects and designers had conceded to official sentiments that pseudoclassicism was closest to the Russian ideal and seemed to abandon the modernist movement in design and architecture of the 1920s and early 1930s.[16] Importantly, in all cases Stalin's imposition of socialist-realist aesthetics in art (including fine art and literature) put an end to the political discussions that had been previously attached to modernism.[17] Henceforth aesthetics and design would become secondary to politics.

Stalin's death in 1953, however, emboldened the dormant modernists. In November 1955 the Soviet Union of Architects renounced "ornamentalism," Stalin's preferred design that included monumental buildings and palatial interior designs that ruled Soviet architecture for a generation.[18] Khrushchev's announcement of de-Stalinization strengthened the resolve of designers in the late 1950s and early 1960s toward a revival. This time the proponents were not arguing for another ideological path to Communism, but argued that modernism was the appropriate style to complement de-Stalinization and the construction of Communism. Designers reignited the call for *nichego lishnego* (nothing superfluous) in the 1960s, but this was not a call for revolutionary culture. Rather, it was an attempt to remove from everyday Soviet life as many vestiges of Stalinist ornamentalist design.[19] The expression had a dual meaning. The first meaning referred to the slogans of constructivism of the 1920s. The second made a direct connection to Khrushchev's de-Stalinization campaign against the *kult lichnosti* (cult of personality). In a strict sense these new movements in design and architecture, being purely aesthetic, were not the same as the movements of the 1920s and 1930s. The aesthetic minimalism of these influences was evident in much of everyday life in the USSR during the 1960s; however, it was not accompanied by the political messages of the previous movement. The designers made no claims to efficiency, durability, or mass utility. Minimalism was readily apparent in the material culture of the space program. However, the messages that these objects carry were not different from their socialist-realist analogues, even in their portrayal of spaceflight. Unlike the modernist movements of the previous generations, these messages did not offer challenges to regime.

Soviet Collecting

By the mid-1960s monuments and museums dedicated to spaceflight were on the increase inside the Soviet Union, and a smaller form of spaceflight material culture was increasing in volume as well. The Twenty-first Congress of the Communist Party of the Soviet Union (CPSU) in 1959 gave official sanction to independent private collecting organizations for the first time in Soviet history. Although stamp collecting had been tolerated in the Soviet Union as unavoidable to generate income from foreign sales of stamps, post officials in the Soviet Union did little to encourage domestic collection before the 1960s.[20] Official sanction of collecting societies was, in part, a concession to rising economic expectations in the Soviet Union, especially among the youth. The generation born after World War II had no firsthand knowledge of the deprivations through which their parents had lived. Therefore they expected more than their parents did. Through official and semiofficial channels the state attempted to meet those expectations.

There were two primary areas of space-themed collecting in the Soviet Union during the early to mid-1960s—stamps and the small lapel pins, the znachki. The former were the products of tightly government-controlled production. The latter came from diverse organizations with little oversight on matters of design and message. Young people expected that these promises made to an older generation would be kept for them as well. The historian Joel Kotek has discussed the importance of directing the youth movement by Khrushchev-era leaders in the Soviet Union during the late 1950s and early 1960s.[21] He has outlined the need for Soviet attention in that matter, including the avid competition with the United States for the post–World War II youth movement. Rising expectations of postwar youth was therefore not unique to the Soviet Union.

Much of the Western-oriented material culture research and writing on collections (and collecting societies) carry the assumption that personal collecting is a consequence of a fully developed consumer society.[22] This assumption excludes noncapitalist societies from the discussion. The logic is that only consumer societies have adequate disposable income to support collecting nonessential goods.[23] This presumption neglects the obvious fact that all economies harbor markets, and governments have limited influence over supply and demand no matter what the ideology of the state. Although the existing literature overlooks collections in socialist societies, especially the Soviet Union, it is possible to draw appropriate conclusions from this literature on the history of collecting in the USSR.

Historians have traced the origin of modern political and social restrictions against collecting and consumerism to the emergence of medieval sumptuary laws, which restricted the material trappings of affluence to the rich and powerful.[24] Centuries ago in European societies, outward signs of affluence were held as an indication of elevated status in society. Socialist and Communist regimes shunned such displays to avoid the appearance of class distinction. When the sumptuary philosophy of Communism in the USSR conflicted with the nascent consumerism of the 1960s, the promise of domestic satisfaction overrode ideology. Although the post-Stalinist turn to consumerism was illusory, the illusion was as important as Marxist ideology was to the state and would be invoked even during declarations of approaching Communism. While Marxism decried consumerism as a philosophy, the impossibility of infiltrating private lives completely and obligatory tolerance of market forces dictated that at least a rudimentary consumerism existed in the Soviet Union. Throughout the history of the Soviet Union there have been periods when the government has publicly tolerated or even encouraged consumerism. The most notable period of toleration was during the period of the New Economic Policy (NEP), when the state sought to harness small-market forces to induce economic growth.[25] The film industry during the NEP was one example of a Soviet state-sanctioned field that developed as a direct consequence of these liberalized economic policies. The implementation of the five-year planning cycles in 1928 ended official tolerance of independent domestic trade.[26]

Even during years in which small profits were tolerated, domestic economic transactions bore the burden of state ideology. The favored transactions were those that increased foreign trade and generated revenues for the state. Few consumer goods were available for domestic consumption. Later, during the period of rapid industrialization followed by World War II, the public had little expectation of consumer goods. By the late 1950s, after Khrushchev's "secret speech," when Stalinist ideology had lost its motivating value, a transformation took place, granting consumer production a new, higher status.[27] This shift in culture is an indication of attempts to provoke consumerism as a driver of economic development. Whereas Soviet rhetoric had been against consumption, its political rhetoric acknowledged an economic multiplier effect that provided economic benefits to society. As a result, Soviet anticonsumerism only campaigned against personal consumption, not state consumption.

One of the consequences of de-Stalinization had been a loosening of the political economy to the point where even if the society had not achieved an "unlimited good" status, the limitations on expectations had relaxed. Although the concept of the unlimited good society might seem to be contrary to Khrushchev's 1961 proclamations of impending Communism at the fall party congress, it was not. The presumption of expanded wealth matches the expectation of having all needs satisfied for the population.[28] It was also consistent with the actions of the state at the time that, while unwilling to acknowledge ideological and economic flaws, it was willing to use tactics that roused consumerist tendencies, especially among the youth in the country. This vicarious support of individual consumerism provided a limited answer to the high expectations among the population for rewards after the sacrifices of World War II.

There are two schools of thought among those who acknowledge and study the growth of consumerism in the Soviet Union during the 1960s. The first is the unmet-demand school that asserts that the Soviet state sought to satisfy built-up consumer demand with illusions consisting of exhibitions of unavailable consumer goods and offers of malfunctioning products.[29] They base their arguments on the growth of exhibitions of consumer goods and the change in interior design during this period.[30] The abandonment of Stalinist aesthetics coincided with the increased appearance of consumer goods. The second argument is a Marxist interpretation that criticizes late Soviet materialism as a departure from Marxist principles.[31] The former approaches the history of Soviet consumerism through the material evidence of the time. The latter argument adheres closely to the philosophical underpinnings of the Soviet state and at times ignores the reality of commercial exchange.

Art historian Susan Reid, in her discussion of consumption in Soviet society, has analyzed Khrushchev's tentative steps to depoliticize consumerism in the Soviet Union. Focusing on the Nixon-Khrushchev "kitchen debate" in Moscow at the American National Exhibition in 1959, Reid traced how Soviet domestic expectations and international politics collided at the display of the General Electric kitchen. Although the "kitchen debate" was between the representatives of the two superpowers, it reflected the conflict that the Soviet Union was having within itself.[32] Even before the declarations of the Twenty-second Party Congress in 1961, Khrushchev had promised that the USSR would pass the West economically, but Soviet domestic economic reality challenged the credibility of that promise. The display of a state-of-the-art American kitchen made the inconsistency even more apparent, revealing that what was a commonplace expectation for American households was beyond fantasy for Soviet ones.[33] Even as the Americans displayed appliances, Khrushchev insisted that space hardware was a surrogate for Soviet domestic appliances, arguing that Soviet space accomplishments compensated for the lack of consumer goods. Soviet washing machines were display objects at the Exhibition of Economic Achievements, as American objects had been at the 1958 Moscow exhibition. Models of spacecraft displaced the appliances at the Exhibition of Economic Achievements (Vystavka Dostizhenii Narodonogo Khoziastvo, or VDNKh) within a few years.[34]

The two types of small collectible items available to the Soviet population in the 1960s, stamps and znachki, illustrated the subject matter of spaceflight. The former did so under the tight control of the Ministry of Post and Telegraph, with its well-established conservative limits on design. The latter did so with little centralized control over design or distribution. These differing situations offer an opportunity to compare the messages on human spaceflight that each presented to the Soviet public. Differences in origins could possibly generate differences in messages.

Stamps

Stamp collecting had a long history in Russia and the Soviet Union. In the nineteenth century, stamp collecting promoted tourism and geographical education among the collecting intelligentsia. In the twentieth century, a strict interpretation of Bolshevik dogma on the part of midlevel postal bureaucrats placed collecting stamps among other bourgeois activities that should never receive domestic encouragement if not prohibited outright.[35] In his history of the pre–World War II Soviet stamp bureaucracy, Jonathan Grant has pointed out that regulating stamp collecting reflected a deeper requirement for Soviet control of society. Grant argues that Soviet strict control of philately during the period between 1929 and 1939 indicates their larger desire to maintain state control of the larger society.[36]

Although postal bureaucrats did not choose to eliminate collectible stamps altogether, the stamps that resulted from this era were largely destined for consumption abroad. The method of restricting collecting to foreign markets was quite simple: stamp denominations determined the market. The more interesting and aesthetically appealing stamps were issued in high denominations. Higher-denomination stamps were airmail stamps that were destined for foreign destinations.[37] Even when they were more aesthetically pleasing, their messages were strict interpretations of Soviet propaganda. They became "visual statements of the values that the regime espoused and desired to foster among the population. In this light, these virtual representations revealed the regime's conception of how Soviet society should be structured."[38] After Stalin's death the organization and methods of Soviet philately did not change significantly. The stamps produced through the 1950s were full of propaganda and continued to recap Soviet industrial, technical, and military accomplishments. Instead of depending on symbols and quick slogans, these stamps took on more ponderous tones: "In the post-Stalin years, Party platforms continued to occupy a prominent place on Soviet stamps but were presented in a different manner. Gone were the brief heroic slogans of the Stalin era that urged economic mobilization and in their place were rather lengthy excerpts from Party congresses."[39] Despite their best intentions, the Ministry of Post and Telegraphs was not producing stamps whose messages drew attention either at home or abroad.[40]

The design for airmail stamps did not vary much from domestic ones, despite the fact that they were destined for consumption abroad. Soviet industrial achievements and social and political milestones were the themes that dominated airmail stamps. This trend continued through the 1930s, when in 1939 at the New York World's Fair the Soviet Pavilion featured stamp exhibits that recounted Soviet aviation endeavors.[41] Moreover, even in the 1960s stamps continued to include long quotations from party congresses. The resulting stamps left an unsatisfied appetite for aesthetically pleasing and inspirational stamps at the dawn of the space age. Furthermore, they were ineffective as instruments of propaganda, spreading the message of Soviet accomplishments to largely capitalist communities that might not learn of these accomplishments otherwise. Around the same time, domestic regulations loosened and stamp collecting became part of an officially sanctioned social organization in the late 1950s and early 1960s. The Twenty-first Party Congress was the first time that collecting organizations were officially recognized as independent social groups, receiving official party sanction. Thus the atmosphere for the domestic collection of stamps was set before the flight of Yuri Gagarin. The first *Vostok* flight provided new imagery for Soviet stamps.

In anticipation of Gagarin's flight on April 12, 1961, the Soviet Ministry of Communications prepared three stamps for distribution in the denominations of three, six, and ten kopeks.[42] The ministry released these stamps within days of the flight. Youth magazines promoted their sale and collection. For example, the magazine *Pioner* devoted the inside back cover of its August 1961 issue to these stamps.[43] Each of the three stamps was consistent with traditional Soviet approaches to the design and marketing of stamps. The three-kopek stamp in a domestic-mail denomination provided only the basic details of Gagarin's flight. The top of the stamp carries the title "Man from the Country of Soviets in Space." Around Gagarin's portrait are the words "First Cosmonaut in the World." On either side are pictures of a generic rocket and an illustration of the Hero of the Soviet Union medal that Khrushchev had awarded him immediately after his flight. The design of the stamp could easily be mistaken for the graphic equivalent of the front page of *Pravda*. There was no effort at aesthetic innovation.

The six-kopek stamp for international mail followed the post-Stalinist tradition of bearing long quotations from party officials. The two-part stamp illustrates *Vostok*, a ballistic missile, and a launch vehicle rocket flying over the Kremlin with a radar dish on the side on the top portion that carries the postage mark and the same title as the three-kopek stamp. The lower portion carries the quotation from Nikita Khrushchev's early statement about the Gagarin flight: "Our country was the first to lay down the path to socialism. He was the first to enter space, and opened the new era in the development of science."[44] The largest denomination stamp in the first Gagarin set was similar to the other two. The ten-kopek stamp, too, features an image of Gagarin's launch vehicle flying over the

Kremlin and the title "Person from the Land of the Soviets in Space." However, this foreign-envelope postage stamp did not have an additional section with a quotation from Khrushchev because a long quote in Russian was of little value to the international public.

These first stamps honoring Gagarin were created and distributed in a short time period. It is not surprising that the ministry made little effort to transform the aesthetic approach to stamp design at that time. There had been no shake-ups within the ministry to change its manner of doing business. It had merely adapted the message of human spaceflight to its format of miniaturizing *Pravda* or *Izvestiia* headlines into a stamp format. Subsequent stamps that honored the flights of *Vostok 2* through *Vostok 6* were similar in detail. For example, the set of stamps that came out in honor of the dual missions of *Vostok 3* and *Vostok 4*, which carried cosmonauts Adrian Nikolaev and Pavel Popovich, respectively in overlapping missions, are little different from the stamp issues the year before commemorating German Titov's first full day in space on board *Vostok 2* in August 1961.[45] In all three cases the stamp featured a portrait of the cosmonaut, his name, the date of the mission, and a stylized illustration of the spacecraft. In all three cases the stylization of the spacecraft did represent an aesthetic effort, but it did not represent an original design on the part of the stamp designer. The stamp merely copied the fictitious illustrations of *Vostok* that had appeared in the national press. As Soviet officials kept the engineering details about the spacecraft secret until 1967, there was no official representation of the craft, only artists' speculation about what a rocket ship might look like.[46]

The stamps from the *Voskhod* (Sunrise) program differed little from the *Vostok* stamps. The Ministry of Post issued a set of identical portrait stamps for each member of the 1964 *Voskhod* crew.[47] Once again, the stamps offered little more in innovation and information than had the pages of the official newspapers. These four-kopek, domestic-use stamps offered no new aesthetic enticements. Virtually identical for each of the three cosmonauts, their only appeal was from the information about this latest space mission that appeared to overtake the United States—namely, the fact that this mission involved, for the first time, a multipassenger crew.

Stamps that commemorated the flight of *Voskhod 2* in March 1965 showed a slightly improved stylization in design.[48] The six-kopek stamp, honoring the commander Pavel Belaev, adapted his official, spacesuit-

Figure 9.1. Aleksei Leonov *Voskhod-2* ten-kopek stamp. This stamp is dramatic, depicting a free-floating Leonov flying alongside his spacecraft with a motion-picture camera in hand while his commander, Beliaev, looks out through the open hatch in the capsule. *Source*: The Smithsonian Institution.

clad portrait into a slightly abstract version. The stamp that commemorated Aleksei Leonov's spacewalk used the official and inaccurate drawings of the spacecraft and airlock that he flew into space. Accuracy notwithstanding, the stamp is dramatic, depicting a free-floating Leonov flying alongside his spacecraft with a motion-picture camera in hand while his commander, Beliaev, looks out through the open hatch in the capsule (figure 9.1). This was the first attempt to depict action in a space stamp. It is significant that this stamp was the highest denomination stamp that the ministry issued during the 1960s. An airmail stand would more likely find its way to the world philately market via a letter or postcard sent from the USSR to the West.

If previous experience is a guide, the Ministry of Post and Telegraph had designed and printed stamps honoring the flight of *Soyuz 1* with Vladimir Komarov before his launch in April 1967. They had done so in the case of Gagarin's *Vostok* flight and released the stamps almost immediately after the flight.[49] If the ministry staff had followed the same procedures of preprinting stamps in advance, in 1967 they stopped the release of any Komarov/*Soyuz 1* stamps after the disastrous end of his flight on April 24, 1967. Nevertheless, the Soviets continued to create and issue space-themed stamps thereafter. By one account in 1975, there were more than a hundred space-themed Soviet stamps. These included stamps that noted Soviet robotic missions to Venus and the moon. The space theme came second in numbers only to World War II themes in Soviet philately.[50]

Soviet human spaceflight stamps continued to receive regular attention in collecting journals and in youth publications that encouraged collecting.[51] Every other issue of *Pioner* and *Semena* featured columns on collecting. Articles noted new stamp issues and made recommendations for completing collections. On occasion, an article would feature a particularly prodigious young collector as an inspiration to others.

Collecting Znachki

Znachki usually run about one to two centimeters in diameter. This is in contrast to the huge scale of space artifacts that include forty-meter-tall launch vehicles. The small size of znachki, as well as their accessibility, transformed the experience of space exploration into one that was palpable to all Soviet citizens through material consumerism. Comprehensive displays of large-scale spacecraft and engineering artifacts have remained rare even today in the former Soviet Union. During the 1960s the secrecy and ambiguity that surrounded the space program hardware made access to such objects nearly impossible for the average Soviet citizen. For those reasons space-themed znachki offered the most complete public image of the Soviet space program.

The small enameled pins that commemorate Soviet space missions are the material culture of the official historiography of the Soviet space program. They surpassed stamps in this distinction because of their unique conception, manufacture, and distribution that transformed an existing object of limited use into one that symbolized mass participation. The pins are distinct from other forms of collectibles because they have a briefer popular history. They offered the opportunity to unsophisticated individuals to collect items without training in other fields and with only the guidance of the popular press. These small pins illustrated a miniature, idealized chronology of the scientific and technical achievements of the space program. The illustrations presented officially sanctioned and occasionally inaccurate images of the spacecraft. They celebrated the firsts and anniversaries of Soviet accomplishments, and thus through repetition and sheer force of numbers, they reinforced the Soviet propaganda mantra of mastery of spaceflight. The pins were ubiquitous throughout the former Soviet Union and reiterated official Soviet accounts of space activities, embodying Soviet efforts to establish claims of superiority through persistence and repetition.

Yet znachki in general, no matter what the subject matter, were unique as consumer goods in the history of the Soviet Union. In contrast to the Soviet government's previous efforts to control and manipulate civil society, znachki emerged from a middle layer of Soviet managers, met an emerging demand for consumer goods, and created a minor source of fundraising. It just so happened that at the same time that this was occurring, the Soviet Union began to fly in space. This coincidence was quite fortuitous for the manufacturers of znachki. They quickly recognized the new and exciting market in space pins. Their popularity quickly transcended borders. During the 1970s American NASA engineers engaged in collecting Soviet space pins, and the jointly designed pins of the Apollo-Soyuz Test Project of 1975 marked the beginning of NASA-inspired pins. In the most general terms these were small, gold-colored pins, often painted with red enamel with a small bent pin on the back to attach for wearing on clothes or display on a wall. There is no exact English equivalent of the word *znachki*, which is the plural of the Russian word, *znachok*, meaning "badge" or "small mark." The word itself is the diminutive form of the word for a sign, mark, or symbol.[52] Anyone who has visited the Soviet Union, or knows someone who did, immediately recognized them as the most common collectable from that country.

There are tens of thousands of unique Soviet znachki. They symbolize significant Soviet events, ranging from Lenin's childhood to the victory in World War II and space exploration. Russian znachki experts and collectors, who call themselves falerists, trace the origins of the pins back to ancient Rome, when soldiers received small pins as acknowledgment of participation in battles. In Russia the creation of znachki dates back to 1722, when the first committee for the description and commission of medals was formed.[53] By the nineteenth century, Russian skilled workers wore the pins as recognition for labor in industrialization projects. The Bolsheviks continued the practice of presenting pins to workers who had participated in construction and industrialization projects and expanded the use to distribution among those who participated in political events, including workers' councils and party congresses. According to collecting experts, the first Soviet-made znachok was issued on May 1, 1918, to coincide with the first May Day (Labor Day) during which the Russian Communist Party (Bolshevik) was in power. The design was a rendition of the hammer and sickle, the symbol of the bond between peasant and worker, with a red-enameled background on a round metal pin. That was the first of many politically associated pins as party delegates took to wearing congress pins much in the way that war veterans wore military medals. Today collectors estimate there to be more than twenty-five hundred znachki dedicated to the memory of Lenin alone.[54] The total count of unique pins remains unknown, as there has been no central authority authorizing or minting the pins and no systematic cataloging of existing collections.

The origin of the popularity of space znachki predates the Soviet space program. Znachki began their expanded career in association with the youth movement of the Khrushchev era that coincided with the public space program. They have developed into the significant objects that they are because of social forces at work within the post-Stalinist Soviet Union and the official government's efforts to meet the demands of a population that had made sacrifices for generations and now held high expectations. The pins became a commodity in a society that was notorious for the absence of consumer goods. In addition, an examination of space-themed znachki offers a unique perspective on the transformation of 1960s culture of the Soviet Union. The space pins combine the optimism of modernism with the reassuring values of socialist realism. The design of many of the pins hearkens back to the constructivist style of the 1920s and 1930s, while the content bears the reassuring tale of incremental Soviet achievement that characterized socialist realism. Finally, the pins are the material remains of the Soviet effort to appeal to the youth market and control the emerging student movements of the early 1960s. Youth organizations introduced znachki to student groups in the late 1950s and encouraged their collection through their official organs.[55] Toward the end of the next decade their popularity was so great that they transcended the youth movement, becoming popular souvenirs among tourists.

During the 1960s space znachki collecting gained an enormous following and the space program was at its zenith in popularity and success. Many collections from that time exist today to demonstrate the peak of its popularity. There are two primary sources for the study of collections in this discussion: the Smithsonian Institution National Air and Space Museum's collection as well as virtual collection resources. The Smithsonian collection has grown over the years through private donations and diplomatic gifts and a much larger private collection that has developed through the advice and recommendations of the international znachki-collecting community. Of the several virtual collection resources, the first is the ever-present market of Russian space memorabilia that is for sale on eBay. These listings frequently offer images of individual znachki that might not be available in an organized collection elsewhere. They also provide insight into the collecting ideals and strategies of Soviet youth during the 1960s, as many of the sellers claim to have amassed their collections in their youth, usually as Pioneers. In addition to the transient exhibitions on eBay, there are a handful of more permanent, and often more comprehensive, Web sites that attempt to catalog znachki according to the preferences of the owners.

Soviet popular journalism dominates the written documentation on the history of znachki. Among the magazines that focused on znachki collecting are the popular collecting journals that announced the release of new designs and encouraged znachki collecting. For the most part these were philatelic and numismatic journals that sought to place znachki within the context of their own disciplines. In doing so, they advocated collecting strategies that paralleled stamp collecting, placing greater emphasis on the breadth of collections than on aesthetics or completeness. The official journals of the Pioneer organization, *Pioner* and *Semena* (Seed), also encouraged their readers to complete their collections, not surprisingly, as editors of collecting journals also wrote the collecting columns for those youth magazines.[56] Popular science journals, such as *Zemliia i vselennaia*, announced newly available pins according to scientific specialization as well.[57] In recent years experts have published monographs on specific collecting areas, including space, which paid closer attention to subject-matter grouping, completeness of cataloging, and design sophistication.[58]

Throughout World War II znachki design and distribution were modest and consistent with the earliest Soviet pins, usually a single-color enamel (most often red) on metal with only the slightest modification to denote an individual event or accomplishment. Until the late 1950s the use of the pins was limited to official events, thus there was no need to encourage people to wear them as an end in itself. It was during the post-Stalinist period that the emphasis on the use of znachki shifted from rewarding work done to acting as souvenirs of national celebrations and mass participation. Innovation in design, materials, and color expanded and increased the diversity of the pins. These changes resulted from related relaxation in Soviet society. Nevertheless, even during this period, distribution and production were tightly controlled to limit the possibility that independent markets might emerge and znachki exchange become unregulated. It was not until the summer of 1957, during the Sixth World Festival of Youth and Students in Moscow, that collecting znachki as souvenirs became an acceptable and evidently an encouraged hobby.

Despite an occasional resemblance to other collectibles, znachki are unique due to their ubiquity. Since 1957, they have been subject to neither officially controlled production nor distribution. Moreover, it is not the rarity of an individual pin but its ubiquity that enhances its value to collectors and historians. Although this might seem counterintuitive, znachki derive value through commonality. A single pin design owned by many carries its message further than a rare pin owned by a few.

For space historians 1957 was a pivotal year because of the launch of *Sputnik*. This year is also significant for falerists for entirely different reasons. The significance for znachki has little to do with successful testing of ballistic missiles and launching satellites into space. That was the year in which collecting znachki began in earnest. During the sixth and largest biennial festival of the International Union of Students (held in Moscow), twenty thousand foreign students—and at least ten thousand Russian students—congregated in the capital. The festival's motto was "For Peace and Friendship," which was a variant of the two elements of all previous and subsequent mottos. However, the primary mission of this festival was to demonstrate Soviet leadership among the growing postwar youth movements. From a political perspective the festival was a success.[59] From the perspective of the youth participants, long-term success could be measured by long-lasting relationships among them. An immediate measure of the outcome was the proliferation of the material remnants of the event. By some estimates there were more than seven hundred distinct types (largely representing Soviet cities) of znachki at the festival, issued in runs that numbered into the thousands. The assembly of tens of thousands of young people in Moscow began a flurry of trading and exchange of znachki among youth.[60] The official znachok of the festival was notable for its six-color rendition of the official flower symbol of the festival. The use of multiple lacquer colors was an obvious departure from previous generations of red pins that celebrated the Bolshevik Revolution. A transition in themes soon followed on the heels of the transition in color.

The first indication that space themes would take a role in the transformation of collecting znachki into a long-term trend occurred a few years after the launch of *Sputnik* in October 1957. Although the znachki exchange among young people at the youth congress in 1957 had caught on, the attempts to recreate this success were cautious. The first space exhibition in the Soviet Union was small, featuring stamps and znachki; it opened at the Moscow Planetarium three years after the launch of *Sputnik*.[61] The exhibit included space-related stamps, postcards, znachki, and commemorative coins. All of the objects portrayed highly stylized representations of the spacecraft that executed the much-celebrated space firsts of the Soviet Union. None revealed technically accurate details of the space hardware, nor were they meant to do so. These pins were decorative and collectible. The exhibit was the brainchild of Moscow Planetarium director V. K. Litskii, who encouraged established collectors, at the time primarily adults, to expand their traditional philatelic and numismatic collections to include space subjects. The exhibit also captured the attention of young people, who had been born in a time when collecting did not meet official approval, and thus paved the way for the next generation of officially sanctioned collectors. The placement of znachki alongside stamps and coins was novel and foretold the dominant role that the pins would play in illustrating the Soviet space program.

Unlike previous znachki, space znachki were never exclusively conceived as a reward for affiliation with a specific project. What makes them most interesting is that the decentralized fabrication of the pins created previously unexplored uses and methods of dissemination. Even though the established mints at Leningrad and Moscow that had long produced and distributed official znachki and aerospace program offices issued their own series of pins, other nonaerospace organizations took the liberty of issuing space-related pins for general consumption. Those pins created for public consumption quickly outnumbered those that had strict institutional uses, as they filled the consumer demands for space-related objects. The range in mission among issuing organizations is also an indicator of how the pins made their way among collectors. By using scrap materials and producing the pins in their own factories, manufacturers that had no relationship to the space program distributed znachki directly to the public at little cost to their official activities.

Nonaerospace organizations timed their issues to coincide with program milestones to capitalize on public attention, issuing pins as soon as missions were announced publicly, albeit after the missions occurred.[62] By echoing the official announcements of missions, even these independent distributors reinforced the official historiography of the space program. Like the official infrastructure, they ignored failures and enthusiastically celebrated heroes. Manufacturers chose sequences of successful projects to form a set of collectible pins and thus define the scope of a successful program. For example, *Vostok* pin sets featured the six spacecraft or cosmonauts and were distinct from a *Voskhod* set in either design or theme. Each set would have a distinct style, separating it visually from another program often sold on a presentation card or box.

When examining the thousands of space znachki that exist, it is useful to organize collections according to materials, manufacturer, purpose of issue, and subject matter. Each approach provides insight into how the pin was used, collected, and by whom. The combination of perspectives helps to organize these objects that are notorious for their ad hoc creation. There were three types of znachki as defined by the purpose of their issue: memorial, jubilee, and souvenir.[63] Memorial znachki honored persons or events (including party congresses, seminars, and scholarly readings), marked anniversaries, or commemorated deaths. The jubilee znachki honored the anniversaries of births and events, usually at ten-year intervals. Souvenir pins came from municipal organizations, museums, sports palaces, and metros to generate revenue and publicity for those places. The more closely that a znachok was issued to the occurrence of a given event, the more likely that the pin was issued individually. Sets of pins, sold in a box or attached to a velour card, usually appeared on the market after an anniversary or after a given program concluded.

Manufacture of znachki had always been decentralized, relying on the issuing organization to commission particular pins on its own instead of going through a central authority. This was the major difference between stamps and znachki. The Ministry of Post and Telegraph controlled both the design and distribution of stamps. There was no single central authority that presided over the many organizations that made znachki. When the space program gained popularity, these already decentralized manufacturers greatly expanded their operations to capture their share of the emerging market. The second edition of the first catalog of space znachki published a list of twenty-three known space znachki manufacturers that included traditional government pin makers such as the Moscow and Leningrad Mints and surprising enterprises such as the All-Russian Choral Society.[64] Each manufacturer displayed its own identifying mark on the back of the pin. Given the range of reporting structures that these twenty-three organizations represented, it was unlikely that they received their content information or design directives from a single source or that any one single body or individual reviewed or approved the designs. They were, in fact, responding to internal values and cultures that had formed throughout the history of the Soviet Union. In the absence of a central power that stamps had had before World War II, the common message of the znachki was an indication of the common values of disparate middle managers at various enterprises throughout the USSR.

The institution of origin is a useful tool with which to categorize znachki. Previously, when enterprises and organizations in the space-flight industry awarded znachki to distinguished individuals for service and achievement, the pins had no marks indicating their origins.[65] There had been no need to do so, because the recipient would likely hold onto this award or remember the circumstances of the award. Souvenirs and collectible pins, however, had a price stamped on the back of the pin— usually a number followed by the letter "K" next to the manufacturer's mark. This indicated the initial sale price and the fact that their distributors anticipated earning money on their sale.[66] Znachki that were issued for more traditional purposes, to honor participation in a project, were more tightly controlled. Because they were not immediately marketed, they did not have the price marking. These issuing organizations ranged from committees within the Academy of Sciences to museums and museum associations and professional societies. With time, both types have found their way to the collectors' market. The awarding organization usually issued a certificate with the pin and kept track of the recipients.[67]

The first space znachki were memorial-type pins that the Shcherbinsk Smelting Factory produced.[68] The initial pins reflected the limited information available on the satellites, but as news services published illustrations of the first sputniks, the earliest znachki makers adapted their designs to incorporate miniature images of the satellites.[69] These pins depicted the first three sputniks accurately. This was in sharp contrast to later depictions of Gagarin's *Vostok* craft that received no accurate public depiction until 1967. However, as early as 1958, eager visitors could see models of these spacecraft on display at the Brussels World's Fair; the Moscow Exhibition of Economic Achievements after in 1958 and the Soviet National Exhibition in New York in 1959.[70] Rectangular or circular shaped, and straightforward in design and message, these pins matched the somewhat reserved claims that the Soviet press made about the sputniks in the press. They marked Soviet mastery of science and technology but made limited claims on Soviet world leadership beyond spaceflight. These claims did not appear until there was a human champion to make them.

Yuri Gagarin's flight around the world in the *Vostok* spacecraft on April 12, 1961, led to spontaneous celebrations in Moscow the next day that matched the celebrations of victory in World War II.[71] Moreover, although party officials had authorized the printing of stamps before his mission, their release was contingent on the success of the mission.[72] Although the Ministry of Communications could control the dissemination of stamps, they had no statutory or institutional authority to impose an embargo on znachki. The pins did not fall under strict regulations that governed the production of stamps and coins that had immediate monetary and trade value. Gagarin's flight inspired the first spontaneously produced znachki. During the festivities in Moscow, participants appeared with small (70-by-55-millimeter or 70-by-45-millimeter) paper portraits of Yuri Gagarin on their chests, which were reproduced newspaper photographs of the cosmonaut.[73] Within days, enterprising producers refined the idea, placing cellophane over a smaller picture (18 millimeters in diameter) of Gagarin (figure 9.2). These photographs were likely taken from newspaper reports of his flight, as there were no prelaunch photographs released.

Three unofficial pins preceded the Shcherbinsk Factory's production of a steel and enamel pin that portrayed Gagarin.[74] Subsequent Gagarin pins from other manufacturers added the detail about his flight as it was released to the public, including approximate launch and landing sites. However, the pin illustrations of the launch vehicle and spacecraft were highly stylized and did not resemble the real objects. Unlike the previous attempts to conceal the design of the *Vostok* spacecraft, in this case the representation was created to reflect the popular conception of a rocket ship, neglecting the spherical simplicity of the *Vostok* craft.[75] Nevertheless, this is consistent with all other illustrations of Gagarin's flight in the popular media, including stamps, posters, and cartoons. The earliest pins had to simplify the illustration of his flight in response to the tech-

Figure 9.2. The first Gagarin znachok. Gagarin's flight inspired the first spontaneously produced znachki. Enterprising producers refined the idea, placing cellophane over a smaller picture of Gagarin. *Source*: The Smithsonian Institution.

nology of making znachki. The elaborate lines of engraving and large pieces of text did not translate into inexpensive metal and enamel. The images became increasingly abstract.

While Gagarin's flight placed greatest emphasis on the accomplishment of spaceflight, and caught officials unprepared for the popularity of the pins more numerous, official znachki appeared immediately after the flight of *Vostok 2*. On August 6, 1961, German Titov became the first human to orbit Earth for more than a day. The design and complexity of the Titov pins had more detail than did the Gagarin pins. The pins immediately sought to identify the complexity of Titov's flight, illustrating multiple orbits around the globe. It was impractical to illustrate all seventeen orbits that Titov made around Earth. Four distinct lines around a representation of a globe on one pin made the point that he had made multiple orbits.

The efforts to provide informative yet aesthetically appealing pins continued through the Vostok and Voskhod programs. The next four Vostok flights were paired flights that implied a maneuvering capability that the Soviets had yet to demonstrate. Translating the dual flights of

Vostok 3–4 and *Vostok 5–6* into pins resulted in similar designs. The Soviet news agency TASS had emphasized the near simultaneous timing of the flights to the point of insinuating active rendezvous—a technical feat of which the Soviets were not capable. The pins that represented those flights echoed this representation. One of the early pins of the flights of Nikolaev and Popovich on board *Vostok 3* and *Vostok 4* show two stylized rocket ships emerging from the tip of the sickle suspended above Earth. The flights of Bykovskii and Tereshkova (*Vostok 5* and *Vostok 6*, respectively) received similar treatment with pins showing two rocket ships orbiting Earth and two ships flying away from Earth in similar trajectories. The Leningrad Mint produced each of these two pins under an official commission.[76]

In the year after the last of the *Vostok* flights, Soviet space designer and manager Sergei Korolev had demanded a redesign of the interior of the spacecraft to accommodate multiple cosmonauts. Soviet engineers built the *Voskhod* spacecraft from the skeleton of the *Vostok* spacecraft, but announced it to be an entirely different species. The plan had been to use the *Voskhod* as a challenge to the Americans' maneuverable *Gemini* spacecraft, but the *Voskhod* was little more than a gutted *Vostok* and could not maneuver in space. There were only two *Voskhod* missions, *Voskhod* and *Voskhod 2*, which flew in October 1964 and March 1965, respectively.[77] One of the first *Voskhod* pins illustrated the literal meaning of the spacecraft name, using the imagery of a sunrise underneath a soaring spacecraft. Other pins emphasized the multiple crew of this first *Voskhod* with images of three helmeted cosmonauts along with the rocket ship, such as one from the Mytishchinsk Experimental and Souvenir Factory. In fact, the three cosmonauts did not wear helmets or spacesuits during the *Voskhod* mission as cramped room in the spacecraft did not allow them to do so.

The last flight of the *Voskhod* spacecraft provided an opportunity for greater artistic representation of the mission because one of the crewmembers, Aleksei Leonov, was himself an artist and drew his impressions of his mission while in orbit. Moreover, his mission reminded the public of ancient dreams of spaceflight. Leonov became the first person to venture outside of a spacecraft and take a walk in space floating alongside his spacecraft. The first *znachki* to represent Leonov's mission used more abstract images to illustrate the flight than had previous ones. Most depictions focused on the distinguishing aspect of the flight, Leonov's walk in space. In contrast to the grainy and unfocused photographs of Leonov's spacewalk, the pins illustrated a crisp image of a human flying through space, untethered and symmetrical (figure 9.3).

Human spaceflight was not the only new thing in the Soviet Union in the early 1960s. Stalin's death and Khrushchev's capitalization on de-Stalinization unleashed other forces within society. Architects and designers found fresh independence with which they could reassert modernism that had been popular in the 1920s and 1930s. Pent-up consumer demand and rising independence of Soviet youth combined to create a palatable dissatisfaction with the current economic situation. This dissatisfaction prompted the government to pay lip service to satisfying the demand for consumer goods. Individual factories and enterprises joined to produce small consumer goods that might satisfy the market. The coincidence of human spaceflight and changes in the material culture of the Soviet Union offered many opportunities for the two to combine.

Stamps and znachki offer the opportunity for comparison of two styles of celebrating national accomplishments. Both embraced the spaceflight subject matter, and each responded to the increased demand for collectibles in the Soviet Union. The Ministry of Post and Telegraph had joined with the rest of the country to relax scrutiny on domestic collecting. Spaceflight prompted manufacturers to expand their production of znachki, which had only recently established them in a souvenir role. There were also differences between the two. Although there were more than a hundred space stamps, there were thousands of individual space znachki, which came from autonomous producers who demonstrated no hesitation about flooding the market. The Ministry of Post, with no competitors in the market, had no reason to attempt innovative designs but conceded public interest through their attention to the new space age subject matter.

The existence and widespread numbers of pins were an indication that the collecting and possession of material goods not only became acceptable in the 1960s Soviet Union; it was also encouraged through official channels. The government encouraged the creation of znachki as a currency for international youth exchanges. Public demand created a domestic market that outstripped official plans. The pin designs hearkened back to a more optimistic time when constructivism and modernism reigned supreme in Soviet art and architecture. Znachki reflected

Figure 9.3. The first znachki to represent Leonov's mission used more abstract images to illustrate the flight than had previous ones. The pins illustrated a crisp image of a human flying through space, untethered and symmetrical. *Source*: The Smithsonian Institution.

this style. In that previous era artists had offered alternative political approaches to those that the Bolshevik politicians had offered. Under Khrushchev, the renewed modernism had no independent implications and reinforced the state's message.

In the absence of systematic exhibits to promote the space program, znachki took on the role of telling the tale of Soviet spaceflight. Children and students learned the lessons of Soviet spaceflight through Pioneer and youth organizations that encouraged collecting through routine articles and columns that announced new issues. Znachki are also significant because they represent a significant departure from previous public culture movements. They shifted public commemoration of national accomplishments from solely mass events to a personal scale. Their manufacture was decentralized with no authority dictating the content and message on all pins. However, as there remained only a single source of information on the space program, pin makers shared the same content as other memorabilia makers. The sole opportunity for innovation was through design. That was the basis of distinction among znachki manufacturers. Finally, the pins are significant for their endurance. Large collections remain intact and, much like modern American baseball cards, they have taken on a following of their own beyond the subject that they illustrated.

10

Cold War Theaters

Cosmonaut Titov at the Berlin Wall

Heather L. Gumbert

On August 6, 1961, the Soviet cosmonaut German Titov became only the second person to orbit Earth. With this accomplishment Titov became a global figure in the race to explore the "final frontier." Less than a month after his spaceflight, Titov visited a frontier of a different kind: the newly built Berlin Wall, on the front line of the Cold War. On an official state visit to the German Democratic Republic (GDR), he met with state officials, received the Karl Marx Medal, appeared at rallies in Berlin, Leipzig, and Magdeburg, and met with East German citizens. Standing at the wall, Titov praised state authorities on their efforts to strengthen socialism. The GDR state media, including the print press, radio, and television, as well as media organizations from around the world, clamored to report on this historic figure.

Titov's appearance in the GDR would have been notable enough under normal circumstances, but it took on a whole new dimension and meaning because it took place in September 1961, just three weeks after the construction of the Berlin Wall. The wall closed the border between East and West Germany, restricting travel to and, to some extent, communication with the West. With the construction of the Berlin Wall, East

Germans' worlds had, for all practical purposes, just gotten smaller: even if they had never been to places like Baden or Bavaria, or writ large Paris, London, or New York, it was unlikely that they now could go. Yet Titov's visit created a new narrative space that allowed East Germans to understand themselves not as hemmed in or excluded, but rather as part of a larger socialist project, one that had made human space travel possible. Why focus on the lost opportunity of "one Germany"—a reunified German state in Central Europe—when the achievements of the community of socialist states pointed toward a brighter future? Titov, a socialist hero par excellence, embodied the superiority of the Soviet Union over the West. And he arrived just as GDR authorities had stepped up their campaign to cultivate a new political consciousness in East Germans—a campaign that situated the GDR firmly in the socialist camp, allied with other socialist bloc countries against the corruption of the West.

GDR media reports on television and in the print press wasted no time locating Titov in the wider vision of Western corruption and socialist achievement. The media drew close connections between Titov and his trip to space on the one hand and the decision to cut off the border in Berlin on the other. Titov was a soldier and comrade in the battle against the West. His trip to space represented an important blow against the West, just as the border closure had been and would continue to be a kind of victory over the expansionist ambitions of the West. Indeed, in this narrative Titov became a symbol of the world saved by the construction of the wall. This is important because what we understand as the "Cold War" was not just a series of incidents and events; rather, it was also comprised by the media narratives created and disseminated about those events.

The goal of this chapter is not to illuminate the Soviet space program, its goals, or its scientific merits per se, but rather to discuss the way in which this revolutionary step into space opened up a whole new world to Soviet citizens as well as to people living in the GDR, at a time when the state faced a potentially explosive crisis of legitimacy. Titov's appearance in the GDR allowed the government to redefine the geopolitical place of East Germans in the Cold War. This was different from their response to the domestic crises of the 1950s—the workers' uprising of 1953, the challenge of de-Stalinization in 1956, and even the early period of the Second Berlin Crisis after 1958. At those moments the regime sought to better educate East Germans about the principles of socialism, training them to be better, more ideologically committed socialists. By 1961, though, the government was using increasingly sophisticated means to deal with domestic crisis. Scholars often focus on the importance of Soviet strength—military strength—in shoring up the legitimacy of Eastern European regimes, especially in the 1950s and 1960s. Yet here is an example where military strength was perhaps not as important as cultural strength. In 1961 the Soviets sent men into space and accomplished that which no one else had yet achieved. For the governing Socialist Unity Party (Sozialistische Einheitspartei Deutschland, or SED), this could not have come at a better time. Although the leader of the SED, Walter Ulbricht, pressed Khrushchev to close the border between the German states, the party had also intensified their ongoing campaign to win ideological adherence to the program of socialism. They prepared to weather this crisis just as they had done over the course of the 1950s: meeting economic and geopolitical crises with political weapons.

Yet this time Titov was the figure at the center of a confluence of events that served to defuse the potentially explosive political upheaval caused by the border closure of August 13; that offered the state a measure of legitimacy that played a part in stabilizing the domestic situation. Titov's visit was a media spectacle that occurred at a moment when one vision of East German socialism began to give way to another, and it became defined in part by the figure of Titov. After the border closure, a political campaign under way for several years aimed at transforming the values and expectations of Germans living in the GDR began to give way to a more conservative vision of socialism. This new socialism was inward-looking, insular, and nationalist and did not require ideological transformation or idealistic fervor. No longer did the government have to fear the economic or ideological repercussions of the relative permeability of the sector border in Berlin, because the possibility of choosing a life in the West had just become more difficult. If during the preceding decade the problem of transforming these Germans into Communists had proven too difficult, it now became enough simply to turn them into *East Germans*.

The political event that was Titov's visit contributed to this new vision in two ways. First, it was a potent visual demonstration of the alliance between the East German state with what could be understood to be the most powerful nation in the world. It shifted the focus away from the GDR's geopolitical relationship with West Germany (that had defined geopolitical rhetoric in the 1950s) and toward their alliance with the socialist world. Second, it allowed East German citizens and government officials to meet one another on neutral ground at the rallies for Titov, giving the regime an opportunity to "stage" a significant visual demonstration of solidarity between the state and the people, even if East Germans were not there for the reasons the state might have hoped.[1]

Crisis Management in the GDR in the 1950s

The foundation of the German Democratic Republic in 1949 was only the first step in the creation of a German socialist state. Throughout the 1950s the authorities faced several challenges to their legitimacy, both from within the party and without. A Stalinist-style party, Ulbricht's SED brooked little internal opposition and had in the late 1940s and early 1950s imprisoned and otherwise disciplined dissenters within the party. At the same time, unrest among the wider population catalyzed primarily around economic problems. During the 1950s authorities increasingly dealt with intractable economic problems through political means: in particular, by campaigning to transform the consciousness of East Germans—turn them into card-carrying socialists who better understood economic issues and no longer adhered to "bourgeois" economic expectations. After a period of relative calm in the mid-1950s, this pattern became clear by the late 1950s, when the SED once again faced economic crises. During the period of the Second Berlin Crisis (1958–62), the SED ramped up the campaign to develop ideological clarity among the people.[2] Titov's visit to the GDR coincided with and contributed to this renewed campaign. Increasingly, though, ideological clarity focused less on understanding of and belief in the tenets of socialism and more on *Parteilichkeit* (partisanship)—adherence to and loyalty for the GDR and the Eastern bloc.

In 1953 problems of economic mismanagement came home to roost in the GDR's first major crisis—and only mass uprising against the East German state. A year earlier the SED had decided that enough of a socialist consciousness had developed among the working class that it was time to systematically develop the foundations of socialism.[3] The government's plan of action included the transition from private to public ownership of property and labor. By year's end the government hoped to nationalize 81 percent of all enterprises in the GDR (to become People's Own Enterprises and cooperatives) and collectivize the land. This was an expensive endeavor, which the state sought to pay for through a variety of economic measures from the judicious to the punitive. The SED raised income taxes, restricted access to health and social insurance from the self-employed, and denied ration cards to East Germans who were self-employed, working in freelance occupations in East Germany, or holding jobs in West Berlin. Prices rose on foodstuffs and other common goods, such as textiles. The government increased taxation of spirits.[4] It expropriated private owners of real estate and commercial interests, such as hotels, pensions, and small businesses, first charging them with crimes like "illegal income" and political unreliability before taking over their property. Legislation for the protection of "socialist" property set off an "avalanche of trials" between October 1952 and March 1953, when more than ten thousand individuals were charged and imprisoned for stealing or diverting supplies from the state economy. The state charged and imprisoned East Germans for crimes as minor as "privatizing" *Pfannkuchen* (pancakes) or stealing 750 grams of sauerkraut.[5] The state also sought to centralize control over decision making across the republic by dissolving the former German states in favor of fifteen new administrative districts. It also targeted potential centers of oppositional authority, most notably the churches, which still appealed to more than 90 percent of the East German population.[6]

Such measures transformed the relationship of East Germans to the state and shook the foundations of their daily lives. When these measures failed to raise the requisite funds for the transition to socialism, the government resorted to increasing production quotas in certain industries by 10 percent. These measures caused concern among Soviet authorities, who worried about the internal stability of the republic, particularly when in March 1953 the numbers of people fleeing for the West reached fifty-eight thousand, its highest point yet.[7] After the new production quotas came into force in June 1953, Soviet authorities' fears seemed to be realized when rising unrest gave way to mass demonstrations.[8] Workers paraded down Stalinallee in East Berlin demanding reductions in the production quotas, a demonstration that grew from three hundred to more than ten thousand people over the course of the day.[9] The following day an estimated three hundred thousand to four hundred thousand people—younger workers, small farmers, and the rank-and-file of the SED—participated in strikes in 270 towns across the GDR.[10] The strikes brought Berlin to a standstill.[11] Although the East German government managed to suppress the demonstrations, the uprising set the SED on a "new course" that rolled back some aspects of the drive for Stalinization, especially the economic reforms that had sparked the riots.

By 1955 the economic basis and social makeup of the GDR had been transformed. The porous border in Berlin allowed many Germans living in the East to leave the republic at will.[12] This Cold War permeability had effected a transformation of the social order. With the departure of so many, especially young, educated males—many of whom were professionals (technicians, engineers, doctors, dentists, lawyers, judges, university teachers, and the like)—it was now workers (agricultural but primarily industrial workers) that comprised the bulk of the population.[13] There were still shortages of necessary goods, and foodstuffs such as meat, sugar, eggs, and oils (including butter) were subject to rationing until 1958.[14] But production from the collective farms showed improvement, and the SED increasingly allowed a consumer-oriented economy to emerge.[15] Despite this, Ulbricht did not enjoy the overwhelming support of his "natural" constituency and still had to work through the economic problems associated with trying to raise East Germans' standards of living.

In 1956 Khrushchev's "secret speech" upset this delicate balance. Ulbricht's government had built a Stalinist-style regime, and Khrushchev's decision to denounce Stalin threw the government and the party into disarray. The possibility of greater openness and the potential for the development of a more organic, German-centered socialism empowered opponents of Ulbricht from within the party. There was a certain "thaw" in domestic politics, during which the government released and, in some cases, rehabilitated dissenters who had been imprisoned in the early 1950s. But Ulbricht's SED was suspicious of the drive to liberalize socialist politics unleashed by Khrushchev, a sentiment that was only reinforced by the Hungarian uprising in November 1956. Thereafter, the fear of the pitfalls of national routes to socialism, identified by the SED as "Titoist revisionism," pervaded politics in the GDR and allowed a "frost" to reemerge. Ulbricht reasserted his authority and, finding himself on stronger ground, targeted internal party opposition that had sought greater de-Stalinization, democratic reforms, and the emergence of a more humane socialism.[16] In this context the SED sought to shore up ideological commitment through a new campaign of ideological transformation, once again meeting economic and geopolitical challenges with political solutions.

During the SED's Thirtieth Party Conference in January and February 1957—the first meeting of the SED since the cessation of protests in Hungary—the party announced the change of course. The SED declared that the GDR belonged to the "socialist camp," rejected further social or political liberalization, and called for greater partisanship among party members.[17] This ideological hardening found expression in an agitation campaign introduced over the course of 1957. The campaign had two goals: to demonstrate the superiority of socialism over the West, and to transform East Germans into socialist citizens by cultivating a "socialist consciousness." The SED hoped to accomplish this through stepped-up agitation against "Western imperialism," renewed emphasis on the lessons of Marxism-Leninism, and the creation of a new, socialist, German culture. Central Committee members denounced manifestations of (Western) "decadence" in East German art and called on East German artists to create a "socialist German culture" following the principles of "socialist realism." At the Bitterfeld Conference of 1959 the SED challenged artists and workers to "overcome the gulf between art and life," by rejecting visual abstraction and bringing art closer to the people, thereby encouraging the transition to socialism.[18]

The campaign to transform East Germans into socialist citizens reached its zenith at the Fifth Party Congress in July 1958. The "construction of socialism" was the main focus of the conference. The SED claimed to view this as primarily an economic problem—transform the economic foundation of society and social transformation will follow—and called for East German production to "overtake" and "outstrip" the West German economy by the early 1960s.[19] But the impatient party also concluded that "the socialist 'education' of the people [was] the key to solving the upcoming economic and political tasks."[20] They called for the unification of entertainment and culture, which should be "put into service for the development of socialist consciousness."[21] Ulbricht promulgated his Ten Commandments, the basis of a new "socialist morality." These commandments included, among others:

1. You always must campaign for the international solidarity of the working class and all working people (*Werktätigen*), as well as for the steadfast connection of all socialist countries.

2. You must love your fatherland and always be ready, to stand up with whole strength and ability for the defense of the workers' and peasants power. . . .

6. You should protect and enhance the People's property.

7. You should always aspire to improve your performance, be economic, and reinforce the socialist work ethic. . . .

9. You should live cleanly and decently, and respect your family.[22]

By 1959 the strategy of raising the living standard alongside a campaign of training people to become socialists appeared to be working: the numbers of people fleeing the GDR had dropped to its lowest point (143,917) since 1949.[23] But the campaign to increase ideological commitment among the people faced renewed challenges, including increasing economic instability that unleashed a new wave of people leaving the GDR, compounded by uncertainty surrounding the future of Berlin. Between 1958 and 1961 there were renewed efforts to conclude the Berlin issue. Khrushchev threatened to sign a separate peace treaty with East Germany, giving the SED control of the Allied transports routes to West Berlin, while John F. Kennedy sought to retain Allied rights and access to West Berlin.

For his part Ulbricht increasingly applied as much pressure as possible on Khrushchev to permit some kind of border closure. The unstable demographic situation helped him make an effective case for closing the border. By early July 1961 the Soviet ambassador to the GDR, Mikhail Pervukhin, estimated that perhaps two hundred fifty thousand people were crossing back and forth across the border each day. That month the SED implemented stricter policies dealing with border crossing, such as registering *Grenzgänger* (border-crossers), demanding Western currency for rent payments, and restricting the purchase of such desirable goods as cars, apartments, and television sets to East Germans who actually lived in the GDR.[24] The numbers of border-crossers who left the GDR jumped sixfold by the end of July.[25] Whatever the reason behind individuals' decisions to cross the German border—including traveling to their places of work or residence, visiting friends or family, going shopping and on other outings, or even leaving for the West (or returning to the East)—media narratives had begun to define the problem using the language of *Abwerbung* (enticement), *Menschenhandel* (people-smuggling), and *Kopfjäger* (headhunters). Such language cast the problem as a criminal matter of the seduction and entrapment of otherwise loyal citizens of the GDR, rather than reporting it as a domestic issue of people choosing to leave the republic.[26] In this charged context Khrushchev finally assented, allowing Ulbricht to proceed with plans to blockade the border.

On August 13, 1961, Germans in East and West awoke to the news that the GDR authorities had closed most of the Berlin border to through traffic. Throughout the night East German soldiers had erected temporary barriers of barbed wire, which were soon to be replaced with less-permeable concrete pylons and later a full-fledged wall. The official decision declared: "For the prevention of enemy activities of the revanchist and militarist forces of West Germany and West Berlin, a control will be introduced on the borders of the GDR including the border to West sectors of greater Berlin, as is common on the borders of any sovereign state."[27] GDR authorities claimed a sovereign right to close the border. Willy Brandt, the mayor of West Berlin, referred to the border closure instead as a "concentration camp" built by a "clique that calls itself a government."[28] The GDR's preeminent television propagandist, Karl Eduard von Schnitzler, described the border blockade as an "antifascist protection barrier."[29]

In the GDR television coverage of the events on August 13 expressed no criticism of the border closure, but rather conveyed the impression of normality and stability in the GDR. The nightly news anchor read the authorities' resolution to close the border, reporting the events of the day as something that had been looming on the horizon since the foundation of the republic. Images supported the announcer's assertion that it was "an entirely normal day" in East Berlin. Across the border, however, there was an atmosphere of crisis: GDR television anchor Klaus Feldmann claimed Chancellor Konrad Adenauer had convened a conference of high-level ministers "in a feverish hurry" in response to the blockade. But the reaction of other Western leaders did not match the anxiety of the West Germans. The East German newscaster was quick to point out that neither Kennedy nor Charles de Gaulle had responded to the "crisis," or even broken off their weekend vacation plans.[30] Thus the initial narrative of the border closure in the state-run media tried to dispel any notion of a crisis, casting it as a defensive measure that would strengthen the GDR state and its citizenry and weaken the power of the Federal Republic and West Berlin.[31]

The period of the border closure marked the beginning of a battle for hearts and minds and against dissent in the republic.[32] Though rooted in the longer-standing campaign to build socialists, this renewed effort sought to define the boundaries between East and West more aggressively. For example, it depicted the Soviet Union as a modern, industrial nation where "per-capita production would overtake that of the most powerful and rich country the USA."[33] By contrast, stories about the Federal Republic focused on the revelation of war criminals in powerful positions of the government, exposed West German militarism, detailed corporate bankruptcies and massive layoffs, and decried the lack of sufficient health care and basic social services in the West.[34]

After August 13 authorities sought to identify and root out border-crossers of a new kind. Now that the borders were impermeable, the border-crossing transgression was purely ideological. State authorities pursued dissenters, so-called slackers and the work-shy. Loyal members of the Free German Youth group purged their troops of those who openly criticized the wall. Newspapers reported with approval malicious attacks on other people for similar transgressions, at least one of whom had to be admitted to hospital. Some denounced their own coworkers for "insulting Comrade Walter Ulbricht" or calling for free elections.[35] Television and newspaper reportage embraced the campaign to prevent ideological border crossing and increasingly moved away from the representation of pan-German themes (previously geared toward preparing Germans for reunification on the basis of socialism) in favor of stories focusing on the GDR's relationship with the socialist countries and their achievements.[36] In the weeks following the border closure, Titov became a central figure in the new narrative; he was a shining example of the superiority of the socialist camp and just the kind of person East Germans might want to have on their side.

Titov in Space

The Soviet space program had been under way for several years by the time German Titov reached space. The Soviets had achieved a number of firsts: the launch of *Sputnik* in 1957, the (ill-fated) flight of the space dog Laika that same year, and the first successful animal flight (of Belka and Strelka) in 1960.[37] The possibility of putting men in space—and at this point authorities had not yet considered women cosmonauts—first arose in January 1959, when authorities began to discuss the parameters for selecting potential candidates.[38] In February 1960, Titov was among twenty young men chosen to train for spaceflight.[39] A year later Yuri Gagarin became the first man in space, with Titov in reserve as his backup pilot. In August 1961, Titov got his chance, becoming only the second man to orbit Earth.

The Soviets appear to have timed the mission to happen shortly before the border closure in Berlin. In early July 1961, Walter Ulbricht had traveled to Khrushchev's vacation house in the Crimea to once again seek the leader's approval to go ahead with the border closure.[40] Soon after, in mid-July, the head of the Soviet space program, Sergei Korolev, made the trip to the Crimea. There he informed Khrushchev that plans were under way for a second *Vostok* flight to follow up Gagarin's successful launch that April. With his promise to Ulbricht in mind, Khrushchev agreed and reportedly requested that such a flight should happen before August 10.[41] Titov's *Vostok 2* mission launched on Sunday, August 6—one week to the day before the border closure in Berlin.

Titov's mission was to extend the amount of time a cosmonaut spent in space, while further determining the effects of weightlessness on human physiology. The spacecraft orbited Earth seventeen times before returning, landing at predetermined coordinates in the Soviet Union. During his flight Titov experienced serious discomfort at times. He became extremely disoriented during the launch and initial orbits, could not differentiate between Earth and space, and reported not being able to shake the feeling of being "upside down."[42] At other points during the flight he felt extreme fatigue, dizziness and nausea, and suffered from vertigo and headaches.[43] He found food unappealing, though Moscow television broadcast pictures of Titov eating lunch.[44] He described reentry into the atmosphere as "staring into the blazing maw of an erupting volcano."[45]

Despite his discomfort, Titov had quite a ride. He observed "dawn" and the subsequent twilight every forty-five minutes.[46] He reported Earth appeared as a "planet enveloped in a blue coating and framed with a brilliant, radiant border," and he marveled at the "terrible intense brightness of the sun contrasting with the inky blackness of the planet's shadow with huge stars above glittering like diamonds." Titov described Earth's stunningly intense colors: the "strangely mottled leopard skin with green jungle" that was Africa; the "rich indigo blue" of the Indian Ocean; the Mediterranean, which "glistened like a vast sea of shining emeralds"; and the "startling salad-green color" of the Gulf of Mexico.[47] He even captured a short film of Earth's horizon with an onboard movie camera. He took manual control of the aircraft for almost twenty minutes and described the sensation as a "tremendous feeling to manipulate with just my hand the mass of a spaceship plunging through a vacuum at nearly eighteen thousand miles per hour!"[48] Titov's ability to control the aircraft would make big news in the coming months.

Media Narratives

As in the case of the Berlin Wall, media narratives were an increasingly integral component of the Cold War, and the space race was no exception. Here was an aspect of the Cold War that was fantastic. By the early 1960s Soviet accomplishments had expanded the boundaries of the "known world" and perhaps even the realm of human understanding. Soviet accomplishments were dramatic; they were visual; they were explosive in their political and scientific implications; and they immediately became wrapped up in the propaganda battle between East and West. In the United States and West Germany newspaper narratives disparaged the accomplishment as mere politics. The *New York Herald Tribune* complained that "the red leader 'turned what might have been a great drama of suspense, which all the world could share, into a tool of Soviet diplomacy—and has, thereby, cheapened it.'" The *New York Times* claimed that "all this brilliance was marred by the transparent Russian propaganda campaign . . . to exploit this latest Soviet space feat for political and psychological warfare ends." West Berlin's *Der Abend* wrote that Khrushchev would use the spaceflight to "blackmail" the West. The *New York Mirror* explicitly drew the connection between the *Vostok 2* mission and the Berlin Wall: Titov's flight was "designed by Khrushchev to intimidate the world and the West in particular on the issue of Berlin."[49] For the *Los Angeles Times* this was but one indication of more nefarious motives; they quoted Bernard Lovell, a renowned British "space watcher," who claimed that "this [was] another important step in the Russian plan to populate the solar system beginning with the invasion of the moon in a few years' time."[50] Western news reports, on the whole, approached the flight with a mixture of awe, skepticism, and fear.

Upon his return Titov, like Gagarin before him and others, like Valentina Tereshkova, who followed him, became an instantly recognizable figure and traveled to other parts of the world as a goodwill ambassador. The Western media treated the cosmonauts with respect as well as some skepticism, expressing doubt about details of their stories, some of which were more earthshaking than others in their implications. During his visit to Canada in 1961, for example, Titov was asked by the press to address rumors that he had not written the account of his flight that had appeared (attributed to him) in the *Atlantic Advocate*.[51] The *Chicago Daily Tribune* asserted that Titov could not have orbited Earth *fewer* than seventeen times and still land in the targeted landing zone, perhaps suggesting that his lack of "choice" in the matter made the feat less remarkable.[52] In Leipzig a Western journalist reportedly asked whether pictures of the *Vostok 2* capsule released to the press were authentic. More profound were questions raised by an American journalist as to whether Titov had even launched into space or left Earth at all.[53]

These components of Western reports of Titov's flight established a story that drew on familiar elements of the Western Cold War narrative of the Soviet enemy. This story defined Gagarin and Titov as cogs in the Soviet space machine—going to space, certainly, but having little to no control over their mission or even their account of it—and performing their parts behind a veil of relative silence and secrecy. Some reports even set them against the free, individualistic, plucky American astronauts Alan Shepard and Gus Grissom. A NASA bio of Shepard perpetuates this narrative still, asserting: "Despite the fact that Gagarin's flight had taken place three weeks earlier, Shepard's flight was still a history-making event. Whereas Gagarin had only been a passenger in his vehicle, Shepard was able to maneuver the *Freedom 7* spacecraft himself. While the Soviet mission was veiled in secrecy, Shepard's flight, return from space, splashdown at sea and recovery by helicopter to a waiting aircraft carrier were seen on live television by millions around the world."[54] Shepard's control over his machine defined the historic nature of his achievement, which was a spectacle of freedom and openness because it was broadcast on live television. In this way Western narratives fit Titov's flight into a longstanding vision of the motivations, goals, and methods of the Soviet state.

The socialist media built uncritical celebrity narratives heroizing the efforts of Titov and the other cosmonauts. The media persistently recounted the details of their personal lives, followed the growth of their young families, and insisted on the unmatched, superbly executed nature of the flights. The significant discomforts (and possible mistakes or failures) of the launches found no place in this narrative. During Titov's flight, for example, he had complained of extreme physical reactions; not only did such complaints not appear in the press, but reports asserted that Titov had not experienced any markedly abnormal changes and had remained "completely fit for work" throughout.[55] There was, then, a certain disconnect between the man and the celebrity. But in the mediated Cold War, who these men were in "real life" was not as important as the social role their mediated personas performed in the GDR.[56] In their study of "socialist heroes" Yuri Gagarin and Adolf Hennecke (an East German Stakhanovite), the historians Silke Satjukow and Rainer Gries have shown how central such figures were to the social construction of the nation. Hennecke, for example, appealed to other East Germans because of his common working-class background, just as Gagarin did. He represented the everyday, but at the same time he represented something extraordinary that could yet become part of the everyday. Worker-heroes such as Hennecke "were supposed to be a role model (for the socialist working people), for the socialist consumer they were supposed to be a glimpse of the future (Vorschein) [sic]. Because just as the hero Hennecke lived today, provided with a good apartment, outfitted with a car and furnished with many privileges and status symbols, so should the many live tomorrow."[57] These representations of Hennecke, Gagarin, and Titov served to bind East Germans to a socialist future.[58]

On the day of his flight Titov became a star overnight in the GDR. The nightly news devoted the August 6 evening broadcast almost exclusively to reporting his flight. It disclosed the details of his personal life and the statistics of his flight that would be reiterated often in the coming weeks: the spacecraft weighed in at 4,731 kilograms, for example; each Earth orbit took 88.5 minutes; at its widest orbit the capsule was 257 kilometers from Earth. It sought to "nationalize" the story by including East Germans' recollections of, and reactions to, the event. The broadcast included short reaction interviews with East Berliners taking in the beautiful summer weather at the beach in southeastern Berlin. It reported on youth who had gathered at a Pioneer camp to listen for Titov's voice over the airwaves and then to write him a letter. It included a sound bite of Titov speaking from space that had been recorded by an East German postal worker and amateur radio enthusiast from Beelitz (southwest of Berlin). The only other substantial reports of this broadcast included a segment on Yuri Gagarin's stay in Brazil and a final item reminding viewers of an upcoming television address by Khrushchev advocating for the conclusion of a peace treaty for Germany.[59]

The official narrative of Titov's trip was celebratory and triumphant, tempered by portentous reminders of the urgent geopolitical situation. In the second week of August the television news reported on the progress of registering border-crossers, the trial of four East Germans for espionage, East German "orphans" of parents who had left the GDR and, of course, Khrushchev's demands for a peace treaty. For some people the increasingly aggressive language of border crossing and espionage, along with renewed demands for a peace treaty took on new, more ominous meaning after the success of Titov's mission. The *Chicago Daily Tribune* published the testimony of a doctor who claimed to have fled Berlin with his family through the still permeable checkpoint at the Brandenburg Gate on August 13. Dr. Ernst Lehnhardt described his life in the GDR as successful and relatively comfortable: "I lived in a good residential area in East Berlin [in] . . . our own house. It was large with a pleasant garden, but run down. . . . I had no serious complaints." But by early August, Lehnhardt had become wary of the possibility that authorities would close the sector border and even build a wall: "Some believed even then that a wall would be thrown up between the two parts of the city. Ulbricht . . . said this never would be done, but we did not trust him. . . . Others soothed themselves with the belief that a wall was impossible. But I thought to myself, what is impossible for a system that sent Titov . . . around the world 17 times?"[60] For Lehnhardt, Titov's triumph represented the growing strength of the socialist bloc and made the prospect of a wall more likely.

The growing strength of the socialist bloc, along with the increasingly aggressive language of border crossing, led some to conclude that it was a good time to leave. Titov did not appear again in the nightly news until August 26, when he led the news with his announcement at a press conference in Moscow that he would be traveling to the GDR. After this announcement, a narrative began to emerge that replaced the contracting space of the East German world with the expanding world of the socialist community.

Titov's Visit

In the GDR the media began crafting the legend of Titov even before his arrival. In its August 20 edition—the first to appear after the border closure—the weekly radio and television magazine *Unser Rundfunk* (Broadcasting) lauded Titov, his flight, and the Soviet Union. The story described Titov's "firm assuredness and steadfast calm, inspiring bravery and boundless energy." His spacecraft, though very complicated, had been utterly reliable, even "flawless" in its operation. The article noted that the craft had even landed at the predetermined coordinates, pointing out that this mathematical feat surely represented a sign of Soviet superiority. With this spaceflight "a new chapter in the scientific exploration of space has been written, composed by the builders of socialism."[61]

German Titov arrived in Berlin on the afternoon of September 1, capturing the imagination of the East German media. East German television covered his arrival in a special simultaneous broadcast for viewers in the GDR, Czechoslovakia, Hungary, and Austria—one of the first of its kind in East German television history.[62] The mood at the top of the broadcast was relaxed, as the moderator introduced the parade route for Titov's motorcade and introduced commentators from Czechoslovakia and Hungary. The moderator then read a letter from Titov to the East German people before a reporter on location set the scene at Schönefeld airport in southeastern Berlin. Titov's arrival at the airfield, at long last, charged the atmosphere. The large crowd surged toward Titov and his official host, Walter Ulbricht. The television camera, still relegated to the back on the crowd in the early 1960s (and not positioned front and center as we might expect in contemporary television coverage of such news conferences), valiantly held its own as the excited throng jostled for the best view of the hero.

After some brief remarks from Ulbricht, Titov took the microphone and praised the GDR as "the great peasant and worker state," which had "accomplished a lot" and was a place where "socialism grows stronger every day." His crowd-pleasing conclusion spoken in German "Es lebe Frieden in der ganzen Welt" (Long live peace in the whole world) set the crowd on fire. Thereafter it took some time for the dignitaries to move through the crowd to their motorcade. The print press presented an equally laudatory picture of Titov's arrival. The *Berliner Zeitung* reported that "the whole of Berlin was on the streets. . . . Everywhere one looked there were smiling faces . . . [and] cheerful songs." At Schönefeld airport the tarmac "teemed" with a crowd of ten thousand; Titov appeared, "beaming," from the door of the aircraft before deplaning with his "picture-perfect" wife, Tamara. "Berlin," screamed the headline, "has never experienced this."[63]

The propaganda value of Titov's accomplishment and subsequent visit so soon after the crisis of the August 13 was laid bare repeatedly in newspaper coverage of the event. The newspaper of the Free German Youth organization reported "Our Successes Prove: We Are on the Right Track."[64] The national daily newspaper *Neues Deutschland* asserted: "Titov's deed announces to all peoples: Socialism is the strongest power in the world."[65] The newspaper of the Free German Trade Union Association, *Tribüne*, declared: "The Roots of Our Success: The Socialist Planned Economy."[66] *Neues Deutschland* quoted Ulbricht's words of welcome: "Cosmonauts herald the great future of Communism."[67] Finally, the *Berliner Zeitung* exclaimed: "He can land anywhere."[68]

In the television coverage as well as the print press, the story of Titov was the story of the superiority—even victory—of the socialist world over the capitalist West. This was a victory both moral and scientific. In a speech welcoming Titov to Berlin, Ulbricht exclaimed: "What a great achievement and precision work of the Soviet scientists, engineers and technicians! What a great success of the Soviet Union and her superior social order! What a triumph of the young heroes of the great Soviet country, who are in the process of putting the forces of nature in the service of man and paving the way into space as fearless pioneers of humanity!"[69]

The *Vostok* missions seemed to lay bare the superiority of Soviet science, particularly when set against the accomplishments of the American space program. NASA had launched two suborbital flights earlier that year, leading the West German publication *Der Spiegel* to claim just days before Titov's launch: "US 2 USSR 1," referring to the number of manned launches that had taken place. The GDR press took exception to the "grotesque equation" of the Soviet and American flights, which clearly were not the same in the scope and breadth of their missions. *Unser Rundfunk* lampooned the *Spiegel* article as an example of the lies told by "bourgeois statistics."[70] This was not the first time this had cropped up. The

American space program had already been skewered in a cartoon reproduced in the GDR (after it first appeared in West Germany and the Soviet
Union) after Gagarin's pathbreaking flight in April 1961. In the cartoon
an American spaceman sits atop an American skyscraper, scratching at
the clouds while above the clouds a Soviet spaceman rides his rocket into
"space" (here, the upper left-hand corner of the image). The skyscrapers
are adorned with well-known brands and slogans, including "Coca-Cola"
and "Mach Mal Pause" (Take a Break), implying that American failure
to reach outer space was the fault of capitalist market culture.[71] During
Titov's visit reporters drew a finer point on the issue, posing the question of whether the flights could indeed be compared. At an international
press conference in Leipzig, Titov argued that in order to "count" as space
travel, the spacecraft had to orbit the earth at least once, which neither of
the American flights had done (figure 10.1).[72]

But media coverage of Titov went beyond simply acclaiming him as
a socialist hero East Germans could claim as one of their own. Instead,
it made close connections between Titov and his trip to space, and the
decision to cut off the border in Berlin. The broadcast of Titov's arrival in Berlin intercut live images from locations along the parade route
with filmed reports on related topics. One report, for example, followed
a group of children as they introduced model rockets they had built to
celebrate the arrival of Titov and concluded with an animated film of children going into space. The most important of these filmed reports, in
terms of the gravity of reportage and the time devoted to its broadcast,
was a film on the subject of Berlin, capital city of the GDR. Ostensibly,
the film introduced Berlin to audiences of the affiliated television organizations in Eastern Europe; its content, however, set out the official argument for the construction of the Berlin Wall. It depicted the geopolitical
problem of "two Berlins," a problem that had been solved by the measures
of August 13 (the border closure). The film used the language of "people-
trafficking," "espionage-central RIAS" (referring to the American radio
station in West Berlin Radio in the American Sector), and the decadent
West that was long familiar to East German viewers. Due to the measures
of August 13, it concluded, "peace is in good hands [in the GDR]."[73] This
film was just one example of a trope that was repeated on television and
in the print press throughout Titov's visit, narratively joining Titov's accomplishment with the "accomplishment" of GDR authorities. Titov was
a soldier in the battle against the West. His trip to space was an important

„Die Amerikaner haben den Vorsprung nicht einholen können. Sie sind dabei, den Weltraum anzukratzen; die Russen beherrschen ihn bereits." („Weltbild", Wiesbaden.)

Zeichnung: G. Würdemann

Figure 10.1. This cartoon is from the East German newspaper *Volksstimme* in 1961, in anticipation of Titov's visit to Berlin. The caption reads: "The Americans couldn't make up the lead. They are trying to scratch space; the Russians already control it." *Source*: *Volksstimme*, May 5, 1961.

blow against the West, just as the border closure had been and would continue to be an important challenge.[74]

Press reports of the visit allowed Ulbricht to bask in the reflected glow of the cosmonaut. Titov was a hero who represented the best of the socialist world; more important, he was impressed by and supportive of the measures taken to close the border. Titov echoed language used by the authorities since August 13, declaring: "It's nice to see the development of the worker-peasant state. All Soviet people are very happy about that and learn with satisfaction how successfully the measures for the protection of the borders are operating. With that, the plans of the West German and international imperialists, who want to interrupt the building of socialism, have been dealt a powerful blow."[75]

Titov stood shoulder to shoulder with Ulbricht, and it could not have come at a better time. Ulbricht expressed this explicitly, thanking Titov for visiting "at a time when the working people of the GDR are putting all their forces into strengthening the Republic and preparing for the conclusion of a German peace before the end of the year."[76] Furthermore, Ulbricht told his audience that Germans all over the republic had clamored to meet the socialist hero; lest they forget who had brought him there, Ulbricht reminded them: "Dear Berliners, as you can see, it did not take long [for Titov to come]."[77] Coverage demonstrated for East Germans that Ulbricht and the GDR had not been shunned by the socialist world (as they had been for some time by the West) because of the border closure. Instead, they could be celebrated for their protection of socialism in Germany and abroad. As Ulbricht argued, the border closure represented the commitment of the GDR to "continue to fight in confraternity with the peoples of the Soviet Union and all the states of the socialist camp, to secure peace and banish war from the lives of the peoples."[78]

In the first week of September there was much talk of peace, but this did not preclude the use of more aggressive language as well. GDR authorities and Titov himself emphasized the growing friendship between Titov and East Germans, and the "unbreakable fraternity" of the GDR and the socialist world.[79] During the Leipzig press conference Titov expressed the view that his flight was but a precursor to the final goal of setting up a long-term, manned, interplanetary station in space, and emphasized that building such a station would require peace.[80] He contrasted what he saw as the confidence and calm with the saber-rattling of the West: "Yesterday as we visited the [border checkpoint at the] Brandenburg Gate, there was upheaval on the Western side. Suddenly a tank drove up. Probably they wanted to terrify us with this jalopy. But we, who have created spaceships and rockets have no fear of tanks. If they had shown us a rocket? We have no fear of that because they have nothing that equals ours [sic]. The Soviet Union pursues exclusively peaceful goals in space. We don't need any razzle-dazzle. We know that the construction of socialism is the best demonstration and testifies to our vitality."[81]

Yet often, deeper warnings followed such pronouncements of peace. Titov drew attention to what he saw as the "recent provocations of some men abroad in the West" and warned that such men should not forget the conclusion of World War II or the effectiveness of the first Soviet missile weapons. Ulbricht boldly reminded the West that "whoever attacks the GDR is against not 17 million, but a billion people of the great family of the socialist countries," who "under the slogan 'All for one, one for all' stand for peace and security." Furthermore, he warned that: "Friends and enemies, especially the lovers of war provocations in West Germany, must say to themselves that a rocket of such enormous propulsive force and precision that transported our comrade Major Titov to space, can also ship other and bigger loads from one place on earth to another easily and with great reliability."[82] With that Ulbricht played on fears in the West that the Soviets' lead in the space race and their development of intercontinental ballistic missile (ICBM) technology jeopardized the security of the West, and the United States in particular, which until now had been relatively safe from Soviet nuclear weapons.

The narrative strategy of drawing the GDR more closely into the socialist fold by linking Titov's achievement and the border closure as two successful battles in the war against the West was only one element—and perhaps not the most important—of the metanarrative value of Titov's visit. Receiving Titov in the GDR just three weeks after the border closure was a propaganda coup. On the one hand, it helped ease public relations between the East German state and its citizens, whose worlds had just gotten smaller. Thousands of people turned out to see Titov wherever he went. In Berlin, Leipzig, and Magdeburg the celebration of Titov was neutral ground upon which state authorities and the East German people could meet and rejoice in the aftermath of the wall. Such crowd scenes were a potent visual demonstration of solidarity; in fact, the SED fairly successfully transformed popular adulation for Titov into evidence of support for the East German state. This is exemplified by press reports that emphasized the signs of support for Titov that came from the East German population, including spontaneous whistles from passing locomotives and celebratory sirens emitting from Berlin factories and, of course, the huge crowds that appeared to greet Titov's motorcades in Berlin and elsewhere in the republic.[83]

The image of thousands of people lining the streets did not approximate the assumption of many in the West that East Germans had retreated to the safety of their homes and families after the border closure. Indeed, the national daily *Neues Deutschland* played this up, contrasting reports from the West German *Welt am Sonntag* that "in Magdeburg they sit under wool blankets and listen to Western radio," with the triumphal pronouncement that "100 000 people" came out to see Titov during his visit to Magdeburg.[84] The East German press thus used Titov's visit to counteract the vision that Easterners lived only in a state of fear for their safety, desperately looking to the West for guidance.

On the other hand, Titov's visit opened a whole new world to East Germans as well, as part of the socialist bloc and ally to the country that had made human space travel possible. Titov's visit was exciting, unique, and most important, it happened in the GDR. On September 2, the television news broadcast Titov's visit to the Berlin Wall. Standing at the wall, he praised state authorities on their efforts to strengthen socialism, while Allied soldiers on the other side sought to catch a glimpse of the space hero. The message was, of course, that East Germans had gotten to experience something they never would have on the other side of the wall. Precisely *because* they lived in the East, it was possible to meet a world-class figure of international fame. Thus Titov's visit exemplifies the ways in which the media, and television in particular, was able redefine the world of the East Germans. This post-wall GDR was no longer the German-centered world of the agenda of reunification in the 1950s; this world looked toward Eastern Europe, the Soviet Union, and beyond.

Notes

Introduction

1. Richard Stites, *Revolutionary Dreams: Utopian Vision and Experimental Life in the Russian Revolution* (New York: Oxford University Press, 1989); and Paul R. Josephson, *Would Trotsky Wear a Bluetooth?: Technological Utopianism under Socialism, 1917–1989* (Baltimore, Md.: Johns Hopkins University Press, 2010).

2. For important works on the place of science and technology in the Soviet Union during the interwar years, see Kendall E. Bailes, *Technology and Society under Stalin: Origins of the Soviet Technical Intelligentsia, 1917–1941* (Princeton, N.J.: Princeton University Press, 1978); Robert A. Lewis, *Science and Industrialisation in the USSR* (New York: Holmes & Meier, 1979); and Nicholas Lampert, *The Technical Intelligentsia and the Soviet State: A Study of Soviet Managers and Technicians, 1928–1935* (New York: Holmes & Meier, 1980). For the generational change in the late 1920s and early 1930s, see also Sheila Fitzpatrick, *Education and Social Mobility in the Soviet Union, 1921–1934* (Cambridge: Cambridge University Press, 1979).

3. David Joravsky, *Soviet Marxism and Natural Science, 1917–1932* (New York: Columbia University Press, 1961); and Loren R. Graham, *Science, Philosophy, and Human Behavior in the Soviet Union* (New York: Columbia University Press, 1987).

4. See, for example, Zhores A. Medvedev, *Soviet Science* (New York: Norton, 1978); Valery N. Soyfer, *Lysenko and the Tragedy of Soviet Science* (New Brunswick, N.J.: Rutgers University Press, 1994); and Paul R. Josephson, *Totalitarian Science and Technology* (Atlantic Highlands, N.J.: Humanities Press, 1996).

5. Michael D. Gordin, Karl Hall, and Alexei B. Kojevnikov, eds., *Osiris*, 2nd series, vol.

23, *Intelligentsia Science: The Russian Century, 1860–1960* (Chicago: University of Chicago Press, 2008); Slava Gerovitch, *From Newspeak to Cyberspeak: A History of Soviet Cybernetics* (Cambridge: MIT Press, 2002); Alexei B. Kojevnikov, *Stalin's Great Science: The Times and Adventures of Soviet Physicists* (London: Imperial College Press, 2004); and Ethan Pollock, *Stalin and the Soviet Science Wars* (Princeton, N.J.: Princeton University Press, 2006). See also the special issue of *Science in Context* 15, no. 2 (2002).

6. For an influential Lysenko-centered narrative of Soviet science, see Nikolai Krementsov, *Stalinist Science* (Princeton, N.J.: Princeton University Press, 1997). For a useful critique of the earlier school, see Michael D. Gordin, "Was There Ever a 'Stalinist Science'?" *Kritika: Explorations in Russian and European History* 9, no. 3 (Summer 2008): 625–39.

7. James T. Andrews, *Science for the Masses: The Bolshevik State, Public Science, and the Popular Imagination in Soviet Russia, 1917–1934* (College Station: Texas A&M University Press, 2003).

8. Lewis H. Siegelbaum, *Cars for Comrades: The Life of the Soviet Automobile* (Ithaca, N.Y.: Cornell University Press, 2008); Scott W. Palmer, *Dictatorship of the Air: Aviation Culture and the Fate of Modern Russia* (New York: Cambridge University Press, 2006); and Asif A. Siddiqi, *The Red Rockets' Glare: Spaceflight and the Soviet Imagination, 1857–1957* (New York: Cambridge University Press, 2010).

9. Asif A. Siddiqi, "Imagining the Cosmos: Utopians, Mystics, and the Popular Culture of Spaceflight in Revolutionary Russia," in Gordon, Hall, and Kojevnikov, *Intelligentsia Science*, 260–88.

10. Lewis H. Siegelbaum, *Stakhanovism and the Politics of Productivity in the USSR, 1935–1941* (Cambridge: Cambridge University Press, 1988); Daniel Peris, *Storming the Heavens: The Soviet League of the Militant Godless* (Ithaca, N.Y.: Cornell University Press, 1998); John McCannon, *Red Arctic: Polar Exploration and the Myth of the North in the Soviet Union, 1932–1939* (New York: Oxford University Press, 1998); Karen Petrone, *"Life Has Become More Joyous, Comrades": Celebrations in the Time of Stalin* (Bloomington: Indiana University Press, 2000); and William Husband, *"Godless Communists": Atheism and Society in Soviet Russia, 1917–1932* (DeKalb: Northern Illinois University Press, 2000).

11. Siddiqi, "Imagining the Cosmos."

12. "Velikaia pobeda v mirnom sorevnovanii s kapitalizmom," *Pravda*, October 9, 1957.

13. Donald. J. Raleigh, *Russia's Sputnik Generation: Soviet Baby Boomers Talk about Their Lives* (Bloomington: Indiana University Press, 2006).

14. See particularly Loren Graham's poignant recollection of the postflight parade for Gagarin at Red Square; see Loren R. Graham, *Moscow Stories* (Bloomington: Indiana University Press, 2006), 18–21.

15. For a social history of the late Stalin years, see E. Iu. Zubkova, *Russia after the War: Hopes, Illusions, and Disappointments, 1945–1957* (London: M. E. Sharpe, 1998).

16. For recent works that explore the construction of Soviet national identity, see Helena Goscilo and Andrea Lanoux, eds., *Gender and National Identity in Twentieth-century Russian Culture* (DeKalb: Northern Illinois University Press, 2006); David Brandenberger, *National Bolshevism: Stalinist Mass Culture and the Formation of Modern Russian National Identity, 1931–1956* (Cambridge: Harvard University Press, 2002); Robert C. Williams, *Russia Imagined: Art, Culture, and National Identity, 1840–1995* (New York: P. Lang, 1997); Stephen M. Norris, *A War of Images: Russian Popular Prints, Wartime Culture, and National Identity, 1812–1945* (DeKalb: Northern Illinois University Press, 2006); Yitzhak M. Brudny, *Reinventing Russia: Russian Nationalism and the Soviet State, 1953–1991* (Cambridge: Harvard University Press, 1998); and Ronald Grigor Suny and Terry Martin, eds., *A State of*

Nations: Empire and Nation-making in the Age of Lenin and Stalin (Oxford: Oxford University Press, 2001).

17. For representative English-language works, see Nicholas Daniloff, *The Kremlin and the Cosmos* (New York: Alfred A. Knopf, 1972); William Shelton, *Soviet Space Exploration: The First Decade* (New York: Washington Square Press, 1968); James E. Oberg, *Red Star in Orbit* (New York: Random House, 1981); Walter McDougall, . . . *The Heavens and the Earth: A Political History of the Space Age* (New York: Basic Books, 1985); and James Harford, *Korolev: How One Man Masterminded the Soviet Drive to Beat America to the Moon* (New York: John Wiley & Sons, 1997). The few academics who have explored the history of the Soviet space program have done so largely from a political science perspective. See, for example, David Easton Potts, "Soviet Man in Space: Politics and Technology from Stalin to Gorbachev (Volumes I and II)" (PhD diss., Georgetown University, 1992); William P. Barry, "The Missile Design Bureaux and Soviet Piloted Space Policy, 1953–1974" (PhD diss., University of Oxford, 1995); and Andrew John Aldrin, "Innovation, the Scientists, and the State: Programmatic Innovation and the Creation of the Soviet Space Program" (PhD diss., University of California, Los Angeles, 1996).

18. See Asif A. Siddiqi's two-volume work *Sputnik and the Soviet Space Challenge* (Gainesville: University Press of Florida, 2003) and *The Soviet Space Race with Apollo* (Gainesville: University Press of Florida, 2003), which were based on a combination of published archival sources, memoirs, official institutional histories, and journalistic accounts in the Russian media. More recently, a few historians have produced scholarship based primarily on a deep reading of primary archival sources, although these works focus on the pre-Sputnik era. See, for example, Matthias Uhl, *Stalins V-2: Der Technologietransfer der deutschen Fernlenkwaffentechnik in die UdSSR und der Aufbau der sowjetischen Raketenindustrie 1945 bis 1959* (Bonn: Bernard & Graefe-Verlag, 2001); Siddiqi, *Red Rockets' Glare*; and James T. Andrews, *Red Cosmos: K. E. Tsiolkovskii, Grandfather of Soviet Rocketry* (College Station: Texas A&M University Press, 2009).

19. For important works on high politics during the Khrushchev era, see William Taubman, *Khrushchev: The Man and His Era* (New York: Norton, 2003); and William Taubman, Sergei Khrushchev, and Abbott Gleason, eds., *Nikita Khrushchev* (New Haven, Conn.: Yale University Press, 2000). For an older but still useful work, see Carl A. Linden, *Khrushchev and the Soviet Leadership: With an Epilogue on Gorbachev* (Baltimore, Md.: Johns Hopkins University Press, 1990).

20. For a sampling of the new work on the Khrushchev era, see Raleigh, *Russia's Sputnik Generation*; Polly Jones, ed., *The Dilemmas of Destalinisation: Negotiating Cultural and Social Change in the Khrushchev Era* (London: Routledge, 2006); Stephen V. Bittner, *The Many Lives of Khrushchev's Thaw: Experience and Memory in Moscow's Arbat*, 2nd edition (Ithaca, N.Y.: Cornell University Press, 2008); Deborah A. Field, *Private Life and Communist Morality in Khrushchev's Russia* (New York: Peter Lang, 2007); V. A. Kozlov, *Mass Uprisings in the USSR: Protest and Rebellion in the Post-Stalin Years* (Armonk, N.Y.: M. E. Sharpe, 2002); Erik Kulavig, *Dissent in the Years of Khrushchev: Nine Stories about Disobedient Russians* (Houndmills, U.K.: Palgrave Macmillan, 2002); and Melanie Ilič, Susan E. Reid, and Lynne Attwood, eds., *Women in the Khrushchev Era* (Houndmills, U.K.: Palgrave Macmillan, 2004). See also Kristin Rothy-Ey, "Finding a Home for Television in the USSR, 1950–1970," *Slavic Review* 66, no. 2 (Summer 2007): 278–306; Andrew B. Stone, "'Overcoming Peasant Backwardness': The Khrushchev Antireligious Campaign and the Rural Soviet Union," *Russian Review* 67, no. 2 (2008): 296–320; Roger D. Markwick, "Cultural History under Khrushchev and Brezhnev: From Social Psychology to *Mentalités*," *Russian Review* 65, no. 2 (2006): 283–301; and Susan E. Reid, "Cold War in the Kitchen: Gender

and De-Stalinization of Consumer Taste in the Soviet Union under Khrushchev," *Slavic Review* 61, no. 2 (Summer 2002): 211–52.

21. For an insightful analysis of the changes in the field of Soviet history as a result of archival research, see Donald J. Raleigh, "Doing Soviet History: The Impact of the Archival Revolution," *Russian Review* 61 (2002): 16–24. See also the articles in the same issue by Lynn Viola and Norman Naimark: Viola, "The Cold War in American Soviet Historiography and the End of the Soviet Union," 25–34, and Naimark, "Cold War Studies and the New Archival Materials on Stalin," 1–15.

22. For useful summaries of the recent literature on the history of Soviet science and technology, see Alexei Kojevnikov, "Introduction: A New History of Russian Science," *Science in Context* 15 (2002): 177–82; and Jonathan Coopersmith, "The Dog That Did Not Bark during the Night: The 'Normalcy' of Russian, Soviet, and Post-Soviet Science and Technology Studies," *Technology and Culture* 47 (2006): 623–37.

23. Some historians have argued that Sergei Korolev, the dean of Soviet rocketry under Khrushchev, can be considered the "father" of Soviet rocketry, while Tsiolkovskii was the luminary and inspirational "grandfather" in the Soviet iconic pantheon. See Andrews, *Red Cosmos*.

24. For an early sociological and theoretical analysis of the process of self-fashioning, see Erving Goffman, *The Presentation of Self in Everyday Life* (Harmondsworth, U.K.: Penguin, 1971). See also Andrews's analysis of Tsiolkovskii's attempts to fashion his own autobiography relative to the Soviet state in his *Red Cosmos*.

25. Fitzpatrick's work is particularly valuable for elucidating the rituals and practices that were a normative aspect of Soviet citizens' lives as they "worked the system" to fashion their identities. See Sheila Fitzpatrick, *Tear off the Masks: Identity and Imposture in Twentieth-century Russia* (Princeton, N.J.: Princeton University Press, 2005).

26. Jochen Hellbeck, *Revolution on My Mind: Writing a Diary under Stalin* (Cambridge: Harvard University Press, 2006).

27. See Natalia Kozlova, "The Diary as Initiation and Rebirth: Reading Everyday Documents of the Early Soviet Era," in *Everyday Life in Early Soviet Russia: Taking the Revolution Inside*, edited by Christina Kiaer and Eric Naiman (Bloomington: Indiana University Press, 2006).

28. Alexander Etkind has taken on the recent Soviet subjectivity school by arguing that, although sincere, some of these edited and resurrected "Soviet life-stories" fail to fully highlight the limited alternatives available to these authors; see Alexander Etkind, "Soviet Subjectivity: Torture for the Sake of Salvation?" *Kritika* 6, no. 1 (Winter 2005): 171–86.

29. Susan Reid, "Toward a New (Socialist) Realism: The Re-engagement with Western Modernism in the Khrushchev Thaw," in *Russian Art and the West: A Century of Dialogue in Painting, Architecture, and the Decorative Arts*, edited by Rosalind P. Blakesley and Susan E. Reid (Dekalb: Northern Illinois University Press, 2007).

1. The Cultural Spaces of the Soviet Cosmos

1. "Forget the pen, pencil it in," newspaper clipping; the publication title and the exact date are unknown.

2. Aleksandr L. Chizhevskii, *Na beregu vselennoi: Gody druzhby s Tsiolkovskim. Vospominaniia* (Moscow: Mysl', 1995), 96.

3. Konstantin E. Tsiolkovskii, "Zhizn' vselennoi," in *Shchit nauchnoi very* (Moscow: Samoobrazovanie, 2007), 207–48.

4. Aleksandr L. Chizhevskii, *Fizicheskie factory istoricheskogo protsessa* (Kaluga: 1-ia Gospolitografiia, 1924).

5. James T. Andrews, *Red Cosmos: K. E. Tsiolkovskii, Grandfather of Soviet Rocketry* (College Station: Texas A & M University Press, 2009); and James T. Andrews, *Science for the Masses: The Bolshevik State, Public Science, and the Popular Imagination in Soviet Russia, 1917–1934* (College Station: Texas A & M University Press, 2003).

6. Richard Stites, *Revolutionary Dreams: Utopian Visions and Experimental Life in the Russian Revolution* (Oxford: Oxford University Press, 1991).

7. Thus the first Soviet science-fiction film, *Aelita* (1924), based on a 1923 novel by Aleksei Tolstoi, combined the ideals of space travel and a social revolution on Mars. The mentality of the revolutionary Soviet youth in the 1920s and their fascination with technology are vividly recalled in B. E. Chertok, *Rakety i liudi: Fili, Podlipki, Tiuratam*, 3rd edition (Moscow: Mashinostroenie, 2002).

8. On the first amateur groups of rocket engineers, see Yaroslav Golovanov, *Korolev: Fakty i mify* (Moscow: Nauka, 1994), 113–63.

9. It has been estimated that there were fewer direct casualties from the V2 launches than among prisoners of war and forced laborers who died while manufacturing those missiles. See Michael Neufeld, *The Rocket and the Reich: Peenemünde and the Coming of the Ballistic Missile Era* (Cambridge: Harvard University Press, 1996).

10. The ultimate (if impractical) example of a synthesis of the highly advanced and primitive technologies was arguably achieved in the design that had a pair of small rockets mounted on and launched from horses.

11. Golovanov, *Korolev*, 223–329.

12. For the most comprehensive account of the Soviet ballistic missile development and space programs, see Asif Siddiqi, *Sputnik and the Soviet Space Challenge* (Washington, D.C.: NASA, 2003); and Asif Siddiqi, *The Soviet Space Race with Apollo* (Washington, D.C.: NASA, 2003).

13. Andrei Sakharov, *Memoirs* (New York: Knopf, 1990), 180–81.

14. For works on the R7 and its testing, see B. E. Chertok, *Rakety i liudi: Fili, Podlipki, Tiuratam* (Moscow: Mashinostroenie, 2002), 142–201.

15. Sergei Khrushchev, *Nikita Khrushchev: Krizisy i rakety. Vzgliad iznutri* (Moscow: Novosti, 1994), 1: 97–114.

16. Golovanov, *Korolev*, 532.

17. On political and media reactions to the first sputnik in the United States, see Walter A. McDougall, . . . *The Heavens and the Earth: A Political History of the Space Age* (New York: Basic Books, 1985), 141–56; and also Paul Dickson, *Sputnik: The Shock of the Century* (New York: Walker Publishing, 2001).

18. Aleksandr Fursenko and Timothy Naftali, *One Hell of a Gamble: Khrushchev, Castro, and Kennedy, 1958–1964: The Secret History of the Cuban Missile Crises* (New York: W. W. Norton, 1998).

19. David Holloway, *Stalin and the Bomb: The Soviet Union and Atomic Energy, 1939–1956* (New Haven, Conn.: Yale University Press, 1994), 337–45.

20. Siddiqi, *Sputnik and the Soviet Space Challenge*, 212–19.

21. The official TASS (the news agency of the Soviet Union) announcement of the first-in-the-world human flight into the cosmic space (April 12, 1961), reprinted in *Bor'ba SSSR za mirnoe ispol'zovanie kosmosa, 1957–1985: Dokumenty i materialy* (Moscow: Politicheskaia Literatura, 1985), 1: 42–43. On Kennedy's reaction, see McDougall, *Heavens and the Earth*, 317–19.

22. The titles of the movies in their original Russian are *Kosmos kak predchuvstvie* (2005) and *Bumazhnyi soldat* (2008).

23. Donald J. Raleigh, *Russia's Sputnik Generation: Soviet Baby Boomers Talk about Their Lives* (Bloomington: Indiana University Press, 2006). This generational issue, and the entire decade of the 1960s, has only recently become the focus of a growing number of detailed investigations by professional historians of the Soviet period.

24. The best existing account of the Soviet cultural 1960s (which actually started around the mid-1950s and ended by the middle of the following decade) is a journalistic and somewhat impressionistic book by Petr' Vail and Aleksandr Genis, *60-e: Mir sovetskogo cheloveka* (Moscow: Novoe Literaturnoe Obozrenie, 1996).

25. In their turn away from glorification of the righteous violence, the shestidesiatniki generation appears to radically differ from the youth that had been similarly traumatized by memories after World War I.

26. After 1954 the public cult of science and computers profited enormously from their association with truth-telling, see Vail and Genis, *60-e: Mir sovetskogo cheloveka,* 100. Also see Slava Gerovitch, *From Newspeak to Cyberspeak* (Boston: MIT Press, 2002), chapter 4.

27. Alexei Kojevnikov, "Russian Science: The Little Ball Made Science Bigger," *Nature* 449 (2007): 542; and "The Phenomenon of Soviet Science," in *Osiris* (Chicago: University of Chicago Press, 2008), vol. 23, *Intelligentsia Science: The Russian Century, 1860–1960,* 115–35.

2. Getting Ready for Khrushchev's *Sputnik*

1. For an overview of Russian utopian thought and the popular cultural crazes of the 1920s, see Richard Stites's monumental study, *Revolutionary Dreams: Utopian Vision and Experimental Life in the Russian Revolution* (New York: Oxford University Press, 1989), 167–89. For a look at aeronautics and its role in popular culture within the context of Soviet exploration of the north, see John McCannon, *Red Arctic: Polar Exploration and the Myth of the North in the Soviet Union, 1932–1939* (New York: Oxford University Press, 1998). Also see Scott Palmer, *Dictatorship of Air: Aviation Culture and the Fate of Modern Russia* (Cambridge: Cambridge University Press, 2006).

2. See I. A. Slukhai, *Russian Rocketry: A Historical Survey* (Moscow: Academy of Sciences of the USSR, 1965).

3. See V. N. Sokolsky, *Russian Solid-fuel Rockets* (Moscow: Academy of Sciences, 1961).

4. Ibid. Sokolsky has argued that these celebratory events were problematic before firework technology was better perfected in the nineteenth century.

5. Michael Stoiko, *Soviet Rocketry: Past, Present, and Future* (New York: Holt, Rinehart and Winston, 1970), 6–7.

6. Evgeny Riabchikov, *Russians in Space* (Garden City, N.Y.: Doubleday & Company, 1971), 115–16.

7. For his collected lectures and information on his rocket designs and interests, see K. I. Konstantinov, *O boevykh raketakh* (St. Petersburg, 1864).

8. For an example of his analysis of rocketry and warfare, see K. I. Konstantinov, "Boevykh rakety v Rossii v 1867," *Artilleriiskii zhurnal,* no. 5 (1867): 6–8.

9. For an elaboration of Gerasimov's design, see A. A. Blagonravov, *Soviet Rocketry: Some Contributions to Its History* (Moscow: Academy of Sciences, 1964).

10. For his classic analysis of dynamics and rocket projectiles in motion, see I. V. Meshchersky, *Dinamika tochki peremennoi massy* (St. Petersburg: Imperial Academy of Sciences, 1897).

11. See Richard Stites, "Fantasy and Revolution: Alexander Bogdanov and the Origins of Bolshevik Science Fiction," in Alexander Bogdanov, *Red Star: The First Bolshevik Utopia*, edited by Loren R. Graham and Richard Stites (Bloomington: Indiana University Press, 1984).

12. See V. N. Chikolev, *Ne byl, no i ne vydumka—elektricheskii raskaz* (St. Petersburg, 1895).

13. For an analysis of these journals and their message, see James T. Andrews, *Science for the Masses: The Bolshevik State, Public Science, and the Popular Imagination, 1917–1934* (College Station: Texas A & M University Press, 2003), 89–91. For an example of the type of articles on exploration published in *Vokrug sveta*, see, for instance, the article cited below on an expedition in 1864 across the Caucasus mountain range by an anthropological team from Russia: "Pereezd' cherez kavkaz," *Vokrug sveta* (1864): 70–77.

14. See his volume of collected science-fiction works: K. E. Tsiolkovskii, "Na Lune" (On the moon), in *Put' k zvezdam* (Moscow: Nauka, 1954).

15. The archival holdings for the Russian Amateur Astronomy Society are located in the Russian State Archival Administration. For an overview of the topics covered in its public meetings and editorial minutes of its journal, see "Otcheti, russkoe obshchestvo liubitelei mirovedeniia 1909–1917," in Gosudarstvennyi arkhiv rossiiskoi federatsii (hereafter cited as GARF), f. 2307, op. 2, d. 365, ll. 1–26.

16. For an analysis of utopianism, cosmonautics, and Russian popular culture, see Asif A. Siddiqi, "Imagining the Cosmos: Utopians, Mystics, and the Popular Culture of Space-flight in Revolutionary Russia," in *Osiris* (Chicago: University of Chicago Press, 2008), vol. 23, 260–88. For a look at the Soviet public's infatuation with flight in air and space in the early period of the twentieth century, also see James T. Andrews "In Search of a Red Cosmos: Space Exploration, Public Culture, and Soviet Society," in *Societal Impact of Spaceflight*, edited by Steven J. Dick and Roger D. Launius (Washington, D.C.: NASA / Smithsonian Institution Press, 2007).

17. See "Otchet M.O.L.A. na pervoe polugodie 1921 i 1922 godax," GARF, f. 2307, op. 2, d. 371, l. 69.

18. For an analysis of cosmic mysticism, the philosopher Nikolai Fedorov, and issues of immortality in Russian philosophy, see Peter Wiles, "On Physical Immortality," *Survey*, nos. 56–57 (1965): 131–34.

19. See Kendall Bailes, *Science and Russian Culture in an Age of Revolutions: V. I. Vernadskii and His Scientific School, 1863–1945* (Bloomington: Indiana University Press, 1990). For a discussion of the biocosmists in the broader context of mystical utopianism in the revolutionary era, see Stites, *Revolutionary Dreams*, 168–70.

20. See N. A. Rynin, *Mechty, legendy, i pervye fantasii* (Leningrad: Nauka, 1930).

21. See N. A. Rynin, *Interplanetary Flight and Communication (A Multi-volume Encyclopedia)* (Jerusalem: Israeli Program of Scientific Translation, published for NASA, 1970). For an overview of the life of N. A. Rynin, see Frank H. Winter, "Nikolai Alexeyevich Rynin (1877–1942), Soviet Astronautical Pioneer: An American Appreciation," *Earth-oriented Applied Space Technology* 2, no. 1 (1982): 69–80.

22. For an example of these types of articles, particularly those explaining the basis of rocketry and overcoming Earth's gravitational forces, see Ia. I. Perel'man, "Za predely atmosfery," *V masterskoi prirody*, nos. 5–6 (1919): 32–33.

23. See Sanktpeterburgskii filial Arkhiva RAN (SF ARAN), f. 796, op. 2, d. 2, l. 60.

24. See Ia. I. Perel'man, *Mezhplanetnoe puteshestvie* (Leningrad: Nauka, 1923).

25. See the editor's biographical entry on Perel'man in *V masterskoi prirody*, nos. 5–6 (1919).

26. For a superb and detailed comparative overview of the early rocket and space societies in America and Europe, see Frank H. Winter, *Prelude to the Space Age: The Rocket Societies, 1924–40* (Washington, D.C.: Smithsonian Institution Press, 1983). For an overview of a variety of public exhibitions and lectures, in Leningrad and Moscow in the 1920s, on popular science in the early Soviet period, see Andrews, *Science for the Masses.*

27. Gosudarstvennyi muzei kosmonavtiki im. K. E. Tsiolkovskogo (GMKT), Kaluga, Russia, f. 1, op. 1, d. 40, ll. 4–12.

28. GMKT, f. 1, op. 1, d. 38, ll. 1–2.

29. GMKT, f. 1, op. 1, d. 15, l. 1.

30. Vladimir Maiakovskii, "Letter from Paris to Comrade Kostrov on the Nature of Love," found in V. Maiakovskii, *The Bedbug and Selected Poetry*, edited by Patricia Blake (Bloomington: Indiana University Press, 1975), 215.

31. GMKT, f. 1, op. 1, d. 38, ll. 15–18.

32. For an analysis of Protazanov's work in the 1920s, especially on *Aelita*, see Peter Kenez, *Cinema and Soviet Society, 1917–1953* (New York: Cambridge University Press, 1992), 46–47. For Soviet criticisms of the film, see a *Pravda* editorial dated October 1, 1924. For the best work on this period regarding film and the Soviet public, see Denise Youngblood, *Movies for the Masses* (New York: Cambridge University Press, 1992).

33. See Alexander Bogdanov, *Red Star: The First Bolshevik Utopia*, translated from the Russian by Charles Rougle (Bloomington: Indiana University Press, 1984).

34. See Nicholas Timasheff, *The Great Retreat: The Growth and Decline of Communism in Russia* (New York: Vintage, 1946). For a more current analysis of cultural practices during the Stalinist 1930s, see Sheila Fitzpatrick, *Everyday Stalinism: Ordinary Life in Extraordinary Times, Soviet Russia in the 1930s* (New York: Oxford University Press, 1999). One can also refer to the work of the historian David Brandenberger for an analysis of the turn toward national themes under Stalin's regime; see David Brandenberger, *National Bolshevism: Stalinist Mass Culture and the Formation of Modern Russian National Identity, 1931–1956* (Cambridge: Harvard University Press, 2002).

35. See David L. Hoffman, *Stalinist Values: The Cultural Norms of Soviet Modernity, 1917–1941* (Ithaca, N.Y.: Cornell University Press, 2003).

36. In the popular journals the 1930s were characterized as years of "Stakhanovite Socialist Aviation." In the summer of 1936, Chkalov, Baidukov, and Beliakov flew their historic nonstop flight in a Soviet *ANT-35*. In 1936, Levanovskii and Levchenko flew from Los Angeles to Moscow, and Molokov flew along the arctic seaboard of the USSR. See L. Khvat, *Besprimernyi perelet* (Moscow: Nauka, 1936). Also see "po stalinskomu marshrutu," *Chto chitat'*, no. 2 (1936): 45–47.

37. See Anatolii Glebov, "Na shturm stratosferi," *Tekhnika* 31 (March 1932).

38. For a comprehensive analysis of the Stalinist campaigns against nature preservations, see Douglas R. Weiner, *A Little Corner of Freedom: Russian Nature Protection from Stalin to Gorbachev* (Berkeley: University of California Press, 1999).

39. See Malte Rolf, "A Hall of Mirrors: Sovietizing Culture under Stalin," *Slavic Review* 68, no. 3 (Fall 2009): 601, 604–5.

40. K. E. Tsiolkovskii, "Osyshchestvliaetsia mechta chelovechestva, Pervomaiskoe prevetstvie K. E. Tsiolkovskogo na plenke," speech taped in his office/laboratory Kaluga, Russia, last week in April 1935; the speech is transcribed in *K. E. Tsiolkovskii, Sbornik posviashchennyi pamiati znamenitogo deiatelia nauki* (Kaluga: N.p., 1935).

41. See Neya Zorkaya, *The Illustrated History of Soviet Cinema* (New York: Hippocrene Books, 1989), 97–98, 127.

42. See *Kosmicheskii reis*, Mosfilm Studios, Moscow, USSR, 1935, director V. Zhuravlev.

43. See I. Golovanov, *Sergei Korolev: The Apprentice of a Space Pioneer* (Moscow: Nauka, 1975). Also see I. Golovanov, *Korolev: Fakty i mify* (Moscow: Mashinostroenie, 1994). Also see S. A. Shlykova, "K. E. Tsilokovskii Correspondence with the Jet Scientific Research Institutes," in *Soviet Rocketry: Some Contributions to Its History*, edited by A. A. Blagonravov (Moscow: Nauka, 1964).

44. See David Holloway, *Stalin and the Bomb: The Soviet Union and Atomic Energy, 1939–1956* (New Haven, Conn.: Yale University Press, 1994).

45. For work on Korolev's team, as well as Khrushchev and the R7s, see Golovanov, *Korolev*; also see Khrushchev's son Sergei's reflections on this because he was a missile guidance systems engineer during his father's time in office. See Sergei Khrushchev, *Nikita Khrushchev: Krizisy I rakety: Vzgliad iznutri* (Moskva: Mashinostroenie, 1994).

46. For a reflective analysis of this communicative discourse done in secrecy between N. Khrushchev and his rocket team of specialists, see Sergei Khrushchev, *Khrushchev on Khrushchev* (Boston: Little, Brown and Company, 1990).

47. See the litany of articles in the Soviet press on this topic, such as those in *Pravda*, November 1957. One article, on November 8, 1957, was entitled "O nabliudenii iskusstvennykh sputnikov zemli." Also see Amy Nelson's chapter in this volume, "Cold War Celebrity and Courageous Canine Scout: The Life and Times of Soviet Space Dogs."

48. Sergei Khrushchev, *Khrushchev on Khrushchev* (Boston: Little, Brown and Company, 1990), 171–72.

49. See Paul R. Josephson, "Rockets, Reactors, and Soviet Culture," in *Science and the Soviet Social Order*, edited by Loren R. Graham (Cambridge: Harvard University Press, 1990), 180–85.

50. For a look at the relationship between science, technology, and propaganda under Khrushchev, see Michael Froggatt, "Science in Propaganda and Popular Culture in the USSR under Khrushchev (1953–1964)" (PhD diss., Oxford University, 2006). See also Cathleen S. Lewis, "The Red Stuff: A History of the Public and Material Culture of Early Human Spaceflight in the USSR" (PhD diss., George Washington University, 2008).

51. See Josephson, "Rockets, Reactors, and Soviet Culture," for his interesting analysis of these letters and debates. For an example of this genre of critique of space travel, see a worker's letter to *Komsomol'skaia Pravda* published under the name Aleksei N., "Ne rano li zaigryvat's lunoi," *Komsomol'skaia Pravda*, June 11, 1960, 1. Also see Slava Gerovitch, "New Soviet Man Inside Human: Human Engineering, Spacecraft Design, and the Construction of Communism," in *Osiris* (Chicago: University of Chicago Press, 2007), vol. 22, 135–57.

52. See Il'ia Ehrenburg, "O lune, o zemle, o serdtse," *Literaturnaia gazeta*, January 1, 1960, 3–4.

53. For an overview of the cultural and public/civic thaw under Nikita Khrushchev, see Priscilla Johnson, *Khrushchev and the Arts: The Politics of Soviet Culture* (Cambridge: MIT Press, 1964). For a more recent anthology of the contours of cultural history in the Khrushchev era, see Polly Jones, ed., *The Dilemmas of De-Stalinization: Negotiating Cultural and Social Change in the Khrushchev Era* (New York: Routledge, 2006).

54. See Paul R. Josephson's analysis of public display of big science in the former Soviet Union in Josephson, "Projects of the Century in Soviet History: Large Scale Technologies from Lenin to Gorbachev," *Technology and Culture* (July 1995).

55. Also see S. Ostrovskii, "Pesenka o sputnike," *Kul'turno-prosvetitel'naia rabota* 1 (1958): 30–33.

56. These claims ranged from the ludicrous assertion of the invention of the electric light, radio, and telegraph, to more specific scientific assertions that Soviets discovered,

for instance, a variety of such disciplines as structural chemistry. Loren Graham believes most of these claims were abandoned later in the Brezhnev era in the 1960s and 1970s. However, he has rightfully asserted that a few of those disciplinary claims (particularly revolving around certain scientific figures) should be investigated more seriously and need to be further analyzed in isolation of the general nationalistic assertions. See Loren R. Graham, *Science in Russia and the Soviet Union* (New York: Cambridge University Press, 1993), 142–43.

57. See Roald Z. Sagdeev, *The Making of a Soviet Scientist: My Adventures in Nuclear Fusion and Space from Stalin to Star Wars* (New York: John Wiley & Sons, 1994), 4–6, 181–82.

58. See Valentin Glushko's reminiscences in his grandiose history of the Soviet space program, *The Soviet Encyclopedia of the Spaceflight* (Moscow: Nauka, 1969). Glushko published this encyclopedia under the pseudonym G. V. Petrovich.

59. See Loren R. Graham, *Moscow Stories* (Bloomington: Indiana University Press, 2006), 18–19.

3. Cosmic Contradictions

1. For the purposes of this discussion, I use "secrecy" to mean deliberate and selective nondisclosure of information. Within this rubric one might consider not only the range of items kept secret, but the degree to which a given piece of information is kept secret. For a discussion of possible definitions and classifications of secrecy, see Raymond Hutchings, *Soviet Secrecy and Non-secrecy* (Totowa, N.J.: Barnes & Noble Books, 1987), 7–35.

2. "Zapiska M. A. Suslova, M. V. Khrunicheva i dr. v TsK KPSS o predstavlenii proekta soobshcheniia TASS o sozdanii iskusstvennogo sputnika Zemli" (August 23, 1955), in *Sovetskaia kosmicheskaia initsiativa v gosudarstvennykh dokumentakh, 1946–1964 gg.*, edited by Iurii M. Baturin (Moscow: RTSoft, 2008), 67–68.

3. "Announcement of the First Satellite," in *Behind the Sputniks: A Survey of Soviet Space Science*, edited by F. J. Krieger (Washington, D.C.: Public Affairs Press, 1958), 311–12.

4. For recent scholarship on the thaw, see Melanie Ilic and Jeremy Smith, eds., *Soviet State and Society under Nikita Khrushchev* (London: Routledge, 2009); Iurii Aksiutin, *Khrushchevskaia ottepel'i i obshchestvennye nastroeniia v sssr v 1953–1964 gg.* (Moscow: ROSSPEN, 2004); Vladislav Zubok, *Zhivago's Children: The Last Russian Intelligentsia* (Cambridge: Harvard University Press, 2009); Polly Jones, ed., *The Dilemmas of Destalinisation: Negotiating Cultural and Social Change in the Khrushchev Era* (London: Routledge, 2006); Stephen V. Bittner, *The Many Lives of Khrushchev's Thaw: Experience and Memory in Moscow's Arbat*, 2nd edition (Ithaca, N.Y.: Cornell University Press, 2008); Deborah A. Field, *Private Life and Communist Morality in Khrushchev's Russia* (New York: Peter Lang, 2007); and Erik Kulavig, *Dissent in the Years of Khrushchev: Nine Stories about Disobedient Russians* (Houndmills, U.K.: Palgrave Macmillan, 2002).

5. "Dekret o pechati" (November 10, 1917), in *Istoriia sovetskoi politicheskoi tsenzury: Dokumenty i kommentarii*, edited by Tat'iana M. Goriaeva (Moscow: ROSSPEN, 1997), 27–28.

6. "Polozhenie o glavnom upravlenii po delam literatury i izdatel'stva (Glavlit)" (June 6, 1922), in *Istoriia sovetskoi politicheskoi tsenzuri*, 35–36.

7. Jonathan Bone, "Soviet Controls on the Creation of Information in the 1920s and 1930s," *Cahiers du Monde russe* 40, nos. 1–2 (January–June 1999): 65–89.

8. Arlen V. Blium, "Forbidden Topics: Early Soviet Censorship Directives," *Book History* 1, no. 1 (1998): 268–82. For Glavlit in general, see Leonid Vladimirov, "Glavlit: How the Soviet Censor Works," *Index on Censorship* (Fall–Winter 1972): 31–43; and Martin Dewhirst and Robert Farrell, eds., *The Soviet Censorship* (Metuchen, N.J.: Scarecrow Press, 1973).

9. "Iz ukaza prezidiuma verkhovnogo soveta sssr ob otvetstvennosti za razglashenie gosudarstvennoi tainy i za utratu dokumentov, soderzhashchikh gosudarstvennuiu tainu" (June 9, 1947), in *Istoriia sovetskoi politicheskoi tsenzury*, 93–94. For the Kliueva-Roskin affair, see Nikolai Krementsov, *The Cure: A Story of Cancer and Politics from the Annals of the Cold War* (Chicago: University of Chicago Press, 2002); Vladimir D. Esakov and Elena S. Levina, *Delo KR: Sudy chesti i ideologii i praktike poslevoennogo stalinizma* (Moscow: IRI RAN, 2001); and V. D. Esakov and E. S. Levina, *Staliniskie 'sudy chesti': Delo 'KR'* (Moscow: Nauka, 2005).

10. Yoram Gorlizki, "Ordinary Stalinism: The Council of Ministers and the Soviet Neopatrimonial State, 1946–1953," *Journal of Modern History* 74, no. 4 (December 2002): 699–736.

11. For example, when a document was lost in a missile design bureau in the fall of 1954, this decree was invoked as a means to bring the situation under control. See Dmitrii F. Ustinov to Central Committee (October 21, 1954), Russian State Archive of the Economy (RGAE), f. 8157, op. 1, d. 1691, ll. 135–36.

12. Stephen Lovell, *The Russian Reading Revolution: Print Culture in the Soviet and Post-Soviet Eras* (Basingstoke, U.K.: Macmillan Press, 2000), 45.

13. Ibid., 6.

14. "Iz spravki glavlita ob itogakh raboty za 1963–65 gg." (August 20, 1965), in *Istoriia sovetskoi politicheskoi tsenzury*, 371–76.

15. For an extensive survey of the pre-*Sputnik* literature on space exploration in the 1950s, see Asif A. Siddiqi, *The Red Rockets' Glare: Spaceflight and the Soviet Imagination, 1857–1957* (New York: Cambridge University Press, 2010), 301–13.

16. N. P. Kamanin, *Skrytyi kosmos: Kniga pervaia, 1960–1963 gg.* (Moscow: Infortekst IF, 1995), 19.

17. Iu. V. Biriukov, "Vsesoiuznaia konferentsiia po primeneniiu reaktivnykh letatel'nykh apparatov k osvoeniiu stratosfery," *Iz istorii aviatsii i kosmonavtiki*, no. 4 (1965): 30–39.

18. Three biographies appeared in 1969: Ol'ga Apenchenko, *Sergei Korolev* (Moscow: Politizdat, 1969); A. P. Romanov, *Konstruktor kosmicheskikh korablei* (Moscow: Politizdat, 1969); and P. T. Astashenkov, *Akademik S. P. Korolev* (Moscow: Mashinostroenie, 1969).

19. "Postanovlenie sekretariata TsK KPSS 'O povyshenii otvetstvennosti rukovoditelei organov pechati, radio, televideniia, kinematografii, uchrezhdenii politicheskii uroven' publikuemykh materialov i repertuara" (January 7, 1969), in *Istoriia sovetskoi politicheskoi tsenzury*, 188–91.

20. "Zapiska otdelov propagandy, kul'tury, nauki i uchebnykh zavedenii TsK KPSS o khode vypolneniia postanovlenii TsK KPSS, napravlennykh na usilenie kontrolia za ideino-politicheskim urovnem knizhnogo rynka, radio, televideniia i kinematografii" (June 27, 1977), in *Istoriia sovetskoi politicheskoi tsenzury*, 210–12.

21. For a brief period in the mid-1960s, Glavlit was subsumed under a new level of bureaucracy, the State Committee for Print.

22. In 1966 this department became the Department of Agitation and Propaganda.

23. Mikhail Suslov served in this position from 1953 to 1957 and then again from 1966 to 1982.

24. The historian S. A. Mikoian, the son of Politburo member A. I. Mikoian and editor of the journal *Latinskaia amerika*, recalled that it was possible to challenge Glavlit directives but not those issuing from the Central Committee. See Sergo A. Mikoyan, "Eroding the Soviet 'Culture' of Secrecy: Western Winds behind Kremlin Walls," Central Intelligence Agency, available online at https://www.cia.gov/library/center-for-the-study-of-intelligence/csi-publications/csi-studies/studies/fall_winter_2001/article05.html.

25. Iaroslav Golovanov, *Korolev: Fakty i mify* (Moscow: Nauka, 1994), 688.

26. Here I draw on some of the work of Hutchings in *Soviet Secrecy and Non-secrecy*; see, particularly, 230–39.

27. "Direktivna zamestitelya ministra oborony sssr no. 45520ss ob obespecheniya sekretnosti provodimykh rabot po raketnomu vooruzheniyu" (July 28, 1955), in *Zadacha osoboi gosudarstvennoi vazhnosti: Iz istorii sozdaniia raketno-iadernogo oruzhiia i raketnykh voisk strategicheskogo naznacheniia (1945–1959 gg.): Sbornik dokumentov*, edited by Vladimir I. Ivkin and Grigorii A. Sukhina (Moscow: ROSSPEN, 2010), 485–88.

28. John Barber, Mark Harrison, Nikolai Simonov, and Boris Starkov, "The Structure and Development of the Defence-Industry Complex," in *The Soviet Defence-Industry Complex from Stalin to Khrushchev*, edited by John Barber and Mark Harrison (Basingstoke, U.K.: Macmillan Press, 2000), 21.

29. For secrecy in the Soviet defense industry, see also Mikhail Agursky, *The Soviet Military-Industrial Complex*, Jerusalem Papers on Peace Problems, No. 31 (Jerusalem: Magnes Press, 1980), 12–16; and Mikhail Agursky and Hannes Adomeit, "The Soviet Military-Industrial Complex," *Survey* 24, no. 4 (Spring 1979): 106–24.

30. Barber et al., "Structure and Development of the Defence-Industry Complex," 21. For military secrecy, see also Arlen Blium, *Kak eto delalos' v Leningrade: Tsenzura v gody ottepeli, zastoia i perestroika, 1953–1991* (St. Petersburg: Akademicheskii proekt, 2005), 35–39.

31. See, for example, two reports prepared in the fall of 1959 summarizing Western speculations on the location of the new Soviet launch base. See "Soobshcheniie No. 863 sluzhebnogo vestnika inostrannoi informatsii TASS o publikatsiiakh v zarubezhnoi presse o sovetskom raketnom poligone v Kazakhstane" (September 17, 1959), and "Stat'ia inzhener I. Pokorny 'Tekhnicheskie svedeniia o kosmicheskoi rakete'" (undated), both in *Zadacha osoboi gosudarstvennoi vazhnosti*, 839–44.

32. The officers were V. D. Iastrebov and A. A. Maksimov. See memoirs of V. D. Iastrebov in *Nachalo kosmicheskoi ery: Vospominaniia veteranov raketno-kosmicheskoi tekhniki i kosmonavtiki, vyp. vtoroi*, edited by Iurii A. Mozzhorin and others (Moscow: RNITsKD, 1994), 320–21.

33. This institutional arrangement has been long known, based on information from such defectors as Leonid Finkel'shtein who, under the pen name Leonid Vladimirov, wrote a number of sensationalist exposés of the Soviet system in the late 1960s and 1970s. Before his defection to Great Britain in 1966, Finkel'shtein had been a journalist for the Soviet popular science journal *Znanie-sila* (Knowledge is power). See Vladimirov, "Glavlit." For his monograph on the Soviet space program, filled with many inaccuracies, see Vladimirov, *The Russian Space Bluff: The Inside Story of the Soviet Drive to the Moon* (New York: Dial Press, 1973).

34. Journalist Evgenii Riabchikov notes that in 1957 an academy scientist, the academician E. K. Fedorov, was responsible for approving the publication of information on the international geophysical year, the international scientific program that served as a backdrop to *Sputnik*. See E. Riabchikov, "Zaria kosmicheskoi ery," *Ogonek*, no. 40 (1987): 1–3.

35. Memoirs of Iu. A. Mozzhorin in *Nachalo kosmicheskoi ery*, 276.

36. See the letter from Smirnov, Afanas'ev, Zakharov, Dement'ev, Zverev, Kalmykov, Butoma, Shokin, and Keldysh to the Central Committee (July 1967) and the draft of an attached decree, RGAE, f. 4372, op. 81, d. 2519, ll. 132–37.

37. Viktor V. Favorskii and Ivan V. Meshcheriakov, eds., *Kosmonavtika i raketno-kosmicheskaia promyshlennost': Zarozhdenie i stanovlenie (1946–1975 gg.)* (Moscow: Mashinostroenie, 2003), 237.

38. Ibid., 233–34.

39. Iurii A. Mozzhorin, *Tak eto bylo . . .* (Moscow: ZAO 'Mezhdunarodnaia programma obrazovaniia,' 2000), 298.

40. A third person, Vladimir Senkevich, also served as Mozzhorin's deputy for the "press group" from 1962 to 1973.

41. "Nagrady-dostoinym," *Voenno-promyshlennyi kur'er* (October 27–November 2, 2004).

42. In a letter dated June 9, 1964, to the Central Committee, Ustinov, Smirnov, Tyulin, Biriuzov, Keldysh, and Korolev recommended displaying the *Vostok*, the *Vostok* descent module, its cosmonaut catapult, the *Vostok* flight plan, and the *Elektron* satellites in exhibitions in the United States. See RGAE, f. 29, op. 1, d. 3443, ll. 1–2.

43. "Postanovlenie Soveta Ministrov sssr 'O podgotovke sovetskoi vystavki "chelovek v kosmose" dlia demonstratsii v zarubezhnykh stranykh'" (November 26, 1965), in *Sovetskaia kosmicheskaia initsiativa*, 307–8. See also Maiorov to Baibakov (November 13, 1965), RGAE, f. 4372, op. 81, d. 1239, l. 11. A later Central Committee and Council of Ministers decree dated July 15, 1966, approved a further set of artifacts acceptable for display, this time at an exhibition in Montreal. Despite initial recommendation that the *Vostok* rocket (with the code name *8A92*) be displayed, officials later recanted their initial decision and withdrew permission to display the vehicle. See "Spravka po vsemirnoi vystavke 1967 g. v Kanade (g. Montreal')" (March 14, 1967), RGAE, f. 4372, op. 81, d. 2519, l. 37.

44. Mozzhorin, *Tak eto bylo . . .* , 301–2.

45. "All Soviet Rockets Orbited by Troops, Soviet General Says," *New York Times*, November 30, 1967.

46. At points other writers were also included in this select club. They included S. A. Borzenko and N. N. Denisov (*Pravda*), B. P. Konovalov and G. N. Ostroumov (*Izvestiia*), N. A. Mel'nikov (*Krasnaia zvezda*), Ia. K. Golovanov and V. M. Peskov (*Komsomol'skaia pravda*), and V. Golovachev (*Trud*).

47. Mozzhorin, *Tak eto bylo . . .* , 304.

48. German Nazarov, "You Cannot Paper Space with Rubles: How to Save Billions" (in Russian), *Molodaia gvardiia*, no. 4 (1990): 192–207.

49. The journalist Angus Roxburgh has noted the following characteristics of the Soviet secrecy system: it sought to maintain the sanctity of the public image of the Soviet "system"; there was an absence of discussion on alternatives to party policy; an absence of information on the personal lives of party officials; no reporting on disputes; and no discussion on policies identified by the party as "progressive." See Angus Roxburgh, *Pravda: Inside the Soviet News Machine* (New York: George Braziller, 1987), 73–75.

50. Slava Gerovitch, "'New Soviet Man' inside Machine: Human Engineering, Spacecraft Design, and the Construction of Communism," in *Osiris* (Chicago: University of Chicago Press, 2007), vol. 22, 135–57.

51. Asif A. Siddiqi, *Sputnik and the Soviet Space Challenge* (Gainesville: University Press of Florida, 2003), 454–60.

52. N. P. Kamanin, *Skrytyi kosmos: Knigaia vtoraia, 1964–1966 gg.* (Moscow: TOO Infortekst, 1997), 174–75.

53. *Soviet Space Programs, 1962–65; Goals and Purposes, Achievements, Plans, and International Implications, Prepared for the Committee on Aeronautical and Space Sciences, U.S. Senate, 89th Cong., 2nd Sess.* (Washington, D.C.: U.S. Government Printing Office, December 1966), 557.

54. N. P. Kamanin, *Skrytyi kosmos: Knigaia tret'ia, 1967–1968 gg.* (Moscow: OOO IID 'Novosti kosmonavtiki', 1999), 35–36.

55. N. P. Kamanin, *Skrytyi kosmos: Kniga chetvertaia, 1969–1978 gg.* (Moscow: OOO IID 'Novosti kosmonavtiki', 2001), 54–55.

56. See, for example, Leonov's claims about Soviet moon missions made while in Japan in June 1969. See Kamanin, *Skrytyi kosmos: Kniga chetvertaia, 1969–1978 gg.*, 63–64.

57. Harry Schwartz, "Soviet Reticent on Space Chiefs," *New York Times*, October 5, 1959.

58. Golovanov, *Korolev*, 553. Emphasis mine.

59. Christian Lardier, "Soviet Space Designers When They Were Secret," in *History of Rocketry and Astronautics*, AAS History Series, vol. 25, edited by Herve Moulin and Donald C. Elder (Novato, Calif.: Univelt, 2003), 319–34.

60. For American astronauts and the challenges of public relations, see, for example, the "tell-all" memoir of former astronaut Walter Cunningham, *The All-American Boys* (New York: Macmillan, 1977).

61. *The First Man in Space*, translation No. 22, Jet Propulsion Laboratory, California Institute of Technology, May 1, 1961. See also Peter Smolders, *Soviets in Space* (New York: Taplinger Publishing, 1973), 115.

62. Iaroslav Golovanov, *Zametki vashego sovremennika, tom 1, 1953–1970* (Moscow: Dobroe slovo, 2001), Knizhka 16, available online at http://epizodsspace.airbase.ru/bibl/golovanov/gol-zap/1/kn1-1.html#10.

63. See, for example, Georgiy Baidukov, *Russian Lindbergh: The Life of Valery Chkalov* (Washington, D.C.: Smithsonian Institution Press, 1991).

64. Jan Plamper, "Abolishing Ambiguity: Soviet Censorship Practices in the 1930s," *Russian Review* 60, no. 4 (October 2001): 526–44.

65. V. P. Glushko to A. M. Prokhorov (May 19, 1983), in *Izbrannye raboty akademika V. P. Glushko, chast' 3* (Khimki: OAO 'NPO Energomash im. akademika V. P. Glushko', 2008), 88–90.

66. For more on the controversy, see Nazarov, "You Cannot Paper Space with Rubles." The encyclopedia in question was Valentin P. Glushko, ed., *Kosmonavtika: Entsiklopediia* (Moscow: Sovetskaia entsiklopediia, 1985).

67. Asif A. Siddiqi, "Privatising Memory: The Soviet Space Programme through Museums and Memoirs," in *Showcasing Space: Artefacts Series: Studies in the History of Science and Technology*, edited by Martin Collins and Douglas Millard (London: Science Museum, 2005), 98–115.

68. See, for example, David King, *The Commissar Vanishes: The Falsification of Photographs and Art in Stalin's Russia* (New York: Metropolitan Books, 1997).

69. For examples, see James E. Oberg, *Red Star in Orbit* (New York: Random House, 1981).

70. See, for example, the configurations show in *Aviation Week*, July 17, 1961, 30; and in *Missiles and Rockets*, December 18, 1961, 16.

71. V. Lavreniuk, "Kosmicheskie miry andreia sokolova," *Voin rossii* no. 4 (2001): 94–96.

72. Iaroslav Golovanov, "Velikie mgnoven'ia torzhestva: K 30-letiiu pervogo poleta cheloveka v kosmos," *Kommunist*, no. 5 (1991): 43–51.

73. Anatolii Agranovskii, *Izbrannoe* (Moscow: Izvestiia, 1987), 18, cited in Thomas C. Wolfe, *Governing Soviet Journalism: The Press and the Socialist Person after Stalin* (Bloomington: Indiana University Press, 2005), 88–89.

74. Sheila Fitzpatrick, *Everyday Stalinism* (Oxford: Oxford University Press, 1999), 9, emphasis mine.

75. Wolfe, *Governing Soviet Journalism*, 30; and Jeffrey Brooks, *Thank You, Comrade Stalin* (Princeton, N.J.: Princeton University Press, 2000).

4. The Human inside a Propaganda Machine

1. Iurii M. Baturin, ed., *Sovetskaia kosmicheskaia initsiativa v gosudarstvennykh dokumentakh, 1946–1964 gg.* (Moscow: RTSoft, 2008), 123–25.

2. Valentina Ponomareva, *Zhenskoe litso kosmosa* (Moscow: Gelios, 2002), 122.

3. Scott W. Palmer, *Dictatorship of the Air: Aviation Culture and the Fate of Modern Russia* (Cambridge: Cambridge University Press, 2006).

4. Ponomareva, *Zhenskoe litso kosmosa*, 122.

5. Baturin, *Sovetskaia kosmicheskaia initsiativa*, 165–66.

6. Iaroslav Golovanov, *Nash Gagarin* (Moscow: Progress, 1978), 190.

7. Missions of exploration in Russian history—from Yermak's Siberian conquests in the sixteenth century to Petr Semenov-Tian'-Shanskii's expeditions to Central Asia in the nineteenth century—often acquired a larger symbolic meaning beyond their narrow utilitarian function. For reform-minded Russian intellectuals in the mid-nineteenth-century, for example, the exploration of the Russian Far East affirmed Russia's unique role as a Eurasian nation, which encompassed Europe and Asia both geographically and ideologically. See Mark Bassin, *Imperial Visions: Nationalist Imagination and Geographical Expansion in the Russian Far East, 1840–1865* (New York: Cambridge University Press, 1999).

8. On the Khrushchev period, see Polly Jones, ed., *The Dilemmas of De-Stalinization: Negotiating Cultural and Social Change in the Khrushchev Era* (London: Routledge, 2006); and William Taubman, *Khrushchev: The Man and His Era* (New York: W. W. Norton, 2003).

9. On the construction of Soviet space myths, see Slava Gerovitch, "'Why Are We Telling Lies?' The Creation of Soviet Space History Myths," *The Russian Review* (forthcoming).

10. See James T. Andrews, "In Search of a Red Cosmos: Space Exploration, Public Culture, and Soviet Society," in *Societal Impact of Spaceflight*, edited by Stephen J. Dick and Roger D. Launius (Washington, D.C.: NASA, 2007), 41–52; Michael Froggatt, "Renouncing Dogma, Teaching Utopia: Science in Schools under Khrushchev," in *The Dilemmas of De-Stalinization: Negotiating Cultural and Social Change in the Khrushchev Era*, edited by Polly Jones (London: Routledge, 2006), 250–66; Michael Froggatt, "Science in Propaganda and Popular Culture in the USSR under Khrushchev (1953–1964)" (PhD diss., University of Oxford, 2006); Paul Josephson, "Rockets, Reactors, and Soviet Culture," in *Science and the Soviet Social Order*, edited by Loren R. Graham (Cambridge: Harvard University Press, 1990), 168–91; Cathleen S. Lewis, "The Red Stuff: A History of the Public and Material Culture of Early Human Spaceflight in the U.S.S.R." (PhD diss., George Washington University, 2008); Walter A. McDougall, . . . *The Heavens and the Earth: A Political History of the Space Age* (New York: Basic Books, 1985); and Trevor Rockwell, "The Molding of the Rising Generation: Soviet Propaganda and the Hero-Myth of Iurii Gagarin," *Past Imperfect* 12 (2006), available online at http://ejournals.library.ualberta.ca/index.php/pi/article/view/1579/1105.

11. Lewis, "Red Stuff," 99–100.

12. Extensive literature on Soviet self-fashioning in the 1930s has followed the pioneering work of Sheila Fitzpatrick, Igal Halfin, Jochen Hellbeck, and Stephen Kotkin. See Sheila Fitzpatrick, *Tear off the Masks! Identity and Imposture in Twentieth-century Russia* (Princeton, N.J.: Princeton University Press, 2005); Igal Halfin, *Terror in My Soul: Communist Autobiographies on Trial* (Cambridge: Harvard University Press, 2003); Jochen Hellbeck, *Revolution on My Mind: Writing a Diary under Stalin* (Cambridge: Harvard University Press, May 2006); and Stephen Kotkin, *Magnetic Mountain: Stalinism as a Civilization* (Berkeley: University of California Press, 1995).

13. See Slava Gerovitch, "'New Soviet Man' inside Machine: Human Engineering, Spacecraft Design, and the Construction of Communism," in *Osiris* (Chicago: University of Chicago Press, 2007), vol. 22, 135–57; the volume is titled *The Self as Project: Politics and the Human Sciences in the Twentieth Century*, edited by Greg Eghigian, Andreas Killen, and Christine Leuenberger.

14. Propaganda in the Soviet Union was directed by the Agitation and Propaganda Department of the Party Central Committee, or Agitprop (later the Ideological Department). Similar departments and positions were established at party committees at all levels—from Soviet republics to regions to cities to individual enterprises. These departments issued ideological work guidelines and implemented them in the media and through various public events, such as mass demonstrations, lectures, and seminars. After the denunciation of Stalin's "personality cult," the propaganda apparatus was undergoing a reform aimed at eliminating dogmatism and falsehoods, "brightening up" propaganda discourse, and expanding into new media, such as television. See Antony Buzek, *How the Communist Press Works* (London: Pall Mall, 1964); and Rockwell, "Molding of the Rising Generation."

15. *Programme of the Communist Party of the Soviet Union* (Moscow: Foreign Languages, 1961), 109.

16. Evgenii Riabchikov, "Volia k pobede," *Aviatsiia i kosmonavtika*, no. 4 (1962): 19; emphasis mine. Unless otherwise noted, all translations are mine.

17. Mikhail B. Chernenko, ed., *V kosmose Nikolaev i Popovich* (Moscow: Pravda, 1963), 92.

18. Iurii Baturin, ed., *Sovetskie i rossiiskie kosmonavty: 1960–2000* (Moscow: Novosti kosmonavtiki, 2001); and Asif A. Siddiqi, *Challenge to Apollo: The Soviet Union and the Space Race, 1945–1974* (Washington, D.C.: NASA, 2000), 246.

19. Iurii Ustinov, *Bessmertie Gagarina* (Moscow: Geroi Otechestva, 2004), 291.

20. German [Gherman] Titov, *Golubaia moia planeta* (Moscow: Voenizdat, 1977), 207–8.

21. Nikolai Kamanin, *Skrytyi kosmos*, 4 vols. (Moscow: Infortekst/Novosti kosmonavtiki, 1995–2001), 1:54.

22. On the symbolic continuity between Stalin-era aviators and Khrushchev-era cosmonauts, see Gerovitch, "'New Soviet Man' inside Machine."

23. John McCannon, *Red Arctic: Polar Exploration and the Myth of the North in the Soviet Union, 1932–1939* (New York: Oxford University Press, 1998), 68.

24. See Jay Bergman, "Valerii Chkalov: Soviet Pilot as New Soviet Man," *Journal of Contemporary History* 33, no. 1 (1998): 135–52; and Katerina Clark, *The Soviet Novel: History as Ritual*, 2nd edition (Chicago: Chicago University Press, 1985), 124–29.

25. Iaroslav Golovanov, *Korolev: Fakty i mify* (Moscow: Nauka, 1994), 665.

26. See Baturin, *Sovetskaia kosmicheskaia initsiativa*, 201–2; Kamanin, *Skrytyi kosmos*, 1:101–2; and Aleksandr M. Pesliak, "Den' kosmonavtiki: Istoricheskie fakty i sovremennyi analiz," *Novosti kosmonavtiki*, no. 6 (2005): 24–25.

27. *Programme of the Communist Party*, 17.

28. Baturin, *Sovetskaia kosmicheskaia initsiativa*, 202–3.

29. Kamanin, *Skrytyi kosmos*, 1:55.

30. Ibid., 2:58.

31. Iina Kohonen, "The Heroic and the Ordinary: Photographic Representations of Soviet Cosmonauts in the Early 1960's," in *Soviet Space Culture: Cosmic Enthusiasm in Socialist Societies*, edited by Eva Maurer, Julia Richers, Monica Rüthers, and Carmen Scheide (London: Palgrave, 2011).

32. Kamanin, *Skrytyi kosmos*, 1:199.

33. Ibid., 2:71.

34. Ibid., 1:221.

35. Ibid., 1:329.

36. Ibid., 1:291.

37. Ibid., 2:125.

38. Ibid., 1:333.

39. Viktor Mitroshenkov, *Zemlia pod nebom: Khronika zhizni Iuriia Gagarina*, 2nd edition (Moscow: Sovetskaia Rossiia, 1987), 317.

40. Kamanin, *Skrytyi kosmos*, 2:332.

41. Ibid., 1:108.

42. Ibid., 2:217.

43. Ibid., 1:346.

44. Ibid., 2:232–33.

45. Ibid., 1:71–72.

46. Ibid., 1:210.

47. Ibid., 2:239.

48. Ibid., 1:313.

49. "Akt o rezul'tatakh ekzamenov," January 18, 1961; Gagarin Memorial Museum Archive, Town of Gagarin, Smolensk Region, Russia.

50. Golovanov, *Nash Gagarin*, 56.

51. Kamanin, *Skrytyi kosmos*, 2:233.

52. Ibid., 2:269.

53. Ibid., 1:219.

54. Ibid., 1:376.

55. Ibid., 1:352.

56. Ibid., 1:369.

57. Ibid., 1:376.

58. Ibid., 1:281.

59. Ibid., 2:29.

60. For a list of cosmonaut biographies and a shrewd analysis of their underlying pattern, see Lewis, "Red Stuff," chapter 2, "Selecting Spacemen, Creating Icons: The First Cosmonauts and Their Stories."

61. Kamanin, *Skrytyi kosmos*, 1:225, 1:236.

62. Ibid., 1:226.

63. Ibid., 4:182.

64. Ibid., 4:152.

65. See Rockwell, "Molding of the Rising Generation."

66. *Programme of the Communist Party*, 108–9.

67. Quoted in Golovanov, *Nash Gagarin*, 272.

68. Ibid., 31.

69. Khodzha Akhmad Abbas [Khwaja Ahmad Abbas], "Rasskaz o Iurii Gagarine," *Aviatsiia i kosmonavtika*, no. 4 (1962): 78–85.

70. Golovanov, *Nash Gagarin*, 281.

71. Vladimir Rossoshanskii, *Fenomen Gagarina* (Saratov: Letopis, 2004), 20.

72. Abbas, "Rasskaz o Iurii Gagarine."

73. Baturin, *Sovetskaia kosmicheskaia initsiativa*, 148–49, 190–91, 227–28, 261–63, 277–78.

74. Richard Stites, *Russian Popular Culture: Entertainment and Society since 1900* (Cambridge: Cambridge University Press, 1992), 145–46.

75. Ponomareva, *Zhenskoe litso kosmosa*, 122.

76. Loren R. Graham, *Moscow Stories* (Bloomington: Indiana University Press, 2006), 18–19.

77. Donald J. Raleigh, trans. and ed., *Russia's Sputnik Generation: Soviet Baby Boomers Talk about Their Lives* (Bloomington: Indiana University Press, 2006), 133.

78. Boris A. Grushin, *Chetyre zhizni Rossii v zerkale oprosov obshchestvennogo mneniia*, vol. 1, *Zhizn' 1-ia: Epokha Khrushcheva* (Moscow: Progess-Traditsiia, 2001), 403.

79. Konstantin Feoktistov, *Traektoriia zhizni* (Moscow: Vagrius, 2000), 188. See also Ponomareva, *Zhenskoe litso*, 242.

80. Kamanin, *Skrytyi kosmos*, 1:164.

81. Ibid., 2:57.

82. Ibid., 2:90.

83. Ibid., 2:10.

84. Ibid., 1:224 and 2:198.

85. Ibid., 2:187.

86. Ibid., 1:170.

87. Ibid., 4:252.

88. Eduard Buinovskii, *Priobshchenie k kosmosu: Zapiski nesletavshego kosmonavta*, chapter 6; available online at http://samlibo.ru/b/bujnowskij_e_i/priobshenie.html.

89. Kamanin, *Skrytyi kosmos*, 1:123.

90. Ibid., 2:57.

91. Golovanov, *Nash Gagarin*, 183.

92. Abbas, "Rasskaz o Iurii Gagarine."

93. Iaroslav Golovanov, *Zametki vashego sovremennika*, vol. 1, *1953–1970* (Moscow: Dobroe slovo, 2001), 278.

94. Kamanin, *Skrytyi kosmos*, 1:57.

95. Ibid., 1:73.

96. Simon Greenhalgh, "Captured on Camera—Gagarin in Trafford," October 4, 2007, available online at http://www.messengernewspapers.co.uk/features/traffordthroughtime/display.var.1731776.0.captured_on_camera_gagarin_in_trafford.php.

97. Kamanin, *Skrytyi kosmos*, 2:187.

98. Ibid., 1:332.

99. Ibid., 1:197–98.

100. Ibid., 1:76.

101. Golovanov, *Nash Gagarin*, 207.

102. Ibid., 211.

103. Kamanin, *Skrytyi kosmos*, 1:75.

104. Ibid., 1:77.

105. Nikolai Kamanin, "Grazhdanin Sovetskogo Soiuza," *Aviatsiia i kosmonavtika*, no. 3 (1962), available online at http://epizodsspace.airbase.ru/bibl/a-i-k/1962/grajdanin.html.

106. Golovanov, *Nash Gagarin*, 211.

107. Kamanin, *Skrytyi kosmos*, 1:369.

108. Major General Leonid Goregliad to Marshal Konstantin Vershinin, February 12, 1962; Russian Government Archive of Contemporary History (RGANI), Moscow, f. 5, op. 30, d. 400, l. 23.

109. Kamanin, *Skrytyi kosmos*, 1:72.

110. Ibid., 4:252.

111. Ibid., 1:321.

112. Ibid., 1:391.

113. Ibid., 1:333.

114. Ibid., 2:9.

115. Ibid., 2:19.

116. Ibid., 2:70.

117. Ibid., 1:57.

118. Golovanov, *Nash Gagarin*, 191.

119. Kamanin, *Skrytyi kosmos*, 1:247.

120. Ibid., 1:231.

121. Boris V. Raushenbakh, *P. S.: Postskriptum* (Moscow: Pashkov Dom, 1999), 87.

122. Rockwell, "Molding of the Rising Generation," 34.

123. Kamanin, *Skrytyi kosmos*, 1:59–60.

124. Ibid., 2:8.

125. Ibid., 1:258.

126. Ibid., 1:189–90.

127. Ibid., 1:98.

128. Baturin, *Sovetskaia kosmicheskaia initsiativa*, 166, 174–77, 194–97, 219–20, 253–55, 266–69, 281–84, 288.

129. Kamanin, *Skrytyi kosmos*, 1:224.

130. Ibid., 2:196.

131. Ibid., 1:98.

132. Ibid., 1:224.

133. Ibid., 2:195.

134. Ibid., 4:116–17.

135. Cited in Sheila Fitzpatrick, *Everyday Stalinism: Ordinary Life in Extraordinary Times: Soviet Russia in the 1930s* (New York: Oxford University Press, 1999), 132.

136. Kamanin, *Skrytyi kosmos*, 2:61.

137. Ibid., 3:283.

138. Ibid., 2:325–27, 332–33.

139. Aleksei Eliseev, *Zhizn'—kaplia v more* (Moscow: Aviatsiia i kosmonavtika, 1998), 120, 93.

140. Kamanin, *Skrytyi kosmos*, 2:26.

141. Ibid., 2:40.

142. Ibid., 2:10.

143. Eventually Leonov agreed to the installation of the bust in his home town of Kemerovo. See Aleksei Leonov, "My mogli obletet' lunu ran'she amerikantsev na polgoda," *Moskovskii komsomolets* (May 29, 2004), available online at http://www.alfabank.ru/press /monitoring/2004/5/29/2.html.

144. German [Gherman] Titov, "Vstrecha s Amerikoi," *Aviatsiia i kosmonavtika*, no. 7 (1962), available online at http://epizodsspace.airbase.ru/bibl/a-i-k/1962/vstrecha.html.

145. Kamanin, *Skrytyi kosmos*, 2:326.

146. Ibid., 1:332.

147. Ibid., 1:374.

148. Ibid., 1:230, 232.

149. Ibid., 2:214.

150. Ibid., 2:239, 250.

151. Yuri Gagarin et al., "The Soviet Union Must Not Lag behind the United States in Space" (1965), translated by Slava Gerovitch, in *Living through the Space Race*, edited by William S. McConnell (Detroit, Mich.: Thomson Gale, 2006), 42–48.

152. Kamanin, *Skrytyi kosmos*, 2:261.

153. Ibid., 2:284.

154. Ibid., 2:262.

155. Vladimir Semichastnyi, *Bespokoinoe serdtse* (Moscow: Vagrius, 2002), 264–66. In May 1967, as a result of Kremlin's internal power struggle, the Soviet leader Leonid Brezhnev forced Semichastnyi to resign, using as a pretext the scandal over Stalin's daughter Svetlana Alliluyeva's defection abroad; see Roy Medvedev, *All Stalin's Men* (Garden City, N.Y.: Anchor, 1985), 75.

156. The cosmonauts followed a venerable Soviet tradition of combining the discourse of space exploration with communist propaganda. James Andrews has argued that in the 1920s and 1930s, the Russian space pioneer Konstantin Tsiolkovskii skillfully employed Bolshevik rhetoric to fashion himself as a sufferer under the tsarist regime and a thinker of a Marxist bent to gain support from the Soviet government. In turn, the government constructed its own propaganda image of Tsiolkovskii. Asif Siddiqi has further documented how Soviet rocket engineers and space enthusiasts created a powerful myth of Tsiolkovskii as the father of Soviet cosmonautics and dexterously manipulated Cold War sentiments to win an approval for the launch of *Sputnik*. See James T. Andrews, *Red Cosmos: K. E. Tsiolkovskii, Grandfather of Soviet Rocketry* (College Station: Texas A & M University Press, 2009); and Asif A. Siddiqi, *The Red Rocket's Glare: Space Flight and the Soviet Imagination, 1857–1957* (New York: Cambridge University Press, 2010).

157. John McCannon, "Positive Heroes at the Pole: Celebrity Status, Socialist-Realist Ideals, and the Soviet Myth of the Arctic, 1932–39," *Russian Review* 56, no. 3 (1997): 347.

158. Slava Gerovitch, "Memories of Space and the Spaces of Memory: Remembering Sergei Korolev," in Maurer et al., *Soviet Space Culture.*

159. Lewis, "Red Stuff," chapter 4, "Death, Destruction, and Mourning: The End of the Golden Age of Spaceflight."

160. In Russian, "Poshatalis', povolynili, ni khruna ne sdelali, ele seli"; see Ponomareva, *Zhenskoe litso kosmosa*, 246.

161. Viktor Stepanov, *Iurii Gagarin* (Moscow: Molodaia gvardiia, 1987).

162. Ustinov, *Bessmertie Gagarina*, 645.

163. David R. Scott and Alexei A. Leonov, *Two Sides of the Moon: Our Story of the Cold War Space Race* (New York: Simon and Schuster, 2004), 229–30.

164. Lewis, "Red Stuff," 161.

165. Clark, *Soviet Novel*, 129.

166. McCannon, *Red Arctic*, 138.

167. Kamanin, *Skrytyi kosmos*, 1:347.

168. Ibid., 3:205.

169. Lewis, "Red Stuff," 99.

170. On April 17, 1961, just five days after Gagarin's flight, *Pravda* had already featured an article, "Unprecedented Exploit of Mastering Outer Space Inspires Soviet People to New Working Victories"; see Rockwell, "Molding of the Rising Generation," 31. On the Stakhanovite movement, see Lewis H. Siegelbaum, *Stakhanovism and the Politics of Productivity in the USSR, 1935–1941* (Cambridge: Cambridge University Press, 1990).

171. McCannon, "Positive Heroes at the Pole," 350.

172. Lewis, "Red Stuff," 158.

5. The Sincere Deceiver

1. Vladimir Ivanovich Rossoshanskii, *Fenomen Gagarina* (Saratov: Izdatel'stvo Letopis', 2001), 210.

2. Gary Minkley and Martin Legassick, "'Not Telling': Secrecy, Lies, and History," *His-*

tory and Theory 39 (December 2000): 2, 5. The historiography of lying is sparse. The December 2000 issue of *History and Theory* was devoted to history and truth-telling. Harry G. Frankfurt, a Princeton philosophy professor, offers many intriguing ideas in his *On Bullshit* (Princeton, N.J.: Princeton University Press, 2005) and *On Truth* (New York: Random House, 2006). Sissela Bok has examined the problem of deception in relation to state regimes of secrecy in *Secrets: On the Ethics of Concealment and Revelation* (New York: Pantheon Books, 1982).

3. As one of Gagarin's teachers once wrote, a study of Gagarin can reveal "who we ourselves are." Serge Mikhailovich Belotserkovskii, *Pervyi kosmonavt: Istoriia zhizni i gibeli* (Lewiston, N.Y.: Edwin Mellen Press, 2000), 10.

4. Cited in Jeremy Campbell, *The Liar's Tale: A History of Falsehood* (New York: Norton, 2001), 242.

5. Alexei Yurchak, *Everything Was Forever, until It Was No More* (Princeton, N.J.: Princeton University Press, 2005); David L. Hoffmann, *Stalinist Values: The Cultural Norms of Soviet Modernity, 1917–1941* (Ithaca, N.Y.: Cornell University Press, 2003); and Sheila Fitzpatrick, *Everyday Stalinism: Ordinary Life in Extraordinary Times: The Soviet Union in the 1930s* (London: Oxford University Press, 1999). The autodidact and father of Russian rocketry, Konstantin Tsiolkovskii, like Gagarin, also attempted to construct his own persona in accordance with Soviet values: see James T. Andrews, *Red Cosmos: K. E. Tsiolkovskii, Grandfather of Soviet Rocketry* (College Station: Texas A&M University Press, 2009).

6. Vladislav Zubok, *Zhivago's Children: The Last Russian Intelligentsia* (Cambridge: Harvard University Press, 2009), 151.

7. The cult of Gagarin is one subject of my forthcoming biography of Gagarin with Northern Illinois University Press; Jenks, *The Cosmonaut Who Couldn't Stop Smiling: The Life and Legend of Yuri Gagarin*. For unpublished letters to the editor, see RGAE, f. 9453, o. 2, dd. 21, 30, 32, 33, 34; and Gagarin Unified Museum, Gagarin, a fond simply titled "Pis'ma v adres pervogo kosmonavta." See also letters sent to the Soviet Academy of Sciences contained in RAN, f. 1647, o, 1, d. 260.

8. "108 minut, kotorye potriasli mir," *Izvestiia*, February 26, 2002, electronic edition, http://main.izvestia.ru/chronicles/article14994; and Iurii Ustinov, *Bessmertie Gagarina* (Moscow: Izdatel'stvo Geroi Otechestva, 2004), 515.

9. Petr Vail' and Aleksandr Genis, *60-e—Mir sovetskogo cheloveka* (Moscow: Novoe literaturnoe obozrenie, 1996), 14.

10. Ibid., 176.

11. Vaclav Havel, *Living in Truth: Twenty-two Essays Published on the Occasion of the Award of the Erasmus Prize to Vaclav Havel* (London: Faber and Faber, 1990), 39.

12. Cited in Campbell, *Liar's Tale*, 214.

13. Ustinov, *Bessmertie Gagarina*, 243.

14. "Text of Soviet Party's Draft Program," *New York Times*, August 1, 1961, 17.

15. Rossoshanskii, *Fenomen Gagarina*, 214, 268; and A. T. Gagarina, *Slovo o syne*, 3rd edition (Moscow: Molodaia gvardiia, 1986), 70.

16. A copy of 1960 and 1961 censorship guidelines for Soviet newspaper editors is in the Partinyi Arkhiv Saratovskoi Oblasti, f. 594, o. 2, d. 4653, ll. 97–122.

17. Kamanin's diaries, published posthumously by his son, provide a rare glimpse into the behind-the-scenes world of the cosmonauts and into Kamanin's active role as a creator of Gagarin's public persona. See volume 1 for Kamanin's role in crafting the public narrative of Soviet space conquest: N. P. Kamanin, *Skrytyi kosmos: Kniga pervaia, 1960–63* (Moscow: Infortekst, 1995), 4 vols.

18. *Stranitsy istorii: Pokrovsk-Engel's*, 4-yi vypusk (March 2004), 8.

19. Valentina Ponomareva, *Zhenskoe litso kosmosa* (Moscow: Fond "Gelios," 2002), 123–24, 161.

20. One American news source did not believe the lie. "Farmers Relate Gagarin Landing," *New York Times*, April 15, 1961, 2. The *New York Times* later pressed the Soviets on the issue of whether Gagarin actually landed in his capsule, but the Soviets maintained the lie: "Could Ride Spaceship to Earth, Russian Says," *New York Times*, August 28, 1962, 13.

21. Ponomareva, *Zhenskoe litso kosmosa*, 248.

22. "Gagarin ne govoril, chto ne videl Boga," *Pravda*, April 12, 2006, online edition, http://www.pravda.ru/print/society/814550-gargarin-o; and Nikolai Denisov, *Khorosho, khorosho, Gagarin* (Moscow: Moskovskii rabochii, 1963), 285. For the various obfuscations perpetrated by Gagarin and his entourage at press conferences following the flight, see Asif A. Siddiqi, *Sputnik and the Soviet Space Challenge* (Gainesville: University Press of Florida, 2000; reprint, 2003), 282–84; and Rossoshanskii, *Fenomen Gagarina*, 210–11. On the ethos of secrecy in the Soviet space program, see Svetlana Boym's essay in the photograph collection, *Kosmos: A Portrait of the Russian Space Age* (Princeton, N.J.: Princeton Architectural Press, 2001), 91.

23. RAN, f. 1647, o. 1, d. 260, l. 7.

24. For Gagarin as an ambassador of peace, see the account of his travels abroad by the *Pravda* journalist who accompanied him: Denisov, *Khorosho, khorosho, Gagarin*.

25. Denisov, *Khorosho, khorosho, Gagarin*, 233; Ustinov, *Bessmertie Gagarina*, 182–83; and "Rocket Warning Issued in Moscow," *New York Times*, April 22, 1961, 9.

26. Valentina Gagarina, *108 minut i vsia zhizn'*, 2nd edition (Moscow: Molodaia gvardiia, 1982), 29, 31; Boym, *Kosmos*, 90.

27. Rossoshanskii, *Fenomen Gagarina*, 285.

28. Valentin A. Gagarin, *Moi brat Iurii: Dokumental'naia povest' / literaturnaia zapis'* (Moscow: ITRK, 2002), 318.

29. Gagarina, *108 minut i vsia zhizn'*, 78–79.

30. Ustinov, *Bessmertie Gagarina*, 103–6.

31. Rossoshanskii, *Fenomen Gagarina*, 268, 294; Ustinov, *Bessmertie Gagarina*, 192, 197, 383, 503, 569.

32. Aleksandr Emel'ianenkov, "A tret'im byl Kheminguei," *Rossiiskaia gazeta*, March 5, 2009, available online at http://www.rg.ru/printable/2009/03/05/leonov.html.

33. Rossoshanskii, *Fenomen Gagarina*, 282.

34. Ibid., 279.

35. Kamanin, *Skrytyi kosmos*, 57–58; interview conducted by author with the cosmonaut Valentina Ponomareva, Moscow, June 28, 2007.

36. Kamanin, *Skrytyi kosmos*, 58–59.

37. Ibid., 57–62.

38. Ibid., 62; Yevgeny Yevtushenko, *Wild Berries*, translated by Antonina W. Bouis (New York: William Morrow and Company, 1981), 9–10.

39. Iulia Turovtseva, "Vam poruchaetsia postoianno nakhodit'sia pri tovarishche Gagarine," *Izvestiia*, April 10, 2009, available online at http://www.izvestia.ru/nystory/article3127306/?print.

40. Sergei Borisov, "45 let poletu cheloveka v kosmos," *Moskovskie novosti*, April 12, 2006.

41. Kamanin, *Skrytyi kosmos*, 66.

42. Ibid., 63, 65.

43. Vail' and Genis, *60-e—Mir sovetskogo cheloveka*, 23.

44. Kamanin, *Skrytyi kosmos*, 60.

45. Gagarina, *108 minut i vsia zhizn'*, 98; Rossoshanskii, *Fenomen Gagarina*, 104.

46. Gagarina, *108 minut i vsia zhizn'*, 85, 92, 96, 98, 123; Gagarina, *Slovo o syne*, 136.

47. On the problem of public and private life, see this collection of essays: Lewis Siegel-baum, ed., *Borders of Socialism: The Private Sphere in the Soviet Union* (New York: Palgrave Macmillan, 2006).

48. Rossoshanskii, *Fenomen Gagarina*, 77, 108; Gagarina, *108 minut i vsia zhizn'*, 91, 98.

49. "Kakovo cheloveku v skafandre legend," an interview with the academician Oleg Gazenko, one of the doctors who checked Gagarin's physical health after his flight; available online at http://www.rtc.ru/encyk/gagarin/bl11.shtml.

50. Gagarina, *108 minut i vsia zhizn'*, 92, 93, 95, 96, 99.

51. Ustinov, *Bessmertie Gagarina*, 504; Gagarina, *108 minut i vsia zhizn'*, 90, 97.

52. Ustinov, *Bessmertie Gagarina*, 155; Belotserkovskii, *Pervyi kosmonavt*, 303.

53. Rossoshanskii, *Fenomen Gagarina*, 77, 87–90, 95, 97.

54. Belotserkovskii, *Pervyi kosmonavt*, 303.

55. Vladimir Vysotskii, "Ia pervyi smeril zhizn' obratnym schetom," available online at http://www.rtc.ru/encyk/gagarin/stihi1.shtml; Gagarina, *108 minut i vsia zhizn'*, 81, 92. Havel referred to citizens in "post-totalitarian" Soviet bloc states as "both victims of the system and its instruments." Havel, *Living in Truth*, 52.

56. Campbell, *Liar's Tale*, 214.

57. Gagarina, *108 minut i vsia zhizn'*, 100.

58. RGAE, f. 9453, o. 2, d. 34, ll. 37–39, 56.

59. RGAE, f. 9453, o. 2, d. 34, ll. 39–41, 76, 190.

60. One legend claimed that the Italian beauty Gina Lollobrigida, who did meet Gagarin, supposedly snuck around KGB officers to get into his hotel room, surprising him in the hotel bathroom. Ustinov, *Bessmertie Gagarina*, 594–95.

61. GARF, f. 4459, o. 43, d. 1011, ll. 98–100, 117, 184, 237, 247; A. A. Lobnev, "Vozvrashchenie pervogokosmonautu," *Gagarinskii sbornik, Materialy XXX obshchestvenno-nauchnykh chtenii, posviashchennykh pamiati Iu. A Gargarina 2003 g. (chast'1)* (City of Gagarin: Ob'edinennyi memorial'nyi muzei Iu. A. Gagarina, 2004), 97–107; *Nash Gagarin: Materialy o prebyvanii letchika-kosmonavta SSSR Iu. A. Gagarina v Kaluzhskom krae* (Kaluga: Zolotaia alleia, 2006), 37.

62. On rumors in the Soviet state, see Timothy Johnston, "Subversive Tales? War Rumours in the Soviet Union, 1945–1947," in *Late Stalinist Russia: Society between Reconstruction and Reinvention*, edited by Juliane Furst (London: Routledge, 2006), 62–78.

63. John Noble Wilford, "Soviet Lifting Veil on Death of Astronaut," *New York Times*, February 7, 1988, 19.

64. Belotserkovskii, *Pervyi kosmonavt*, 102–3. Gagarin's wife had little faith in the government commission that investigated his death. Gagarina, *108 minut i vsia zhizn'*, 124.

65. Ustinov, *Bessmertie Gagarina*, 594; Alvin Klein, "Play on Cosmonaut Lands in Sea of Vacuity," *New York Times*, April 26, 1981, LI 15; and Rossoshanskii, *Fenomen Gagarina*, 199–205, discusses the many popular explanations of Gagarin's death, including twenty different popular versions in 1996.

66. Rossoshanskii, *Fenomen Gagarina*, 201–4; Belotserkovskii, *Pervyi kosmonavt*, 188–201; see also S. M. Belotserkovskii, *Gibel' Gagarina: Fakty i domysly* (Moscow: Mashinostroenie, 1992).

67. Serguei Alex. Oushakine, *The Patriotism of Despair: Nation, War, and Loss in Russia* (Ithaca, N.Y.: Cornell University Press, 2009), 74; and Belotserkovskii, *Pervyi kosmonavt*, 307.

68. Cited in Bok, *Secrets*, 199.

69. "Elena Gargarina: 'v zvezdnom . . . gorodke byla chudesnaia zhizn,'" *Izvestiia*, March 3, 2004, online edition, http://www.ru/person/article44900; Ustinov, *Bessmertie Gagarina*, 338.

70. Denis Tukmakov, "Gagarin i natsiia," *Russkii zhurnal*, April 12, 2006, online edition, http://www.ru/comments/115335709?mode=print; Ustinov, *Bessmertie Gagarina*, 277, 386.

71. See "Yuri Gagarin: His Life in Pictures," at http://www.russianarchives.com/gallery/gagarin/index.html.

72. David King, *The Commissar Vanishes: The Falsification of Photographs and Art in Stalin's Russia* (New York: Metropolitan Books, 1997).

6. Cold War Celebrity and the Courageous Canine Scout

1. On the significance of the often unacknowledged but shared legacy of the enlightenment in the cultural Cold War, see David Caute, *The Dancer Defects: The Struggle for Cultural Supremacy during the Cold War* (Oxford: Oxford University Press, 2003), 4, 38–39; and Susan Buck-Morss, *Dreamworld and Catastrophe: The Passing of Mass Utopia in East and West* (Cambridge: MIT Press, 2002).

2. In the voluminous and rapidly expanding interdisciplinary field of animal studies, historians have taken methodological inspiration from environmental history as well as the traditions of social and cultural history. For the former, see Harriet Ritvo, "Animal Planet," *Environmental History* 9 (2004): 204–20; and Edmund Russell, "Evolutionary History: Prospectus for a New Field," *Environmental History* 8 (2003): 204–29. For the latter, see such pioneering studies as Harriet Ritvo, *The Animal Estate: The English and Other Creatures in the Victorian Age* (Cambridge: Harvard University Press, 1989); Kathleen Kete, *The Beast in the Boudoir: Petkeeping in Nineteenth-century Paris* (Berkeley: University of California Press, 1995); and Nigel Rothfels, *Savages and Beasts: The Birth of the Modern Zoo* (Baltimore, Md.: Johns Hopkins University Press, 2002). Recent studies of particular interest to historians include Dorothee Brantz, ed., *Beastly Natures: Animals, Humans, and the Study of History* (Charlottesville: University of Virginia Press, 2010). For an introduction to animal studies in the Russian field, see Jane Costlow and Amy Nelson, eds., *Other Animals: Beyond the Human in Russian Culture and History* (Pittsburgh: University of Pittsburgh Press, 2010).

3. Daniel Todes, *Pavlov's Physiology Factory: Experiment, Interpretation, Laboratory Enterprise* (Baltimore, Md.: Johns Hopkins University Press, 2002), 93–101. On animals as technologies versus organisms, see Stephen Pemberton, "Canine Technologies, Model Patients: The Historical Production of Hemophiliac Dogs in American Biomedicine," in *Industrializing Organisms: Introducing Evolutionary History*, edited by Susan R. Schrepfer and Philip Scranton (New York: Routledge, 2004), 191–213; and Bruno Latour, "The Costly Ghastly Kitchen," in *The Laboratory Revolution In Medicine*, edited by Perry Williams and Andrew Cunningham (Cambridge: Cambridge University Press, 2002 [1992]), 295–303.

4. Anita Guerrini, *Experimenting with Humans and Animals: From Galen to Animal Rights* (Baltimore, Md.: Johns Hopkins University Press, 2003), x. On the sociological concept of "boundary object," see Susan Leigh Star and James R. Griesemer, "Institutional Ecology, 'Translations,' and Boundary Object: Amateurs and Professionals in Berkeley's Museum of Vertebrate Zoology, 1907–39," *Social Studies of Science* 19 (1989): 387–420.

5. Star and Griesemer, "Institutional Ecology," 412–13.

6. An emerging scholarly consensus sees domestication as a collaborative relationship

with ongoing evolutionary consequences for both species. This is the premise of recent innovative work by such ethologists as Vilmos Csányi and Ádam Miklósi. On the implications of this collaborative view of domestication for human history, see Richard W. Bulliet, *Hunters, Herders, and Hamburgers: The Past and Future of Human-Animal Relationships* (New York: Columbia University Press, 2005).

7. Ádam Miklósi, *Dog Behavior, Evolution, and Cognition* (Oxford: Oxford University Press, 2007), 165.

8. Donna J. Haraway, *When Species Meet* (Minneapolis: University of Minnesota Press, 2008), 16.

9. Asif A. Siddiqi, *The Red Rockets' Glare: Spaceflight and the Soviet Imagination, 1857–1957* (Cambridge: Cambridge University Press, 2010).

10. James T. Andrews, *Science for the Masses: The Bolshevik State, Public Science, and the Popular Imagination in Soviet Russia, 1917–1934* (College Station: Texas A&M Press, 2003), 85–86; also see James T. Andrews's chapter in this volume, "Getting Ready for Khrushchev's *Sputnik*," as well as his book, *Red Cosmos: K. E. Tsiolkovskii, Grandfather of Soviet Rocketry* (College Station: Texas A&M Press, 2009).

11. Peder Anker, "The Ecological Colonization of Space," *Environmental History* 10 (2005): 239–68.

12. The most important scholarship on the early Soviet space program includes Asif A. Siddiqi, *Sputnik and the Soviet Space Challenge* (Gainesville: University of Florida Press, 2000); Asif A. Siddiqi, *The Soviet Space Race with Apollo* (Gainesville: University of Florida Press, 2000); James Harford, *Korolev: How One Man Masterminded the Soviet Drive to Beat America to the Moon* (New York: John Wiley & Sons, 1997); Yu. A. Mozzhorin et al., eds., *Dorogi v kosmos: Vospominaniia veteranov raketno-kosmicheskoi tekhniki i kosmonavtiki*, 2 vols. (Moscow: Izdatel'svto MAI, 1992); Yaroslav Golovanov, *Korolev: Fakty i mify* (Moscow: Nauka, 1994); and B. E. Chertok, *Rockets and People*, vols. 1–3, translated by Asif A. Siddiqi (Washington, D.C.: NASA History Division, 2006–9).

13. On the Americans' preference for animals "closer to man" versus the Soviets' choice of dogs, see Clyde R. Bergwin and William T. Coleman, *Animal Astronauts: They Opened the Way to the Stars* (Englewood Cliffs, N.J.: Prentice Hall, 1963), 57–69; Colin Burgess and Chris Dubbs, *Animals in Space: From Research Rockets to the Space Shuttle* (New York: Springer, 2007), 39–40, 63, 189–90, 239–71; Strel'chuk and Gartsshtein, "Chertveronogie pomoshchniki uchenykh," *Kresnaia zvezda*, August 27, 1960, 3; V. Borisov and O. Gorlov, *Zhizn' i kosmos* (Moscow: Sovetskaia Rossiia, 1961), 136–39; and P. Sharov, "Dorogi v kosmos liudiam prolozhili sobaki," *Novosti kosmonavtiki* 19, no. 1 (2009): 65.

14. Mozzhorin et al., *Dorogi v kosmos*, 2:124–25.

15. Accounts of the space dog program in English include Amy Nelson, "The Legacy of Laika: Celebrity, Sacrifice, and the Soviet Space Dogs," in Brantz, *Beastly Natures*, 204–24; Asif A. Siddiqi, "There It Is! An Account of the First Dogs-in-Space Program," *Quest* 5, no. 3 (1996): 38–42; Colin Burgess, "Dogs Who Rode in Rockets," *Spaceflight* 38 (December 1996): 421–23; and Burgess and Dubbs, *Animals in Space*, 61–84, 143–65, 213–18. The most accessible sources in Russian are participants' memoirs: V. I. Iazdovskii, *Na tropakh vselennoi. Vklad kosmicheskoi biologii i meditsiny v osvoenie kosmicheskogo prostranstva* (Moscow: Slovo, 1996); A. Ivanov, *Pervye stupeni. Zapiski inzhenera*, 2nd edition (Moscow: Molodaia gvardiia, 1975); Ivan Kas'ian, "My, kosmicheskie mediki," in . . . *Tri, dva, odin!* edited by V. K. Chanturiia (Moscow: Sovetskaia Rossiia, 1989), 257–98; and A. I. Ostashev and Elena Iur'evna Bashilova, comps., "Prelestnaia, spokoinaia Laika byla slavnoi sobaki: K 45-letiiu so dnia zapuska vtorogo ISZ," *Istoricheskii arkhiv* 6 (2002): 11–18. Accessing the archival records of the program remains challenging for foreign researchers. A chronolog-

ical listing of the dog flights based on archival materials is provided in I. B. Ushakov, V. S. Bednenko, and E. V. Lapayev, eds., *Istoriia otechestvennoi kosmicheskoi meditsiny* (Voronezh: Voronezhskii gosudarstvennyi universitet, 2001), 17. At least fifteen dogs flew more than once, and several were renamed, making an overall calculation of the quantity of dogs involved in these experiments difficult.

16. Sharov, "Dorogi v kosmos," 65.

17. Mozzhorin et al., *Dorogi v kosmos*, 2:127; Sharov, "Dorogi v kosmos," 66; and Siddiqi, *Sputnik and the Soviet Space Challenge*, 92–96.

18. Mozzhorin et al., *Dorogi v kosmos*, 2:132–39; Ushakov, Bednenko, and Lapayev, *Istoriia*, 6–7; Burgess, "Dogs Who Rode in Rockets," 422–23; and Burgess and Dubbs, *Animals in Space*, 70–78.

19. Siddiqi, *Sputnik and the Soviet Space Challenge*, 145. On the role of Korolev and the Soviet and American print media in the origins of the space race, see Asif A. Siddiqi, "Sputnik Fifty Years Later: New Evidence on its Origins," *Acta astronautica* 63 (2008): 529–39; and Asif A. Siddiqi, "Korolev, Sputnik, and the International Geophysical Year," in *Reconsidering Sputnik: Forty Years since the Soviet Satellite*, edited by Roger D. Launius, John M. Logsdon, and Robert W. Smith (Amsterdam: Harwood Academic Publishers, 2000), 43–72.

20. Mozzhorin et al., *Dorogi v kosmos*, 2:138–39; and Burgess and Dubbs, *Animals in Space*, 79.

21. A. V. Pokrovskii, "Vital Activity of Animals during Rocket Flights into the Upper Atmosphere," in *Behind the Sputniks: A Survey of Soviet Space Science*, edited by F. J. Krieger (Washington, D.C.: Public Affairs Press, 1958), 156–63.

22. The phrase from "Vse vyshe" is "iz skazki stanet iav'iu." K. Raspevin, "Pervye puteshestvenniki v kosmos," *Trud*, February 16, 1957, 3.

23. "Dogs Unharmed Sixty Miles Up," *The Times*, February 18, 1957, 6; "Dogs in Seventy-mile Rocket Flights," *The Times*, June 3, 1957, 10; "Soviet 'Rocket Dogs' Get Geophysical Year Role," *New York Times*, June 9, 1957, 7; and *Literaturnaia gazeta*, June 8, 1957.

24. "An Old Hand at Space Travel, the Russians Say," *New York Times*, March 25, 1957.

25. "O neobyknovennom 'gode' i o tekh, kto pobyval v kosmose," *Iunyi naturalist*, no. 9 (1957): 10–12.

26. "Vtoroi iskusstvenyi sputnik vrashchaetsia vokrug zemli," *Izvestiia*, November 5, 1957, 1; and "Soobshchenie TASS," *Pravda*, November 4, 1957, 1.

27. "Half-ton Satellite Circling Earth: Dog inside Reported in 'Good' Condition," *The Times*, November 4, 1957, 10; "U.S. Smarting under the Satellites," *The Times*, November 5, 1957, 10; and "Anniversary Display of Soviet Power," *The Times*, November 8, 1957, 10.

28. *New York Times*, November 4, 1957, 8; *New York Times*, November 5, 1957, 12; and *The Times*, November 4, 1957, 10.

29. V. Polynin, "Sovetskim sputnikam privet!" *Ogonek* 46 (1957): 6.

30. "Vse dal'she v kosmos," *Krasnaia zvezda*, November 5, 1957; "O dvizhenii vtorogo iskusstvennogo sputnika zemli," *Izvestiia*, November 5, 1957; and "Russian Indicates That Dog Will Die," *New York Times*, November 5, 1957.

31. Irina Volk, "Zhivoe suchshestvo v kosmose," *Literaturnaia gazeta*, November 5, 1957; and "Name of Satellite Dog Breeds Confusion Here," *New York Times*, November 5, 1957.

32. S. Morozov, "Pervyi puteshestvennik v kosmos," *Ogonek*, no. 46 (1957): 7.

33. "Soobshchenie TASS," *Pravda*, November 4, 1957, 1; "Vtoroi iskusstvenyi sputnik vrashchaetsia vokrug zemli," *Izvestiia*, November 5, 1957, 1; "O dvizhenii iskusstvennykh sputnikov zemli," *Krasnaia zvezda*, November 6, 1957, 2; and "O dvizhenii iskusstvennykh sputnikov zemli," *Izvestiia*, November 7, 1957, 12.

34. "O nabliudenii iskusstvennykh sputnikov zemli," *Pravda*, November 8, 1957, 2.

35. "O nabliudenii iskusstvennykh sputnikov zemli," *Izvestiia*, November 11, 1957, 1.

36. Max Frankel, "Satellite Return Set as Soviet Goal," *New York Times*, November 16, 1957, 1; and *Pravda*, November 13, 1957, 2.

37. Osgood Caruthers, "Soviet Space Dog Survives Fourth Trip," *New York Times*, July 14, 1959. Otvazhnaia may have flown twice in August 1958 under the name Kusachka.

38. *The Times*, July 9, 1959, 6.

39. A. Golikov, "Piat' poletov 'Otvazhnoi'," *Ogonek* 28 (1960): 30.

40. "Kosmos stal blizhe," *Izvestiia*, July 8, 1959.

41. Boris Chertok, *Rockets and People*, vol. 3., *Hot Days of the Cold War*, edited by Asif Siddiqi (Washington, D.C.: NASA History Division, 2009), 40–41; Alexander Milkus, "Do 'Belki' i 'Strelki' v kosmose pogibli Laika, Chaika i Lisichka," *Komsomol'skaia pravda*, August 18, 2000, 37; and Kelly Kizer Whitt, "Reluctant Astronauts: How Other Creatures Paved the Way for Human Space Travelers," *Astronomy* 29, no. 4 (2001): 42.

42. Chertok, *Rockets and People*, 3:50.

43. Seymour Toppings, "Two Dogs Frisky after Space Trip; Condition 'Perfect,' Soviet Says," *New York Times*, August 22, 1960, 1; "Satellite Dogs Shown in Moscow," *New York Times*, August 23, 1960, 3; "Vydaiushcheesia dostizhenie sovetskoi nauki i tekhniki," *Krasnaia zvezda*, August 25, 1960, 3; and "Krugovorot prirody v kabine kosmicheskogo korablia," *Literaturnaia gazeta*, August 27, 1960, 1.

44. "Sdelan novyi shag na puti k poletu cheloveka v kosmos," *Krasnaia zvezda*, August 20, 1960, 1; "Kosmonavt, gotov'sia v put'," *Literaturnaia gazeta*, August 23, 1960, 1; and *Ogonek* 35 (1960).

45. Osgood Caruthers, "Five-ton Soviet Space Craft with Two Dogs Put in Orbit," *New York Times*, December 2, 1960, 1; Seymour Toppings, "Soviet Space Craft with Dogs Aboard Burns on Re-entry," *New York Times*, December 3, 1960, 1; "Tretii kosmicheskii v polete," *Krasnaia zvezda*, December 2, 1960, 1; "O polete tret'ego sovetskogo korablia-sputnika," *Krasnaia zvezda*, December 3, 1960, 1; and Chertok, *Rockets and People*, 3:52–53.

46. Siddiqi, *Sputnik and the Soviet Space Challenge*, 259–60; and Chertok, *Rockets and People*, 3:53–54.

47. *Krasnaia zvezda*, March 11, 1961.

48. "Kosmonavty, tovs'!" *Krasnaia zvezda*, March 29, 1961, 4.

49. "Svershilos'!" *Krasnaia zvezda*, April 13, 1961, 3.

50. "Kennedys Get Puppy as a Gift from Khrushchev," *New York Times*, June 21, 1961, 4; and "Soviet Space Pup for Mrs. Kennedy," *The Times*, June 21, 1961, 12.

51. "O polete sputnika Kosmos-110," *Izvestiia*, February 27, 1966, 6; "Eksperiment prodolzhaetsia," *Izvestiia*, March 19, 1966, 5; "Biologicheskaia laboratoriia na orbite," *Izvestiia*, March 1, 1966, 5; "Soviet Orbits Two Dogs for Biological Study," *New York Times*, February 23, 1966, 1; Evert Clark, "Flight a Puzzle to U.S.," *New York Times*, February 24, 1966, 7; "Soviet Says Two Orbiting Dogs Provide Test for New Space Step," *New York Times*, February 24, 1966, 7; and "Soviet Space Dogs Seen Moving About," *New York Times*, February 28, 1966, 2.

52. "Otchet of rabote po sozdanuiu bazy dlia odnovremennogo oblucheniia 330 sobak po programme 'khronicheskogo eksperimenta' (1965)," Rossiisskii gosudarstvennyi arkhiv nauchno-tekhnicheskoi dokumentatsii (RGANTD), fond 4, opis 1, delo 45; Peter Grose, "Soviet Space Dogs Returned to Earth," *New York Times*, March 17, 1966, 1; Raymond H. Anderson, "Soviet Dogs Lost Muscular Control in Space," *New York Times*, May 17, 1966, 1; John Noble Wilford, "First Spanish Rocket," *New York Times*, October 16, 1966, 78; and Thomas J. Hamilton, "Report on Space Dogs Indicates Astronaut Health Peril on Long

Flights," *New York Times*, November 21, 1968, 18; and "Soviet Subjecting Dogs to Radiation Like That in Space," *New York Times*, October 20, 1968, 4.

53. Introduction to Adam Bartos, *Kosmos: A Portrait of the Russian Space Age*, 1st edition (New York: Princeton Architectural Press, 2001), 89.

54. W. Patrick McCray, *Keep Watching the Skies! The Story of Operation Moonwatch and the Dawn of the Space Age* (Princeton, N.J.: Princeton University Press, 2008), 142–64; also see James T. Andrews's chapter in this volume.

55. Siddiqi, *Sputnik and the Soviet Space Challenge*, 169. Also see Asif Siddiqi's chapter in this volume.

56. Golikov, "Piat' poletov Otvazhnoi," 30.

57. "Belka, Strelka, i shcheniata," *Ogonek* 8 (1961): 32–33.

58. A. Golikov and I. Smirnov, "Mezhzvezdnye puteshestvenniki," *Ogonek* 35 (1960): 2.

59. V. Borisov and O. Gorlov, *Zhizn' i kosmos* (Moscow: Sovetskaia Rossiia, 1961), 135–58; O Gorlov and V. Borisov, *Zhivotnye v kosmose* (Moscow: Znanie, 1960), 51–62; M. Vasil'ev, "Zhizn' v kosmose," *Iunyi naturalist* 8 (1960): 1; Igor Artem'ev, *Iskusstvennyi sputnik Zemli* (Moscow: Gosudarstvennoe izdatel'stvo detskoi literatury Ministerstva Prosveshcheniia RSFSR, 1958), 83, 91; and I. Strel'chuk and N. Gartsshtein, "Chertveronogie pomoshchniki uchenykh," *Krasnaia zvezda*, August 27, 1960, 3.

60. Amy Nelson, "A Hearth for a Dog: The Paradoxes of Soviet Pet Keeping," in *Borders of Socialism: The Private Sphere in the Soviet Union*, edited by Lewis Siegelbaum (New York: Palgrave Macmillan, 2006), 123–44. The reemergence of pet keeping tied into broader reformulations of domesticity and materialism as well. See Susan E. Reid, "Cold War in the Kitchen: Gender and the De-Stalinization of Consumer Taste under Khrushchev," *Slavic Review* 61, no. 2 (Summer 2002): 211–52; Susan E. Reid, "The Meaning of Home: 'The Only Bit of the World You Can Have to Yourself,'" in Siegelbaum, *Borders of Socialism*, 145–70; and Polly Jones, ed., *The Dilemmas of De-Stalinization: Negotiating Cultural and Social Change in the Khrushchev Era* (Oxford: Routledge, 2006).

61. Nikolai Vasil'evich Demidov and Miron Borisovich Rivchun, *Sobaki i koshki v bytu*, (Moscow: Gosudarstvennoe izdatel'stvo meditsinskoi literatury, 1959), 3; and A. M. Chel'tsov-Bebutov and N. N. Nemnonov, *Nashi vernye druz'ia* (Moscow: Prosveshchenie, 1974), 5.

62. Demidov and Rivchun, *Sobaki i koshki v bytu*, 8–10; "Tol'ko li drug?" *Sovetskaia Rossiia*, July 16, 1971; and B. Bialik, "Zhizn' i smert' Belogo Bima," *Komsomol'skaia pravda*, September 17, 1971.

63. Kenneth Love, "Britons Protest Dog in Satellite," *New York Times*, November 5, 1957, 12.

64. Chel'tsov-Bebutov and Nemnonov, *Nashi vernye druz'ia*, 5; Demidov and Rivchun, *Sobaki i koshki v bytu*, 5; and B. Riabinin, *Moi druz'ia* (Moscow: Gosudarstvennoe izdatel'stvo detskoi literatury, 1963).

65. V. Nemtsov, "Fantasy, A Book and Life," *Soviet Union*, no. 12 (December 1957): 39.

66. Diane L. Beers, *For the Prevention of Cruelty: The History of Animal Rights Activism in the United States* (Athens: Swallow Press / University of Ohio Press, 2006), 162–80.

67. Susan E. Lederer, "Political Animals: The Shaping of Biomedical Research Literature in Twentieth-century America," *Isis* 83, no. 1 (1992): 61–79.

68. Peter L. Smolders, *Soviets in Space*, translated by Marian Powell (New York, 1974), 103–4. M. A. Gerd and N. N. Gurovskii, *Pervye kosmonavty i pervye razvedchiki kosmosa* (Moscow: Izdatel'stvo Akademii nauk SSSR, 1962); Strel'chuk and Gartsshtein, "Chertveronogie pomoshchniki," 3; and V. Borisov and O. Gorlov, *Zhizn' i kosmos* (Moscow: Sovetskaia Rossiia, 1961), 136–38.

69. Catriona Kelly and David Shepherd, eds., *Constructing Russian Culture in the Age of Revolution, 1881–1940* (Oxford: Oxford University Press, 1998), 254–55; Todes, *Pavlov's Physiology Factory*, 123–52.

70. Volk, "Zhivoe suchchestvo," 2; Gorlov and Borisov, *Zhivotnye v kosmose*, 63; and Borisov and Gorlov, *Zhizn' i kosmos*, 135.

71. Strel'chuk and Gartsshtein, "Chetveronogie pomoshchniki," 3

72. Ostashev and Bashilova, "Prelestnaia, spokoinaia Laika," 13.

73. Golikov and Smirnov, "Mezhzvezdnye puteshestnenniki," 2.

74. V. N. Chernov and V. I. Yakovlev, "Research on Animal Flight in an Artificial Earth Satellite," *Iskusstvennye sputnik zemli* (English) 1 (1960): 108–10.

75. Kas'ian, "My kosmicheskie mediki," 271.

76. For details about the testing regimen, see Gerd and Gurovskii, *Pervye kosmonavty i pervye razvedchiki*; N. M. Sisiakian, ed., *Problemy kosmicheskoi biologii,* (Moscow: Izdatel'stvo akademii nauk SSSR, 1962), vol.1:377–91; N. Sisiakin, ed., *Problemy kosmicheskoi biologii* (Moscow: Izdatel'stvo akademii nauk SSSR, 1962), vol. 2:226–406; and M. A. Gerd, *Reaktsii i povedenie sobak v ekstremal'nykh usloviiakh* (Moscow: Nauka, 1976).

77. Siddiqi, *Sputnik and the Soviet Space Challenge*, 96; Gazenko also adopted one of the dogs that survived the crash landing in Siberia in December 1960. See "Interviu: Olegom Georgievichem, zapisannoe 7 ianvaria 2006," online at http://sobaka.udmweb.ru/zv22 .html.

78. Chertok, *Rockets and People*, 3:41–42.

79. Golovanov, *Korolev*, 550.

80. Volk, "Zhivoe sushchestvo"; and Ostashev and Bashilova, "Prelestnaia, spokoinaia Laika," 13.

81. For a current summary of these rumors, see "Memorial to Laika," available online at http://www.novareinna.com/bridge/laika.html; and Ted Strong, "Laika the Russian Space Dog!" available online at http://tedstrong.com/laika-trsd.shtml.

82. Mozzhorin et al., *Dorogi v kosmos*, 1:60; and Golovanov, *Korolev*, 551.

83. Sven Grahn, "Sputnik-2, Was It Really Built in a Month?" available online at http://www.svengrahn.pp.se/histind/Sputnik2/Sputnik2.htm; David Whitehouse, "First Dog in Space Died within Hours," *BBC News Online*, October 28, 2002, available online at http://news.bbc.co.uk/1/hi/sci/tech/2367681.stm; and Tim Radford, "Fate of First Canine Cosmonaut Revealed," *The Guardian*, October 30, 2002, available online at http://www .guardian.co.uk/international/story/0,3604,822152,00.html.

84. Justine Hankins, "Lost in Space," *The Guardian*, March 20, 2004, available online at http://www.guardian.co.uk/weekend/story/0,3605,1172484,00.html. On the guilt that several researchers experienced in conjunction with Laika's voyage, see Kas'ian, "My kosmicheskie mediki," 273–75.

85. A. Golikov and I. Smirnov, "Chetveronogie astronavty," *Ogonek* 49 (1960): 2.

86. The Soviet Union and several other Eastern bloc countries issued stamps of other space dogs, especially Belka, Strelka, Chernushka, and Zvezdochka.

87. "Soviet Smokers Now Have Filters," *New York Times,* September 11, 1958.

88. On the ongoing resonance of Laika in contemporary global culture, see Amy Nelson, "The Music of Memory and Forgetting: Global Echoes of Sputnik 2," in *Remembering the Space Age*, edited by Steven J. Dick (Washington, D.C.: NASA History Division, 2008), 237–25; and Amy Nelson, "Der abwesende Freund. Laikas kulturelles Nachleben," in *Ich, das Tier: Tiere als Persönlichkeiten in der Kulturgeschichte*, edited by Jessica Ullrich, Friedrich Weltzien, and Heike Fuhlbrügge (Berlin: Reimer Verlag, 2008), 215–24.

89. Star and Griesemer, "Institutional Ecology," 393.

90. Sisiakin, *Problemy kosmicheskoi biologii*, vols. 1–2 (1964); Gerd, *Reaktsii i povedenie sobak*; M. A. Gerd and N. N. Gurovskii, *Pervye kosmonavty i pervye razvedchiki kosmosa*, 2nd edition (Moscow: Izdatel'stvo Akademii nauk SSSR, 1965).

91. Star and Griesemer, "Institutional Ecology," 408.

92. Leonid Vysheslavsky, "Pamiati Laiki" (In memory of Laika), in *Zvezdnye sonety* (Moscow: Sovetskii pisatel', 1962), 71. I am grateful to Andrew Jenks for bringing this poem to my attention.

93. Walter A. McDougall, . . . *The Heavens and the Earth: A Political History of the Space Age* (Baltimore, Md.: Johns Hopkins University Press, 1997 [1985]), 3–4.

7. Cosmic Enlightenment

The author wishes to thank numerous institutions that supported this work and research, including the University of California at Berkeley's History Department and Graduate Division, the Allan Sharlin Memorial Fellowship of UC Berkeley's Institute of International Studies, the ACTR/ACCELS Advanced Research Fellowship, Fulbright-Hays, and the Charlotte W. Newcombe Doctoral Dissertation Fellowship in Religion and Ethics. I am also very grateful to Galina Zhelezniak and Vladimir Kozhanov for permission to use the wonderful images in this chapter. *Epigraph*: Vladimir Maiakovskii, "Listen!" in *An Anthology of Russian Literature from Earliest Writings to Modern Fiction: Introduction to a Culture*, edited by Nicholas Rzhevsky (Armonk, N.Y.: M. E. Sharpe, 2004), 443.

1. Viktor Pelevin, "The Code of the World" (Kod mira), *Frankfurter Allgemeine Zeitung*, 2001, available online at http://pelevin.nov.ru/rass/pe-kod/1.html. All translations are mine, unless otherwise indicated.

2. Ibid. On the material culture of the Soviet space program, see Cathleen Lewis, "The Red Stuff: A History of the Public and Material Culture of Early Human Spaceflight in the U.S.S.R." (PhD diss., George Washington University, 2008).

3. I borrow the term "dreamworld" to describe utopian ideology from Susan Buck-Morss; see Susan Buck-Morss, *Dreamworld and Catastrophe: The Passing of Mass Utopia in East and West* (Cambridge: MIT Press, 2002).

4. Numerous accounts exist on the political and technological dimensions of the space race in the context of the Cold War. See Matthew Brzezinski, *Red Moon Rising: Sputnik and the Hidden Rivalries That Ignited the Space Age* (New York: Times Books, 2007); Nicholas Daniloff, *The Kremlin and the Cosmos* (New York: Alfred A. Knopf, 1972); Walter A. McDougall, . . . *The Heavens and the Earth: A Political History of the Space Age* (New York: Basic Books, 1985); Asif A. Siddiqi, *Sputnik and the Soviet Space Challenge* (Gainesville: University Press of Florida, 2003); and Von Hardesty and Gene Eisman, *Epic Rivalry: The Inside Story of the Soviet and American Space Race* (Washington, D.C.: National Geographic Society, 2007).

5. There are numerous hagiographic accounts of Soviet cosmonauts, and "insider" accounts, by engineers in the space program or cosmonauts themselves, were especially popular. Some examples include E. Petrov, *Kosmonavty* (Moscow: "Krasnaia zvezda," 1963), and Titov's hagiographic biography of Yuri Gagarin; see German Stepanovich Titov, *Pervyi kosmonavt planety* (Moscow: "Znanie," 1971). Children's books were also a popular genre. On the myth of Gagarin, see Trevor Rockwell, "The Molding of the Rising Generation: Soviet Propaganda and the Hero Myth of Iurii Gagarin," *Past Imperfect* 12 (2006): 1–34.

6. Jay Bergman, "Valerij Chkalov: Soviet Pilot a New Soviet Man," *Journal of Contemporary History* 33, no. 1 (January 1998): 135–52; Georgii Baidukov, *Russian Lindbergh: The*

Life of Valery Chkalov, translated by Peter Belov; edited by Von Hardesty (Washington, D.C.: Smithsonian Institution Press, 1991); Von Hardesty, *Red Phoenix: The Rise of Soviet Air Power, 1941–1945* (Washington, D.C.: Smithsonian Institution Press, 1982); Robin Higham, John T. Greenwood, and Von Hardesty, eds., *Russian Aviation and Air Power in the Twentieth Century* (Portland, Ore.: Frank Cass, 1998); and Kendall E. Bailes, *Technology and Society under Lenin and Stalin: Origins of the Soviet Technical Intelligentsia, 1917–1941* (Princeton, N.J.: Princeton University Press, 1978).

7. *XXII S'ezd KPSS* (Moscow: Politizdat, 1962), 411.

8. On December 19, 1917, the Bolshevik government transferred the legal jurisdiction over changes in civil status from the church to the newly created Department for the Registration of Acts of Civil Status. On January 23, 1918, the Bolsheviks separated church and state and secularized education, thereby gaining unprecedented power over the population.

On antireligious campaigns in the early Soviet period, see Mikhail Ivanovich Odintsov, *Gosudarstvo i tserkov': Istoriia vzaimootnoshenii, 1917–1938 gg* (Moscow: Znanie, 1991); Valerii Arkadevich Alekseev, *"Shturm nebes" otmeniaetsia?: Kriticheskie ocherki po istorii bor'by s religiei v SSSR* (Moscow: Rossiia molodaia, 1992); Glennys Young, *Power and the Sacred in Revolutionary Russia: Religious Activists in the Village* (University Park: Pennsylvania State University Press, 1997); Arto Luukkanen, *The Religious Policy of the Stalinist State, A Case Study: The Central Standing Commission on Religious Questions, 1929–1938* (Helsinki: Suomen Historiallinen Seura, 1997); Daniel Peris, *Storming the Heavens: The Soviet League of the Militant Godless* (Ithaca: Cornell University Press, 1998); William B. Husband, *"Godless Communists": Atheism and Society in Soviet Russia, 1917–1932* (DeKalb: Northern Illinois University Press, 2000); Edward E. Roslof, *Red Priests: Renovationism, Russian Orthodoxy, and Revolution, 1905–1946* (Bloomington: Indiana University Press, 2002); Heather J. Coleman, *Russian Baptists and Spiritual Revolution, 1905–1929* (Bloomington: Indiana University Press, 2005); and Paul Froese, *The Plot to Kill God: Findings from the Soviet Experiment in Secularization* (Berkeley: University of California Press, 2008).

On prerevolutionary and early Soviet enlightenment efforts, see Jeffrey Brooks, *When Russia Learned to Read: Literacy and Popular Literature, 1861–1917* (Princeton: Princeton University Press, 1985). On the early Soviet period, see James T. Andrews, *Science for the Masses: The Bolshevik State, Public Science, and the Popular Imagination in Soviet Russia, 1917–1934* (College Station: Texas A&M University Press, 2003). Importantly, the Soviet enlightenment campaign extended beyond education and the inculcation of high culture to a broader "civilizing" agenda. The *kul'turnost'* campaign emphasized personal hygiene, social propriety, and correct behavior. On *kul'turnost'*, see Vadim Volkov, "The Concept of *Kul'turnost'*: Notes on the Stalinist Civilizing Process," in *Stalinism: New Directions*, edited by Sheila Fitzpatrick (New York: Routledge, 2000); and Catriona Kelly, *Refining Russia: Advice Literature, Polite Culture, and Gender from Catherine to Yeltsin* (Oxford: Oxford University Press, 2001).

The Soviet state's concern with the persistence of religiosity is evident in the renewed antireligious campaign during the Khrushchev era after the relative calm in church-state relations in the second half of Stalin's reign. See Joan Delaney Grossman, "Khrushchev's Antireligious Policy and the Campaign of 1954," *Europe-Asia Studies* 24, no. 3 (January 1973): 374–86; John Anderson, *Religion, State, and Politics in the Soviet Union and Successor States* (New York: Cambridge University Press, 1994); Mikhail Shkarovskii, *Russkaia Pravoslavnaia Tserkov' pri Staline i Khrushcheve: Gosudarstvenno-tserkovnye otnosheniia v SSSR v 1939–1964 godakh* (Moscow: Krutitskoe patriarshee podvor'e, 1999); Tatiana A. Chumachenko, *Church and State in Soviet Russia: Russian Orthodoxy from World War II to the*

Khrushchev Years, translated and edited by Edward E. Roslof (Armonk, N.Y.: M.E. Sharpe, 2002); Nathaniel Davis, *A Long Walk to Church: A Contemporary History of Russian Orthodoxy* (Boulder, Colo.: Westview Press, 2003); and the works of Dimitry V. Pospielovsky, especially *A History of Marxist-Leninist Atheism and Soviet Antireligious Policies* (New York: St. Martin's Press, 1987) and *Totalitarizm i veroispovedanie* (Moscow: Bibleisko-bogoslovskii in-t sv. Apostola Andreia, 2003).

9. *22nd S'ezd KPSS*, 411.

10. "Piat' let shturmu kosmosa," *Nauka i religiia*, no. 10 (October 1962): 3–8.

11. Ibid.

12. "Address of the Central Committee of the KPSS, the Presidium of the Supreme Soviet and the government of the Soviet Union," *Komsomol'skaia Pravda*, April 13, 1961.

13. "Estafeta pokolenii," *Nauka i religiia*, no. 9 (September 1962): 4.

14. "Piat' let shturmu kosmosa," 5.

15. Ibid.

16. Ibid., 7.

17. Peter L. Berger, *The Sacred Canopy: Elements of a Sociological Theory of Religion* (Garden City, N.Y.: Doubleday & Company, 1967), 112–13. On the classic secularization thesis and its numerous detractors, see David Martin, *On Secularization: Towards a Revised General Theory* (Burlington, Vt.: Ashgate, 2005); Brian Wilson, "Secularization and Its Discontents," in his *Religion in Sociological Perspective* (New York: Oxford University Press, 1982), 148–79; and Steve Bruce, ed., *Religions and Modernization: Sociologists and Historians Debate the Secularization Thesis* (New York: Oxford University Press, 1992).

18. Berger, *Sacred Canopy*, 112–13.

19. P. V. Liakhotskii's *Zavoevanie kosmosa i religiia* (Groznyi: Checheno-Ingushskoe knizhnoe izdanie, 1964) is typical of a genre that emerged at this time depicting space conquest as a weapon in the war against religion. See also Sergei Fedorovich Anisimov, *Nauka i religiia o smysle zhizni: Otvety na voprosy* (Moscow: Znanie, 1964); V. N. Komarov, *Kosmos, bog i vechnost' mira* (Moscow: Gozpolitizdat, 1963); E. T. Fadeev, *O cheloveke, kosmose i boge* (Moscow: Znanie, 1965); G. I. Naan, *Chelovek, bog i kosmos* (Moscow: Sovetskaia Rossiia, 1963); *Zavoevanie neba i vera v boga: Sbornik statei*, edited by K. K. Gabova (Moscow: Znanie, 1964); B. M. Marianov, *Otvoevannoe nebo* (Moscow: Moskovskii rabochii, 1971); *Voprosy mirovozzreniia v lektsiiakh po astronomii: Sbornik* (Moscow: Znanie, 1974); and "Kosmos, kosmogoniia, kosmologiia (Podborka statei i interviu)," *Nauka i religiia*, no. 12 (December 1968).

20. Speculation on the cosmological significance of space travel was not confined to the Soviet press but permeated religious and secular media abroad. For a thorough discussion of the range of religious responses to human space travel, see Ryan Jeffrey McMillen, "Space Rapture: Extraterrestrial Millennialism and the Cultural Construction of Space Colonization" (PhD diss., University of Texas at Austin, 2004).

21. "1000 Pisem," *Nauka i religiia*, no. 2 (February 1960): 8. Unless otherwise noted, all translations in this chapter are mine.

22. Editorial, "Survey of Letters: What Is God? [Two letters from former believers who have abandoned religion since Gagarin's spaceflight]," *Izvestiia*, May 23, 1961, 4. In *Current Digest of the Soviet Press* 13, no. 21 (1961): 28.

23. C. L. Sulzberger, "Foreign Affairs: Paradise and Old Noah Khrushchev," *New York Times*, September 9, 1961, 18. Quoted in McMillen, "Space Rapture," 121.

24. "Presidential Prayer Breakfast," *New York Times*, March 2, 1962, 3.

25. For a more detailed discussion of the escalation of the space theological debate between the American and Soviet sides, see McMillen, "Space Rapture," 115–37.

26. The widespread claims about Gagarin's statement (about not encountering heavenly bodies in space) are never cited, and I have yet to find a direct quote from him on the subject, yet there is no doubt that it was widely propagated, especially within the USSR. In his autobiographical *Moscow Stories*, Loren R. Graham, one of the most prominent historians of Soviet science, mentions that a pamphlet about this supposed statement by Gagarin was sold in the antireligious bookstore in Zagorsk (Sergeev Posad); see Loren R. Graham, *Moscow Stories* (Bloomington: Indiana University Press, 2006), 178.

27. Louis Cassels, "Religion in America," *Chicago Defender*, May 26, 1962, 8; "Titov, Denying God, Puts Faith in People," *New York Times*, May 7, 1962. "Gherman Titov, Soviet Cosmonaut, Comments at World's Fair, Seattle, Washington, May 6, 1962," *Seattle Daily Times*, May 7, 1962, 2.

28. G. Titov, "Vstretil li ia boga?" *Nauka i religiia*, no. 1 (January 1962): 10.

29. Ibid.

30. In his study of Russian popular culture, the historian Richard Stites notes that Gagarin's brother described hundreds of letters that the cosmonaut received from former believers testifying to their atheist conversions; see Richard Stites, *Russian Popular Culture: Entertainment and Society since 1900* (New York: Cambridge University Press, 1992), 175.

31. The editorial cites believers who "came to the same conclusion" as Danilova—three Orthodox women (from Moscow, Odessa, and Vinnitsa) and another three Baptist women (one Nina Velikanova and her two friends). The editorial also mentions the conversion of the priest Pavel Darmanskii, whose faith was called into doubt during a scientific-atheist lecture on astronomy. "Piat' let shturmu kosmosa," 8.

32. Danilova's letter is originally published in "Survey of Letters: What Is God?" *Izvestiia*, May 23, 1961, 4. Danilova is also cited in Liakhotskii, *Zavoevanie kosmosa i religiia*, 64–68; and V. Bazykin, "V nebesakh chelovek, a ne bog," *Sovetskie profsoiuzy*, no. 13 (1961): 28. For other examples of "conversion" stories, see *Komsomol'skaia Pravda*, August 13, 1962; "Estafeta pokolenii" *Nauka i religiia*, no. 9 (September 1962): 5; "Piat' let shturmu kosmosa," 3–8; and *Izvestiia*, May 22, 1961.

33. Rossiiskii gosudarstvennyi arkhiv sotsial'no-politicheskoi istorii [henceforth RGASPI], f. 599, op. 1, d. 211, ll. 116–21.

34. Ibid., 117–18.

35. On Soviet atheist depictions of religious beliefs and practices as antisocial, see Sonja Christine Luehrmann, "Forms and Methods: Teaching Atheism and Religion in the Mari Republic, Russian Federation" (PhD diss., University of Michigan, 2009).

36. RGASPI, f. 599, op. 1, d. 211, l. 121.

37. In my interviews with former atheist agitators, the argument that space travel proved that heaven and deities did not exist was almost unanimously invoked as an example of the "vulgar atheism" from which the subject sought to distance himself or herself. Olga Brushlinskaia, the editor-in-chief of the journal *Science and Religion* (Nauka i religiia), interview with author, Moscow, Russia, December 7, 2008.

38. Ernst Kolman, "Chelovek v epokhu kosmicheskikh poletov," *Voprosy filosofii*, no. 11 (November 1960): 124–32.

39. Kolman came to Russia as a prisoner of war. He studied at Moscow State University, worked with Khrushchev and Kaganovich in the Moscow city government over the course of the 1930s, and was head of the Moscow Mathematical Society (from 1930 to 1932) and deputy head of the science department of the Moscow party organs. See Arnosht (Ernst) Kolman, *My ne dolzhny byli tak zhit'* (New York: Chalidze Publications, 1982); and William Taubman, *Khrushchev: The Man and His Era* (New York: Norton, 2003), 91–93. I am grateful to Professor John Connelly for drawing my attention to Kolman's biography.

40. Kolman proposed actual space colonies as humans made their way to the moon, Mars, and Venus, then the rest of the galaxy, and finally beyond.

41. Kolman, "Chelovek v epokhu kosmicheskikh poletov," 132.

42. For an excellent analysis of the physical and psychological preparation of Soviet cosmonauts, see Slava Gerovitch, "'New Soviet Man' inside Machine: Human Engineering, Spacecraft Design, and the Construction of Communism," *Osiris* (2007): 22, 152.

43. Kolman, "Chelovek v epokhu kosmicheskikh poletov," 127.

44. Ibid., 128.

45. Mark Borisovich Mitin was chairman of the "Knowledge" Society (from 1956 to 1960) and the editor of the journal *Voprosy filosofii* (Problems of philosophy) (from 1960 to 1968).

46. Gosudarstvennyi arkhiv Rossiiskoi Federatsii [henceforth GARF], f. 9547, op. 1, d. 1209, l. 287.

47. Ibid.

48. Letchik-kosmonavt A. A. Leonov i kandidat meditsinskikh nauk Lebedev, "Proniknovenie v kosmos i otrazhenie chelovekom prostranstva na Zemle," *Voprosy filosofii*, no. 1 (1966): 3.

49. Letchik-kosmonaut Yuri Gagarin and kandidat meditsinskikh nauk Lebedev, "Osvoenie Luny chelovekom," *Voprosy filosofii*, no. 3 (1966): 25. (Cosmonaut) Georgii Timofeevich Beregovoi, "Shagi po zemle, shagi v kosmose," *Ia—ateist: 25 otvetov na vopros 'Pochemu vy ateist?'* (Moscow: Izdatel'stvo politicheskoi literatury, 1980), 17–21. (Cosmonaut) Oleg Grigorievich Makarov, "Ia-veriashchii," *Ia—ateist: 25 otvetov na vopros 'Pochemu vy ateist?'* (Moscow: Izdatel'stvo politicheskoi literatury, 1980), 22–27. (Cosmonaut) Konstantin Feoktistov, "Neskol'ko slov o bessmertii," *Nauka i religiia*, no. 4 (1966).

50. On the intellectual history of atheism in imperial Russia, see Victoria Sophia Frede, "The Rise of Unbelief among Educated Russians in the Late Imperial Period" (PhD diss., University of California–Berkeley, 2002).

51. On antireligious propaganda and policies, see Dimitry Pospielovsky, *A History of Marxist-Leninist Atheism and Soviet Antireligious Policies* and *The Orthodox Church in the History of Russia* (Crestwood, N.Y.: St. Vladimir's Seminary Press, 1998).

52. See Husband, *"Godless Communists"*; Froese, *Plot to Kill God*; Young, *Power and the Sacred in Revolutionary Russia*; Alekseev, *"Shturm nebes" otmeniaetsia*; and Peris, *Storming the Heavens*.

53. Two studies that do focus on scientific education provide insight into the broader context of atheism and enlightenment: see Brooks, *When Russia Learned to Read*; and Andrews, *Science for the Masses*, 6.

54. The historian Jeffrey Brooks has argued that for many intellectuals involved in the enlightenment project the battle was against superstition rather than religion. He points out that priests and teachers were allied with authors of popular literature in the task of enlightening the population. Superstition was "clearly not equated" with religion, "nor was atheism considered a necessary concomitant to the rational world view." See Brooks, *When Russia Learned to Read*, 251. James Andrews has demonstrated that the primary goal of science popularizers was to demystify natural occurrences and explain evolutionary phenomena from a scientific perspective; see Andrews, *Science for the Masses*, 104–5, 172.

55. The first Soviet atheist works that strove to get beyond the political battle against religious institutions presented religion as a phenomenon with a predetermined life cycle (and therefore destined to decline and, finally, to become extinct). Because the source of religion's vitality was the ignorance of believers, the principal weapon against it was edu-

cation. Emblematic of this approach are the works of Emelian Iaroslavskii, the leading Soviet atheist of the prewar period and the chairman of the League of Militant Atheists. See Emelian Iaroslavskii, *Kak rodiatsia, zhivut i umiraiut bogi i bogini* (Moscow: Sovetskaia Rossiia, 1959) and *Bibliia dlia veruiushchikh i neveruiushchikh* (Leningrad: Lenizdat, 1975).

56. On utopian and mystical scientific thought, see Asif A. Siddiqi, "Imagining the Cosmos: Utopians, Mystics, and the Popular Culture of Spaceflight in Revolutionary Russia," *Osiris* 23 (2008): 260–88; James T. Andrews, "In Search of a Red Cosmos: Space Exploration, Public Culture, and Soviet Society," in *Societal Impact of Spaceflight*, edited by Steven J. Dick and Roger D. Launius (Washington, D.C.: National Aeronautics and Space Administration, History Division, 2007); Alexander C. T. Geppert, "Flights of Fancy: Outer Space and the European Imagination, 1923–1969," in Dick and Launius, *Societal Impact of Spaceflight*; Igor A. Kazus, "The Idea of Cosmic Architecture and the Russian Avant-garde of the Early Twentieth Century," *Cosmos: From Romanticism to the Avant-garde*, edited by Jean Clair (Montreal, Quebec: Montreal Museum of Fine Arts, 1999). On Fedorovism and Russian Cosmism, see Michael Hagemeister, "Russian Cosmism in the 1920s and Today," in *The Occult in Russian and Soviet Culture*, edited by Bernice Glatzer Rosenthal (Ithaca, N.Y.: Cornell University Press, 1997), 185–202; and Olga Matich, *Erotic Utopia: The Decadent Imagination in Russia's Fin de Siècle* (Madison: University of Wisconsin Press, 2005).

57. Brooks, *When Russia Learned to Read*, 259.

58. Richard Stites has shed light on the contradictory nature of the early Soviet scientific enlightenment, arguing that the fascination with immortality and space travel "illustrate[s] vividly the relationship between the futuristic speculation and pathos of the period and the reality from which it arose: immortality yearned for in a land still groaning from a decade of holocaust; space flight, in a land where wooden plow and horse-cart were everyday sights"; see Richard Stites, *Revolutionary Dreams: Utopian Vision and Experimental Life in the Russian Revolution* (New York: Oxford University Press, 1989), 169.

59. On the intellectual world of Tsiolkovskii, see Siddiqi, "Imagining the Cosmos"; James T. Andrews, *Red Cosmos: K. E. Tsiolkovskii: Grandfather of Soviet Rocketry* (College Station: Texas A&M University Press, 2009); and McMillen, "Space Rapture," 53. McMillen describes Tsiolkovskii as "more metaphysicist than engineer." This intertwining of mystical and technological utopianism, Svetlana Boym has suggested, is "part of a history of technology in Russia, an 'enchanted technology' founded on charisma as much as calculus, on pre-modern myth as well as modern science"; see Svetlana Boym, "Kosmos: Remembrances of the Future," in *Kosmos: A Portrait of the Russian Space Age* (New York: Princeton Architectural Press, 2001), 83.

60. As if to underscore the thin line between the metaphorical and the literal, the Militant Atheists raised funds for the construction of a "Bezbozhnik" airplane (later followed by a "Bezbozhnik" tank and submarine). The league ceremonially presented the airplane as a gift to the Red Army in June 1929. Resources were mobilized with calls for donations in the league's periodicals. See "SVB v bor'be za mobilizatsiiu sredstv," *Antireligioznik*, no. 6 (1935): 62. On atheist propaganda in the Soviet industrial complex, see V. N. Kuriatnikov, "Vlianie religioznoi obstanovki SSSR na stanovlenie neftianogo kompleksa Uralo-Povolzhia v 30-50ee gg. 20th veka," *Religiovedenie: Nauchno teroeticheskii zhurnal*, no. 4 (2006): 42–47.

61. *Bezbozhnik* contained articles linking flight and religion, such as "The Church and Aviation" (*Bezbozhnik*, no. 8 [1935]), and illustrations of technology colonizing the sky: an airplane with "Bezbozhnik" written across the body pursuing God and a cupid as they fly off into the distance (cover of *Bezbozhnik*, no. 22 [November 1928]); a woman parachuting

in front of a church with an airplane flying in the background, and a zeppelin serenely floating above the city. See the covers on the following *Bezbozhnik* issues: no. 11 (1928); no. 2 (1935); and no. 8 (1935).

62. See the works of Nikolai Petrovich Kamenshchikov, and Grigorii Abramovich Gurev's *Kopernikovskaia eres' v proshlom i nastoiashchem i istoriia vzaimootnoshenii nauki i religii* (Leningrad: GAIZ, 1933) and *Nauka i religiia o vselennoi* (Moscow: OGIA, 1934). See also Gurev's articles in the atheist journal *Antireligioznik*: G. Gurev, "Vopros o nachale i kontse vselennoi v propagande bezbozhiia," *Antireligioznik*, no. 7 (July 1926): 17–26; G. Gurev, "Vopros o nachale i kontse vselennoi v propagande bezbozhiia (prodolzhenie)," *Antireligioznik*, no. 9 (October 1926): 55–62; and G. Gurev, "Vopros o nachale i kontse vselennoi v propagande bezbozhiia (konets)," *Antireligioznik*, no. 10 (October 1926): 11–21.

63. For instance, Kamenshchikov's *Pravda o neve: Antireligioznye besedy s krest'ianami o mirozdanii* (The truth about the sky: Antireligious conversations with peasants about the origins of the world) (Leningrad: Priboi, 1931), covered such folk beliefs as "how Kuzma forecast the weather" and "the beginning and the end of the world." Kamenshchikov's *Mir bezbozhnika* (The world of the atheist) (Leningrad: Priboi, 1931) asserted the authority of science over the cosmos with chapters like "The world is not as it seems, and is not as it is presented by the church"; "The construction and evolution of the universe"; and the past and future of Earth. Besides his prolific atheist publications, Professor Kamenshchikov also set up an astronomical exhibit of Foucault's Pendulum at the St. Isaac Cathedral in Leningrad, which briefly served as an antireligious museum. Kamenshchikov published other works that used astronomical findings in atheist propaganda as well as prominent and widely used astronomy textbooks. See N. Kamenshchikov, *Astronomiia bezbozhnika* (Leningrad: Priboi, 1931); Kamenshchikov, *Astronomicheskie zadachi dlia iunoshestva* (Moscow: GIZ, 1923); and Kamenshchikov, *Nachal'naia astronomiia* (Moscow: GIZ, 1924).

64. N. Kamenshchikov, *Chto videli na nebe popy, a chto videm my* (Moscow: Ateist, 1930).

65. The letter was published in *Izvestiia* on March 27, 1930, and reproduced in the popular science journal *Mirovedenie*, nos. 3–4 (1930): 141–49. A response to an alleged comment made by the pope about the repression of culture and science in the Soviet Union, the letter was a Soviet critique of the Vatican's historical repression of astronomers and science in general.

66. *Sovremennaia arkhitektura* 3 (1927): 79.

67. Designed by architects M. Barshch and M. Siniavskii, the Moscow Planetarium, a brilliant example of constructivist architecture, was conceived as a monument to technology and scientific materialism. Considering the material conditions of the Soviet Union in the 1920s, the mobilization of resources for a planetarium is a testament to the faith in the potential of scientific enlightenment. The art historian Catherine Cooke has pointed out that progressive Soviet architects hoped that the construction of the planetarium would jump-start bureaucratic inertia to promote more rational Soviet construction practices and progressive city planning; see Catherine Cooke, *Russian Avant-Garde: Theories of Art, Architecture, and the City* (London: Academy Editions, 1995), 133–35.

68. Aleksey Gan, "Novomu teatru—novoe zdanie," *Sovremennaia arkhitektura* 3 (1927): 80–81. Interestingly, Gan sees the theater in general as a regressive, rather than a progressive, force. The theater, Gan writes, is nothing other than a space to satisfy a primitive instinct for spectacle, an instinct that will persist "until society grows to the level of a scientific understanding [of the world] and the instinctual need for spectacle comes up against the real phenomena of the world and technology." The planetarium, then, while still satisfying the instinct for spectacle, "goes from servicing religion to servicing science."

69. Ibid., 81.

70. B. A. Vorontsov-Veliaminov, *Astronomicheskaia Moskva v 20e gody: Istoriko-astronomicheskie issledovaniia* (Moscow: Nauka, 1986); and V. N. Komarov and K. A. Portsevskii, *Moskovskii planetarii* (Moscow: Moskovskii rabochii, 1979).

71. Il'ia Il'f and Evgenii Petrov, *Dvenadtsat' stul'ev: Zolotoi telenok* (Moscow: Eksmo, 2006), 456.

72. Ibid., 458.

73. Nicholas Timasheff's classic work explains the abandonment utopianism for more traditional values in the mid-1930s as a "great retreat"; see Nicholas Timasheff, *The Great Retreat: The Growth and Decline of Communism in Russia* (New York: E. P. Dutton & Company, 1946).

74. On the reversal of Soviet church-state relations during World War II, see M. V. Shkarovskii, *Russkaia pravoslavnaia tserkov' i sovetskoe gosudarstvo v 1943–1964 godakh: Ot 'premiriia' k novoi voine* (St. Petersburg: DEAN + ADIA-M, 1995); S. Merritt Miner, *Stalin's Holy War: Religion, Nationalism, and Alliance Politics, 1941–1945* (Chapel Hill: University of North Carolina Press, 2003); and Davis, *Long Walk to Church*.

75. Emblematic of this ideological turn away from antireligious rhetoric was the disbanding of the League of Militant Atheists and the shutting down of most Soviet atheist periodical publications in 1941.

76. For an overview of the history of the "Knowledge" Society, see James T. Andrews, "All-Union Society for the Dissemination of Political and Scientific Knowledge ("Znanie" Society)," in *Modern Encyclopedia of Russia and the Soviet Union*, vol. 2, entry #124, edited by Donald R. Kelley (Gainesville, Fla.: Academic Press International, 1990).

77. Lectures of the period include V. A. Shishakov, *Nebo i nebesnye iavleniia* (Moscow: Izdatel'stvo Moskovksogo planetariia, 1940); M. I. Shakhnovich, *Sueverie i nauchnoe predvidenie* (Leningrad: Lenizdat, 1945); B. A. Vorontsov-Veliaminov, *Vselennaia* (Moscow: Gostekhizdat, 1947); M. V. Emdin, *Nauka i religiia: Stenografiia publichnoi lektsii, prochitannoi v 1948 g v Leningrade* (Leningrad: Obshchestvo po rasprostraneniiu politicheskikh i nauchnykh znanii, 1948); and V. A. Shishakov, *Nauka i religiia o stroenii vselennoi: Nauchno-populiarnaia lektsiia s metodicheskimi ukazaniiami* (Moscow: Pravda, 1950).

78. Shkarovskii notes that atheism was barely mentioned as late as the Nineteenth Party Congress in 1952; see Shkarovskii, *Russkaia pravoslavnaia tserkov' i sovetskoe gosudarstvo v 1943–1964 godakh*, 46.

79. On July 7, 1954, the party issued a decree titled "On Great Insufficiencies in the Propagating of Scientific Atheism and on Measures for Its Improvement," criticizing the low level of attention that antireligious propaganda and atheist education had received in previous decades. Yet the direction of the party line was so ambiguous that interpretations on the local level fell on both sides of the spectrum—from excessive permissiveness to excessive force against believers and the church. Reports from local organs about believers protesting state measures against them called for a second decree to provide party cadres with a more clear direction. "On Errors in Scientific-Atheist Propaganda among the People," issued on November 10, 1954, criticized the "administrative methods" employed to harass the clergy believers. On the developments and reception of the 1954 atheist decrees by party, state, and church, see Chumachenko, *Church and State in Soviet Russia*, 129–34.

80. The Third Party Program underscored the increasingly important role of "communist morality" as "the administrative regulation of the relations among people decreases." See *Programma Kommunisticheskoi Partii Sovetskogo Soiuza priniata XXII s'ezdom KPSS* (Moscow: Izdatel'stvo politicheskoi literatury, 1971), 116–21. As the historian Stephen Kotkin has observed, in the evolving definition of socialism, the few constants were a commitment to modernization and Soviet distinctiveness. See Stephen Kotkin, *Magnetic*

Mountain: Stalinism as a Civilization (Berkeley: University of California Press, 1997). On the importance of values in communist modernity, see David L. Hoffmann, *Stalinist Values: The Cultural Norms of Soviet Modernity, 1917–1941* (Ithaca, N.Y.: Cornell University Press, 2003). On communist morality in the Khrushchev era, see Deborah A. Field, *Private Life and Communist Morality in Khrushchev's Russia* (New York: Peter Lang, 2007). Arguably, then, what made Soviet modernization distinct was its promise of a morally superior modernity.

81. Historian Mark Sandle has noted that the Third Party Program "made it clear that the definition of 'needs' would be highly circumscribed. The inculcation of Communist consciousness through extensive agitprop work would result in the population itself moderating their demands"; see Mark Sandle, "Brezhnev and Developed Socialism: The Ideology of *Zastoi*," in *Brezhnev Reconsidered*, edited by Edwin Bacon and Mark Sandle (New York: Palgrave Macmillan, 2002), 177.

82. See David E. Powell, *Antireligious Propaganda in the Soviet Union: A Study of Mass Persuasion* (Cambridge: MIT Press, 1975).

83. The society had an expansive institutional structure organized around the All-Union "Knowledge" Society and extending down through the republic, regional, and local level. Corresponding local branches of the party exercised control over each local branch of the society. GARF, f. 9547, op. 1, d. 1048, l. 5.

84. The party's renewed interest in atheist education was also made evident by the reintroduction of "Foundations of Scientific Atheism" (Osnovy nauchnogo ateizma) in higher education. See Michael Froggatt, "Renouncing Dogma, Teaching Utopia: Science in Schools under Khrushchev," in *The Dilemmas of De-Stalinization: Negotiating Cultural and Social Change in the Khrushchev Era*, edited by Polly Jones (New York: Routledge), 250–67.

85. See Estonian astronomer G. Naan's article "Chelovek, bog i kosmos," *Nauka i religiia*, no. 2 (1961): 5–10; "Veril li Tsiolkovskii v boga?" *Nauka i religiia*, no. 3 (1962): 25; the Ukrainian astronomer S. Vsekhsviatskii's "Tainy nebesnykh stranits," *Nauka i religiia*, no. 1 (1963): 8–13; and "Mogli li kosmonavty videt' boga?" *Nauka i religiia*, no. 1 (1963). A number of articles authored by cosmonauts themselves were also published, such as Iu. Gagarin, "Na poroge griadushchikh shturmov," *Nauka i religiia*, no. 4 (1964): 10 and K. Feoktistov's "Neskol'ko slov o bessmertii," *Nauka i religiia*, no. 4 (1966). The journal also dedicated an entire issue to space exploration and cosmology; see "Kosmos, kosmogoniia, kosmologiia (Podborka statei i interview)," *Nauka i religiia*, no. 12 (1968).

86. See the inside cover of *Nauka i religiia*, no. 1 (1959).

87. On the transfer of the Moscow Planetarium, see GARF, f. 9547, op. 1, d. 1429; and Tsentral'nyi arkhiv goroda Moskvy (TsAGM), f. 709, op. 1, d. 177.

88. TsAGM, f. 709, op. 1, d. 177, l. 75. In 1959 the Moscow Planetarium had an income of 1,906,000 rubles, while its expenditures constituted 2,071,000 rubles—that is, it had a 165,000 ruble deficit.

89. GARF, f. A-561, op. 1, d. 492.

90. In 1974 planetariums across the USSR hosted 3,586,000 lectures on science in general and 897,000 lectures on atheism in particular. This includes lectures conducted beyond planetarium buildings by "mobile" planetariums. See Iu. K. Fishevskii, "Obshchestvo 'Znanie' i propaganda nauchnogo mirovozzreniia," *Voprosy nauchnogo ateizma* 19 (1974): 76.

91. TsAGM, f. 709, op. 1, d. 177, l. 75, Decision of the Council of Ministers (April 17, 1959) and the Mosgorispolkom (June 29, 1959).

92. Ibid.

93. Some prominent examples include the Gorky/Nizhnyi Novgorod Planetarium,

which opened in 1948 in the space of the Alekseevskaia Church of the Blagoveshchen-skii Monastery; the Barnaul Planetarium, which was constructed in the space of the Kre-stovozdvizhenskaia Church and opened in 1950; and the Kiev Planetarium, the oldest in Ukraine, which was opened in 1952 in the former Aleksandr Catholic Cathedral.

94. For an excellent description of day-to-day enlightenment work conducted through the planetarium, see the memoirs of Kharkiv Planetarium lecturer Natal'ia Konstanti-novna Bershova, "Esli zvezdy zazhigaiut . . . Zapiski lektora Khar'kovskogo Planetariia," available online at http://kharkov.vbelous.net/planetar/index.htm.

95. In 1963 the cosmonauts A. G. Nikolaev and G. S. Titov lectured at the Moscow Planetarium. GARF, f. 9547, op. 1, d. 1324, l. 9.

96. GARF, f. 9547, op. 1, d. 1048, l. 14.

97. Ibid.

98. GARF, f. 9547, op. 1, d. 1324, ll. 26–27. Based on my archival research, this un-willingness on the part of scientists, and the intelligentsia in general, to agitate against religion was evidently widespread.

99. GARF, f. 9547, op. 1, d. 1048, l. 15.

100. TsAGM, f. 1782, op. 3, d. 183.

101. TsAGM, f. 1782, op. 3, d. 183, l. 4.

102. Ibid., 6.

103. Ibid., 7.

104. Ibid.

105. GARF, A–561, op. 1, d. 492, ll. 25–28.

106. Ibid., 36–39.

107. GARF, f. 9547, op. 1, d. 1048, l. 22.

108. Rossiiski gosudarstvennyi arkhiv noveishei istorii (RGANI), f. 71, op. 1, d. 15, l. 171.

109. Ibid., 151–53.

110. The first expeditions to study religiosity were conducted in the late 1950s by the Institute of History of the Soviet Academy of Sciences (under the guidance of the historian Aleksandr Il'ich Klibanov) and the Department of Atheism at Moscow State University.

111. For a succinct discussion of the development of the sociology of religion in the post-Stalin period, see Mikhail Smirnov, "Sovremennaia rossiiskaia sotsiologiia religii: Otkuda i zachem?," *Religiovedenie: Nauchno-teoreticheskii zhurnal*, no. 2 (Moscow 2007), and M. M. Shakhnovich, "Otechestvennoe religiovedenie 20-80kh godov XX veka: Ot kakogo nasled-stva my otkazyvaemsia," in *Ocherki po istorii religiovedeniia*, edited by M. M. Shakhnovich (Saint Petersburg: Izdatel'stvo SPBGU, 2006).

112. RGASPI, f. 606, op. 4, d. 37, l. 31.

113. RGASPI, f. 606, op. 4, d. 156, l. 29.

114. Ibid.

115. Ibid., 47.

116. Ibid., 48.

117. Ibid., 139.

118. RGANI, f. 72, op. 1, d. 15, ll. 151–53.

119. M. B. Mitin, "O soderzhanii i zadachakh nauchno-ateisticheskoi propagandy v sovremennykh usloviiakh," in *Nauka i religiia: Sbornik stenogramm lektsii, prochitannykh na Vsesoiuznom soveshchanii-seminare po nauchno-ateisticheskim voprosam* (Moscow: Znanie, 1958), 17.

120. Naan, "Chelovek, bog i kosmos," 6.

121. Ibid., 7.

122. RGANI, f. 5, op. 55, d. 72, l. 53.

123. RGASPI, f. 606, op. 4, d. 126, ll. 33–34.

124. RGASPI, f. 606, op. 4, d. 37, l. 85.

125. V. N. Komarov and V. V. Kaziutinskii, eds., *Voprosy mirovozzreniia v lektsiiakh po astronomii: Sbornik* (Moscow: Znanie, 1974), 4.

126. Gerovitch, "'New Soviet Man' inside Machine," 152.

127. RGASPI, f. 606, op. 4, d. 133.

128. Vladimir Voinovich, "Moskva 2042," in *Utopia i antiutopia XX veka* (Moskva: Progress, 1990), 387–716.

129. Boris Groys, "Nelegitimnyi kosmonavt," *Khudozhestvennyi zhurnal/Moscow Art Magazine* 65–66 (June 2007), available online at http://xz.gif.ru/numbers/65-66/kosmonavt/.

130. Pelevin, "Code of the World."

8. She Orbits over the Sex Barrier

Funding for this research has been provided by the Spencer Foundation, the American Philosophical Society, and DePaul University. The title phrase, "She Orbits over the Sex Barrier," is borrowed from a headline in *Life Magazine* 54, no. 26 (June 1963): 28.

1. There have been a number of popular biographies of Tereshkova but few scholarly investigations of her moment in Soviet history. Recent work by historians has begun to fill the gap. This scholarship includes Cathleen Susan Lewis, "The Red Stuff: A History of the Public and Material Culture of Early Human Space Flight in the U.S.S.R. (PhD diss., George Washington University, 2008); Sue Bridger, "The Cold War and the Cosmos: Valentina Tereshkova and the First Woman's Space Flight," in *Women in the Khrushchev Era*, edited by Melanie Ilic et al. (New York: Palgrave Macmillan, 2004), 222–37; and Erica L. Fraser, "Masculinities in the Motherland: Gender and Authority in the Soviet Union during the Cold War, 1945–1968" (PhD diss., University of Illinois at Urbana-Champaign, 2009). Historians interested in female participation in the American and Soviet space programs and the Cold War "space race" more generally also mention Tereshkova. See Bettyann Holtzmann Kevles, *Almost Heaven: The Story of Women in Space* (New York: Basic Books, 2003); Margaret A. Weitekamp, *Right Stuff, Wrong Sex: America's First Women in Space Program* (Baltimore, Md.: Johns Hopkins University Press, 2004); and others.

2. This language was ubiquitous in the press coverage of Tereshkova. See, for example, the extensive coverage of Tereshkova's flight in *Literaturnaia gazeta*, June 18, 1963.

3. See, for example, the letter attributed to the famous French scientist and popular science writer Albert Ducrocq in *Literaturnaia gazeta*, June 19, 1963.

4. Tereshkova was frequently referred to as "our Valia." See, for example, *Pionerskaia pravda*, June 25, 1963, 1. Although she does not mention Tereshkova, the historian Svetlana Boym has discussed Soviet children's dreams of space travel and the enthusiasm generated among them by the flights of *Sputnik* and Yuri Gagarin; see Svetlana Boym, "Kosmos: Remembrances of the Future," in *Kosmos: A Portrait of the Russian Space Age* (Princeton, N.J.: Princeton Architectural Press, 2001), 83.

5. There are still relatively few historical studies of Soviet childhood. The most comprehensive in terms of scope is Catriona Kelly, *Children's World: Growing Up in Russia 1890–1991* (New Haven, Conn.: Yale University Press, 2007). Specialized studies of particular eras include Lisa A. Kirschenbaum, *Small Comrades: Revolutionizing Childhood in Soviet Russia, 1917–1932* (New York: Routledge Falmer, 2001); Ann Livschiz, "Growing Up Soviet:

Childhood in the Soviet Union, 1918–1958" (PhD diss., Stanford University, 2007), and her article, "De-Stalinizing Soviet Childhood: The Quest for Moral Rebirth, 1953–1958," in *The Dilemmas of De-Stalinization: Negotiating Cultural and Social Change in the Khrushchev Era*, edited by Polly Jones (New York: Routledge, 2006). Literary scholars have also begun to investigate various aspects of Russian children's culture. Anindita Banerjee's work is particularly relevant; see Anindita Banerjee, "Between Sputnik and Gagarin: Space Flight, Children's Periodicals, and the Circle of Imagination," in *Russian Children's Literature and Culture*, edited by Marina Balina and Larissa Rudova (New York: Routledge, 2008), 67–89. Also notable is Margaret Peacock, "Contested Innocence: Images of the Child in the Cold War" (PhD diss., University of Texas at Austin, 2008).

6. According to the American Academy of Pediatrics, children in middle childhood (from ages six to twelve) become increasingly aware of the world and their place in it, demonstrating enhanced self-awareness through their emerging ability to articulate thoughts and feelings and describe life experiences. They also begin to think more about the future and seek to be more independent from their parents and families. At the same time, though, children's desire to be accepted and liked by their peers gains intensity. The years of middle childhood are thus critically important in the development of self-esteem, as children gain or lose confidence in their abilities to successfully navigate the worlds of home, school, and society. See "Developmental Stages," American Association of Pediatrics, available online at http://aap.org/healthtopics/stages.cfm. See also "Child Development," U.S. Department of Health and Human Services Center for Disease Control, online at http://www.cdc.gov/ncbddd/child/default.htm.

7. See Lewis, "Red Stuff"; Bridger, "Cold War and the Cosmos"; Fraser, "Masculinities in the Motherland"; Kevles, *Almost Heaven*; Weitekamp, *Right Stuff, Wrong Sex*; and others.

8. See especially Fraser, "Masculinities in the Motherland," 155–71. Slava Gerovitch talks about Tereshkova's futile efforts to remain active in the cosmonaut corps. See Slava Gerovitch, "'New Soviet Man' inside Machine: Human Engineering, Spacecraft Design, and the Construction of Communism," *Osiris* (2007): 22, 152.

9. "Devushka iz Iaroslavlia," *Pionerskaia pravda*, June 18, 1963, 2. For more on the female cosmonaut corps, see Lewis, "Red Stuff," 143–58.

10. The findings discussed in this paragraph are in keeping with those presented in Kelly, *Children's World*.

11. Even a cursory inspection of *Pionerskaia pravda* for the years 1963 through 1965 shows that representations of boys outnumbered those of girls by at least five to one.

12. For a sampling of photos of girls engaging in these activities, see *Pionerskaia pravda* on the following dates: May 21, 1963; May 28, 1963; September 3, 1963.

13. Such images were ubiquitous. See, for example, photos in *Pionerskaia pravda* on January 25, 1963; March 17, 1963; March 26, 1963; May 14, 1963; August 13, 1963; February 11, 1964; March 10, 1964; March 17, 1964; March 20, 1964; April 24, 1964; April 28, 1964; May 29, 1964; and many others.

14. For examples on sewing, knitting, fashion, and hair styling, see *Pionerskaia pravda* on January 4, 1963; January 15, 1963; February 8, 1963; April 5, 1963; and October 22, 1963. Examples of arts and crafts, music, drama, and dancing can be found in *Pionerskaia pravda* on January 25, 1963; February 1, 1963; February 26, 1963; March 1, 1963; May 15, 1963; July 2, 1963; July 19, 1963; August 27, 1963; February 11, 1964; February 14, 1964; March 3, 1964; and March 10, 1964.

15. Images of girls engaged in sports and recreational activities typically appeared several times a month in *Pionerskaia pravda*. See January 4, 1963; January 18, 1963; January

25, 1963; February 22, 1963; March 5, 1963; May 17, 1963; May 21, 1963; June 4, 1963; June 11, 1963; July 23, 1963; August 9, 1963; August 16, 1963; November 15, 1963; January 3, 1963; January 17, 1964; February 4, 1964; and March 13, 1964.

16. For examples of stories about mothers as role models, see especially the International Women's Day issues of *Pionerskaia pravda*: March 8, 1963; March 3, 1964; and March 6, 1964. For an illustrative piece about teachers, see "Moia uchitel'nitsa," *Pionerskaia pravda*, May 12, 1964. For World War II–era heroines, see June 14, 1963; September 24, 1963; January 24, 1964; and January 31, 1964. For stories about female political and party figures as role models, see February 8, 1963; February 19, 1963; and February 25, 1964.

17. See *Pionerskaia pravda*, February 19, 1963; March 9, 1963; April 9, 1963; July 9, 1963; February 11, 1964; March 17, 1964; and April 28, 1964

18. See, for example, *Pionerskaia pravda* on March 5, 1963; March 26, 1963; May 7, 1963; May 24, 1963; November 19, 1963; December 10, 1963; February 11, 1964; and April 3, 1964.

19. Compare "Kogda stroikh mashinu sam" with drawings of girls collecting grain in a field and watering a house plant, in *Pionerskaia pravda*, February 12, 1963, 2–3.

20. *Pionerskaia pravda* was full of references to space and space exploration, both in the context of nonfiction references to Soviet accomplishments and plans for the future and in science fiction stories, which appeared with great frequency. In the months before Tereshkova's flight, space-themed items appeared on January 4, 1963; January 11, 1963; January 15, 1963; February 5, 1963; February 12, 1963; March 1, 1963; March 24, 1963; April 5, 1963; April 9, 1963; April 12, 1963; April 16, 1963; May 10, 1963; May 28, 1963; and May 31, 1963.

21. In this, my interpretation differs somewhat from that of the historian Erica Fraser, who has argued against the notion that media representations of Tereshkova associated her in a robust way with scientific and technological competence. See Fraser, "Masculinities in the Motherland," 156, and below.

22. For more on girls' enthusiasm, see Roshanna P. Sylvester, "'Let's Find out Where the Cosmonaut School Is': Soviet Girls and Cosmic Enthusiasm in the Aftermath of Tereshkova," in *Soviet Space Culture: Cosmic Enthusiasm in Socialist Societies*, edited by Eva Maurer, Julia Richers, Monica Rüthers, and Carmen Scheide (London: Palgrave, 2011).

23. *Moscow News*, June 18, 1963.

24. Quoted in *Pionerskaia pravda*, June 18, 1963.

25. Boym, *Kosmos*, 83.

26. Quoted in *Ogonek*, no. 15 (April 1963): 17.

27. "Sbudetsia, Sveta, tvoia mechta!," *Pionerskaia pravda*, June 18, 1963, 1.

28. *Pionerskaia pravda*, June 21, 1963.

29. *Krokodil*, June 30, 1963.

30. *Ogonek*, no. 26 (June 1963).

31. K. Iur'ev, "Devchonki sogodnia imenninitsy," *Ogonek*, no. 26 (June 1963): 30–31.

32. Tereshkova's Red Square speech as well as speeches by Soviet Premier Nikita Khrushchev, official state and Communist Party decrees, and transcripts of official conversations associated with her accomplishments were widely reprinted in the Soviet Union's major newspapers. Here, and below, I quote the officially approved English-language translations in *Moscow News*, June 23, 1963, 6.

33. *Moscow News*, June 22, 1963.

34. Ibid.

35. *Izvestiia*, June 18, 1963.

36. *Moscow News*, June 18, 1963.

37. *Moscow News*, June 23, 1963.

38. *Izvestiia*, June 17, 1963.

39. *Literaturnaia gazeta*, June 20, 1963.

40. *Literaturnaia gazeta*, June 25, 1963.

41. *Moscow News*, June 23, 1963.

42. *Pionerskaia pravda*, June 25, 1963.

43. Ibid.

44. For evidence of this see, for example, the article by V. Parin in *Izvestiia*, June 18, 1963, 3.

45. This line of thinking has been evolving in large part thanks to the pioneering work of Susan E. Reid. Her article "Cold War in the Kitchen" did much to inspire scholarly investigation of Soviet consumerism and gender in the Khrushchev and Brezhnev eras; see Susan E. Reid, "Cold War in the Kitchen: Gender and the De-Stalinization of Consumer Taste in the Soviet Union under Khrushchev," *Slavic Review* 61, no. 2 (Summer 2002): 211–52. Some of the work she inspired is collected in Susan E. Reid and David Crowley, eds., *Socialist Spaces: Sites of Everyday Life in the Eastern Bloc* (New York: Berg, 2002). Larissa Zakharova's work on the Soviet fashion industry and its connections to Paris is also a fascinating addition to the literature; see Larissa Zakharova, "S'habiller à la soviétique: La mode sous Khrouchtchev: Transferts, production, consommation" (thesis, Centre d'etudes des mondes russe, caucasien et centre-europeen, 2006), and her articles, including "Dior in Moscow: A Taste for Luxury in Soviet Fashion Under Khrushchev," in *Pleasures in Socialism: Leisure and Luxury in the Eastern Bloc*, edited by David Crowley and Susan E. Reid (Evanston, Ill.: Northwestern University Press, 2010).

46. "Ia 'Chaika,'" *Ogonek*, June 23, 1963, 6–7.

47. Kelly, *Children's World*, 132–34, discusses the continued influence of Stalin-era and particularly World War II–era role models in children's periodical literature of the 1950s and 1960s and their conflation with narratives about cosmonauts.

48. *Literaturnyaia gazeta*, June 23, 1963.

49. Lewis, "Red Stuff," 143–58, provides a summary of Russian women's accomplishments in the realms of aviation and space technology.

50. "Ee predshestvennitsy," *Znanie—Sila*, no. 7 (July 1963): 5.

51. Nikolai Denisov, "Kosmicheskaia nedelia: Iz zhurnalistskogo dnevnika," *Ogonek*, June 23, 1963, 12–13.

52. The transcript of the phone conversation was widely published in Soviet newspapers on June 18, 1963. See, for example, *Izvestiia*, *Literaturnaia gazeta*, and *Komsomolskaia pravda*. Here I am quoting from *Moscow News*, June 18, 1963, a special issue that featured on its cover a smiling Tereshkova in her space helmet under the headline "The First Woman Astronaut in the World."

53. For an example of this, see *Literaturnaia gazeta*, June 20, 1963.

54. As the scholar Erica L. Fraser has argued, Tereshkova "epitomized a particular postwar and Cold War version of the female celebrity, which was limited to the gendered realm of the family. Her celebrity was highly contingent on the political elite's insistence on fashioning her as a wife and mother, first and foremost, in contrast to the masculine embodiments of military might, science, technological progress, and diplomatic skill ascribed to her male colleagues"; see Fraser, "Masculinities in the Motherland," 156.

55. Reported in T. A. Babushkina and V. N. Shubkin, "The Statistics and Dynamics of Occupational Prestige: From the Findings of the Comparative International Research Project 'The Life-Paths of Young People in Socialist Society,'" translated in *The Social*

Structure of the USSR: Recent Soviet Studies, edited by Murray Yanowitch (New York: M. E. Sharpe, 1986), 132–35.

56. V. N. Shubkin, "Youth Starts out in Life," in *Sociology in the USSR: A Collection of Readings from Soviet Sources*, edited by Stephen P. Dunn (White Plains, N.Y.: International Arts and Sciences Press, 1969), 28. Originally published in *Voprosy filosofii*, no. 5 (1965).

57. Norton T. Dodge, "Women in the Professions," in *Women in Russia*, edited by Dorothy Atkinson et al. (Palo Alto, Calif.: Stanford University Press, 1977), 212–13.

58. See the statistics compiled by the American Institute of Physics Statistical Research Center from NSF data, available online at http://www.aip.org/statistics/trends/highlite/women05/figure7.htm.

59. Dodge, "Women in the Professions," 212–13.

60. For a recent example, see Organization for Economic Co-operation and Development Global Science Forum, "Evolution of Student Interest in Science and Technology Studies: Policy Report," May 2006, available online at http://www.oecd.org/dataoecd/16/30/36645825.pdf.

61. From first through ninth grade, pupils studied mathematics for six hours a week. Children in second, third, and fourth grades spent two additional hours on the natural sciences. By fifth grade Soviet pupils added two hours a week of biology. Physics and chemistry entered the curricula in sixth and seventh grades, becoming a still more substantive part of the science program in higher grades. In tenth grade Soviet sixteen-year-olds had five hours of math, five hours of physics, three hours of chemistry, two hours of biology, and one hour of astronomy every week. This meant that sixteen of thirty of their compulsory lesson hours were in math and science. Sarah White, ed., *Guide to Science and Technology in the USSR* (Guernsey, U.K.: Francis Hodgson, 1971), 64.

62. M. Ia. Sonin, "Equal Rights, Unequal Burdens," *Ekonomika i organizatsiia promyshlennovo proizvodstva*, no. 3 (May–June 1977): 5–18; and M. Pankratova, "The Soviet Woman—A Social Portrait," *Sotsiologicheskie issledovaniia*, no. 1, 1978. Both are available in translation online at *Seventeen Moments in Soviet History*, available at http://www.soviethistory.org.

63. Svein Sjoberg and Camilla Schreiner, "How Do Learners in Different Cultures Relate to Science and Technology?" *Asia-Pacific Forum on Science Learning and Teaching* 6, no. 2 (December 2005): 10–13, available online at http://www.ied.edu.hk/apfslt/.

64. Bridger, "Cold War and the Cosmos," 234–35. Cathleen Lewis, "Red Stuff," 151–52, has argued that at least part of the explanation for the decline in the female cosmonaut program was that, in the latter half of the 1960s, the Soviet space program as a whole lost its most powerful patrons with the premature death of the chief designer, Sergei Korolev, and the removal of Nikita Khrushchev as general secretary of the Communist Party.

65. Quoted in Ron Laytner and Donald Mclachlan, "Ride, Sally Ride: Her Place in Space," *Chicago Tribune*, April 24, 1983.

66. NASA reports that as of May 2009, forty-nine women have flown to space, "including cosmonauts, astronauts, payload specialists, and foreign nationals." Of those, forty-three participated on NASA flights, but only five on Soviet/Russian space expeditions. For more, see the NASA History Division Web site at http://history.nasa.gov/women.html.

9. From the Kitchen into Orbit

1. Walter H. Waggoner, "Brussels Invites the World to Its Fair," *New York Times*, March 2, 1958, XX: 6.

2. "U.S. and Soviet Agree to Exchange of Exhibits," *Washington Post and Times Herald*, December 30, 1958, A5.

3. The U.S. *Vanguard TV-3* launch attempt, two months after the Soviet's successful *Sputnik*, failed on December 6, 1957. The United States successfully launched *Pioneer 1* on January 31, 1958, before the spring opening of the Brussels World's Fair but too late for inclusion in the exhibition.

4. Susan E. Reid, "Cold War in the Kitchen: Gender and the De-Stalinization of Consumer Taste in the Soviet Union under Khrushchev," *Slavic Review* 61, no. 2 (Summer 2002): 211–52.

5. Jeffrey Brooks, *Thank You, Comrade Stalin! Soviet Public Culture from Revolution to Cold War* (Princeton, N.J.: Princeton University Press, 2000), xvii–xviii.

6. Susan E. Reid and David Crowley, eds., *Style and Socialism: Modernity and Material Culture in Post-war Europe* (Oxford: Berg, 2000).

7. Iurii Gerchuk, "The Aesthetics of Everyday Life in the Khrushchev Thaw in the USSR (1954–64)," in Reid and Crowley, *Style and Socialism*, 81–100.

8. Jonathan Grant, "The Socialist Construction of Philately in the Early Soviet Era," *Comparative Studies in Society and History* 37, no. 3 (July 1995): 476–93.

9. Nina Tumarkin, *Lenin Lives! The Lenin Cult in Soviet Russia* (Cambridge: Harvard University Press, 1983); Jeffrey Brooks, *Thank You, Comrade Stalin! Soviet Public Culture from Revolution to Cold War* (Princeton, N.J.: Princeton University Press, 2000); and Karen Petrone, *Life Has Become More Joyous, Comrades: Celebrations in the Time of Stalin* (Bloomington: Indiana University Press, 2000).

10. The Lenin All-Union Pioneer Organization (Vsesoiuznaia pionerskaia organizatsiia imeni V. I. Lenina), known as the Pioneers, was a mass, scoutlike organization for children ages ten through fifteen in the Soviet Union. Komsomol, the Communist Youth Union (Kommunisticheskii soiuz molodëzhi), was the youth wing of the party for students ages fourteen through twenty-eight, after which one could petition to full party membership.

11. Catriona Kelly, "'Thank You for the Wonderful Book': Soviet Child Readers and the Management of Children's Reading, 1950–75," *Kritika: Explorations in Russian and Eurasian History* 6, no. 4 (Fall 2005): 719–20.

12. Grant, "Socialist Construction of Philately in the Early Soviet Era," 476–93.

13. Both economic and social studies of the Soviet postwar population have indicated that the need to rebuild the economy and continue economic growth that would maintain the USSR's role in world affairs built expectations among the populace that the victor against fascism would reward its population with some portion of its new status and building wealth. Susan J. Linz, "World War II and Soviet Economic Growth, 1940–1953," in *The Impact of World War II on the Soviet Union*, edited by Susan J. Linz (Totowa, N.J.: Rowman and Allenheld, 1985); and Elena Zubkova, *Russia after the War: Hopes, Illusions, and Disappointments, 1945–1957*, translated by Hugh Ragsdale, in the New Russian History series, edited by Donald J. Raleigh (Armonk, N.Y.: M. E. Sharpe, 1998).

14. Stamps and *znachki* were not the only miniature objects that were for sale and collection in the former Soviet Union. There existed also *palekh*-style miniatures (*palekh* are the traditional Russian lacquered miniatures that were originally religious icons, but under Soviet rule they became secular and marketed for export) that portrayed Gagarin and other space themes. See in Boris Groys, *Ilya Kabakov: The Man Who Flew into Space from His Apartment*, installation review (London: Afterall Books, 2006), plates 20–23: 20. K. V. Kukulieva, B. N. Kukuliev, and O .V. An, portrait of Yuri Gagarin, lacquer painting; 21. K. V. Kukulieva, B. N. Kukuliev, and O .V. An, portrait of Konstantin Tsiolkovsky; 22. K. V. Kukulieva, B. N. Kukuliev, and O .V. An, portrait of Yuri Gagarin and Sergei Ko-

rolyov, lacquer painting; 23. K. V. Kukulieva, B. N. Kukuliev, and O .V. An, portrait of Yuri Gagarin, lacquer painting, from book of postcards Syn Rossii (Son of Russia) (Moscow: Izobrazitel'noe iskusstvo, 1987).

15. Vladimir Paperny, *Architecture in the Age of Stalin: Culture Two*, translated by John Hill and Roann Barris (Cambridge: Cambridge University Press, 2002).

16. Arthur Voyce, "Soviet Art and Architecture: Recent Developments," *Annals of the American Academy of Political and Social Science* 303 (January 1956): 104–15. The issue theme is "Russia since Stalin: Old Trends and New Problems."

17. Christina Kiaer, *Imagine No Possessions: The Socialist Objects of Russian Constructivism* (Cambridge: MIT Press, 2005).

18. The Union of Architects issued the 1955 "Directive of the Party Design and Construction"; see Victor Buchli, "Khrushchev, Modernism, and the Fight against 'Petit-Bourgeois' Consciousness in the Soviet Home," *Journal of Design* 10, no. 2 (1997): 161–76. "Ornamentalism" was the euphemism for Stalinist neoclassical "wedding cake" architecture. The Directive of the Party Design and Construction used the term in 1955 when overturning Stalin's directives on design.

19. Ibid., 175.

20. Stamp collecting had its origins in British and American industrial capitalism, and these origins might have tainted the hobby for midlevel Soviet officials who determined stamp issues. Steven M. Gelber, "Free Market Metaphor: The Historical Dynamics of Stamp Collecting," *Comparative Studies in Society and History* 34, no. 4 (October 1992): 742–69. Until the official allowance of independent-collecting societies in 1961, Soviet sanction of domestic philately was grudging at best. The philately journals appeared sporadically over the years and the Philately Society reported directly to the NKVD; see Grant, "Socialist Construction of Philately in the Early Soviet Era," 476–93.

21. Joel Kotek, *Students and the Cold War* (New York: St. Martin's Press, 1996).

22. Russell Belk, *Collecting in a Consumer Society* (London: Routledge, 1995); and Philipp Blom, *To Have and to Hold: An Intimate History of Collectors and Collecting* (Woodstock, N.Y.: Overlook Press, 2003). Belk and Blom assume that collecting societies develop as consequences of leisure and affluence of a well-developed capitalist society.

23. Belk, *Collecting in a Consumer Society*, 3; and Steven M. Gelber, "Free Market Metaphor: The Historical Dynamics of Stamp Collecting," *Comparative Studies in Society and History* 34, no. 4 (October 1992): 742–69.

24. Belk, *Collecting in a Consumer Society*, 6–7.

25. The New Economic Policy (NEP) took place between 1921 and 1928. The Tenth Party Congress approved the policy in recognition of the fact that the peasantry withdrew from economic exchange under the policy of War Communism that sanctioned mass state appropriation of goods. The policy allowed peasants and other small producers to sell their surpluses for a small profit and thereby encouraged production as the Bolsheviks sought to rebuild the Russian economy after World War I and the Civil War. This period also coincided with a relaxation of Civil War–era restrictions on cultural activities. In both cases the relaxed rules were considered short-term ideological sacrifices to regain pre–World War I economic and social stability; see E. A. Preobrazhensky, *The Crisis of Soviet Industrialization: Selected Essays*, translated by Donald A. Filtzer (White Plains, N.Y.: M. E. Sharpe, 1979) and *Russia in the Era of NEP: Explorations in Soviet Society and Culture*, edited by Sheila Fitzpatrick, Alexander Rabinowitz, and Richard Stites (Bloomington: Indiana University Press, 1991).

26. Stalin instituted central planning in the form of the First Five Year Plan in 1928

to extract as much wealth as possible from the countryside to control the economy and finance industrialization.

27. Alex Levant, "The Soviet Union in Ruins" (MA thesis, Methodologies for the Study of Western History and Culture Master's Program, Trent University, 1999), 102.

28. The Marxist definition of Communism is "from each according to his abilities, to each according to his needs." This is distinct from socialism, which is defined as "from each according to his abilities, to each according to his work."

29. Brooks, *Thank You, Comrade Stalin!*, xvii–xviii, states the philosophy behind Khrushchev's belief: "After Stalin's death, Khrushchev increased public expectations about the quantity and quality of the state's gift to society, but his promises to match and surpass Western Living standards went unfulfilled. . . . Along with the emphasis on consumerism, Khrushchev opened society to a degree by limiting repression as easing censorship. Intellectuals took advantage of Khrushchev's 'thaw' to champion 'sincerity,' the antithesis of the formative tethos, but nonetheless left much of the performative culture intact. In the end, neither Khrushchev not his successors were willing to discard the ritualistic certainties from which they derived legitimacy. Their performative culture lingered on in a semi-moribund state until Brezhnev inadvertently turned it into self-parody." Reid, "Cold War in the Kitchen," explains the practical significance of Khrushchev's activities.

30. Buchli, "Khrushchev, Modernism, and the Fight against 'Petit-Bourgeois' Consciousness in the Soviet Home," 161–76.

31. Levant, "Soviet Union in Ruins," 97.

32. The "kitchen debate" was an impromptu debate between Nixon and Khrushchev at the opening of the American National Exhibition in Moscow, on July 24, 1959, among the American household appliances display that had been a focus of the United States's exhibit at the 1958 Brussels World's Fair.

33. Reid, "Cold War in the Kitchen," 223–24.

34. Marquis Childs, "Moscow Exhibits Stress Sputniks," *Washington Post and Times Herald*, June 24, 1958, A16.

35. Grant, "Socialist Construction of Philately in the Early Soviet Era," 476–93.

36. Ibid., 476.

37. Ibid., 481.

38. Ibid., 484.

39. Ibid., 492–93.

40. The Soviet Ministerstvo sviazi is the Ministry of Communications; however, the traditional translation is Ministry of Post and Telegraph, alluding to the pre-twentieth-century origins of the name.

41. Anthony Swift, "The Soviet World of Tomorrow at the New York World's Fair, 1939," *Russian Review* 57 (July 1998): 376.

42. The Ministerstvo sviazi issued stamps in five denominations in 1961 (after revaluation of the ruble in 1961): one, three, four, six, and ten kopeks. The one-kopek stamp paid for delivery of domestic postcards. The four-kopek stamp delivered domestic envelopes. The six- and ten-kopek stamps delivered international postcards and letters, respectively.

43. "Marki dlia kollektsii," *Pioner* (Moscow), August 1961, n.p. (inside back cover).

44. *Vostok Stamp with Khrushchev Quote, 6 k*, in *Moscow, USSR*, postage stamp, Smithsonian Institution National Air and Space Museum, USSR Ministerstvo Sviaz, April 1961.

45. *Vostok 3* launched on August 11, 1962, with Adrian Nikolaev on board. While that craft was still in orbit, Pavel Popovich launched on board *Vostok 4* on August 12, 1962. Both craft remained in orbit until August 15, 1962.

46. The first model of a *Vostok* went on display inside what was soon to become the Kosmos Pavilion at the Exhibition of Economic Achievements in Moscow: "Vostok Model Is Shown to Public in Moscow," *New York Times*, April 30, 1965, 10.

47. *Voskhod 1* launched on October 12, 1964, and landed on October 13. The mission's technological significance was that the craft carried a crew of three, making it the first multipassenger human space mission. The mission's added political significance came from the fact that the crew was in orbit at the time when the Politburo removed Nikita Khrushchev from power.

48. *Voskhod 2* was the second mission of the modified *Vostok* hardware. Pavel Belaev commanded the mission and pilot-cosmonaut Aleksei Leonov performed the first space-walk on this daylong mission beginning March 18, 1965.

49. "Marki Dlia Kollektsii," *Pioner* (Moscow), August 1961, n.p. (inside back cover).

50. Samuel A. Tower, "Looking into New Soviet Issues," *New York Times*, June 22, 1975, 143.

51. The Pioneer organization magazines, *Pioner* and *Semena*, continued to run "Marki dlia kollektsii" (Stamps for collectors) and "Dlia kollektsioner" (For the collector) articles on an alternating basis in the monthly magazines throughout the 1960s. The latter followed the stamp issues. The former announced the release of znachki, coins, and special issue medals.

52. Sergei Ivanovich Ozhegov, *Slovar' russkogo iazyka* (Moskva: Izdatel'stvo "Sovetskaia entsiklopediia," 1968), 228.

53. German Evgenevich Kruglov, *Chto takoe faleristika* (Minsk: Polymia, 1983), 9.

54. Ibid., 20.

55. V. N. Il'inskii, *Znachki i ikh kollektsionirovanie (Posobie dlia fileristov)*, 1976, *Izdanie vtoroe pererabotannoe i dopolnenie* (Moscow: Izdatel'stvo "Sviaz'," 1977); and V. A. Omel'ko, *Nagradnye znaki obshchestvennykh organizatsii u muzeev*, vol. 1, *Nagrady za osvoenie kosmosa catalog* (Moscow: N.p., 2002).

56. These were the official magazines of the Pioneer organization.

57. The voluntary Znanie Society promoted public scientific education and published this journal.

58. V. N. Il'inskii, *Znachki i ikh kollektsionirovanie (Posobie dlia fileristov)*, 1976, *Izdanie vtoroe pererabotannoe i dopolnenie* (Moscow: Izdatel'stvo "Sviaz'," 1977) describes the history of the collection of the pins. Kruglov, *Chto takoe faleristika*, offers a history of the pins themselves, including useful information on their production and materials. V. N. Il'inskii, V. E. Kuzin, and M. B. Saukke, *Kosmonavtiki na znachkakh sssr, 1957–1975: Katalog* (Moscow: Izdatel'stvo "Sviaz'," 1977), is the most comprehensive catalogue of space-related znachki.

59. Frederick C. Barghoorn, "Soviet Cultural Diplomacy Since Stalin," *Russian Review* 17, no. 1 (January 1958): 41–55.

60. Kruglov, *Chto takoe faleristika*, 10.

61. "Neobychnaia Kollektsiia," *Ogonek* (Moscow), February 12, 1961, 26.

62. Il'inskii, *Znachki i ikh kollektsionirovanie (Posobie dlia fileristov)*, 6.

63. These are the official terms that Russian falerists use in classifying their collections. Other historians use a more elaborate classification system that addresses all znachki, not focusing specifically on space-related ones; see Victor C. Seibert, "Falerists and Their Russian Znachki," *Numismatist* (June 1979): 1,198–202.

64. Il'inskii, Kuzin, and Saukke list at least twenty-three enterprises that manufactured space znachki as of 1975; see V. N. Il'inskii, V. E. Kuzin, and M. B. Saukke, *Kosmonavtika na znachkakh sssr, 1957–1975: Katalog* (Moscow: Izdatel'stvo "Sviaz'," 1977), 143–44.

65. V. A. Omel'ko, *Nagradnye znaki obshchestvennykh organizatsii u muzeev*, vol. 1, *Nagrady za osvoenie kosmosa Katalog* (Moscow: N.p., 2002), 6.

66. The "K" stands for *kopeek*, the Russian penny.

67. Omel'ko, *Nagrady za osvoenie kosmosa katalog*. This is a catalog of these awards. Although it does not list the recipient of each award, it does state the issuing organization, the purpose of the award, and the starting dates and cycles for each award.

68. Il'inskii, *Znachki i ikh kollektsionirovanie (Posobie dlia fileristov)*, 9, 112, and 143. Tompak is a copper and zinc alloy that is an inexpensive alternative to copper and gold in costume jewelry. The Shcherbinsk Factory is an optical facility in the suburbs of Moscow.

69. Ibid., 9.

70. Childs, "Moscow Exhibits Stress Sputniks," A16; Waggoner, "Brussels Invites the World to Its Fair," 6; "U.S. and Soviet Agree to Exchange of Exhibits," *Washington Post and Times Herald*, December 30, 1958, A5; and "Text of Speeches by Nixon and Kozlov at Opening of Soviet Exhibition," *New York Times*, June 30, 1959, 16.

71. Iurii Sal'nikov, director, *Iurii Gagarin*, film (Moscow: Ekran, 1969).

72. Grant, "Socialist Construction of Philately in the Early Soviet Era," 493.

73. Il'inskii, Kuzin, and Saukke, *Kosmonavtiki na znachkakh sssr, 1957–1975: Katalog*, 6.

74. Il'inskii, *Znachki i ikh kollektsionirovanie (Posobie dlia fileristov)*, 15.

75. Frank H. Winter, "The Silent Revolution or How R. H. Goddard May Have Helped Start the Space Age," paper presented at the Fifty-fifth International Astronautical Federation Congress, October 4–8, Vancouver, Canada, 2004. Winter goes into some detail about how the image gained popular international acceptance.

76. Il'inskii, Kuzin, and Saukke, *Kosmonavtiki na znachkakh sssr, 1957–1975: Katalog*, 143.

77. *Voskhod* launched on October 12, 1964, with commander Vladimir Komarov, engineer Konstantin Feoktistov, and physician Boris Ëgorov. The March 18, 1965, launch of *Voskhod 2* carried commander Pavel Belaev and pilot Aleksei Leonov.

10. Cold War Theaters

1. I am not arguing that the government "staged" the events in the traditional use of the word. Rather, I think it is important to recognize the narrative value of convening large, enthusiastic, celebratory demonstrations of the people so soon after the border closure.

2. On Khrushchev's role in the Berlin Crisis, see, for example, Vladislav M. Zubok, "Khrushchev and the Berlin Crisis (1958–62)", in *Cold War International History Project (CWIHP): Working Paper No. 6* (Washington, D.C.: Woodrow Wilson International Center for Scholars, 1993). On the events leading up to the construction of the Berlin Wall, see Hope M. Harrison, *Driving the Soviets up the Wall* (Princeton, N.J.: Princeton University Press, 2003) or Harrison, "Ulbricht and the Concrete 'Rose': New Archival Evidence on the Dynamics of Soviet-East German Relations and the Berlin Crisis, 1958–61," *CWIHP: Working Paper No. 5* (Washington, D.C.: Woodrow Wilson International Center for Scholars, 1993).

3. Dietrich Staritz, *Geschichte der DDR* (Frankfurt: Suhrkamp, 1996), 96.

4. Ibid., 101.

5. This was meant to perform a deterrent effect: to convince people that it was not worth it to steal from the government (ibid., 104). Staritz uses the pancake example to show that prosecutors did not pursue every case—this baker was given a fifty-deutschemark fine for "privatizing" ten pancakes. For his reluctance to imprison the baker, however, the court sentenced the prosecutor to three years in prison.

6. Staritz (ibid., 105) has noted that by 1950 the percentage of East Germans claiming no religious affiliation had risen by less than 2 percent (to 7.6 percent from 5.9 percent).

7. Ibid., 105.

8. Collectivization had previously unleashed revolts in the countryside (ibid.). Workers in Leipzig already had begun striking in May because of falling wages; see Gareth Pritchard, *The Making of the GDR* (Manchester: Manchester University Press, 2000), 202. See also Hermann Weber, *Geschichte der DDR* (Munich: Deutscher Taschenbuch Verlag, 2000), 164–65.

9. Weber, *Geschichte der DDR*, 164.

10. Volker Berghahn, *Modern Germany: Society, Economics, and Politics in the Twentieth Century* (Cambridge: Cambridge University Press, 1982), 219.

11. Weber, *Geschichte der DDR*, 164.

12. Although new passport laws restricted the number, legal trips across the border were increasingly restricted after 1956, allowing the number of cross-border trips to drop from 2.5 million in 1956 to just 700,000 in 1958. Christoph Klessmann, *Zwei Staaten, eine Nation: Deutsche Geschichte, 1955–1970* (Bonn: Bundeszentrale für politische Bildung, 1997), 320.

13. Weber, *Geschichte der DDR*, 201. Klessmann, *Zwei Staaten*, 321.

14. Klessmann, *Zwei Staaten*, 309. Then the government lifted postwar rationing in 1958, before reinstating it for a time in the early 1960s because of continuing supply crises. Ulrich Mählert, *Kleine Geschichte der DDR* (Munich: C. H. Beck, 1999), 103.

15. Weber, *Geschichte der DDR*, 201. Klessmann, *Zwei Staaten*, 309.

16. Weber, *Geschichte der DDR*, 196.

17. Ibid., 198.

18. Ibid., 211.

19. Andreas Malycha, "Von der Gründung bis zur Mauerbau," in *Die SED. Geschichte, Organisation, Politik. Ein Handbuch*, edited by Andreas Herbst (Berlin: Dietz Verlag, 1997), 3.

20. This according to a contemporary periodical, *Neuer Weg*, cited in Weber, *Geschichte der DDR*, 209. Also (uncited) in Jürgen Winkler, "Kulturpolitik" in Herbst, *Die SED*, 396.

21. Bundesarchiv (BArch), DR 6 280, Staatliches Rundfunkkomitee, "Für ein interessantes, massenwirksames Fernsehprogramm," [1958], 8.

22. Cited in Mählert, *Kleine Geschichte der DDR*, 88. Translations by the author.

23. Klessmann, *Zwei Staaten*, 558.

24. Weber, *Geschichte der DDR*, 219. Harrison, *Driving the Soviets up the Wall*, 189.

25. Harrison, *Driving the Soviets up the Wall*, 189.

26. For more on this, see Heather L. Gumbert, "Constructing the Berlin Wall: East German Television Narratives and the Second Berlin Crisis," in *Propaganda and the Mass Media in the Making of the Cold War*, edited by Christoph Müller and Judith Devlin (London: Palgrave, forthcoming).

27. Cited in Klessmann, *Zwei Staaten*, 322.

28. Excerpts from Willy Brandt, "Erklärung des Regierenden Bürgermeisters von Berlin, Willy Brandt, auf einer Sondersitzung des Abgeordnetenhauses am 13. August 1961," Deutsche Teilung, Deutsche Einheit: Willy Brandt zum Mauerbau, Bundeszentrale für politische Bildung, available online at http://www.bpb.de/themen/58KKAK,0,0,Erkl%E4rung_des_Regierenden_B%FCrgermeisters_von_Berlin_Willy_Brandt_auf_einer_Sondersitzung_des_Abgeordnetenhauses_am_13_August_1961.html.

29. Klessmann, *Zwei Staaten*, 322.

30. See transcript: "Es war ein ganz normaler Tag . . . normal auch deswegen, weil sich etwas vollzog, was sich seit Gründung unserer Republik zu vollziehen pflegt. . . . " Deutsches Rundfunkarchiv (DRA) Babelsberg, Ostaufzeichnung, "Die aktuelle Kamera: Hauptausgabe," August 13, 1961.

31. Gumbert, "Constructing the Berlin Wall."

32. Weber, *Geschichte der DDR*, 223.

33. "Die aktuelle Kamera," August 3, 1961, article 5, in DRA Babelsberg, Ostaufzeichnung.

34. "Die aktuelle Kamera: Sonderbericht—Menschenhändler vor Gericht," July 27, 1961. For example, on August 4, 1961, in DRA Babelsberg, Ostaufzeichnung; "Aktuelle kamera" reported a "polio epidemic" in the Federal Republic, implying a lack of basic social services. "Die aktuelle Kamera," August 4, 1961, in DRA Babelsberg, Ostaufzeichnung.

35. Weber, *Geschichte der DDR*, 225–26.

36. Also noted by Peter Hoff in Knut Hickethier, *Geschichte des deutschen Fernsehens* (Stuttgart: Verlag J. B. Metzler, 1998), 284.

37. Consider, for example, the work of the historian Amy Nelson on dogs in the Soviet space program (see her chapter in this volume).

38. Asif Siddiqi, *Sputnik and the Soviet Space Challenge* (Gainesville: University Press of Florida, 2003), 243.

39. Not, as the author William Shelton has reported, "a few months after *Sputnik*." William Shelton, *Soviet Space Exploration: The First Decade* (New York: Washington Square Press, 1968), 107.

40. Harrison, *Driving the Soviets up the Wall*, 186.

41. Siddiqi, *Sputnik and the Soviet Space Challenge*, 292.

42. Shelton, *Soviet Space Exploration*, 121. Siddiqi, *Sputnik and the Soviet Space Challenge*, 292–93.

43. Shelton, *Soviet Space Exploration*, 121. Siddiqi, *Sputnik and the Soviet Space Challenge*, 294.

44. Shelton *Soviet Space Exploration*, 121. Siddiqi, *Sputnik and the Soviet Space Challenge*, 293.

45. Shelton, *Soviet Space Exploration*, 122.

46. Ibid., 120.

47. Ibid., 119.

48. Ibid., 120.

49. All excerpts cited in "World Press Reaction to Space Flight: Western Writers Cite Propaganda Value of Feat," *Los Angeles Times*, August 8, 1961, 7.

50. Bernard Lovell, quoted in "Scientists See Feat as Red Triumph," *Los Angeles Times*, August 7, 1961, 8.

51. The USSR Embassy in Canada, *Gherman Titov in Canada* (Ottawa: USSR Embassy in Canada, [1962]), 11.

52. "17 Orbit Trip Only Choice Open to Titov," *Chicago Daily Tribune*, August 8, 1961.

53. Titov attributed the latter question to an article that had previously appeared in the *New York Herald Tribune*. "Alles was ich lernte, gab ich dem Kosmosflug" *Junge Welt*, September 5, 1961, in DRA Babelsberg, Pressearchiv. The latter was also the subject of a speech Titov gave in Berlin. "Unsere Erfolge beweisen: Wir sind auf dem richtigen Weg," *Junge Welt*, September 2, 1961, in DRA Babelsberg, Pressearchiv.

54. Tara Gray, "Alan B. Shepard, Jr.," NASA 40th Anniversary of the Mercury 7, available online at http://history.nasa.gov/40thmerc7/shepard.htm.

55. *Pravda* article cited in *Berliner Zeitung*. "Er kann überall landen," *Berliner Zeitung*, September 9, 1961, in DRA Babelsberg, Pressearchiv.

56. Audience participants at "The Cultural Impact of the Cold War Cosmonaut" panel of the 2006 convention of the American Association for the Advancement of Slavic Studies emphasized that the disconnect between the image of prominent Soviets and their real-life personalities sometimes caused awkward situations when they traveled abroad. A favored example was Gagarin, who had already begun to tarnish his own reputation by jumping from a hotel window, possibly drunk, to prevent his wife from catching him in flagrante with another woman.

57. Rainer Gries and Silke Satjukow, "Von Menschen und Übermenschen: Der 'Alltag' und das 'Ausseralltägliche' der 'socialist heroes,'" *Aus Politik und Zeitgeschichte* 17 (2002): 43.

58. Tamara Titova played her own role in this narrative: that of the supportive young wife. Whether she was in the West or the GDR, reporters questioned her on a limited range of topics, including how she felt when Titov was in space and especially what she thought of the current fashions. In the GDR she praised the selection of fabrics: "There are so many pretty things to see here, that it would be hard for any woman to choose. I find the many new textiles especially lovely." East Germans may have been surprised to hear this, given the problems of provisioning the population with consumer goods the government had at the time. "Tamara Titowa bei Frau Mode zu Gast," *Junge Welt*, September 5, 1961, in DRA Babelsberg, Pressearchiv.

59. "Die aktuelle Kamera," August 6, 1961, in DRA Babelsberg, Ostaufzeichnungen. Unfortunately no audio-visual record of this particular program remains, only a partial written transcript that was created by West German authorities. In the period before it was possible to record programs for broadcast, and East Germany did not acquire the technology to do so before 1964, the television service had to broadcast programs live, sometimes including slides (still images) or filmed excerpts. The fragments of film that remain from this early period were collected by the West German authorities, who created and preserved kinescopes of certain (but certainly not all!) programs, filming televised images from the television screen. They did this in part to learn something about the current state of the GDR and in part to find material that they could rebroadcast in anticommunist commentary programs, such as *Rote Optik* (Red spectacles). They were not alone; the GDR did the same thing. After the fall of the Berlin Wall, the respective broadcasting authorities each "returned" these audio-visual archives to their rightful owners. For the television researcher this is a serendipitous product of the Cold War, making available sources that otherwise would no longer exist. It is an incomplete record, however, and subject to whatever the transcribers felt was important to preserve at the time. The scribes of this particular transcript did not see fit to record the comments of East German bathers on the subject of Titov, only that such comments appeared in the broadcast. Similarly, the last item of this transcript recorded only that the broadcast informed viewers of a Khrushchev television speech, but not what that speech was about. The next transcript, though, from August 8, 1961, suggests that it was a television speech about the conclusion of a peace treaty.

60. Ernst Lehnhardt, quoted in "Doctor Tells Why He Fled East Berlin: Wants to Live Under Freedom, Not Reds," *Chicago Daily Tribune*, August 26, 1961, 4.

61. "Wostok II," *Unser Rundfunk*, August 20, 1961.

62. This was a special broadcast for the affiliated national broadcasters of the International Radio and Television Organization (OIRT).

63. "Das hat Berlin noch nicht erlebt," *Berliner Zeitung*, September 2, 1961, in DRA Babelsberg, Pressearchiv.

64. "Unsere Erfolge beweisen: Wir sind auf dem richtigen Weg," *Junge Welt*, September 2, 1961, in DRA Babelsberg, Pressearchiv.

65. "Titows Tat kündet alle Völker: Der Sozialismus ist die stärkste Macht der Welt," *Neues Deutschland*, September 3, 1961, in DRA Babelsberg, Pressearchiv.

66. "Die Ursache unserer Erfolge: Sozialistische Planwirtschaft," *Tribüne*, September 5, 1961, in DRA Babelsberg, Pressearchiv.

67. "Walter Ulbricht: Kosmonauten künden von der grossen Zukunft des Kommunismus," *Neues Deutschland*, September 6, 1961, in DRA Babelsberg, Pressearchiv.

68. "Er kann überall landen," *Berliner Zeitung*, September 9, 1961, in DRA Babelsberg, Pressearchiv. Media reports persistently mobilized the language of space and place. Titov claimed that the GDR was the first place he had wanted to visit after his spaceflight, iterating this point several times. The press also reported repeatedly that Titov could have landed anywhere he wanted. (Unlike Gagarin's flight six months earlier, Titov had manual control of the spacecraft for a short time at the end of the flight, and the spacecraft itself was more advanced.) Questioned on this point by the press, Titov replied: "Why not? Of course it would have been possible. But it was not a part of the plan." "Alles was ich lernte, gab ich dem Kosmosflug."

69. "Titows Tat kündet alle Völker." The *Berliner Zeitung* similarly wrote: "You have shown the world the ability of the socialist people and the certain victory of the great cause of Communism. Your spaceship and the scientific instruments of highest precision were as good as your social order" ("Karl-Marx Orden für Titow," *Berliner Zeitung*, September 2, 1961, in DRA Babelsberg, Pressearchiv). And, as Titov left the GDR, Ulbricht iterated that Titov was for East Germans "an emissary of freedom, a harbinger of the victorious nature of the great program of the Soviet Communist Party." "Walter Ulbricht."

70. According to *Unser Rundfunk*, "bourgeois statistics" were a good example that there were three kinds of lies: "useful lies, necessary lies and statistical conclusions." See "Lügen-Vorsprung" (Taking the lead in lies), *Unser Rundfunk*, August 20, 1961.

71. The cartoon, from an unnamed West German publication, was reproduced in its entirety in the East German *Volksstimme*, May 5, 1961, alongside an article from the April 23, 1961 issue of *Pravda*, in German translation.

72. GDR coverage asserted repeatedly that the Soviet space program could have achieved this already five years earlier, in 1956. "Alles was ich lernte, gab ich dem Kosmosflug."

73. "Kosmos-Moskau-Berlin," September 1, 1961, in DRA Babelsberg, Ostaufzeichnung.

74. Indeed, *Neues Deutschland* reported that the GDR government had effected three blows against the West. The first was the border closure, struck by the working people of the GDR and the armed forces against "German militarism and their agents." Then, on August 31, the Soviet government "came down like a ton of bricks on the nuclear warmongers of NATO." (The paper did not spell it out here, but it was referring to Khrushchev's repeal of the moratorium on nuclear testing.) The final blow exacted was the arrival of Gherman Titov in Berlin, received by crowds of Berliners at a massive rally for German-Soviet friendship. These quotations are all from *Neues Deutschland*. "Titows Tat kündet alle Völker," in DRA Babelsberg, Pressearchiv.

75. "Triumphfahrt des Kommunisten Titow," *Neues Deutschland*, September 4, 1961, DRA Babelsberg, Pressearchiv.

76. "Walter Ulbricht," DRA Babelsberg, Pressearchiv.

77. "Titows Tat kündet alle Völker."

78. "Walter Ulbricht."

79. The latter is from "Walter Ulbricht." Also "Triumphfahrt des Kommunisten Titow."

80. "Alles was ich lernte, gab ich dem Kosmosflug."

81. "Triumphfahrt des Kommunisten Titow."

82. Quotations from "Titows Tat kündet alle Völker."

83. And lest we suspect that the press simply overestimated the numbers, we must remember that television footage of Titov's arrival indeed suggests the attendance of large, curious crowds. "Kosmos-Moskau-Berlin," September 1, 1961, in DRA Babelsberg, Ostaufzeichnung.

84. "Triumphfahrt des Kommunisten Titow."

Contributors

—————————

James T. Andrews is full professor of modern Russian and comparative EurAsian studies in the Department of History at Iowa State University (ISU), where he is director of the University Center for Excellence in the Arts and Humanities (CEAH). At ISU he has also been director of Eurasian Studies and director of the Center for the Historical Studies of Technology and Science. He is the author of *Red Cosmos: K. E. Tsiolkovsksii, Grandfather of Soviet Rocketry* (2009); *Science for the Masses: The Bolshevik State, Public Science, and the Popular Imagination in Soviet Russia, 1917–34* (2003); and editor of *Maksim Gor'kii Revisited: Science, Academics, and Revolution* (1995).

Asif A. Siddiqi is associate professor of history at Fordham University. He specializes in the history of science and technology and modern Russian history. He is the author, most recently, of *The Red Rockets' Glare: Spaceflight and the Soviet Imagination, 1857–1957* (2010). He has published numerous books, articles, and edited volumes on Soviet history and the history of technology. He is also serving as series editor of the four-volume English-language memoirs of academician B. E. Chertok, entitled *Rockets and People* (2005–).

Slava Gerovitch is a lecturer in the Science, Technology and Society Program at the Massachusetts Institute of Technology. He specializes in the history of Soviet cosmonautics, computing, and cybernetics with a particular interest in the politics, language, and culture of Cold War science. He is the author of *From Newspeak to Cyberspeak: A History of Soviet Cybernetics* (2002), numerous articles in journals, and book chapters in *Science and Ideology, Universities and Empire, Cultures of Control*, and *Critical Issues in the History of Spaceflight*. Gerovitch is currently working on a book on the technopolitics of automation in the Soviet space program.

Heather L. Gumbert is an assistant professor of history at Virginia Tech. She is the author of "Split Screens: Television in East Germany," in *Screening the Media: Mass Media, Culture and Society in Twentieth-century Germany*, edited by Corey Ross (2006). She has also written on debates surrounding the placement and construction of the iconic Berlin television tower. She is currently writing a book, *Envisioning Socialism*, which examines the ways in which the emergence and growth of television shaped the lives and worldviews of Germans living in the German Democratic Republic (GDR) in the postwar period.

Andrew Jenks is associate professor in the department of history at California State University, Long Beach. He is the author of *Russia in a Box: Art and Identity in an Age of Revolution* (2005) and *Perils of Progress: Environmental Disasters in the Twentieth Century* (2010). He has published articles on a variety of topics in *Kritika: Explorations in Russian and Eurasian History, Environmental History, Technology, and Culture*, and *Cahiers du Monde Russe*. Jenks is now completing a study of the cosmonaut Yuri Gagarin entitled *The Cosmonaut Who Couldn't Stop Smiling: The Life and Legend of Yuri Gagarin*.

Alexei Kojevnikov is associate professor of history of science and Russian/Soviet history at the University of British Columbia in Vancouver, Canada. His publications in English and Russian include *Stalin's Great Science: The Times and Adventures of Soviet Physicists* (2004); *Rockefeller Philanthropies and Soviet Science* (1993) as well as articles in *Isis*,

Historical Studies in the Physical and Biological Sciences, Osiris, Russian Review, VIET, and other journals. Kojevnikov also edited *Science in Russian Context* (a special issue of *Science in Context,* 2002) and co-edited (with Michael Gordin and Karl Hall) *Intelligentsia Science: The Russian Century, 1860–1960* (a special issue of *Osiris,* vol. 23, 2008).

Cathleen S. Lewis is a curator of International Space Programs and Spacesuits at the Smithsonian Institution's National Air and Space Museum, specializing in Soviet and Russian programs. Her current research is on the history of the public and popular culture of the early years of human spaceflight in the Soviet Union. She has completed degrees in Russian and East European Studies at Yale University and holds a PhD in history from George Washington University. Lewis's dissertation and current book project is "The Rise and Fall of the Red Stuff: A History of Russian Cosmic Enthusiasm."

Amy Nelson is associate professor of history at Virginia Tech. She is the author of *Music for the Revolution: Musicians and Power in Early Soviet Russia* (2004) and the recipient of the Heldt Prize for the Best Book by a Woman in any area of Slavic/East European/Eurasian Studies, awarded by the Association for Women in Slavic Studies in 2005. Her recent articles have focused on Soviet pet keeping, the animal protection movement in imperial Russia, and the cultural legacy of Laika the space dog. She is writing a collective biography of the Soviet space dogs and is editor (with Jane Costlow) of *The Other Animals: Beyond the Human in Russian Culture and History* (2010).

Victoria Smolkin-Rothrock holds a PhD in modern Russian history from the University of California at Berkeley (2010) and is currently an assistant professor of Russian history at Wesleyan University. Her publications in English and Russian include articles in the journal *Neprikosnovennyi zapas: Debaty o politike i kul'ture* and the book *Petersburg/Petersburg: Novel and City* (edited by Olga Matich) Smolkin-Rothrock's current book project is tentatively titled "A Sacred Space Is Never Empty: Scientific Atheism, Socialist Rituals, and the Soviet Way of Life, 1954–1991."

Roshanna P. Sylvester is associate professor of Russian history at DePaul University, where she has been director of graduate studies in history. She is the author of *Tales of Old Odessa: Crime and Civility in a City of Thieves* (2005). Her articles have appeared in *Slavic Review,* the *Journal of Urban History,* and the *Jahrbücher für Geschichte Osteuropas.* Sylvester's current book project is a comparative study of girls, science, and technology in Cold War America and the Soviet Union.

Index

Note: Illustrations are indicated by page numbers in italic type.